P9-CEN-082

ALSO BY ANDY COHEN

Most Talkative

The Andy Cohen Diaries

SUPERFICIAL

SUPERFICIAL

MORE ADVENTURES FROM
THE ANDY COHEN DIARIES

ANDY COHEN

HENRY HOLT AND COMPANY   NEW YORK

Henry Holt and Company
Publishers since 1866
175 Fifth Avenue
New York, New York 10010
www.henryholt.com

Henry Holt® and 🏛® are registered trademarks of Macmillan Publishing Group, LLC.

Copyright © 2016 by Andrew Cohen
All rights reserved.

Library of Congress Cataloging-in-Publication Data is available.

ISBN: 978-1-2501-1648-2

Henry Holt books are available for special promotions and premiums.
For details contact: Director, Special Markets.

First Edition 2016

Designed by Meryl Sussman Levavi

Printed in the United States of America

10 9 8 7 6 5 4 3 2 1

ISN'T LIFE JUST A SERIES OF IMAGES
THAT CHANGE AS THEY REPEAT THEMSELVES?

—ANDY WARHOL

I AM A DEEPLY SUPERFICIAL PERSON.

—ANDY WARHOL

SUPERFICIAL

INTRODUCTION

This diary, like the last, is inspired by *The Andy Warhol Diaries*, which were published after the artist and pop icon died. I continued keeping a diary starting a week after volume 1 (*The Andy Cohen Diaries*) ended; this one runs from September of 2014 through June of 2016. I wrote every day, but for the purposes of space and not boring you to tears, I've cut or combined some days in this book.

It's absolutely not essential for you to have read my last book to understand this one. (The title *is* "Superficial"—you can do it!) Like the last one, I continued to write this book in diary form. I try to explain names when you won't know them, but sometimes I don't because, again, background on every single person I interact with every single day would turn this book into an encyclopedia of inessential information.

My title is both dead on and yet somewhat misleading, because I think I get more personal in this book than the last, deeper into my feelings about myself and others. I was in such a zone after writing the first one that it felt easier and more honest to share more about what's really going on in my head and personal life. A lot happens in these pages: my dating life picks up, I take you behind the scenes of a book tour, my V card is in play, and Wacha has PTSD. I launch a radio channel, make major moves in real estate, cause a few celebrity scandals, go on tour with Anderson Cooper, and continue to completely humiliate myself—and pinch myself—along the way.

Sometimes I think this can't be my life; and maybe that's part of the reason I write everything down—it's too good to forget. It goes deeper than that, too. I'm usually moving too fast to take a step back and take stock of where I am; I'm not the most introspective fella. But keeping this diary—for almost three years now—has forced me to "go there." Now I understand why Oprah begged us all to keep a journal for all those years! I can happily report I'm not the same person today as I was when I started this journey.

I want to thank all my friends for allowing me to share their names and our moments together in these pages. Also, thanks to my family, who I am sure are reading things here that they themselves never wanted to know about me. Thanks to Joe Mantello for coming up with a genius title for me and to Robert Risko for bringing it to life in illustration. Last, thanks to my team at Holt, led by my brilliant editor, Gillian Blake, for being great partners.

FALL 2014

IN WHICH . . .

> THE *NEW YORK TIMES* IS FATIGUED BY ME,

> I AM CONSIDERED SEXY BY *PEOPLE,*

> I GO ON A BOOK TOUR,

> AND MY VIRGINITY IS IN PLAY.

Even Joan Rivers can't make a funeral fun. Well, I bet she could if she was there and not the one being buried, but no such luck today. It was a big media event on Fifth Avenue with barricades, screaming fans, satellite trucks—everything Joan would've wanted. As always, Temple Emanu-El looked like a big Roman cathedral packed with fancy-pants New Yorkers. I walked in with Whoopi Goldberg, who told me she was feeling really shaky from this and Robin Williams's death. Luckily I had reserved seating— in a row with SJP, Matthew Broderick, Kristin Chenoweth, Kathy Griffin, and Rosie O'Donnell.

Of all the eulogies, Howard Stern's was my favorite. He and Joan were kindred spirits. He opened by talking about how dry her vagina was. That was his *opener*! The New York City Gay Men's Chorus sang, as did Audra McDonald. Hugh Jackman sang "Quiet Please, There's a Lady Onstage," which I never liked in *The Boy from Oz* but was a killer today, and bag-pipers played "New York, New York." I hate bagpipers. Barry was there, which I thought was really stand-up of him given that Joan publicly blamed him for her husband's downfall. He told me he had been invited and felt it would be rude not to go. The silent procession out of the church-y temple took forever and of course I was right next to Kathy, with whom I started to make small talk before wondering why I was trying to make this less awkward for her when I'd heard that she'd been shit talking me earlier in the week. So we walked out in silence, which I hate more than bagpipers.

There were crowds cheering in front as I left and that felt . . . *weird* at a funeral. People don't know what the hell to do with themselves anymore. I couldn't find a cab on the Upper East Side and wound up walking to a diner and eating at the counter, where I was soon joined by Liza and Brian. After we were done reviewing the funeral, as you do—high marks all around for Howard, big debate about Deborah Norville—we got back to business: the question of whether or not I should shave my summer beard.

At home I gave Wacha a doggie-frozen-yogurt treat, which he wolfed down, then puked up a little bit, and then while I was getting a rag to clean it up, he ate the puke. Efficient!

The sun streaming in the windows of Spring Studios turned DVF's fashion show into a hotbox. Still in our funeral clothes, Whoopi and I chatted again on our way in—that's twice in one day. She said Joan's funeral affected her profoundly and will change her attitude about work. Maybe she'll be less miserable than she's been seeming on *The View*? Sat next to Bryan at the show and the first lady of NYC was two seats over. I was hoping she'd break out some slam poetry, but that didn't happen. DVF's curtain call is always my favorite part of her fashion show. Naomi Campbell closed the show again and we ran into each other on the street and she complained that I never take her out to dinner. She's right! What am I *thinking*?

Went to *Watch What Happens: Live* for our first show of the fall. Tonee gave me a haircut and we took a vote about my beard—the consensus was to shave it, so off it went. We taped two shows, the first with Steve Harvey and Nick Jonas, who were totally incongruous but really worked. Harvey forgot his wedding ring in the car and we couldn't start until someone went down and got it. It's off brand for him to be seen without his ring, apparently. I liked him, though. And I was pervy with Nick Jonas. Speaking of pervy, it is male model week on *WWHL* in honor of fashion week. The models always look hotter in their pictures than in person. The guests for the live show were Rosie and Kathy from *Real Housewives of New Jersey* and we did a lovely tribute to Joan. Mom texted at the end of the night: "Not a great show but you look fab." I will always get points from her for shaving.

▶ MONDAY, SEPTEMBER 8, 2014

"You lost your toughness, man!" Surfin greeted me with that bon mot this morning. Negative points for shaving from the doorman! You don't necessarily want to start your day feeling like your mojo was shaved off the night before, but then again it's nice to have a trusted friend keeping you in check.

There's nothing better than walking into a show with enthusiasm and excitement, but the longer I do this job (I've done more than seven hundred shows) the harder it is to get it up. I was fully erect today, though (I love a #bonermetaphor) for Kristen Wiig and Bill Hader, who we were taping at noon for air Thursday. My team had had advance warning that Kristen was sick, wouldn't be drinking, and was barely up for the show. Turns out she had a scratch in her throat and was everything I wanted her to be, and that's saying something. I think she'll be back. Then Ramona came in to discuss her future on *Real Housewives of New York*. She arrived wearing hot pants, a tank top, pumps, and her hair in a topknot (business casual!) and though I was dreading it, the conversation actually went well. She profusely apologized for how she treated me at the reunion, and I said I just wished she'd *listened* to my questions because they weren't so bad— but that the viewers had turned on her and she needed to rehabilitate herself. I may have even used the "I want to be in the Ramona business for a long time" line. (I really do, though!)

I had to sign a zillion bookplates—and by "a zillion" I mean a thousand— which Target will insert in my book, which wasn't fun, and then plan for our Friends In Deed gala next month, then go through tax payments with Daryn and write thank-yous for the very random gifts I got all summer from viewers (paintings of myself, paintings of Wacha, dog leashes, Cardinals stuff, Peanuts stuff). Then I grabbed my executive producer, Michael Davies, and we went to the men's finals of the U.S. Open. We were in the Heineken suite (David Schwimmer was too and he looks very good, very "Ross") and it was too bad my dad didn't come this year (Mom and Dad are getting ready for their tour of Nazi hot spots in Europe) not only because they showed me on the big screen but also because I could've used him by my side: they showed me at the exact moment that Michael went to get a Heineken Light (Delicious! Full bodied, but half the cals!) so I was sitting there alone like a douchelord. Last year I'd made fun of Kevin Spacey for wearing makeup to the match, but I was glad I'd kept mine on from the earlier taping because, despite seeming like a lonely loser, I didn't look half bad up there. The match was over in a flash—the Croat won— and in the car back to the Clubhouse, as we watched the incredible sunset over Manhattan, we marveled at how lucky we are to live in this city. I signed more pieces of paper, then a reporter from *Details* showed up to follow me around behind the scenes of the live show, which was a half disaster. Let me just say this: I think Zosia Mamet was not very amused by this little show of ours, or by me. Then the phones went out somehow and I wound up objectifying Patrick Wilson and talking about his tits, further alienating Zosia. And it turns out the sponsor got up during a commercial break and changed the placement of their product on the bar, which later sent me into a tailspin. The best thing about the show, as it sometimes is, was Wacha. He came out and picked his favorite Girl from *Girls* by picking his favorite treat. He chose Shoshanna, so that was fun for her. After the show Mom texted, "I don't know who that girl is but she wasn't having fun."

"What the fuck are we doing up at five forty-five, homeboy?" That was the look Wacha gave me when the alarm went off this morning. I tried to tell him that Daddy had a paid speaking gig in Greensboro, North Carolina, but he didn't get it. In my ongoing bid to roll with a deeper posse (even freaking Zosia Mamet had ten people with her last night—WTF?), I made Daryn come with me. Also, she had booked the private plane, so I figured the best way to ensure that she was invested in the safety of the plane was to make her a passenger. I wrote my speech on the plane—it was great, if I can be objective (probably not?). The venue was a corporate retreat for a big outlet mall and the owner of the company ended his speech, right before I went on, with "God bless the United States of America," which made me aware that perhaps I should rethink some of my saltier material. I did this thing that was very Tom Cruise in *Magnolia* where I talked about how similar we all are and how people think we have the most glamorous jobs and everybody wants to go to outlet malls and everybody wants to go to a talk show. I started to believe my own BS: for sure outlet malls and talk shows are the two most glamorous places to work, right?

I was back in New York City by one forty-five and tried to nap but my first dream out of the gate was that Wacha got hit by a car. We had two *more* shows tonight—I feel like a machine. The first one was Connie Britton and Justin Long. Connie brought her baby in to meet Wacha and I brought Wacha in to meet Connie (she has a private Instagram account and "likes" a lot of his pictures). She is lovely. I don't know what came over me but when Justin came in to the studio I did something I've never done in all these years: jumped into his arms. He grimaced, caught me, and said, "I just had hernia surgery!" So that was an epic fail. Poor guy!

While I was signing a few hundred more bookplates the Clark Kent lawyer I met on Fire Island a few weeks ago started drunk texting me some provocative stuff, which I was fully on board with and which led to a marriage proposal, then more realistically to planning a date for Saturday night. He said he wants to take me out to prove to me that he isn't a gold digger, which is exactly the first time that thought ever crossed my mind. *Is he* actually a gold digger? So confusing. I told him he was gonna wake up tomorrow and look at his text history and cancel the date. The live show was Jenna Dewan Tatum and Tyson Beckford. I got Tyson to strip down to his undies. During the show Mom texted me, out of nowhere (and after all these years), her *Housewives* tagline: "I may be shrinking, but I'm no shrinking violet!" Slow. Claps.

▶ WEDNESDAY, SEPTEMBER 10, 2014

Woken up from a deep sleep by Wacha flipping out because the window washer was cleaning our bedroom window. Then two more appeared outside the living room window and all hell broke loose. He was barking at the washers, running from window to window and then looking back at me with eyes that said, *"Do you not SEE what is HAPPENING out the WINDOW??? We are being ATTACKED from the OUTSIDE!!!"* He had certainly never before entertained the possibility that a human could appear outside our twelfth-story window. I took tons of pictures. I got a text from the Clark Kent lawyer this morning telling me how drunk he had been last night. Oy. But it seems the date is still on. I didn't follow up on the marriage proposal.

Worked out with my Ninja for the first time since before vacation in mid-August. He made me get on the scale and I was sure it was going to read between 170 and 175 but it was 167. I hugged him. Then he kicked my ass and I almost barfed. Did work at home and Wacha slept next to me and, since I am an adrenaline junkie, I woke him up when the window washer appeared again. He lost his shit once again and I immediately regretted it. I went to my formal interview with *Details* at Morandi and the reporter asked if it was my brand to always wear a gray suit. I told him I wear all kinds of suits but I do have a lot of gray ones. At the end of the interview I started to think he wanted something deeper and I went into a whole riff that, if he uses it, is going to make me look like an idiot. First we talked about drugs, then I was saying how hard it is to not turn into a douchebag if you're hosting your own talk show every day, which just opens up the debate about whether I, myself, am a douchebag. We'll see.

There were about twenty people at Jessica Seinfeld's birthday dinner at Charlie Bird—Consueloses and Ali Wentworth included—but I had to leave early for the show. Got a late-night massage and kept falling asleep during it, which always makes me wonder what he was doing while I was out of it. Did he keep massaging or was he happy to have a break and catch up on email? I guess I wouldn't blame him.

▶ THURSDAY, SEPTEMBER 11, 2014

Just how clean do our windows need to be that these men are out there first thing every morning? Wacha freaked out again. I finally calmed him down, we went back to bed, and then I was awoken by an urgent text from Kelly, who had a guy from Guinness on her show measuring tongues for a new world record. Knowing that I had won a long-tongue contest at a gay bar in Miami a few years back, she wanted me to measure mine, take a photo, and get it to her stat so she could put it on the air in ten minutes. So then there was me frantically running around trying to take a selfie of my tongue despite my bedhead and gross #morningface (if that's not a thing, it should be). My tongue is three and a half inches long from the back and I almost puked putting the measuring tape that far in my mouth. I almost puked again working out with the Ninj. And then I *looked* like I was gonna puke at the photo shoot for the *Details* spread this afternoon because they wanted me looking really serious and Blue Steel. I told them I am a smiley, smirky guy, but they said everyone had seen me smile enough. We'll see how that turns out.

Dinner with SJP and Hickey for our annual September 11 gathering at Raoul's. Hickey and I walked down there remembering walking down that same route on 9/11; they let us right past all the barricades that night because we were with SJ and Matthew. As surreal as it was, some of the workers that night wanted pictures with them. I think everybody was walking around in a haze like it was some bad dream in a parallel universe, with papers flying around everywhere—all over the place—and from the World Trade Center that unbearable stench. Now I wish I would've thought to save some of those papers. Is that morbid? We had that same chic, older French lady waitress we always do at Raoul's and ordered three artichokes and three steak frites. It was perfect.

⋗ FRIDAY, SEPTEMBER 12, 2014

How did I know he was going to cancel? Clark Kent Lawyer's birthday is coming up and he wants to postpone our date so he can "party really hard" on Saturday night. Shelli Azoff simultaneously invited me to see the Eagles at Madison Square Garden on Saturday night, so I'm gonna ask Liza to go and I'll be with all the white senior citizens rocking to the oldies instead of with the young, hot revelers at Viva. In other news, the window guys aren't window guys; they're cleaning the exterior of our building, so this trauma isn't over. (And, now that I think of it, my windows aren't getting any cleaner.) I boxed with the Ninj and weighed myself after and I have *gained* two pounds since Wednesday—thank you, steak frites at Raoul's. Recorded the last of my audio book. Man, do I hate doing that. Dinner with John Hill, then opening night of Benjamin's new bar, LoveGun, in Brooklyn, which was a total happening. Kelly was wearing a sequined outfit almost identical to one I've seen on that fun little person, Joey, who hosts the Low Tea on Fire Island. Kelly can stand on a banquette and dance like a whirling dervish for three hours straight completely sober, which is incredible. I spent most of the night talking to Anderson and flirting with guys: in other words, my kind of night. Jacqueline Laurita thinks I hate her. She DMed me on Twitter.

⋗ SATURDAY, SEPTEMBER 13, 2014

This morning at the dog run Wacha slammed into a pole at full speed, squealed loudly, and limped over to me to cry in my arms. It was traumatic and bonding for us all at once. At the appointed time Liza and I arrived backstage at Madison Square Garden, where Shelli Azoff (with bone-straight hair and a manicure to die) grabbed us and said, "You *have* to meet Don [Henley] and Glenny [Frey]." She's the wife of his manager, so I guess she can call him Glenny, but then I called him Glenny and for a second it looked like he was going to have me kicked out of Madison Square Garden. But he was cool. Those guys are older gents at this point but they still are who they are, the motherfucking *Eagles*. Shelli was with Patty Smyth and John McEnroe, who confirmed he was, as always, wearing Björn Borg undies. I wondered if he thinks it's weird that I ask him every time I see him, but then he got approached by a friend of Shelli's who asked if he remembered staying at his house in Paraguay in 1980. Of course he did, he said. I felt less bad about the underwear. Shelli took us into the Dolans' suite, which is right off the floor, and the minute we walked in Liza loudly proclaimed to the entire room of swells: "Oh my God, look how big the SHRIMP are!!!" I think I screamed "NOOOO!" to her in slow motion and asked if she was Thelma Evans on her first trip out of the projects, or a girl who grew up in Malibu. The concert was fantastic. As Liza the walking blurb machine said, it was three and a half hours of "only songs you want to hear." Joe Walsh killed, that's my blurb. I didn't see one black face in all of Madison Square Garden. Maybe no Latinos either. There's another blurb.

▶ SUNDAY, SEPTEMBER 14, 2014

The West Village is one empty storefront after the next because no one can afford the rents. The old lady from the dog run with the golden retriever had to put her dog to sleep yesterday. I went to see Mark and Kelly's beautiful new town house on the Upper East Side. Couldn't find anything to buy in Ralph Lauren. Mindy Kaling and Meredith Vieira were on the show. Loved them both. Mindy and I exchanged numbers. We will wind up making love before the year is over. (Kidding.)

▶ MONDAY, SEPTEMBER 15, 2014

Twenty-five years after I came out of the closet, sitting in a doctor's office waiting for the results of an AIDS test hasn't gotten any easier. How can that be? I have only had safe sex my entire life, but once again every scenario runs through my head and all roads lead to the inevitable moment where everything changes. That didn't happen today, and I breathed yet another sigh of relief. Oh, and my cholesterol and blood pressure are good, news I was sure to email Mom and Dad on their trip through Nazi territory. They love reports on my cholesterol and blood pressure. Dinner with the *RHONY* producers—the big discussion was how do we reveal to the rest of the women that Bethenny is coming back to the show. One scenario we love is her just showing up at Countess LuAnn's party in the Hamptons unannounced, kind of an "I'm baaaaaaack!" thing. But we're having second thoughts because, well, the other women may feel set up—or worse, for a Housewife, excluded.

▶ TUESDAY, SEPTEMBER 16, 2014

There are no Jews or young people on the Nazi riverboat tour, so naturally my parents are eating each other alive. My mom said it's all church ladies and they are in a part of Germany full of Christmas stores. I saw the Ninj this morning, then went to the dentist, then to meetings at Bravo. Bill Simmons was there—he's starting a basketball show on ESPN, and apparently he loves *WWHL*, which made me go nuts and get defensive and crazy and jokingly ask him if he was here to rip off ideas from us, in a most un-jovial tone of voice. The first thing Craig Ferguson (who was on with Jessica Chastain) asked me was whether I had gone crazy yet. Apparently all talk show hosts do. So I guess I have, is the answer. I got him to say that Macy Gray was the worst guest on his show and when we went off the air, he felt horribly for saying it.

▶ WEDNESDAY, SEPTEMBER 17, 2014

I actually *gained* weight: I weigh 169.9 pounds; very upsetting. But a great workout. Brought Wacha to Holt for a meeting to go over plans for *The Andy Cohen Diaries*. It comes out in November. At this point I am honestly so sick of the book and I never want to see it again. Good attitude! Wacha was good in the meeting, running around the conference room, which is the tenth floor tip of the Flatiron Building. (He loves landmarked buildings—maybe because there are rats running around under the floors?)

We had Liam and Hickey on the show and it was a triumph—I made Liam do so many things. He was like a monkey, poor guy. After, Hickey and I joined Liam at the Boom Boom Room for his premiere party. Seth Meyers lost ten pounds on a cleanse. He's very thin and I was jealous. Some woman came up to me and told me she wants to develop a lollipop with me—branded freaking lollipops, are you kidding? Branded *pot* lollipops might actually be a good idea, now that I think about it. Hickey and I went to this horrible bar with go-go boys and some Portuguese dancer named Yugo came up to us and I don't know what was worse, his teeth or his breath, which told us everything we needed to know about the joint. We were out in ten minutes.

⟫ THURSDAY, SEPTEMBER 18, 2014

Two women, Debbie from San Francisco and Laura from Chicago, paid an inordinate sum to have lunch with me. It was a charity thing, and they must be pretty rich because they've bought charity tickets to *WWHL* too. Laura had a long, single-spaced list of good questions for me, which we went through ("Which Housewives have been to your house?" "Was *Southern Charm* your idea?" "Who would you want to sell your apartment from *Million Dollar Listing Los Angeles*?" "Which guest have you hated?"). At other tables were Hoda and Kathie Lee, Whoopi (I complemented the new *View* and she said she yelled at Rosie yesterday), and Bethenny. Had dinner with Amanda at this great old Italian place on the Upper West Side. We talked about whether twenty-five years ago we would imagine ourselves to be where we are in our lives now and we agreed it was pretty obvious. Had a two-hour massage very late and, once again, I kept falling asleep on the table.

⟫ FRIDAY, SEPTEMBER 19, 2014

The pitch with Martha Stewart and Bethenny at Bravo went pretty well. (The show is like *Shark Tank* meets *The Apprentice*, with Martha as Trump and Bethenny as Tim Gunn.) Martha was yammering on about hydrangeas. She is going to Newport for the weekend with seven friends, and Frances said "Road trip?" and she said "Yes, but on a plane." Talked to B about her arrival on *RHONY*. I said it would seem like we were setting her up to be the villain if we didn't tell the other women. She suggested telling them that there is someone joining who will be great for the show, and that we think it'll be good for them to find out who while cameras are rolling, but if they object, we will tell them in advance. I got home and spoke with Heather Thomson, who I'm not sure is coming back to *RHONY*. So Bethenny's entrance into the show may be a moot point to Heather—and probably Carole, who isn't sure she's coming back either.

Saw Bridget Everett's show at Joe's Pub with Anderson and Benjamin. My highlight was her pretending she was pregnant and Cole Escola coming out in a diaper as her unborn son begging her not to abort him. LoveGun was really fun. Anderson and I avoided that nasty writer who is always writing shit about us.

▶ SATURDAY, SEPTEMBER 20, 2014

Read Norman Lear's book for most of the day. I can't believe how much he accomplished. Sounds like *Good Times* was a real pain in the ass to produce. Conversely, *The Jeffersons* was on for nine seasons and was a completely happy set. Went to Gant and got a shitload of clothes—and by "shitload" I mean three bags.

Had a spontaneous dinner with SJP and James Wilkie; we tried to go to John's Pizzeria but there was a line down the block. We found another good pizza joint. Kim Cattrall is coming on the show next week and we hatched an idea for SJP to ring our "doorbell" and come out and give Kim the Mazel of the Day for being so great on *Sex and the City*. That'd really be something.

▶ SUNDAY, SEPTEMBER 21, 2014

I opened up the *New York Times* and saw the wedding announcement of a guy I went on a couple dates with about seven years ago. He was very handsome, with a good job, and he married another handsome guy who I recognize from the beach in East Hampton. I sat and wondered if I was letting all the great guys slip away, and what is my impossibly high standard for dating? I am hanging on to "cute" by a thread at this late stage in my life, and it's all downhill from here. Time goes by in a minute. Would I rather be with this guy—who I rejected, by the way, but I can't remember the reason—or doing my thing now? Well, I guess I know my answer. I dared Mom and Dad to buy space cake in Amsterdam. I don't think that'll happen. Lunch with Troy Roberts at Bubby's. Melissa and Joe were on the show. The lady who is @WachaCohen on Twitter was there. She's also @YolandasFridge. Hilarious.

MONDAY, SEPTEMBER 22, 2014

Bruce is back in town from LA for the week, so after both our workouts we got coffee and went to the dog run, like Real Housewives of NYC. Dinner with Ricky Van Veen and Allison Williams at Café Cluny. We talked about Zosia Mamet (Allison said she's not as awkward as I think she is), *Peter Pan Live!* (she goes to flying lessons every day for a few hours), and their wedding (Wyoming, this time next year). I don't know what the hell happened to the roast chicken in that place, but now it's all fancy and the plate looks like it's being submitted for a competition. I just want a roast chicken, that's all. Chloë Grace Moretz was on the show with Billy Bush. I've been anti–seventeen-year-olds on our show since Abigail Breslin came on—she was nice and fun but it just seemed inappropriate to be drinking in front of her—so when Chloë was having a dance-off to Taylor Swift in our bullpen area, I was worried, but she turned out to be great. Oh, and there were paparazzi for her when I arrived at the studio and I somehow dropped my phone and I think my man Ray ran over it. It's shattered. Emailed back and forth with SJP about walking on to the show tomorrow—seems like it's going to happen. My team is very excited.

TUESDAY, SEPTEMBER 23, 2014

Had a very frustrating, fairly circular conversation with Carole Radziwill today about the show, which is especially unfun because of our friendship, which predates *RHONY*. I got a new iPhone 6 and even though it's the small one, it's too big and looks like a whole new headache. We taped Sofía Vergara and Sam Rockwell this afternoon, and Sofía was stuck in United Nations traffic so our poor "audience" was in the Clubhouse waiting about an hour for her and I kept going in trying to take questions from them but nobody had any. Afterward, I had a pitch meeting with Isaac Mizrahi and a whole group of Upper East Side animal people for a potential show. Could be good. Threw on a Shipley & Halmos tux for the New York City Ballet opening; they'd made it for me when I hosted the CFDA Fashion Awards and the pants are now too big in the waist and seem to be too short. So, I got thinner and taller in the last two years, I guess?

Picked SJ up and ate Bolognese in her kitchen with Matthew, the twins, and James Wilkie while she got ready (Matthew was on the way to his show) and ultimately appeared looking very Jackie Susann in a Mary Katrantzou dress. On the way uptown, we discussed whether SJ should walk on to my live Kim Cattrall show and she was concerned that it would somehow be misconstrued, so I went with her flow and told her we shouldn't do it. In the line of cars, we watched as Baryshnikov walked undetected amongst the crowd and SJ was marveling at the sight of the greatest living dancer, and her former costar, quietly slipping into the ballet opening. On the way into Lincoln Center that lady from the *Daily News* who always trips me up did it again. I was waxing poetic to her about how much I loved the ballet, then she asked if I'd ever slept with a ballet dancer and I said, "But of course, and they are fantastic, like finely tuned machines," then spent much of the performance wondering why I'd fallen into her trap and why I felt it necessary to be honest when I know that this is going to wind up making me look horrible in the paper. That being said, the ballet was beautiful. We were sitting by the demon Koch brothers, and I sat there trying to think of something horrible yet memorable I could say to them during intermission but couldn't. So, I *had* to answer the *Daily News* lady but I couldn't muster up any balls with those evil billionaire brothers?

What *did* happen during intermission was that Scott Wittman and Alison Benson thought the Cattrall idea was kind of great, so the momentum turned back to SJP doing it. There was a dinner with gorgeous waitstaff and a whole slew of highly dateable guests, and of course I had to leave for the show before even the appetizer was served. I barged into Kim's dressing room full of praise for her and excitement that she was finally at *WWHL*. She was lovely, and I said I had just left the NYC Ballet opening and SJP, but she didn't hear the SJP part and said, "Oh, you're having a very *Sex and the City* night!" and then asked, "Are we talking about menopause tonight?!" because she was there to promote some menopause website. I said, "Of course we're talking about menopause!" but what I was thinking was, "SJP is going to walk through that door and I hope you love it as much as I will." I asked her what question I could ask that would provoke the exact words she wanted to say about menopause, she told me, and then I split to change. There was much blocking and coordination of our possible SJ doorbell, then I got an email from her at 10:55 that they were just serving the main course so all the excitement was for naught. (She tweeted something instead.) It was the doorbell that never happened. The show was pretty good, but I was kind of scared of Kim Cattrall for some reason and Frank Grillo (the other guest) started laughing out loud when I began earnestly talking about menopause. How could *I* be seriously bringing up menopause to Kim Cattrall, was what we both were thinking.

▶ WEDNESDAY, SEPTEMBER 24, 2014

When the building washers went by the window this morning, Wacha stood up, let out a little growl, looked at me, and returned to his nap. Hope that's his new normal. Neicy was here today and I realized (too late) I left a huge check on the counter from Bravo. You don't want your housekeeper knowing about your finances, but I guess it's inevitable. If they know where the lube is, is anything sacred? I grabbed the check and deposited it on the way to the gym. When I was getting ready for the show I realized I left my receipt from the ATM on the counter, so now Neicy saw not only the check but also how much is in my account. I am officially an idiot! Taped JHud and André Leon Talley—we played What's! Under! That! Caftan! and beneath André's caftan, which was covered in black bunnies, was a pink Cadillac sedan with my bobblehead driving and Anna Wintour Barbie (homemade) in the passenger seat. John Hill was controlling the car, so he drove it out from the caftan at the end. André—who we *loved*—was shrieking about the clubhouse being so Warhol: "Look at Wacha eating that cup! It's *so Warhol*!" "Lite Brites!?—*Warhol*!!" He worked with Warhol, so I was thrilled, and he was excited about my book, which he thought was very meta—"Andy doing Andy."

Went with Bruce to a new restaurant called BEA in Hell's Kitchen where we were discussing Natasha Richardson's love of Esca, across the street, and just as we were reminiscing about her someone walked by us carrying a big image of her face on a window sign for *Streetcar*, starring Tash. *Freaky.* There's too much going on in that new restaurant—movies on the walls, a piano, TVs. The food is good; they don't need all this junk. And Nick Lachey was there. We hugged twice. I think he's hot (Bruce doesn't). He said next time I talk to Lizzie from *Real Housewives of Orange County* on TV maybe I don't need to ask her about dating him and I said it was fascinating and I wanted to hear all about it! Then we went to Fantasia at Atlas Social Club, which is Asian night there. I met a very Waspy guy who said we connected at the last night of Beige, five years ago, and I didn't know if that meant we did something more than connect or what. What does "connect" mean, anyway, in this day and age?

ᐅ THURSDAY, SEPTEMBER 25, 2014

Happy New Year, Jews! Ninj said Cristiano Ronaldo's body double is going to come work out with him. What does that even mean? Is he a stunt man for his underwear shoots? I did a pre-call for a Q and A I am doing during Advertising Week and I was so anxious to get off the phone I kind of yessed the woman to death, and now what will happen is she's gonna ask me about marketing, branding, and blah blah blah onstage and I will not know the answers. Speaking of me looking like an idiot, the *Daily News* never ran anything about me fucking ballerinas. Phew. The Bethenny news is leaking out, it seems, so now all the NY Housewives are texting me asking if it's true and so there goes that surprise. Mom and Dad are back from the Nazi tour and full of piss and vinegar. Went to 30 Rock and had wine with Frances at Morrell. Me and the Bravo boss talked about all this and more: the Martha Stewart pitch, the possibility of my doing a podcast, SXSW sponsorship, *RHONY*, *RHONJ*, Kim and NeNe, *WWHL* ratings, my book, and a Bravo book party in LA.

I went to Amanda's for Rosh Hashanah. I brought wine that I got at Morrell and a challah and babka, both which were given to me yesterday by an audience member. You really aren't supposed to eat "fan food," but here I was serving it to my friends. We talked about if we all died, Jonestown style, from the challah how long it would take for someone to discover us and Liza thought Brian would be pounding on the door before sunrise, which is amazing and comforting, I guess, even though we would be dead. The headline news of Rosh Hashanah is that I found myself looking at Liza sexually—I was attracted to her physically! She was wearing this kind of light, clingy DVF-y dress with major cleavage and her legs showing and I was looking at her legs and she was kind of draped on the couch and it was totally new. Amanda had difficulty processing that, and I don't blame her. We've all been friends for thirty years. In the cab home I watched Derek

19

Jeter's last career at bat in Yankee Stadium, which wound up being a walk-off single. I had tears streaming down my face the entire time. Baseball is so romantic. I got home and grabbed Wacha for a walk—we took selfies with four really cute girls in front of Equinox and their two guy friends said, "We like your shit," and I said, "I like your shit too!" and then as I was walking away they both howled, *"What a douchebag!!!"* I started walking at a crazy brisk pace, saying to Wacha, *"OMG, this is so bad; this is so bad."* I hated it; it felt like some nightmare high school bullying experience (that I never had). Wacha was clueless.

▶ FRIDAY, SEPTEMBER 26, 2014

Surfin's off on Fridays, so Big Mike is on the door today and he's just about the biggest Yankees fan there is; all day it's been a flurry of Jeter talk in the lobby. Everybody's walking around with an extra bounce in their step. I saw *Gone Girl* with John Hill at the opening of the New York Film Festival and forgot I would be photographed. I looked unshaven and bloated and butterscotch teethed. We loved the movie. Afterwards we ate outside at Café Fiorello on Broadway. You could feel dust particles in the air. Or maybe I was a little high. I won't rant about how depressing the Upper West Side has become, because it's just a boring topic, but it's all chain stores. And the West Village is all for rent. What's the end game here? I got home and John and I read the *Times* review of the movie and realized Manohla Dargis was right about it being too tilted toward Affleck's character's POV. In the book you didn't find out she was a psycho until halfway through or more.

▶ SATURDAY, SEPTEMBER 27, 2014

Gorgeous day. Indian summer. Howard Stern is doing a tribute to Eric the Actor all weekend—they're playing every call he ever made to the show. I listened to about four hours, then I got a headache. After a hard workout with the Ninj, I met Ralph Fiennes for coffee and we sat outside and analyzed people on the street. I couldn't fathom how he could possibly be attracted to this tits-y, whore-y girl who walked by, then a tits-y, whore-y *guy* walked by and I understood. Then I went, date-less, to John Shea's wedding. It was the first non–TV wedding I officiated, and I didn't even think in advance of the possibility of bringing someone. Walking in alone felt really funny, kind of Miranda-like, for the first ninety minutes, until I married them. How amazing to officiate the wedding of a friend that I've known for twenty-five years! The ceremony was lovely and emo—the guests thought they were just going to a party for the wedding but were surprised with an actual wedding. I met John in LA at the pool at Sofitel in the early nineties, both of us there on business. He gave me tickets to the MTV Movie Awards that night and I brought Nancy Burns. We became friends, and one summer he had a share in the Sag Harbor house (those were the days, sharing my little house with others) and he and I were going to bed in those little nun's beds downstairs, and after the lights were out it sounded like he was wheezing a little. I said, "Wanna hit of my asthma inhaler?" and he made me repeat the question a couple of times. He thought I was saying, "Wanna eat my ass, maybe later?" We died.

After the wedding I met John Mayer at the Carlyle where he was with BJ Novak, who informed me he's doing my show on Wednesday, and I felt dumb not knowing. John played me two super emo, super good demos from his new album. At around one-thirty I stumbled out of the Carlyle elevator right into Rita Wilson. I hitched a ride with her and then her driver took me the rest of the way home. We talked *Housewives* and how much jail time Teresa and Joe will get. I am supposed to interview them next Friday, the day after their sentencing; I'm trying to think of the tone for that one.

▶ SUNDAY, SEPTEMBER 28, 2014

Wacha seems depressed. He was no fun on two visits to the dog park today. I asked Ryan at *WWHL* to describe his personality, and he said "aloof." Indeed, a week after I got him Liza said he was like Hugh Grant. The Cardinals clinched the National League Central Division so they're play-off bound again. Bruce was at George Clooney's wedding yesterday and took his shirt off—it's his thing at weddings—and TMZ called him the drunk guy without a shirt. It was Jeter's last game ever today, at Fenway. The sold-out crowd of Yankees haters all gave him a 112-second ovation. I cried again. The live show was Jacqueline and Rita Wilson. (We made a barter deal that she could come on if she gave me the ride. I am *completely* kidding; she had already been booked, we love her.) I told Jacq that I don't hate her. She said another Housewife told her I did. I told her to just base it on how I've treated her but then I realized I let her go last season, so why *wouldn't* she think that? I don't, though! I love everybody! Okay, I don't love *everybody*, but I don't hate Jacqueline.

▶ MONDAY, SEPTEMBER 29, 2014

In the hot haze of August I agreed to do two panels this week and the first one was this morning, something Lincoln Center put on for Advertising Week. I was interviewed by a *New York Times* reporter about . . . what? Branding, I guess. Marketing. The Future. It was sparsely attended, so I felt like a loser up there, and even more like a loser for saying yes in the first place, but I was home by eleven. Oh, we were waiting to go on and Daryn (I enjoy making my assistant join me at dubious events) told me she's been dating a girl named Evan. So it's two girls with boys' names—Daryn and Evan—dating each other. I had nothing to do until my show, other than figure out a way to avoid doing cardio at the gym. I wandered around the neighborhood for an hour with Wacha, who went into almost every store. He was in a better mood, and no wonder: he got treats at Gant, Marc Jacobs, and Steve Madden, then slept on my foot for an hour while I dealt with the Bethenny story, which is gonna break in *Us Weekly* on Wednesday. Carole texted and LuAnn wants to talk to me before the show tonight. The natives are getting restless. I was walking by Nourish on Greenwich Avenue and a tall ginger on a bench winked at me. We got to chatting as Wacha pissed on the flowerpot next to him. I asked him what he does for a living and we decided to play twenty questions about his profession. After twenty-five questions I was still circling around it—turns out he's a piano teacher and opera singer. He said his name was Tim but I thought he said Kim, and he said his mom used to date a guy named Kim but he wound up being gay. Which is now the second story of the day about girls' and boys' names pre-defining them as homosexuals! Got home and hung with Surfin and Big Mike in front of the building and talked about Jeter's last game. The window people had a little transistor and were speaking Spanish outside the window when I got upstairs at sunset. I felt like I was in *West Side Story*.

Wacha felt like he was in *The Amityville Horror*. Got a text from Cher whilst rehearsing and just knowing she thought of me put a smile on my face. She's scared about Ebola.

Jeff Garlin and the Countess were on the show, an odd combo that worked. She wants to talk about her future on the show but we were both preoccupied, so that call is coming tomorrow. Wacha almost ate the squeaky part out of his toy and choked and died on the after show. I realized on the massage table that I am officially lonely and have felt this way since John Shea's wedding. It's only when the noise stops that I even pause to think about it. Maybe that's why I keep it so noisy.

▶ WEDNESDAY, OCTOBER 1, 2014

The Bethenny news was everywhere when I woke up and I had texts from Housewives wanting to know what was up. Rosie O'Donnell was supposed to be on the live show with Melissa Etheridge but had to cancel, which is bad enough but made worse by the fact that *CBS Sunday Morning* is coming to shoot me tonight for the segment that will air when my book comes out. Erin Moriarty is doing the piece and Jay Kernis is producing, which is crazy full circle considering I was their intern twenty-five years ago at CBS. Erin is bartending, so I don't want someone shitty with Melissa. I lost another pound with the Ninj today. Cristiano Ronaldo's body double was at the gym and he is a beauty. I stared at his ass while doing plank leg raises and it was the best diversion ever. Ninj says I need a diversion; he likes when I have to take a business call but keep working out. We booked Gretchen Mol. Did my main interview with Erin for *Sunday Morning* at Morandi, and I think I was producing the piece in the back of my mind the whole time and thinking we didn't have enough stuff, that I wasn't being smart and funny or whatever. Erin thinks it's groundbreaking that I talk about being gay so much in the book, but maybe that's because she knew me when I was "straight"? We were supposed to tape Caroline Manzo today for Sunday's show but realized Teresa's sentencing is tomorrow and it would be weird for it to air on Sunday without Caroline's reaction to it, so we postponed that until tomorrow afternoon. Get this: Page Six ran a piece headlined "Andy Cohen Throws 'Housewives'-Sized Hissy Fit," saying that the "flamboyant" host—which means "queen"—showed up ninety minutes late (what?) to the Advertising Week panel on Monday and stormed out after a question about Aviva Drescher. Then TMZ texted me (does TMZ just have everybody's number?) asking for a comment. I didn't respond.

► THURSDAY, OCTOBER 2, 2014

Holy shit—Teresa's going to jail. We should've had a crew as I sat with her sworn enemies, the Manzos, waiting for the verdict before taping *WWHL*. We expected Joe to get time, and he got three and a half years, but Teresa getting fifteen months, and being sentenced first, was a surprise and seemingly due to omissions in the paperwork. We were all stunned and sad for her.

I brought Dr. Kyle from the Hamptons to see Rita Wilson at the Café Carlyle. Ran into Brian Williams with Allison and Ricky, and the anchor started giving me shit about my "creation," Teresa, and I said I feel clean, but she is a representative of *your* home state, New Jersey. I told him he should be jealous because I was doing a hard-hitting interview with her tomorrow. Kyle was a few drinks in when he arrived to our date. I realized that he was nervous—maybe because we were being joined by Mark and Kelly? It doesn't cross my mind that someone would ever be nervous to be out with me, but could I be misjudging the situation? Rita was great—her voice is lovely, very southern Cali. She had a thing upstairs after—Christine Baranski and Jann Wenner were there. Then we went to Kelly's for her birthday. Anderson and Ben came. Anderson told us he doesn't think Ebola will make it to the United States, but he thinks there will start to be ISIS-copycatting beheadings here. So that's a mixed bag of news. Naomi Campbell left a message after midnight. What's that about?

► FRIDAY, OCTOBER 3, 2014

Tonight is Kol Nidre, the night of atonement, and I spent the day trying to get some out of Teresa and Joe. I spoke to Dina, who was in a state of shock about the sentencing. She can't believe Teresa is doing this interview or that we're still doing the reunion Sunday. I called Naomi back. She had a message for me to give to Lisa Vanderpump and also told me to please tell Teresa she was praying for her.

The interview was very somber. Teresa seemed numb. Joe has zero remorse: He doesn't think he did anything wrong, he just thinks he got caught. They told Gia but not the other kids, even though the other kids are in school. Teresa's crisis manager was running in and out telling Joe to shut up and listen to the questions and not offer anything more. The crisis manager has also worked with Lindsay Lohan, Jill Zarin, and The Situation—all of whom still seem to be in varying levels of crisis, so . . . I was asking Teresa how she's going to feel in an orange jumpsuit because she likes the finer things. She said, "I don't even know if it will be orange," and I asked, "Well, how do you look in orange?"—the whole thing came off really mean, like I was kicking her when she's down. Teresa and I have a long history of joking with each other, but I actually felt bad. We won't use it. Went straight to dinner with Amanda and I gorged, knowing we had to fast tomorrow, then headed to temple. No cute guys at the gay temple this year, and that's okay because I was so preoccupied and still in shock from the sentencing and the interview. I've never known anyone who went to jail. I couldn't help wondering if this was the last time I would see her in the Clubhouse.

It was the Cardinals' first play-off game against the Dodgers, and I might've been a little preoccupied with that too. We won. I went home and watched *The Grand Budapest Hotel*—I loved it. Ralph was *perfect*.

▶ SATURDAY, OCTOBER 4, 2014

Fasting. Richard Johnston wrote a bitchy item saying I was cheering so much for Rita Wilson I should've just been up her ass. So I guess he has it in for me because that's what you call an opinion piece from someone who has a bad one. I forgot to tell Teresa that Naomi is praying for her. I wonder if I will remember tomorrow. Broke fast at the Levys' again; ate a tremendous amount but took it slow and steady.

SUNDAY, OCTOBER 5, 2014

Draining day at that *RHONJ* reunion, which we shot at some random place in the West Forties, for reasons unknown. When I saw Teresa, she said this would be her last reunion so she was going out with a bang, and she pointed to her shiny gold dress. I loved that she was in full Jersey drag. With her sentencing hanging in the air, it was a low-key reunion for sure. SJP came at a boring time and sat in the truck for about forty-five minutes. At the end of the day I turned to Teresa on camera and said remind me of what you said to me backstage about your dress. "That I didn't like my hair up so I put it down?" No. "That I was wearing gold?" No. Finally she said that it would be her last reunion. I wanted to hear her say it, I admit it, and we got choked up walking her through her years on the show. We had a weepy goodbye hug right after the show and she left.

MONDAY, OCTOBER 6, 2014

After weeks of avoiding walking under the ladder that's perched over the sidewalk on Hudson between Perry and Eleventh, I did it today. Kolten Wong hit a big home run tonight. The Teresa interview aired in prime time, but I was at the Friends In Deed event. Hickey was being honored, and the two of us gathered two tables but then he couldn't come because he's shooting in Australia. So I felt responsible for the two tables of people I'd gathered and was codependent the whole time. Mike Nichols spoke, which was amazing. In the midst of it all, my Joe and Teresa interview was airing. I built a barricade of napkins around my iPhone and was scrolling through Twitter, which John Hill correctly said was the rudest thing ever given that it was my event. I was trending on Twitter, though! Should there be some kind of etiquette loophole that if you're trending, you can look even if it's *your* charity event? In retrospect, absolutely not. Ron and Iva Rifkin, Matthew, Victor Garber and Rainer, Kevin Kline and Phoebe, Ralph, John Slattery and Talia Balsam, Scotty Wittman, Jeff, Mark Consuelos and Albert Bianchini, Marc Shaiman and Lou were all there. After, we all went to Anfora and then with Bryan and Matthew to watch the Cardinals at Corner Bistro. The burgers were magnificent and the Cardinals won.

TUESDAY, OCTOBER 7, 2014

Interesting to see what gets under your skin and what doesn't. Today the *Daily News* had an item on the gossip page saying I was partying at Atlas Social Club on Yom Kippur, which is a total lie based on a Facebook "friend" who I've never actually met tagging me as being there. I never care enough about this stuff to have Bravo PR call and complain, but I was so pissed because that is the holiest night of the year on the Jewish calendar and the single solitary only night of the year that I stay home after temple. Bravo let them know I went home to watch the end of the Cardinals game and then watched *The Grand Budapest Hotel,* and told them to call Benjamin to ask him if I was at the club. They said sorry, their sources have me there and that Ben is my friend and would cover for me. They doubled down, told Jen at Bravo that either she was lying to them or I was lying to her. I was going out of my mind about it all day. I had a fitting at Gucci, and maybe my mood is the reason I picked out a made-to-measure puke-greenish poo-colored suit. Went to Gordon's and looked at bathroom fixtures for the new apartment, which I have no set plan to begin work on but apparently need bathroom fixtures for. I think I have opinions about everything *but* bathroom fixtures.

I did a Q and A at the Jewish Community Center on the Upper West Side with a rabbi, and I guess they don't read the *Daily News* because no one brought up my alleged sin. The show was *Below Deck* people. Wacha shit inside, so maybe he is depressed again? After the show I had a Tinder date for which I had low expectations but that turned out to be nice. A Sicilian from Long Island. Big nose. His dad is a French lit professor. He loves *The Comeback*, which of course tells me everything I need to know about him. He wants to make me pasta. I felt very *Moonstruck.* The Cardinals beat the Dodgers and are moving on to the next round.

WEDNESDAY, OCTOBER 8, 2014

Wacha jumped up during the Tarzan yell with Carol Burnett. Hilarious. Totally spontaneous, and best of all, Carol was laughing from her gut and couldn't stop after. She was still giggling at the step and repeat. She was holding her chin after she did it, so I wondered if he nipped her, but she wasn't bleeding. Can you imagine? We played a game of *All My Children* trivia and Susan Lucci surprised her as the MC. Also hilarious.

MediaPost ran an article saying my Teresa interview was as good as any network news division could do. It made me think we should be in the business of scandal interviews, air them in prime time—the one-on-one is a great extension of what we're already doing. Then again, what's *MediaPost*? I never heard of it before today. Went to the *Top Five* (new Chris Rock movie) screening with Jackie. It bugged me for the first half, then I kind of got it and enjoyed it. Larry David was sitting in front of us. Some rapper was next to me and had no idea who I was but wanted my card. I said I didn't have one, which is the truth. Wacha shit inside again. Does he not like it when I leave him in the apartment—is he telling me he wants to be in the crate? If he does it again tomorrow I will leave him in the crate. The Italian dude is cooking me pasta next Friday night.

▶ THURSDAY, OCTOBER 9, 2014

It's decided—Wacha wants to be in the crate. He shit in the apartment again. Ran into Sean Avery on my way home from the gym sitting outside eating the most overbuttered pancakes and bacon—I don't know how he has the body he has eating like that. Then he said he'd just worked out for two hours. So that answers that. He was riding me like a horse about my workout outfit: blue sweat shorts, Cardinals sweat shirt, blue socks. He said I should be in all black Nike. John Hill and I went to Matthew's opening of *It's Only a Play*, which was really funny. Stockard Channing was unbelievable. That face! There were a few seventy-five-year-old/twenty-two-year-old duos who I couldn't stop staring at for the entire production. The arrangement begs so many questions (is it financial or a daddy complex, is the biggest one), which John and I discussed endlessly. We also were starstruck by Angela Lansbury—seeing Jessica Fletcher in the theater district is like seeing a mirage. We were turned away at Bar Centrale after—pretty sure that lady who runs it don't like me one bit—so we went to Joe Allen for dinner; we both had eggs and salmon.

Then I stopped back by the opening-night party, where I was talking to the Slatterys, who introduced me to their friend Maura Tierney. I told her how beautiful she smelled and she said she didn't know if she could believe me, and I said she had no reason not to believe me. I followed up with "I'm not trying to fuck you," but it came out sounding a little aggressive and she said something like "Wow." And so I realized I had to make it better and I said, "I mean, I *will* fuck you if you want me to, but I'm not trying." And that turned out to be the worst thing I could say. I knew it was all wrong as the words hung in the air. "Oh, you *will* fuck me if *I want to*??" She had a smile on her face, but it was incredulous. For ten minutes I stood there unsuccessfully trying to talk myself out of the hole, until these two agents came over to talk to me and I just gave up. I met Eddie Izzard, who was wearing heels and long nails and says he is running for mayor of London. Later the Slatterys came over and asked, "So you'll fuck Maura if she wants you to, but you're not trying to?" I think everybody had heard by the end. We all—Slatterys, Brodericks, my new best friend Maura, Scott Wittman, etc.—went to Bar Centrale after, so then it was me showing back up right at the spot where I'd been turned away, which you always think is going to be victorious but it never is.

▷ FRIDAY, OCTOBER 10, 2014—NYC—SAG HARBOR

I just missed the Cristiano Ronaldo body double at the gym. So upsetting. I need diversions! Had a pitch meeting with Jason Blum and his team about a scripted idea I'd had over a year ago when we were on Barry Diller's boat with the grandkids called *The Sophisti-kids*. Initially it was going to be about a group of super-rich, wise-beyond-their-years kids who solve murders. All ideas morph into others, and this one is now about people trying to figure out which rich people have sold their souls to the devil and which haven't, meaning somehow we've lost the kids entirely. So we added some and made the devil a woman—that was my contribution to the creative. The drive to the beach took four hours. I was supposed to have Sam's with Sandy Gallin tonight but that somehow turned into dinner at Tutto Il Giorno with him, Calvin Klein, and Ross Bleckner. We talked about bad plastic surgery for a long time. I was asleep really early.

► SATURDAY, OCTOBER 11, 2014—SAG HARBOR

It rained all day, which was perfect for me. Spontaneous lunch with Amanda and Jim. Two-hour nap, got Sam's to go, and stayed home and watched the game (we lost) with a fire and red wine. Mom is terrified I'm gonna be like Joe Giudice and drink three bottles alone, but I didn't even finish one. Kolten Wong kind of screwed up and of course Mom texted. I told her she had bad juju.

► MONDAY, OCTOBER 13, 2014

I'm at war with my eye doctor. The man is so thorough and meticulous, but along with that he's passive-aggressive, or maybe just mean. No bedside manner. All day I was dreading going but my vision is getting worse. His assistant lady examined me and figured out my new contact prescription and I was hoping I wouldn't have to see him, but she dilated me and said no such luck. Dr. Personality came in and questioned me. "You *say* you can't see distances that well, right?" Yes, I told him, starting to doubt myself. *Could I* see distances after all? "But there's only a slight change in your prescription here, so you don't really need a new one." He didn't believe me that I needed a new prescription?! He said my eyelids were kinda dry, and hadn't he told me a few years ago to moisturize them once every couple of weeks? I said yes and he asked if I do it. I confessed that I haven't. "Don't you think it's about time you listened to me?" he demanded. I felt like he had chopped my dick off. The lady at the desk said they don't take insurance—none of the fancy doctors in New York City do—and I asked if she would just send in the bill to my insurance company. No, they won't do that. I said, "You really don't want to help me, do you?" She kind of chuckled. The whole thing was humiliating. Dinner with Jason at Good. Got a text from someone named Tim who is in my phone as "rower" and looking back at my text history, it looks like we met very late at ASC months ago. He wants to grab a drink later this week. I have a vague memory that he is very tall and rowed in college—or maybe that's just because I named him "rower" in my contacts. We made a plan for Wednesday after the show. I thought about the dog for most of my massage; I'm pretty sure he's getting fat. I don't want a fat dog. He is definitely stout. I keep feeling to see if it's fat, but there isn't any, but then he looks it.

▶ TUESDAY, OCTOBER 14, 2014

When I dressed for the gym I thought of Sean Avery and did all black, then I ran into him on my way to the gym. He approved. They put an insanely aggressive Halloween display up in our lobby. Surfin has been staring at it quizzically.

The Cardinals pulled Seth Maness from the mound in the tenth inning and Randy Choate lost the game for us. I went nuts and for the first time started questioning Mike Matheny's motives in tweets. The Sicilian guy who is supposed to make me pasta on Friday night texted and said, "Let's eat out instead, my week is too crazy to make pasta." I know I'm not a chef, but don't you just boil the water and . . .

▶ WEDNESDAY, OCTOBER 15, 2014

I guess if *I* was ever going to be embroiled in a controversy surrounding the Cardinals it'd actually be about the *wives* of the Cardinals, and that's exactly what's happened! It turns out that some baseball blog noticed that Seth Maness retweeted my tweets questioning why Matheny would take him out. It's highly unusual for a player to retweet a fan's comments going against team management, and this morning the *New York Post* reported that Maness' *girlfriend* was actually tweeting on his account. The girlfriend tweeted me confirming that she says "amen" to all I was tweeting. All the retweets were deleted by this morning, as was the girlfriend's account. I texted Jon Jay, who said it was a real shitshow there, with emergency meetings about the girlfriend's behavior and a whole scandal going down. I kind of loved it, to be honest.

Wacha almost pissed on the Halloween display. Tamra texted me and is furious about the amount we talked about her last night. I said you can dish it but then you need to either take it or ignore it. Went to the Jeff Koons exhibit and some queen was FREAKING OUT because they wouldn't let him take his backpack inside but they let women take purses in. He kept screaming, *"Think of it as a purse!"* I stood and watched for a couple minutes then went through the exhibit, where I wanted to rub my grubby hands on every single shiny surface in there. Stopped by Mark and Kelly's fancy new town house but they weren't there. I ate Parmesan Goldfish in the kitchen with Lola for ten minutes then got a cab going down Fifth, where the driver gave me the bad news that his phone informed him it would take thirty-five minutes to get downtown, but the FDR would only be twenty minutes. I said okay but then we were stuck in traffic going to the FDR, which is the totally wrong direction from my house, and I panicked and started heckling him from the back seat—never an effective strategy. Then we finally got on the FDR and *flew* downtown and I *was* home in twenty minutes, so I gave him eight bucks on a twenty-eight-dollar fare. Wacha is being extra cuddly and keeps falling asleep on top of me. It is the loveliest thing. Maybe he's settling in to his life, since it'll be a year with me this weekend. John Hill is gonna plan something for us to do on Saturday to celebrate.

Kolten Wong keeps hitting home runs. This time last year Mom was heckling him and he was losing games for us; now Kolten Wong is the hero. We completely fell apart midway through the game and I was getting in a violent mood the closer we got to air. Minnie Driver and James Marsden chatted like schoolkids while my attention was diverted by the game. (Deirdre is a great EP but is not gifted at doing play-by-play into my earpiece. She doesn't understand that I want *every* play. She's very incomplete: "Two outs," she'll say—but she'll leave out that they moved to the bottom of the inning.) We lost. The mystery rower who I had a date with texted to cancel, which was fine because I had totally forgotten about the date. I stayed and partied with the kids from the show. Straight Pat made two comments about Wacha being fat.

▶ THURSDAY, OCTOBER 16, 2014

Turns out everyone at the dog run had been talking about how fat Wacha is too, because I brought it up and Lola, the golden retriever's owner, said, "We've been waiting for you to notice." Now I feel stigmatized on behalf of the dog. How did I not see this was happening? Maybe I'm too obsessed with my own weight! I don't *want* a fat dog! I mean, who does? I want *him*; I just don't want him fat. All I do every day is plan this book launch: the tour, the press, and the signings. I had lunch with Gillian so she could bring me my first copy, and there's nothing quite like the feeling of holding your own book for the very first time. (I guess I think I'm F. Scott!) It looks gorgeous and elegant.

All day long I was regretting saying yes to hosting the charity thing tonight for the Hudson River Park—which was happening at exactly the same time as the do-or-die Cardinals play-off game—and trying to remember why I had, and I was finally reminded: Gladys Knight is performing, and they agreed to throw a plaque on the back of a bench with my name on it. I'm a whore for posterity, I guess. And Gladys. When I arrived at the event, I was seated between Kevin Bacon and Kyra Sedgwick (both are very lovely) and two down from Michael Bloomberg. I have a thing where I always want to talk to famous people about their most iconic thing, whether on my show or off, so in no time I was talking *Footloose* and *The River Wild* with Bacon. (No, he was not a professional dancer and yes, he loved the river movie and it is his favorite death scene on film.) I think they were regretting saying yes too, but Kyra said she considers it "doing service" and I agreed. Somebody has to do it. And by the way, it *felt* like I was doing charity work MCing this thing because not one person listened to me while I was onstage. They had me interviewing these Asian violin prodigies and then they performed and no one listened. People are beasts, is the thing. I wonder if they would listen in St. Louis or if it's really just New Yorkers who are the animals. I, meanwhile, was sitting to the side of the stage following the game on my MLB app for much of the night, and it looked like we were going to win for most of it. Gladys performed and did the classic intro ("Thank you for making this next song our biggest hit—sing along to the record you made number one!") right into "Midnight Train," to which I was flailing wildly as Bloomberg sat like a stone next to me. How many of these things has he been to in his life, I wondered. He turned to me and wanted to hear about what's on Bravo because, as he told me three times, he has never seen Bravo. So I classed it up a little and told him about the cooking and the real estate shows. I asked what he thought of the Comcast/Time Warner deal and he said he saw nothing wrong with it. And I said, "Well it's a monopoly, right?" but he didn't really hear that part. I went to the stage hoping to get a chance to talk to Gladys and was chatting with her road manager as a woman came up to take a picture of her, and the manager said, "Get a good look, because we are *out* after this song. *Gladys has to roll.*" And just like that she finished singing ("That's What Friends Are For") and was on a golf cart and off like Cinderella into the night. The Cardinals game was tied up in the ninth inning and I flew out of there at the speed of Gladys to watch for myself. When I arrived home, I realized it was to be a very bad night for Wachas everywhere. Mine was in his crate with a pile of barf in front of him, poor fella. And on TV his name-sake was on the mound, losing the game for us and ending the season. It was awful. I turned it off and went to ASC to meet up with Billy Eichner, which was incredibly fun. Went to bed wondering where the hell Gladys ran off to . . .

▶ FRIDAY, OCTOBER 17, 2014

Worked out on the piers with the Ninja and Wacha sat in the corner watching, next to these people drinking gin out of a bottle and smoking dope. Juxtapositions! Took him to the vet and he turned into a nasty, growling *animal*. It turned out he was having white-coat syndrome, said the doctor. We were unable to get him to do anything but get on the scale—he's gained three pounds since his last visit and eight since I got him, and she said I'm overfeeding him. So that's the end of that. He's officially on a diet.

Got together with Phaedra at 30 Rock and finally met her son Ayden. I got him an Empire State Building Lego set, so we made that while I tried to convince Phaedra to do a one-on-one special with me for the *Real Housewives of Atlanta* premiere night. She *so* doesn't want to. She's this weirdly private person who is on a reality show about her life, so that's a life-sized oxymoron. We were talking in code about Apollo in front of Ayden, saying he is working in a hospital, so I guess that's what they told him. I got home from the show and drunkenly was looking through my book and noticed we spelled Billy, as in Joel, "Billie." There's nothing quite like holding your own book in your hands for the first time and finding a mistake.

SATURDAY, OCTOBER 18, 2014

It's Wacha's Andyversary! As planned, John Hill came over to celebrate. I can't give him tons of treats as I'd intended to because he is morbidly obese. We saw *On the Town* with Jason and Lauren and I absolutely loved it. It's old-school perfection. So romantic and epic—the dancing and sailors and Jackie Hoffman all killed me. So I guess the stink of *Spider-Man: Turn Off the Dark* has left the Lyric Theatre. After the show they brought us right back to take pictures with the cast onstage, which was exhilarating. I was a blabbing fool about how much I loved them all. Okay, maybe I was a little high. Or very high. During a long dance break in the show I convinced myself that the *Details* piece about me is going to come out and be a disaster—I said some dumb stuff—so that's something to look forward to this week. Went to Orso and got the worst table in the restaurant, right by the kitchen. So I'm a real heavy hitter there.

SUNDAY, OCTOBER 19, 2014

Watched *Notting Hill* on TV. The Julia Roberts character is a real bitch and I have no faith that they stayed together. At *WWHL*, Caissie pointed out that Julia Roberts always plays bitches. The mystery guy wanted to make another date, so we made one for Tuesday. I still have no idea who he is. He rows?

MONDAY, OCTOBER 20, 2014

I told the Ninj that I am done obsessing over the scale. I can't freak out over a few pounds—I'm just going to go by how I feel, and that's it. No more weighing. We announced the Bethenny news; it's great to have that out there. I feel like it's the calm before the storm of the book-tour madness. *People* is coming here Wednesday and shooting Wacha and me to promote the book in the magazine, and today they said they want to do a separate shoot of me for their Sexiest Men issue without my shirt on. Maybe I picked the wrong day to stop weighing myself.

Matthew Broderick was on the show with T.I., and T.I. seemed very stoned. We got word before the show that Oscar de la Renta had died and I asked Matthew about it top of show and he said that they swam with him in Greece a summer ago and he was even elegant while swimming. So T.I. thought this was quite funny and was giggling, which of course was highly inappropriate. I hung with Matthew and Wacha in my office having cocktails after the show. *Details* came out and the piece is great. It might wind up being the best thing that'll ever be written about me; the writer basically calls me a pop genius. Michael Davies forbade me from going shirtless in *People* magazine, and thought that if I was straight they wouldn't be asking. So now I am a victim of homophobia!

⟩ TUESDAY, OCTOBER 21, 2014

My PR rep suggested I pose with the sheets up to my pecs for *People*. I said we will see. My arms and pecs actually look pretty good; it's the stomach I don't love. There's a big Microsoft deal brewing for me that might mean I have to do a live commercial on Thanksgiving and Mom would be in it too. I Skyped her to tell her and she was quite wound up. "I'm doing WHAT in a commercial??? WHAT AM I GONNA WEAR? How will I know what to SAY?" They'll tell you what to say and we will rehearse, I told her. I told her not to stress, that it's thirty seconds and no one watches commercials. She said, "You're right, I haven't seen one IN MY ENTIRE LIFE!" Which is her refrain, she swears she's never seen a commercial. Dad wanted to know if there's a part for him and she kept saying "He's a MEDIA MONGER." I told her the term is "media whore." "Media WHORE! He loves the CAMERA! I'm OVER IT."

Met Carole and cleared the air. She had stuff to say to me and I to her—so it was very *Housewives*. I told her I am not inviting her *or* Bethenny to my Anderson-hosted book party because it's not fair to the others. She asked about my Christmas party, and I said that too. These are her friends too, she said. Who knew becoming a Housewife would get her uninvited to a party she's been attending for years? But I feel funny inviting her and not all of them.

Ty Burrell and John Leguizamo were on the show, and Ty and I discovered that we were both working at Faneuil Hall in 1987; he was a bouncer and I was selling Grateful Dead–y Mexican pullovers. I'm hosting these *GQ* awards tomorrow and haven't given a moment's thought to jokes so I asked Caissie to think of some ways to make fun of old *GQ* pics of myself. She thought of some good stuff, like, "Here's me on a Tinder date with a blue purse." Then I went on the date with the mystery rower. Turns out we met *a year ago* at ASC, *not* this September as I had thought. So I have no frame of reference for time. He is a nice guy, only twenty-six and a half. He's six foot six, which is a plus, but maybe not enough of a reason to see him again. I realized when I got home that I have a tentative plan with Grac for Saturday night, which is the same night as Allison Sarofim's legendary fancy Halloween costume party, and this is a huge opportunity for us so we have to take it! Her themes are always really high concept and everyone takes them really seriously, and this year's is Italian futurism. So I have to figure out what the hell that means.

▶ WEDNESDAY, OCTOBER 22, 2014

Wacha is very over being famous. We had twenty people from *People* magazine here all day bossing him around, trying to get him to do stuff that he had no interest in, like sit on the counter looking cute while I read the paper, sit with me on the couch pretending to interview me, and lie on the bed looking seductive with me for the "sexy" shot. The compromise was me in a tank top. I did pushups beforehand, but I still think I look kinda chub. My bedroom was full of people, with me sprawled on the bed in a tank top feeling like an old bloated Jew kissing my dog. It's amazing how you can feel so hot when you're alone, like you're ready to shoot a naked *Playgirl* spread, then you actually book a photo shoot and you look awful.

We taped Alan Cumming and Victor Garber and played What's! Under! That! Kilt! and I swear it's so hard not to sexually harass these models who are lifting up their kilts on command. I feel like someone is trying to trap me. God? Is it you? I sloshed in the rain (well, I walked from my car under an umbrella) to the *GQ* Gentlemen's Ball. The awards were for celebrity do-gooders and a few real do-gooders too. It was Zachary Quinto, Joshua Jackson (Pacey!), Taylor Kitsch (Riggins!), and Andrew Garfield. The blue purse line got a big laugh.

The live show was Jenny McCarthy and Tom Bergeron. Jenny wants to set me up with a Croatian chef. He looks very hot. Wacha grabbed Donnie

Wahlberg's hat at the end of the show and ripped it up. And Bergeron was playing tug of war with him and he kind of bit Bergeron. After the show Deirdre and John Jude were very serious with me, saying that maybe I should get Wacha under control and he could hurt a guest, and my position was that Bergeron had it coming because he was winding him up—kind of a Kenya/Porsha situation in my eyes. They didn't seem to agree, and we all hung out drinking after the show and Anthony said Donnie had remarked that the hat was his favorite, so then I started kind of feeling bad. I am playing the celebrity edition of *Who Wants to Be a Millionaire* tomorrow and half my crew works for the show and I am getting advice from as many people as possible. They say to listen very closely—there are clues in many of the questions, and many of the answers are common sense.

⯈ THURSDAY, OCTOBER 23, 2014

My new contacts arrived from my eye doctor who accused me of lying about not being able to see and I swear they are the wrong prescription. I was up at the crack of dawn to tape some "The More You Know" spots, which should be called "The Less You Know" because they seem to be for people who don't have common sense. Mine were about unplugging your appliances to save electricity, meeting people you only know from social media in public, and not sharing personal information online. *Rocket science!* Matt Lauer came in the studio toward the end of my taping and he and I had a jovial bro-chat.

Someone from *GQ* posted a pic of me hosting last night—me in front of a blown-up pic of myself with the blue purse—and the comments were about how self-centered I am and that I make everything about me. It pissed me off so bad I commented and said I was actually making fun of myself. I am so sick of everyone's opinion. Went to 30 Rock and had a meeting about that potential Microsoft endorsement deal that would mean I have to shoot like eight commercials sometime before the book comes out in two weeks. Hmm. And met with Randy and Fenton from World of Wonder about potential shows for me to produce and host with them. I love those guys.

Schlepped to *Millionaire*—in Stamford, Connecticut—with Daryn and Ryan. Daryn is obsessed with game shows, so my playing celebrity

Millionaire is her dream come true. So we arrived at this building that looks like a junior high school (they also seem to shoot *The People's Court* here) and here's how it went down:

They take us to a conference room (the teachers' lounge) where Michael Gelman and Laurie Hibberd are waiting; he's taping *Millionaire's* Daytime Talk Show Week and Laurie is his lifeline, and then mine arrives in the form of my friend Dave. I gorge on food from the spread—lots of cheese and Doritos—and Dave comments on my consumption. The lawyer comes in and briefs us about how the game is played and I realize I am a complete idiot for not having watched since they changed the format a few years ago. And why, exactly, did they change the format of a show that was perfect? I start to wonder, and consider that *The Price Is Right* is still going strong after all these years. I manage to wander back into the tutorial before I go off the rails. They take Michael and me through eight sample questions. Some seem like tricks—though they're not—some have clues in the questions, as I'd been advised, and some are just hard. But we're getting the hang of it and they're giving us intel. You basically have to eyeball the audience, who are bussed in, to see if they're smart or dumb. If you say you're leaning in one direction and then ask the audience, they'll go with wherever you said you were leaning. The biggest lesson is to *play the game*. Michael goes down to the studio to tape his show, and I don't know a few of his questions and neither does he. He walks away with ten thousand dollars, which is the minimum you can get. You're guaranteed that amount, as a matter of fact. I am playing for Doorways, Mom's AIDS charity in St. Louis. I don't want to fuck it up.

I go in the studio, which is all blue lighting and feels like a spaceship about to blast off. You have to get ten questions right to get to $68,000 and "Classic *Millionaire*"—I still barely understand how it works beyond having to get ten right. The first question is about Salt-N-Pepa. Got it. Next is Peter Pan—what does a tinker do? I don't know what the hell a tinker does. I ask the audience (I had identified the college section before the show and implored them to help me). A tinker fixes pots and pans, says 79 percent of the audience. That's a landslide, and I get it right. I get tripped up on "What musician was originally going to play Clint Eastwood's role in *Dirty Harry*?" The choices are Sinatra, Elvis, Harry Belafonte, and Mick Jagger. I know that Belafonte and Jagger are out and I think it's Elvis, weirdly. I don't think Dave would know so I don't use him. (He did; it was Sinatra.) I skip the question and lose $5,000 out of my pot. The next question to stump me is which French designer made the bag that Grace Kelly made famous. I narrow it down to Hermès and Louis Vuitton, don't ask Dave (he didn't know), and guess Hermès. I'm right! I think I jumped into Terry Crews's arms at that point. (I did it twice.) I carry over to the next episode so we have to go change our clothes because it's another "day." (Yes, that's how it works!) At the hundred-thousand-dollar round, the question is a whopper: "Kim Kardashian's wedding ring weighs fifteen carats and is worth one point five million dollars"—promising so far, and then—"how many times bigger is the Hope Diamond?" No fucking clue. I call Dave out; he wants to bet four times and I think he's right. The deal is, get it right, win $100,000, get it wrong, leave the game with $25,000. I decide not to guess and I leave with $77, 000.

Mom was thrilled. After there was John Hill's birthday dinner at Elmo and then drinks and video games at Barcade. Liza is an *animal* at Centipede! Who knew?!

▶ FRIDAY, OCTOBER 24, 2014

Mom doesn't believe I'm one of *People*'s Sexiest Men. "Do you HAPPEN to be in the issue? I mean there's a LIST, YOU KNOW. Are you on THE ACTUAL LIST?" She actually got under my skin. I emailed around and they said, yeah, you're in that issue on the list of sexy guys. I am in a real limbo kind of situation with these contact lenses. I don't want to go back to the eye doctor because I can't stand him, but my reading on my phone and computer is all fucked up. What do I do? I'm frozen. And blind. Daryn found some kind of pixelated suit at Patricia Field for the Halloween party that seemed like Italian futurism to her so I sent Mike Robley to pick it up during the *Below Deck* reunion taping today, which was three hours of fun. Man is that Kelley hot. I had dirty fantasies about him as we taped. I tried on the pixelated suit and it's really cheap. The search isn't over and the party is tomorrow.

Went to Allan and Suzi—which moved from the Upper West Side to SoHo at some point. It's smaller and not as great as I remember it being. Allan kept saying how tiny I am in person, and then Suzi called and he said loudly into the phone, "Guess who's here: Andy Cohen. *You can't believe how tiny he is!*" They had nothing resembling Italian futurism. He brought out a huge pair of silver jeans that only illustrated how tiny I am. I was a little stoned and wandering all over the city with Wacha looking for Italian fucking futurism clothes and wound up in Paul Smith, where I spontaneously bought a bright purple suit, black shirt, and silver and black tie—does anything scream Italian futurism more than that ensemble? I felt good about myself and they sent me to this alteration place on Thompson Street which would do it in an hour. The dude in that store said I couldn't bring Wacha in, and I couldn't tie him up with his weird leash so I stood waiting for a fan to walk by and say hi. One did and asked for a selfie and I said how do you feel about watching Wacha for three minutes while I get these pants hemmed? The guy asked if he could bring Wacha down the street to show him off to his friends. I said yes and then asked the alteration guy if he thought that was the last time I would ever see the dog. He didn't want to engage me on this topic but the other tailor said it was dumb of me to let a stranger take care of the dog and I should've just tied him up. I tried to explain the leash, and that really what would've been swell is if I could've just brought him inside. None of it translated. But the dog was returned unharmed. I hung out in a park and talked to John Hill, Jackie, and Bruce on the phone while waiting for the suit. Grac came by and we listened to the B-52s and had a lot of pot lolly and then walked to the party in matching white round sunglasses—she was all in Pucci.

Got to the party and the theme had changed from Italian futurism to the Future, and I hadn't gotten the memo! Patrick McMullan was dressed as a fairy so maybe he didn't either. There were some crazy costumes—people in astronaut outfits who must've been so hot, and some sexy robots. I was pissed about agonizing over the wrong theme all week! I take these things seriously! The Diamond Horseshoe, which was a big vaudeville kind of supper club in the forties, is revived and amazing and tonight was the opening and I forced Grac to come with me after the party for old times' sake. Erich Conrad put us in a booth and we danced a lot and met a group of hot bisexual guys from Bay Ridge. Grac left at one forty-five and I at two-thirty but I went to that pizza place on Forty-Eighth and Eighth where slices are five dollars but you're too drunk to care. Or maybe they just charge the drunk people that because you will pay anything at that hour for a slice. I sat there and motioned for this very cute kid with a backpack eating alone to come over and wound up eating with him; it was Brett who played Spider-Man on Broadway. I was drunk and looking at him with one eye squinted.

▶ MONDAY, OCTOBER 27, 2014

Listened to Amy Poehler promote her book on Howard Stern. I'm prepping myself. Had a conference call about potential game shows to host and produce. I love the excitement and possibility of a game show; I hope I can find one. Jenny McCarthy emailed me about the Croatian chef who is going to be in her radio studio when I am on her show. I asked her about Donnie's hat that Wacha ate, and she said he has two thousand hats and not to worry the least bit about it.

It was our *American Horror Story* Halloween show. I asked Angela Bassett her secret and if it was a "black don't crack" kind of thing and Kathy Bates was mortified. She thought it was racist. The live show was Nathan Lane and Andrea Martin. Nathan said he likes the version of me who hosts a show better than the real me, so that was nice.

▶ TUESDAY, OCTOBER 28, 2014

All day was spent trying to find a guest for tonight because Rene Russo cancelled. The booked guest is Joey McIntyre. We had Antonio Sabàto Jr. as a backup but he wasn't getting anybody too excited. He got kicked off *Dancing with the Stars* last night. We were after Nicole Wallace, Jenna Bush Hager, Tom Colicchio, John McEnroe, Bob Costas, and a whole list. We listened to a steady stream of reasons why each person couldn't do it. Grac interviewed me about the book for *Entertainment Tonight* at the Cubbyhole—a hilarious concept, letting an old friend turn the tables on me.

While I waited on a bench in front of Café Cluny for them to get set up, a woman walked by with three dogs and one got off his leash and started running down West Fourth Street. I ran after him and thought I had him cornered but he tore off toward Twelfth Street, then Eighth Avenue, where I lost him. He was so fast. Someone else had eyes on him and was far ahead of me. The lady was gone when I got back to the bench. It was all so traumatic and fast. Grac was adorable in the interview. She had her hair done and was playing games with me. She asked me what minute of fame I'm at on Warhol's fifteen-minute scale. (I said I hoped I was on my second minute—in actuality I fear I'm on my tenth or eleventh.) Around five o'clock we booked Antonio Sabàto Jr., who was looking bad at ten this morning and great seven hours later.

Liza came over and we watched the first episode of *The Comeback,* which was incredible (and would've been even if I wasn't in it). Got an email from Tracey at the dog run with a picture of that cute dog I chased around the West Village today—Ruby! Ruby is still missing. Oh man.

▶ WEDNESDAY, OCTOBER 29, 2014

Awoke to an email from Tracey at the dog run saying Ruby was found. Wacha has a vet appointment on Friday and now that he has white-coat syndrome, they're recommending I give him some drugs before he goes. Today was the test dose and he was totally looped; he could barely walk. Legless, I believe is the term. It was beyond heartbreaking. His eyes were glassy and open the whole time. He wouldn't go to sleep. His expression was saying, "What the FUCK did you put in my peanut butter an hour ago!?" The doc said to give him a little less on Friday. Okay!

▶ THURSDAY, OCTOBER 30, 2014

Not feeling great. Met with Gordon the architect and went over plans for the apartment. It looks great but the whole process involves an incredible amount of minutiae. We're talking about beginning construction early next year. Stayed home obsessing over the book coming out in two weeks. *New York* magazine wants nothing to do with me; they don't want to cover me or the book, not even online. Tried to figure out why *New York* hates me during my two-hour massage. Decided I am widely considered a douchebag among some circles in New York (and thus, in *New York*).

▶ FRIDAY, OCTOBER 31, 2014

Happy Halloween. I guess *Vanity Fair* hates me too because they won't mention the book—they "don't put reality TV stars in the magazine." Except, I guess, Ryan Seacrest, Jessica Simpson, Paris Hilton, etc. Took Wacha to the vet and got the dose wrong again, I guess—it was too mild or else he is just totally full of PTSD where the vet is concerned. He was full of rage, Cujo, terrifying. Thus, we didn't get very far. He needs his shots, but the lady just fed him treats. That was our big success. The streets were a shitshow. Hickey and I went to Good and then watched *The Comeback*. It never gets old.

▶ SUNDAY, NOVEMBER 2, 2014

The vet came for a house call, which was a total trauma. Wacha was legless when she arrived, totally drugged, but saw the stethoscope and totally flipped out and became a wolf! He fought through the drugs. I was able to put a muzzle on him and they were able to give him three shots and take blood. It was truly exhausting. Don't get me started on how much I hate the muzzle, though nowhere near as much as he does. Dinner for DVF's new E! show with Hammy, the Rourkes, Benjamin, Barry, Allison and Ricky, etc. Caroline was on *WWHL* post-reunion and I had to ask her about all this shit Dina said at the reunion and it's a never-ending cycle of family drama I am stirring up and I feel bad. I have a conscience, people!

▶ MONDAY, NOVEMBER 3, 2014

Felt sick all day. Taped Lisa Kudrow and Martin Short, who said Kevin Lee (the *Real Housewives of Beverly Hills* "shi shi shi" guy) is *not* the inspiration for his *Father of the Bride* character so we had to kill the mash-up comparing them. The premiere of *The Comeback* is Wednesday in LA and I can't go because of work. Lisa said all the Friends are gonna be there. Wowza. I think I said on the show the other night that *Friends* wasn't funny, so now I regret it. Or I would've if I went to LA Wednesday night. But I hate to miss a party, and let's get real: I like the idea of all the Friends in a theater seeing me on *The Comeback*. Lunch with Hickey at Village Den. Delicious turkey burger. I was telling him about being on *Millionaire* and he told me to use my inside voice, which he has to tell me constantly. Went to Dr. Katchen about my hair, which I think is falling out. He says it's fine but I should have a consultation with a guy in LA. Everyone on Mom's side lost their hair. He said, "Who do you look like?" I said my dad's side. Is it as simple as that? Spoke to Jacob Bernstein, who said that the *New York Times* Style Section won't be covering the book at all because "there is Andy Cohen fatigue at the *New York Times*." Let me just repeat that sentence so it can really sink in because I heard it ringing in my ears all afternoon: The *New York Times* is fatigued with me. Well isn't that ironic because I haven't read today's paper and I think I will just pitch it right out because I am fatigued with *it*. The *whole* paper—the old Gray Lady—is fatigued with me?! So I guess the *Times* and *New York* magazine have something in common. We had a Friends In Deed board meeting. Dinner with Ted Harbert, where we discussed the possibility of bringing *Match Game* back. I am *in*! Back to the show for an interview about the book with E! and a fitting, then the live show which was *Vanderpump Rules* people. I drank tea on the air. I've been doing these interviews for the book but the truth is that no one has actually read it. They ask about something that happens on the first page and then about a quote on the back of the book. (I learned that with my first book.) And that has made me do more prep for people with books who come on my show. I read Marty Short's and Andrea Martin's in advance of them coming and can't stop patting myself on the back.

▶ TUESDAY, NOVEMBER 4, 2014

Two phone interviews with people who hadn't read the book. The lady from the *Philadelphia Inquirer* just wanted to pitch *The Real Housewives of Philadelphia*. So that'll be a boring piece. The radio interview was all about trying to set me up with the gay guy from the radio show who seemed from his Twitter profile pic to be wearing a paisley scarf—not promising. I am terrified no one will come to the signings next week. The 92nd Street Y is almost sold out—nine hundred people—but who knows who will actually turn up. I had a real crisis in my head today about that. Speaking of signings, we are pretaping some shows for next week so I can take selfies at these signings for four hours (or one, depending on whether anyone shows) in New Jersey and Long Island. Today we taped Dick Cavett and Megan Mullally. The energy was a little off. You just don't want to cut off Dick Cavett, and it was one time I wished our format had room to just chat without me shoving another game down everyone's throats. He told some good stories, and I read him a bit from the Warhol diaries about him seeming a little gay on *Letterman* in 1985 but that he killed on the show. He seemed a little pissed at first but I guess it was okay. Did an interview for the *Los Angeles Times*'s website—they won't cover me in the actual paper but perhaps are not fatigued enough by me to forbid coverage of me online—and then went to the Palm where I sat with a reporter from the Associated Press for an hour until Amanda came and we had a fast dinner before *The Last Ship*. I realized that not only had I forgotten to take my makeup off, I hadn't stopped home to get money or my wallet. So Amanda had to give me twenty bucks for a cab at the restaurant *and* pay for dinner. I was like the queen of England. Loved *The Last Ship*—Joe Mantello directed it (beautifully) and all the music is by Sting and it's like *Billy Elliot* without the gay and with better music. That being said, I was trying to figure out which of the shipbuilders is gay—someone has to be, it's Broadway, plus they're all essentially clogging bears with beards and bellies so it looks either very butch or like Sunday night at the Eagle. We went backstage and ran into Gloria Estefan who is in town working on her musical *On Your Feet!* She said it's more about resilience than dancing and I don't know what that means. I like her. We encountered Sting backstage and the photographer asked to take a picture of the three of us and I just felt bad for the two of them that they were being sullied by my stink in that music-legend pic. I was about to leave when a bearded fellow from the cast breathlessly appeared, saying he'd heard I was here and had to come tell me that he and his boyfriend love me. I told him I was trying to figure out who in the cast was gay and that I had pegged this guy in a track jacket in the bar scene. He said nope, he's the only gay guy in the whole show. When I got home I saw a new guy in the elevator—tenth floor, big ass, sexuality in question—and watched an old episode of *Concentration* to see if I wanted to host it but the game seemed so boring. I couldn't concentrate!

▶ WEDNESDAY, NOVEMBER 5, 2014

Asked Surfin about the guy with the big ass but he didn't have a lot of information. The day was absolutely nuts and I was sick as a dog and in a foul mood. I cancelled the Ninj as a result and did phone interviews all morning—blessedly, with reporters who had actually read the book, which I found incredibly gratifying. My *Today* show pre-interview made me dubious about my ability to get the book's point across in the three minutes allotted. Had another meeting about game-show possibilities with Jimmy Fallon's production company people. We are narrowing in on *Match Game* and *Concentration*—both have issues, though. I am worried I would get physically bored hosting *Concentration*, like checking my phone while I was up there hosting the show. That's no good. And I'm worried *Match Game* is only nostalgia. Went down to the show to pretape Naomi Judd and Rob Riggle. I went into Naomi's dressing room and she said in her kind of country deadpan drawl, "I'm not afraid of you, Andy Cohen. I raised *Wynonna Judd* and *Ashley Judd*." I love it when the Judds mention other Judds! She said she only came to see Wacha, so we had the doorbell ring at the top of the show and he ran in, at which point she dumped out a bag of treats and toys she had brought him and I went apoplectic because he's on a diet but was slurping up a mountain of Judd dog treats with abandon. To make matters worse, one of the toys was a squeaky one so during Plead the Fifth you could hear "squeak squeak squeak." She told me during a commercial break that I seem lonely and she wanted to give me her "private line." Then on the after show she asked where I was spending *Thanks*giving (that's how she says it, real country) and I said with my family and she said that sometimes the family we make is the most important, not our *blood family*. Here is exactly how the conversation went:

NAOMI: I worry about you.

ANDY: You do?

NAOMI: I dunno. I just get an intuition sometimes. . . . You're too good to be alone.

ANDY: Thank you. You think I'm a sad guy, don't you?

NAOMI: *(closes her eyes)* I just think you are so stinkin' sensitive . . .

ANDY: Uh-huh.

NAOMI: *(eyes still closed)* And I think you are hypervigilant.

ANDY: Uh-huh.

NAOMI: And I think you're . . . *(opens eyes directly into her camera, smiling)* Well, I don't want to analyze you on TV, but—

ANDY: I have no problem with it.

NAOMI: HAHAHAHA! Okay. You have your *blood* relatives *(glances around her for reassurance)*, you know, that you're born with. I personally think that the stork was drunk and dropped me at the wrong house. You know, that kind of thing. So, what we've done, um, we have created our family of choice.

ANDY: Yes . . . yes. Right. So are you saying you would be like an auntie to me?

NAOMI: *(possibly paraphrasing* Golden Girls *theme song)* I would be your confidante and your friend.

Was Naomi Judd trying to turn me against my family? She said so many weird things, like that she and Ashley went to DC for Ashley to get "vetted" to be a senator (wha???) and they realized everyone in DC is legally insane and so they held each other in the hotel-room bed at night and sobbed. Um.

After the show I had a demo from the Microsoft white-glove team to show me the attributes of the Surface. They want Wacha at the shoot tomorrow and I begged them to leave him out of it. Now I see why Patsy Ramsey killed JonBenét (wait, did she?)—she got sick of having to lug her around to perform. If I didn't already feel like shit the rest of the night would've made me sick: I had a haircut and a photo shoot, shot a mock episode of *WWHL* with Lisa Edelstein in character from *Girlfriends' Guide to Divorce*, then did an *Access Hollywood* interview, voice-over for a *RHONJ* Secrets Revealed episode, and *then* the live show, with the stars of *Hot in Cleveland* minus Betty White—we had a cardboard version of her behind the bar. Wacha knocked over Wendie Malick's champagne but she loved it. Got to bed at one forty-five. Did I mention I'm sick?

▶ THURSDAY, NOVEMBER 6, 2014

You want the day of your book party to be like your wedding day, essentially doing spa activities til the magic hour, but I had a 6:00 a.m. wake-up call to shoot the Microsoft spot on Long Island, where I wondered all day if I'd make it back in time for the party. Once again, Liza was spot on about the weather; it rained like a bitch all day. The first shot was me and Wacha watching the Westminster Kennel Club dog show and he was just wild and out of nowhere a dog wrangler appeared with a huge bag of treats and cheese and liver, which made him a ravenous wolf and made me an insane bear. A couple hours of him jumping on and off the couch actually yielded what I am sure will be a really cute spot. And sometime after we finished shooting I realized that even though I still have a cough I am feeling better, I think, which made me forget how tired and cranky I was and just made me anxious for my book party tonight. I had a solid twenty minutes at home to shit/shower/shave and refresh for the party, which like the last one was at Anderson and Benjamin's house and included people from every facet of my life (college/Bravo/Holt/gays/high school/CBS/randoms but no family—parents coming next week), which sounds fun until you are the only one at the party who knows everyone and you feel codependent about not paying enough attention to each person. The second most talked about person at the party was also the only Housewife there: NeNe Leakes, who happened to be in town and came. I snapped a selfie with her and Monica Lewinsky, which was all I needed to make me extremely happy. When worlds collide! Monica at a party is always the most talked about and stops even the most jaded people in their tracks. Willie Geist arrived breathless because he'd walked in with her (Willie is not jaded, BTW). She looks very pretty. I introduced her to Erin Moriarty, who said I was her intern back in the day, and Monica said, *"I was an intern too!"* You go, girl! The last people at the party were Mark and Kelly, Jeanne and Fred, Padma, Anderson and Ben, and we all slid down the fireman's pole.

FRIDAY, NOVEMBER 7, 2014

6:30 a.m. wakeup. Jessica Seinfeld posted an Instagram saying the stuffed monkey at AC's (they have lots of taxidermy) was giving my book side-eye because I wrote about Jerry's mom's shiva. So that not only made me paranoid that I crossed a line writing about the food at the shiva but made me wonder (for the hundredth time) what else was in the book that could piss off my friends and acquaintances. Had a pit in my stomach all day about it while I shot the Microsoft stuff for twelve hours. Dinner at the Consueloses' and got home and talked to Lynn, who terrified me about the *Sunday Morning* piece that airs in two days. Somehow Erin was being very cautious with me at the party and kept saying she hoped it was okay. I hung up thinking the piece was going to be all about what a starfucker I am. Isn't publishing a book supposed to be *fun*? Well, it's not.

SATURDAY, NOVEMBER 8, 2014

Very mellow, quiet day. John Hill came by. Sandy said my book is kind of boring if you're not reading about yourself. Dinner with Jamie and Liza. They were telling each other things they already know about each other, like what drugs they've done and stuff. Watched *Olive Kitteridge* on HBO. The book was a hundred times better.

SUNDAY, NOVEMBER 9, 2014

Woke up early to walk Wacha before *CBS Sunday Morning* aired. Checked Amazon and the book was number 540 (can anyone stop me from obsessively checking?). I watched the whole piece standing up and let out a big sigh at the end. It was great. My only problems were that it seemed like I worked at CBS News for one minute (it was ten years) and that the *Housewives* clips were all insane—drink toss, table flip, limo fight. Oh, and I looked sweaty. I am so relieved. Lunch with Hickey, Jeffrey, and Scott Wittman. Went to New Jersey for Michael Rourke's dad's viewing. I didn't view. Barry invited me to the Philippines for Christmas; I have no plans and want to go. NeNe was on fire on the live show but I was horrible. Went to the apartment of the Italian guy who I had the mellow date with to watch the premiere of *The Comeback*. It was all gay guys I didn't know and it was kinda weird because I was *on* the episode. Book was number 155 on Amazon when I went to bed. So it begins.

⯈ MONDAY, NOVEMBER 10, 2014

Book was number 55 when I woke up! Of course checking the number was the first thing I did. On the *Today* show Anjelica Huston and I went back to back plugging our books. They did a tease with us both and it came off a shot of Al nuzzling Matt's ear and Savannah kind of prodded me to do that to Anjelica, which I did and immediately regretted. I am a monkey. (With a wig on.) Savannah interviewed me and she's as sweet as pie and I think it went well. From there I had phone interviews, then went back to my real job and did a pretape in the afternoon with Kenya and Sherri Shepherd which was all sorts of wrong. We played a game with NeNe last night called Silk du Soleil where I showed her people and she said who she would save and who she would drop. We showed Wendy Williams and she said she'd drop her. So I hear from CAA that Wendy and her manager-husband are furious at me for "dissing Wendy" and now don't want to do the *Judge Judy*-type show I was going to produce for Joan Rivers that we'd reformatted for Lifetime starring Wendy. Wendy is perfect for the show and I really want to be in business with her. Are they so thin-skinned that a game of Silk du Soleil could kill the deal? Hopefully they'll be over it in a couple days and we'll get it back on track.

Backstage at *The Colbert Report* I was really nervous running through the questions with Emily (thank God my very old friend produced my segment so she could brief me hard), but also the problem is he doesn't really *ask* questions. He just says things like, "You're as shallow as a kiddie pool." I almost always travel solo but finally had a (motley) posse in the greenroom— Aunt Sheila and Robert, Daryn, Ryan, Emily, Tommy, and Charlotte. Colbert came in before the show to say hi to me and remind me that he is playing a loud, dumb character, which is their warm-up to make you even more scared. I was pacing backstage but the truth is that it was a funny segment. My show was Tom and Ariana from *Vanderpump Rules* and they were jet-lagged or something and Tom couldn't get his sentences together and I was mugging to the camera and people thought I was either a genius or very rude. Or both. Jon Jay from the Cardinals was behind the bar and his wife told me my whole tweet thing with the girlfriend of Seth Maness was a massive scandal within the Cardinals. I love it. I was so excited about doing Howard Stern in the morning that I couldn't fall asleep.

▶ TUESDAY, NOVEMBER 11, 2014

Publication day! I woke up like it was Christmas morning—at five-thirty, after four hours' sleep—kissing Wacha as he wondered WTF was going on. Took a pic of the sunrise, and you know you're feeling zen when you do that. I am such a Howard fan, and just being lucky enough to be interviewed by my broadcasting role model is a win for me. It felt so natural and so great sitting across from him; I took it all in. But he reawakened all my fears when he said the Seinfelds would be pissed I wrote about their kid's bat mitzvah and Madonna would hate that I said she was singing to her own music at my Christmas party. I turned it around and explained myself. We talked about weed, molly, poo, me being a power top, what makes me a great houseguest, Eric the Actor, baseball players' asses, Joan, Wacha, John Mayer—everything *except* the Housewives, which I loved.

Got to Kelly right before the show and Michael came into her dressing room as I was telling her about Howard. I'd just seen pictures of Strahan with washboard abs and told him I wanted to punch him. I did twice and maybe it was weird; Kelly told me to stop. She sold the fuck out of my book. I need to send her something. Then I was on the radio with Seacrest, and I realized I was going to have to own everything that's in the book so I told him about how I write that he always says "you're crushing it." He liked that. Or pretended to. While I was on the phone with Seacrest a hot window-washer dude appeared outside and I secretly took his pic. The book was in the twenties on Amazon at midday and I think Holt was freaking out that it wasn't higher because they started giving me media-training tips that were kind of contradictory, like to lose the Warhol reference. I pointed out I'm going on *Morning Joe* and *Imus in the Morning* and I would think they would like that. I was at my breaking point. Got off the phone and napped for half an hour. When I woke up I opened the window and offered the hot window washers a beer, which I know would lead to us having a successful three-way marriage. Then tried to get them to pose for a pic, which they didn't love. Took their pic anyway, the second of the day. *Radar Online* picked up me saying I love molly on Howard Stern, so I am sure I will be media trained one more time before the week is up. And Fox Sports picked up me talking about Anthony Recker's ass. So now Anthony Recker knows how I feel about his ass.

Schlepped two hours to Huntington, on Long Island, where I signed 450 books. During the Q and A there were a few precocious kids—one wanted to be a reality star and I said to go to school instead; the other looked like the bee girl from that Blind Melon video and asked if I keep up with the Kardashians. She and her mother thought it was a hilarious question. A lady raised her hand and asked if I ever want to do a "real" late night show. Nice. They all had glitter cases on their phones. This one lady said, "I'm the pipe cleaner lady!" and handed me a bag of pipe-cleaner cocktail rings and some glasses that said "mazel" in pipe cleaner. I took them with me. Another lady had the most gorgeous kid ever, who I picked up to discover a terribly poopy diaper. Ooh. It was 90 percent women, some couples, and some really sweet misty-eyed gay guys. I got two numbers. Neither will I use. At the end of the line was a dude who introduced himself as Big Fat Joe and he had a big fat son named Joseph. I loved them. Went to bed and the book was number 8 on Amazon. Wacha's in Brooklyn, and I needed a hug from him so bad after this day. Sherman said he and Tico are having a blast. I asked who Tico is and it turns out he's Trey Anastasio's dog. Another famous dog friend for the Wach-star!

❧ WEDNESDAY, NOVEMBER 12, 2014

Radio interviews first thing in the morning. John Hill came over and told me about his great Tinder date last night, then said he likes normal-looking guys and I was like *um*, didn't *we* date for three years? Taped *The Meredith Vieira Show*; they had Doritos in the greenroom (I guess they paid attention to the book) and I gorged on them. Ryan got sick watching me suck the flavor off and asked if that's what I do. So I guess my own Bravo publicist didn't read my book in which I detail sucking the flavor off Doritos? The scuttlebutt backstage was that Streisand had been there the day before and wanted all the orange removed from the set. Any trace of orange had to be gone. But she asked for *cantaloupe and cheddar cheese* in the green-room. Both orange! *What does it mean?* Meredith had me rat out Barbara Walters for yelling at me. All day there have been stories about the book on *Radar*, first saying that Theresa Caputo is called out in my new book for "fishing," then it was that Naomi Campbell told me to fire Kenya at the Met Ball. You never know what's going to get pickup. Wacha is still in Brooklyn living it up with Tico Anastasio and I am starting to get jealous. Literally.

On my way to New Jersey, I got a text from Naomi Campbell saying to call her. It's highly unsettling to get a text from someone saying to call. The signing went by like a flash. Signed 450 books. The crowd was great. Very few black people, but more men tonight than last night. Fell in love with a lady named Lil' Shirl, who is short, not so little, but full of personality. I love anybody that calls themselves "Lil'," or "Big." I wonder if she knows Big Fat Joe from last night? Maybe they should date! On the way home I told Leslie, my publicist at Holt, that I'd stopped looking at Amazon because it was killing me, and she told me we're number 6, which is outstanding! Called Naomi on the way home and she said, "Have you gotten me in a scandal, darling?" I told her I had not and she said, "Don't worry, but it will be in the UK because they make a scandal out of anything. And any-way, darling, what did you *say?*" I told her what it was and she said it was fine and would I walk in her Fashion Against Ebola show and I said of course I will. She asked what designer and I said Ralph Lauren. So there's that. When I hung up I realized she never said *when* the thing is. Went to Hickey's and ordered a salad, which I crammed in my mouth while talk-ing to him and Denise, then went home and Eli Lehrer came over for vodka and gossip. Done by twelve-thirty.

▶ THURSDAY, NOVEMBER 13, 2014

Woke up at the crack of my ass to go do *Morning Joe*. Saw Willie in the makeup room and he and I gossiped about the *Today* show, *GMA*, and Josh Elliott. The show went well. It was me, Joe, Nicolle Wallace, and Thomas Roberts. I was feeling weird because Thomas is in the book but I came clean and told him, so that's that. From there I went to Imus and that was a trip. The man is in his eighties and his hair still looks like it's *from* the eighties, like a big poufy thing that you would think is a wig but I really don't think it is. He must get it blow dried in the morning. I wonder who does it—him? His wife? A paid employee? Will I have that much hair when I'm his age? I fear not. There's been a story around about the door on Bono's private plane coming open in mid-flight so it was the perfect segue way to start my interview with a recollection of our plane sinking with Dan Rather all those years ago, which he remembered but didn't realize it was me who was the producer with them. I had a meeting with FremantleMedia and Jimmy's team about game shows and decided to narrow it down to either inventing a new one or *Match Game*. *WWHL* was Anjelica and Wendi McLendon-Covey with my parents at the bar. We played Cohen to the Movies and they had to give clues, and Mom said, "CALL HOME!" for *ET*. All night Dad kept talking about Brandi. "There's a picture of Brandi . . . when is Brandi coming on?" Mom had a bad cold. She said she thinks celebrities like reading about themselves in other people's books. Really TCBed it at *WWHL*—signed books, dealt with staff Christmas present (Adidas track jackets with logo), met about creative for the *five* shows we're crashing in two days, next Monday and Tuesday.

Mom and Dad and I went to the Village Den and ate comfort food as it rained outside, then I did a signing at Barnes and Noble in Union Square. Finally had a lot of black people in the crowd. And men. And everyone was so calm and well behaved compared to the ruffians in Jersey and Long Island! Someone asked who my fave bartender was and Mom raised her hand, furious I didn't think of my parents first. Some women from the #CherCrew were there asking all kinds of fanatic Cher questions—"Can you get us backstage? How is her health? Do you want to come with us to see her in Allentown, Pennsylvania?" I said no but mentioned that I used to jerk off to the Billy Joel "Allentown" video, which was unsatisfying to her. Mom connected with every gay guy there, especially a kid named Fernando who works with people with MS and almost didn't eat because he was so nervous to come and begged her to have me follow him on Twitter (I did). Met a gal with a stack of eight by tens of herself auditioning to be a Housewife. At the end of the night I got a DM on Twitter from Fernando asking can I please follow him on Instagram—is it ever enough? After Insta will be Snapchat!

Met Jon Jay and Nikki for drinks at Anfora. Talked more about the Cardinals wives scandal. Heaven.

Phone interviews, then Mom and Dad arrived, she with a bad cold and in a mood. We went to the Palm for the first of six book signings at Palm locations that Bruce and I concocted. Quickly signed 240 books (fifteen minutes) and downed a steak. Mom came in and said, "Your father and I are sitting WITH THE PEOPLE! People DROVE HERE for you! From BUFFALO! CLEVELAND! Some lady stopped me in the bathroom and said 'YOU'RE MY MOTHER' and I said 'No I'm NOT!' and she said that I could be because she's JUST LIKE YOU!" Stern Wack Packer Mariann From Brooklyn was there and I just couldn't get enough of the full circleness of sitting in the back looking at her tweeting selfies with my parents. I wandered the room of women—a ravenous bullseye of a Venn diagram of Palm People and Andy People—and answered questions for a half hour and then took pics with all as they were hustled in via a line. Got out of there and did an hour-long Twitter chat and #AskAndyCohen was trending for the whole hour, which seemed like a mix between homemade and 2014.

Went up to the 92nd Street Y for the interview with Anderson, which I'd been looking forward to. He and I were chatting in the greenroom when all of a sudden I heard my shrieking mother's voice: "We were ATTACKED in the LOBBY!" she announced as she charged into the room with an air of just having fought—and lost—a battle. "We were getting our TICKETS and they started CIRCLING with CAMERAS. For FIFTEEN MINUTES! WE DON'T WANT TO DO THIS! WE'RE NOT FAMOUS! We're OLD!" My father seemed resigned to—if not tickled about—it all. "They are very excited to see you, Andy," was his gentle way of processing the pandemonium. "There's a lady from PARIS out there who flew here just to see you! She watches ON THE INTERNET!" AC had just met with the Ferguson cop and gave my parents a little intel on him, and we all speculated on when the verdict would be. I won't be home for two weeks yet so I'm sure it won't affect my trip at all. They are planning for protests in St. Louis—in Clayton, specifically—and Mom and Dad's building has a plan for people to walk their dogs in the garage. She thinks it's a lot of hype, but Em is fully engaged in the hysteria. Anderson's intro was a version of the intro he says I will be getting on the book tour, which is a mangled version of my Wikipedia page. It was perfect. The interview itself was an hour of rollicking fun. He said no one has more fun being famous than me and I protested but upon introspection, he's right. We both gave each other a lot of shit and had great chemistry. As the lights went up I realized Margaret Russell was in the front row and she gave me a pass to an amazing design show which I will miss because of the book tour. Can't believe she was there. I want my new place in *Architectural Digest*! When it was over Anderson and I went in the greenroom and I said, "That was an hour of host chat! I hope there were syndicators in the audience!" and on cue his agent, Carole Cooper, entered and said she could book us in theaters like she does with Bill O'Reilly and Dennis Miller, an idea to which we both perked up. My parents raved too. "Now THAT was fun. We're OUTTA HERE though. We're gonna go GET A COOKIE somewhere." (How cute is that?) I signed three hundred books; they sold out, and the organizers were in a frenzy because the line was so long. Met a lady wearing an "I'm a Fandy" shirt and "Lil' Fandy" pointing to her baby bump. Guess who she was there with? *Lil' Shirl from Jersey!* I greeted Lil' Shirl like she was my long-lost sister.

Left the signing and met Amanda, Jim, and Liza for drinks. They loved the event, which made me happy. They couldn't believe how ravenous the audience was—apparently fights were breaking out. Amanda was sitting behind a fourteen-year-old boy, there with his mother, who was paying *rapt* attention. I love that. Dropped them all off on the Upper West Side and met Hickey and his family at Tavern on Jane for a pop and crashed hard at twelve-thirty. Why don't we go to Tavern on Jane anymore, was the question of the night. Need to change that.

❧ SATURDAY, NOVEMBER 15, 2014—NYC—ATLANTA

Here are names that make me a little nuts when they appear on the yellow Post-it to the left of the title page in the frenzy of a signing: Jennifer, Jessica, Danielle. They're just long, is all. And my writing gets sloppy. The book is number 14 on Amazon now, so it's still high but going in the wrong direction. Looked for it in the Delta terminal at LaGuardia and couldn't find it, so this begins the torture of being at airports without my book on sale. Landed in Atlanta and went straight to visit Grac who happened to be here visiting Andrea for the weekend with the kids. Went to the Palm for a signing and was interviewed by Robin Meade from HLN, who appears to be the person with the chunky side braid in my last book. Full circle! It felt so sweet to be at the Palm—they all love Bruce so much and I feel like an extension of him since he's my best friend. Plus they'll make me whatever I want (today, a chicken Caesar salad). There were 150 people who were not normal Palm People, very well behaved. Some had flown from Seattle or driven from Jacksonville, in Florida. Half hour Q and A and then photos. Then I went to the hotel to close my eyes for twenty minutes before Grac met me and we went to the Jewish book festival, which was 1,200 people in a gymnasium. It felt like a dead house but I guess it was enjoyable despite my outfit, which I got all wrong—cargo pants and denim shirt. Tomorrow will be worse because I'm whipping out the yellow plaid Gant shirt that Madonna made fun of on the plane. I have nothing but clothes and still sometimes I can't figure it out. Interesting. Right before the Q and A I got an URGENT text from Kathy Griffin asking me to call her, saying she needed fifteen minutes of me talking to her with no one around. What is it with women texting me to call them? I told her I couldn't and she said it was urgent and to call after the signing. I texted after and said I would call tomorrow. Was she calling to apologize for shit talking me? I have no clue. This man introduced me at the book fair signing and gave the *exact* butchered Wikipedia intro that Anderson parodied last night, to the note.

After the Q and A (during which I hugged a lady, then a guy asked for one and came up and squeezed my ass, which I liked), I got ready to sign by chewing a pot lolly and the Jewish ladies were *freaking out* that the line was longer than anything they'd ever seen and I would never get through it and basically it was a similar deal to last night, Jews breathing down my neck predicting doom and all of us seeing the sun rise. So that made me sign so fast—like a maniac; I tried to give everyone a moment but I was freaking out and people were being shuttled through super fast. I got crazy gifts: Some lady made me "Disco Andy," which is a doll wearing the exact outfit I wore while dancing with the B-52s with Grac, which was nuts given that Grac was sitting five feet away watching the whole spectacle, taking pictures, it turns out, of all the girls' high heels in line. Some girl, all done up, gave me a T-shirt for her charity that she wanted me to pose with (all while the book fair people are screaming "No posed pictures!") and then she asked for me to write a paragraph in her book and then for a selfie with her coming behind the table, which is a no-go for these ladies, and with each new request I started to lose it and crumble. By the time she walked away I had kind of lost my shit internally and then it seemed the end of the line was near so I calmed down and was able to focus and I am glad I did. There were some really sweet people near the end of that line—a group of girls who drove all the way from Kentucky, a couple who drove from Tennessee and the woman was in tears of happiness. I wound up signing six hundred or so books. Then I recorded a video for a lady who works at the cash register, telling her family that she and her husband are expecting a child. I said, "I have big news about them—they're not splitting up, though they have had troubles." Then: "It turns out Jared *is* the father"—it's a great video. I was high on the lolly by that point, so it better have been.

I left feeling a sense of accomplishment for signing six hundred books and taking pictures with all until I read my Instagram in the car and saw a post from a woman who said that I was the rudest person she ever met, that she left in tears after I wouldn't look her in the eye and her image of me was ruined, and in turn she basically ruined the entire experience for *me* of meeting all the people who *were* happy. I apologized profusely to her but it went on and on and I had a pit in my stomach about it all night. Met Lindsay Denman and Matt Anderson at Swinging Richards and laughed, partied, and celebrated the end of a great week of hard work. Oh, and we felt up a couple strippers. I was asleep by three.

❧ SUNDAY, NOVEMBER 16, 2014—ATLANTA—DETROIT—NYC

Was up at seven forty-five, so that wasn't enough sleep. I still feel like shit about this girl who was my biggest fan whose life I ruined; that's hanging over me. The whole plane ride I was worried about Wacha, who had a shoot with Jerry Seinfeld today in Central Park for I don't know what. I checked with Jessica, who said he behaved himself. Wacha did too. (Hahaha, get it?) Heard later in the day that he went completely nuts on the hansom cab people—he hates a horse! My sister, Em, is having agita because she is meant to come to meet me in San Francisco on Wednesday but the Ferguson verdict is fucking everything up. They're talking about closing schools and rioting and she doesn't have childcare and it's a mess. Landed in Detroit and the driver was a half hour late and I was freaking out by the baggage claim, irritated that I wouldn't have time to run and see Hitsville U.S.A.

before having to be at the JCC at one o'clock. The driver finally showed up; they had the wrong times at the car place and I came *this close* to letting the guy have it, but didn't, and wound up completely falling in love with him. He's a Russian Jew and has been here twenty-five years. He'd never heard of Hitsville U.S.A., but now he knows all about it and about using both my phones (I'm using the Microsoft phone as part of my deal) to take many variations of pics of me in front of the building where Motown started: me cheering, holding my arms open, one over my head in triumph. We had time to kill and he took me to Leeza's Cafe, a deli-type breakfast place that felt like home, and I sat at the counter and had an amazing egg scramble with chicken sausage, mushrooms, and onions, plus hash browns.

Everywhere I go people say they heard me on Howard, which made me happy. There's a club of Howard people out there. Went to the venue, which had a beautiful theater with 650 sold-out seats, but I think we only sold 250 books, which seems low. I did the signing in an hour; it was frenetic but effective. Tons of suburban Jewish ladies around and I absolutely loved them. The Detroit Jews are also my people.

I was having paranoid feelings the whole flight home about a variety of issues. Sarah Silverman and Rashida Jones are interviewing me onstage next week—what if they hate the book and those nights go horribly wrong? Why haven't I heard from certain people to whom I sent the book? What about people I know who are mentioned in it and haven't said anything? Are people mad at me? Did I sell them out? Did I sell *myself* out? I thought I got the tone right, but maybe I grossly got it wrong. I was an insecure mess. Got home and had one of those quiet, deep hugs with Wacha when he comes out of his crate and he sits in front of me and I hold him and his tail is wagging like crazy but he is otherwise still. He was so insanely sweet and instead of his usual spot by my legs in the bed he was cuddled up by my chest. It's like he knew my head wasn't right and he gave me exactly what I needed.

❧ MONDAY, NOVEMBER 17, 2014

I dreamed there was a hatchet job on me on the front page of the *New York Times* Style Section. It was so bad, calling me out on having written a shitty book, for selling people out, for being a fraud. But in the dream I didn't read the piece, I just knew it was there and all my friends had read it. I felt so proud of myself in this hypothetical situation for not reading it that I hope if there is a hatchet job on me somewhere I will choose not to read it. I've actually found solace in the fact that the *New York Times* has Andy Cohen fatigue. That being said, there are also terrible reviews going up on Amazon and I have a feeling that they are by online allies of fired Housewives—this is how I think—because of things that we said on *WWHL: Uncensored* last week. I'm getting a lot of Twitter hate from Housewives' armies trying to protect their women—or maybe from the women themselves, running fake accounts? The fan from Instagram who now hates me has a blog post about her horrible experience with me and is emailing Bravo to let them know what a sham I am. So I hit my limit and blocked her from all my social media. Bye, Ashy.

Worked out. Almost puked. Texted Anderson that I was so bored of myself I felt like I was gonna rip all of my skin off me. I texted with Barkin, who assured me that my tone was perfect in the book. But it was Bruce who talked me off the ledge.

Finally connected with Kathy Griffin, who wanted advice about whether to take Joan's job on *Fashion Police*. I picked up and she said, "Should I do it???" *This* was what was so urgent on Saturday night. A *Time* magazine piece came out saying the book is the most important piece of gay literature in the 2010s *but* it also paints me as a lonely, body-image-obsessed representative of a generation that never thought that we could settle down. Once I got over the shock of the picture he painted, I loved that this guy read between the lines and identified something real that I never said explicitly about my identity and who I am. And he's right. I felt ashamed of my sexuality for so many years, hid everything, denied myself any true intimacy with another man in favor of casual relationships, focused on my job and my life—and now suddenly I can have kids and get married, but I'm alone. I looked at two apartments in my building to see about a place to move during construction—neither was great. (I have a fantasy about moving into a big, nondescript high-rise, on the fiftieth floor, and seeing what it feels like to live in the sky for a year. I wonder what my *Time* reviewer would read into that.) But man, would it ever be convenient to live in this building while this construction is going on.

I am gearing up to hit the road for ten days on Wednesday, so it's five shows in two days and Wacha is making my leaving hard because he was so snuggly all day. Pretaped Allison Williams and Allison Janney. I made a joke in the Mazel about French kissing and showed a video of Cloris Leachman and I doing it and then Janney and I somehow started French kissing. It was kind of amazing. The live show was Lisa Vanderpump alone. I was stumbling all over my words but it was okay, I guess. She couldn't wait to meet Wacha and we brought him out with a doorbell and he kind of wanted nothing to do with her and was still being huggy with me. Behave, JonBenét! Came home and watched the rest of *Olive Kitteridge*.

▶ TUESDAY, NOVEMBER 18, 2014

Woke up early and raced to the United Jewish Appeal where I was speaking about—what else—*being Jewish* to three hundred ladies and then signing books. When I got there I kept thinking of something my mom told me when I was impatient at an event a few years back—that this is something people have worked on for months and months so if they are hyper or irritating you have to get over it because to you it's one morning, but to them it is the culmination of tons of work. Maybe SJP said that, actually. But my mom agreed, and it is a good tool for me. So I was patient and enjoyed talking to the women. All I have to do is start talking about my mother and I get their attention and they love it. Mom is my secret weapon. All of the Jewish women looked like people I know. I could walk into any of their houses, hit the kitchen, go straight for the pantry, and help myself. I was flirting with a too-young intern who was helping me sign books and we took a selfie and the lady in charge yelled at him and I was trying to tell her that it was my fault because I was flirting with him. So many women came up to me and said, "*I'm* the one *in charge* of this lunch," "This is *my* lunch," "I'm *the chair* of this event"—literally seven women at a minimum. (They aren't all in charge but they all think they are—which is the definition of a Jewish woman, by the way. Everybody wants to be the *macher*!)

On the way home I did a radio interview with Joan Hamburg—another Jewish lady I love. She was kvelling over the book, and over my mother, which made me so happy. I went home, grabbed the dog (still being sweet), and went to the Clubhouse for an afternoon taping with Brooke Shields and Russell Brand, where I discovered a huge amount of food from Barney Greengrass, who were apparently thrilled that I had mentioned them on

Howard Stern the other day. So that's great! Being famous is good today. Russell Brand was late and Brooke and I caught up. She told me she is in Warhol's *Diaries*, which I need to look up. The Muppets were bartending but they have many restrictions, so there was no drinking word and Russell and I did espresso shotskis (he doesn't drink) and we pretended Brooke's drink was water but it was really tequila. She drank beer during the show. She can drink! She said during Plead the Fifth that Liam's dick was as huge as reported (I asked) so I wonder how long it'll take for that news to get to Liam. Not that he doesn't already know that his dick is huge, of course. Went home and paid bills and talked to my agent about Wendy Williams; she still doesn't want to do this show with me producing because I "disrespected" her. Losing a whole show over NeNe saying she would drop her? Maybe I should just call the husband/manager? Grabbed two suits and hit the Clubhouse again, where we taped Kandi and Lisa Wu. Then the live show was with the former OGs of *RHOBH*, Taylor, Camille, and Adrienne. Someone called in and asked which *BH* husband was the biggest drama queen and Taylor laughed and said, "Well, I guess *mine*?!" which is of course not funny but is quite shocking and so, yeah, maybe is funny, but not funny at all.

After the show there was a staff party but I needed to go home and pack because I'm getting picked up at the crack of dawn tomorrow to leave for San Fran. So I left a party in progress—the worst kind to leave—and started rolling off when I realized my keys were in another suit and went to the door of the building where my show is taped, which was locked, the chatty doorman nowhere to be found as I was banging on the door with no coat in the freezing cold. At the end of my glass rope, I kicked the door and shattered the glass. I was shocked! Turned around to Ray, who was sitting in the car watching everything, absolutely beside himself laughing. I had to go upstairs and explain to the entire staff that there is most likely surveillance video of their host having a hissy fit and kicking the door in, which was both hilarious and humiliating.

I was packing this morning and Wacha knew. *He knew*! Got to the airport early and then my flight for San Francisco was horribly delayed. So I had plenty of time to kill at JFK with my carry-on full of pot candy—my secret medicine to power me through long signings, making them as fun for me as for everyone I get to meet. Em isn't coming to meet me, but the verdict hasn't come. I know that will bug her because it turns out she could've come, but how could she know? I signed stock at Hudson Booksellers in the airport, which made me feel productive. Then, I don't know how I did it, but I took a poop in the American Airlines lounge. Highly unusual. Right before we took off I got a PDF of my pic in *People* mag's Sexiest Men issue. It looks great—and Wacha is *beautiful.* He's in my arms sleeping in the Sexy Guys and Their Dogs section! Surreal! I posted it and spent the rest of my flight online on my phone, getting a distinct attention high from the comments on the picture and a new batch of Instagram DMs. I texted AC that the DMs are gonna keep me from getting into a relationship until it's too late. Too many possibilities. The flight was *endless* and made no better by the flight attendant who first got my attention with her incredibly pungent lotion smell, which on the one hand I admire for being very antiseptic but on the other made my eyes water. She got in *real close*, looked at my Ralph Lauren Olympic zip-up sweatshirt (not the ugly Christmas sweater *or* the turtleneck Olympic ski sweater referenced in volume 1) and asked in all sincerity if I was travelling with an Olympic team. She thought gray-haired me was on an *Olympic team*! I got a DM on Twitter from Anthony Recker asking if I knew of a dog walker and letting me know he heard me on Stern and so did all his friends. I told him I was sorry for objectifying his ass and he said maybe it's an ASSet and I said he should market himself as the JLo of baseball but he didn't seem to like that idea.

The *WWHL* staff was texting me pictures of the cone in front of the broken window; they were in hysterics about it. For the whole flight I read the funniest comments from people reading the book about things they relate to (walking into people's farts, pooping at work). It felt like a victory lap. John Mayer texted asking if I will be his guest on the *Late Late Show* when he fills in for Grammy Week. I said yes immediately. Five hours into the flight the email came from Gillian that the book entered the *New York Times Best Sellers* list at number 4 and is number 1 on the ebook bestseller list and number 3 on combined print and ebook. I was elated, and of course commenced to tell everyone I knew via text. I emailed Mom who said, "I AM SO PROUD OF MY BOY," and then, "Amazing. You could sell a dead horse to a race track!! (I just made that up.) I don't mean your book is a dead horse but that you have done a fantastic job!!!" I thought that was pretty clever. I do feel a real sense of accomplishment. I landed and called Mom and Dad, who brought me down to earth when I confirmed to her that I am in *People*'s Sexiest Men issue. "SEXIEST MEN? Just because you are IN the issue, ARE YOU ONE OF THEM? Like, DO YOU HAVE A NUMBER? What NUMBER are you?"

Got to the hotel and Lynn arrived and I debated whether to wear a T-shirt and sport coat or a button down and sport coat for twelve minutes, then did an exhaustive pre-interview with Conan's producer on the way to meet Bravo people at an ad sales event across the street from the event at the Castro Theatre. Signed books, did a tequila shot, and went over to the theater, which was sold out—1,200 seats or so—saw Uncle Dick on the way in, grabbed him, got Aunt Kay, and went backstage, where I talked to a *San Francisco Chronicle* reporter who made me very nervous because she wasn't writing anything down. Rashida arrived and we went over the run of the show quickly and hit the stage to thunderous applause and enthusiasm, at which time I had a flashback to the horrible moment during the last Q and A at the Castro when I was overserved on pot candy. Rashida was perfect and we sipped tequila on ice and I could feel the love from the audience. There were people lined up around the block and around another block, and they were magnificent, all full of energy and love, the coolest group of people I could ever hope to have as "fans." Here's what they gave me: a *lot* of pot (buds, pot Rice Krispies treats, pot caramels), five separate penis pastries from the place next door, poppers, a bag of beautiful Snoopys, snacks from some small town in wine country, bottles of booze, some cards, and more pot. I gave some of the pot to a cute bear who was loitering but the edibles are being shipped to New York, unwittingly, by the nice people from the Commonwealth Club. I filmed another video telling a woman's family that she is pregnant. Took a lot of pictures and I pray everybody left as happy as I was. The gay guys touch me the most at these events. In general, judging by what I read online, I feel hated by the gays, so it is nice to connect with some of them personally.

I stood in front of the hotel on Geary in the moist night with a roadie, laughing with Lynn about the hysteria we'd seen. I was flying from all the love and energy from the great San Franciscans, and all the wonderful news of the day. Lynn is worried about me eating the edibles or smoking the dope; she thinks someone might try to kill me, and I said I looked into these people's eyes and felt their love and am a good judge of character and that she has been working for *20/20* for too long. She's still skeptical. Went to bed around midnight.

▶ THURSDAY, NOVEMBER 20, 2014— SAN FRANCISCO—LOS ANGELES

I barely slept and woke up to the news that Mike Nichols passed away. It feels like everybody is dying. Saw online that there's "news" that I outed Kevin Spacey in the book. I did? I'm staying away from that one if anyone asks. And isn't that old news—like, hasn't he been outed twenty times? Went from LAX straight to *The Talk* at the CBS Radford lot, where Diane Ronnau met me and we walked around. It's where they shoot all the TV Land shows and *Brooklyn Nine-Nine* and I guess *Community* because we bumped into Joel McHale. From there I went to the Beverly Hills Palm, where Pierce Brosnan was eating with the Armani team. It was so good to see Bruce, and the restaurant looks great. Went to the hotel, where I closed my eyes for five minutes, and then headed to *Conan*, where I bombed. The audience was dead or I was bad or I don't know what. The second it was over Conan turned to me and said, "That was *great*!! That was *amazing*!" but I knew it wasn't. Wound up having a conversation about John Stamos with Andy Richter and Conan during the break that was way more interesting than my segment.

Went to the Montalbán Theatre to prep for my event with Sarah Silverman and was told I was to go into the basement and call into *Wait Wait . . . Don't Tell Me!*, which I did like a robot, not realizing I didn't know what I was getting myself into. All I know about the show is that smart people love it. From the basement of the Montalbán I was connected to Chicago, where Paula Poundstone, P.J. O'Rourke, Bill Kurtis, and a theater full of people were itching to attack me about the Housewives. I felt like I was on 'shrooms and everybody was laughing at me on the other end of the line, but I won out over their snotty tone about the Housewives, then got every question right in a quiz about bees, so I turned it around. The *Writers' Bloc* thing was hectic. Sarah told some really funny Holocaust jokes, which are her specialty. Some man got up and asked about Blouse, our housekeeper when I was a kid and a minor star of *Most Talkative*, which really warmed my heart and felt surreal. (By the way, Blouse is in love with Eddie and going to be a bride at seventy-four. I'm definitely going home for that wedding!) Some German guy asked a question and I flirted with him. A lady got up and dropped all these names and said she has had a lot of famous people in her house in Pasadena because it's huge and she was just rambling on and on and she got booed off the mic! And I was the only one coming to her defense because she was like Play-Doh for Sarah Silverman. The signing was bedlam—one pen, no line, a mess. Sold four hundred books and met some really cool people.

Met Jenn Levy and Comis for a drink after at the Tower Bar and Dimitri came up in his usual happy fluster (I call him Aunt Blabby in the book—will he see it?) saying, "You can't believe the night, it was amazing, you missed it," and I said well, the night is still going, I didn't miss anything and he said, "No, no, you can't believe what happened *here*," and I said well, I am still in the present so let me feel like it's still happening. They wouldn't serve me food at the bar—it was 11:10—but Dimitri wound up making it happen. Then I met two girls who said they were in the middle of reading my book and was *this* maître d' the one I was talking about, so that's funny!

▶ FRIDAY, NOVEMBER 21, 2014—LOS ANGELES

I got five hours' sleep and woke up still wired from the pot lolly last night. Is it possible that I am overindulging in pot lollies, or are they helping me get through this insane book tour? Met Dan and Jane for breakfast and talked about maybe doing a Magical Elves/Most Talkative Productions documentary together or an anthology series. A while later I read a tweet from someone saying they were listening to a girl talking loudly about herself and reality stars and it turned out to be *me* at *breakfast!* Mean! Went to Kitson for my signing wondering if Paris Hilton would be there (wasn't she a Kitson girl in the day?) and the Egbers from *The People's Couch* were there. So was TMZ, who asked me about Kevin Spacey. I said, "It was a passing comment about something that's been discussed in the media for fifteen years," and moved on. Then I signed books and the names were so SoCal: Linzy,

Britnee, Pippin, Monsy, Summer. "Linzy" kills me! The German guy from last night showed up and gave me his card but I think it's Dead in the Water. From there I had a little time to kill so I went to Fred Segal, where they really do such a hard sell on shit that never ever looks good outside the store. This justifies a retelling of the story about the time when, in the mid-nineties, I bought what can only be described today as a ladies' mid-length faux-mink coat with shoulder pads, from the *Mildred Pierce* collection. I got it back to NYC and was quickly horrified by what I saw in the light of NYC reality (not a dressing room in West Hollywood with possibility in the air and two queens chirping to buy it from over my shoulder). A week later Jess Cagle told me that he'd found the *most* cool fur coat at Fred Segal that he had been lamenting not buying and had gone back in to see that it was gone. I said, "You'll never believe this," and sold him mine. Today I bought a John Varvatos zip-up sweater that looks like a motorcycle jacket. Then today's pot lolly started kicking in and I was rendered paranoid when I looked at my schedule, which had an interview that I'd forgotten about. I called Hickey and Anderson for advice about how to handle the Kevin Spacey situation and they both told me that I had done nothing wrong. AC reminded me that I don't need to talk to TMZ if they are at my *OMG! Insider* interview; I can walk by and not say anything. A novel thought! Turns out the *Insider* guy didn't even ask me about Kevin Spacey.

The event at the Palm was really low key. I think the real Beverly Hills housewives are really dosed up on pills. After, we went to Bruce's and I napped for a while, gave Ava her present, and then went back to the Palm for a lovely dinner in my honor. It was Lynn, Eli and Sari Lehrer, Jake Shears, Rebecca Romijn and Jerry O'Connell, Sandy and Bryan, Henry Winkler and Stacey, Jason and Lauren, Simon Halls, Jess Cagle (we discussed the fur coat story), Ricki Lake, Bruce, and Ralph Fiennes. Jake, Rebecca, and Jerry kept talking *Housewives* and Ralph would say, "Who are you talking about?" and they would try to explain Teresa or Apollo. Jerry is obsessed with Apollo, by the way. Henry made a touching toast about my evolution and the achievement of writing two best-selling books. We got Sandy telling us Michael Jackson stories, which are my favorite. I realized while I was showing Jason pictures of Wacha that Lauren is pregnant with an actual baby and I felt immediately inferior and idiotic. I was exhausted and when we left at midnight there was a guy from TMZ screaming at me about invading Kevin Spacey's privacy and could I explain myself and, by the way,

I look very guilty not answering and getting in the car, where the light by the seat wouldn't turn off and the guy kept videoing me sitting there like a fucking idiot trying to turn the light off. I texted Billy Eichner saying I had to go crash, that I couldn't meet him, and simultaneously got a text from a special friend in LA to whom I thought I responded but instead sent something slightly provocative to Billy so it was like I had sexted him and he *loved* that. Lots of big laughs, and I did in fact wind up going to bed before one o'clock, completely exhausted.

▶ SATURDAY, NOVEMBER 22, 2014—LOS ANGELES—MIAMI

Woke up wired at six-thirty, as is my new custom. Packed sleepily for Miami. The flight attendant wanted to bond with me for the whole flight about how horrible the plane was, so with every question I asked he was serving me a lot of sass: "Is there Wi-Fi on the plane?" "No, it's *nineteen ninety-FIVE* in here if you haven't checked." "Do you have chocolate chip?" "Oh, they *definitely* aren't serving you two kinds of cookies up here!" We were girl-friends, I guess. And she was serving lots of tea. Landed and got a text from Hickey (I talked him into joining me at the Delano so we could have a vacation happening simultaneous to my book events) and I told him to meet me at the pool in half an hour for a quick pre-massage dip. It was very overcast and muggy but the second I hit that water I felt like I was on vacation. Took a long nap, and Hickey and I hit Casa Tua for a 9:00 p.m. dinner, followed by a stroll on Lincoln Road and a stop into the stripper hut behind Twist. We were perched right by the strippers' storage closet and we were transfixed, watching as these 'roidy lunkheads showed up for work and dumped off fanny pack after fanny pack and assorted lube- and grease-filled backpacks. There has got to be a lot of theft in a strippers' locker room, wouldn't you think? Our experienced analysis showed that the Cubans were the hottest strippers with the best personalities (that counts too). They are all hustling you for a lap dance, and I bought one (twenty bucks) and Hickey made fun of me for waiting for the song to start to ask for one (they go the length of one song). I'm thrifty, and I want the full lap dance! Or so I thought. As hot as the Cubano (Joe—not his real name; he could barely come up with it when I asked) was, it was just a soulless, sad experience and I wound up feeling bad for him and ending it before the song ended.

Tell me your hopes and dreams, Joe. Do you support immigration reform? We left and went to Score which was a blast. Asleep by 5:00 am. When in Miami . . .

⏩ SUNDAY, NOVEMBER 23, 2014—MIAMI

The alarm at eight forty-five for my Miami Book Fair International event was just rude. I was hoarse and more sick of myself than I have ever been in my entire life, but there was a theater full of people waiting for me to blather on about myself and sign my books. And Daddy needs to make a living, so he got out of bed and bucked it up like a big boy. The people were nice. A boy asked me to marry him, a lady asked for a hug, I got a ton of presents for Wacha, and I can't remember what else happened except that I signed about three hundred books for customers and another two hundred for stock after the speech and it went by like a breeze (I didn't even mind that no one upon no one knows how to use their cameras and that people wait in line for over an hour but don't care to have their camera ready when they get to the front of the line) and I was with Hickey at the pool by noon, where I felt like a king. The vibe was magical—chill-out jams but not too many people. We got a bottle of rosé and Jon Jay came and joined us for an hour before he left for Europe for Manny Machado's wedding (the baseball life). Left for the Palm at three-thirty and I had completely hit a wall—all the talking and smiling for pictures and being patient and hospitable to perfectly nice people completely slammed down on my last gay nerve. Now I wanted to not only rip the skin off myself, but then burn it, and *then* throw the remains of myself back into the fire. And initially the crowd was so lovely and warm and Jewy, my people. There were five yentas in the front row with excellent face work; a bunch of husbands; Marqueeta, who I used to work for when I interned at KMOV when I was seventeen; and a whole lot of personality which made the Q and A a total blast. A woman in a white dress kept asking two-part questions and talking over people who had not had a chance to ask anything, which was triggering me. The rule at these Palm events is to only take pics with groups, because it's a happy-hour type environment. The lady in the white dress stopped me as I was going back to take pictures with everybody to ask if I could take a selfie with her so she didn't have to wait in line. I said it was against the rules but yes, let's do it! She was the one squeaky wheel in the room, so it seemed like a good way to appease her. People brought so many gifts for Wacha it was unbelievable. Lots of chewy dreidels and a cute Chewbacca chew. (*Star Wars* dog toys? How rich *is* George Lucas?)

I was close to done and deeply in love with everyone until the white dress lady appeared again and announced that on top of a picture with her friends, she wanted another one alone with me. I told her we would not be doing that because it was against the rules and she and I had already taken a selfie. She wanted another, she declared. When her friends stepped away, she said ONE MORE I WANT ANOTHER. At which point all the sleep I haven't gotten in the past week and all the cameras in my face and the endless thirst for selfies all came to a head in my brain and I basically lost it. I grabbed her and said, "I am gonna give you a *big hug* instead, and that is what you're going to get," and I proceeded to grab her and squeeze her so hard that I thought her head might pop off her body. I mean, I was *violently* squeezing her. She emerged from the stranglehug a little stunned, a little out of breath, and a lot confused about what had just happened. Upon regaining my composure, I realized that I had just tried to kill a woman with a hug and quickly tried to make up for it by carrying on about how much I loved her gorgeous dress. I was manic, as hyper as she was. She took the compliment and I moved on. I continued with the photos and left to go to the Gilt event, where I did five interviews for local magazines (there are a lot of press outlets in Miami, it turns out) and had great reunions with Miami Housewives Adriana, Marysol, Alexia (who wore a jumpsuit for me and proudly announced she had no camel toe—upon inspection she was correct), and Lea. I introduced them before the Q and A and said I knew the first question was going to be when is *Real Housewives of Miami* coming back and I said, "Never say never," but I could see from the women's faces that they didn't believe me and then *I* kind of didn't believe me, but I was getting nostalgic for them. I was Phil Donahue-ing around the room when someone asked me to pick my *Real Housewives* all-stars, one from each city, to be in a dream cast. I chose Teresa, NeNe, Vicki, Vanderpump, and Bethenny and then I realized I was going to have to choose one of the Miami women standing in front of me. Adriana, I announced. You would've thought I'd just given her a yacht, and I couldn't even turn to look at Lea; I just immediately moved to the next question.

I raced out of there to pick up Hickey to take him to the Palace, an experience I was so excited to share with him. If anyone could enjoy margaritas with sidewalk performances from fierce drag queens it is John Hickey. We got there kind of late—eight-thirty—but the place was still thumping and I was happy to see Tiffany Fantasia as the MC. The performances weren't great at first and I was worried it was going to be a bust, but then I went to the bathroom and the manager brought me into the drag queens' dressing room for the private loo, where I got to see the queens in various stages of dress. Lots of smells in there, and I took selfies with them all and maybe offended Tiffany Fantasia by telling her she looked like "NeNe Leakes Beyond Thunderdome." I don't think she liked it, but when she took the "stage"—which is what they call the sidewalk—she gave us exactly what we were looking for, running around the street and beach across from us and finally doing a drop to the floor just as the song dropped—she had us on our feet roaring. Tiffany joined us at our table later and we went deep. She has three jobs, including being an Uber driver by day. I love it! I want to keep Ubering in Miami until I get Tiffany Fantasia. She was making her final announcement of the night and closed with "Don't be a dry ho, be a greasy bitch. Good night, everybody!" I asked her if that was her sign-off and she said yes, that's her little tag line. As we sat at the table the incident with the lady in the white dress flashed through my mind and I decided that I was completely insane.

▶ MONDAY, NOVEMBER 24, 2014—MIAMI—ST. LOUIS

Got a text from Anderson this morning saying the verdict in the Ferguson case was coming in tonight and he was heading to St. Louis. The white suburbanites are in a total panic, expecting riots in Clayton, which is where the courthouse is and right where my parents live. Mom doesn't seem worried. We will see! Of course this is happening the day I get home, after all these weeks of waiting. I had a great Delano breakfast and three hours by the pool being fed grapes. A waitress who came up to us with frozen mint coladas announced, "Mint is my signature! Expect a lot of it today!" *Mint is her signature!* I couldn't stay long enough to get the full suite of poolside mint snacks because I had to go to St Louis. Went into the bookstore at the airport and they haven't had my book in stock since it came out and were getting some tomorrow, which made me insane. I wanted to hug the dude to death like I did the lady with the white dress. I'm getting some nasty tweets about the book. One lady is furious at me for being ageist toward flight attendants (I told her to burn my book because if she couldn't handle my flight attendant jokes she was going to be in for an upsetting 350 pages) and gays are pissed about this Kevin Spacey thing. Went straight to Left Bank Books from the airport and signed 950 copies, then home for flank steak and to watch the verdict. The prosecuting attorney's speech was a total joke; the policeman got off and there was rioting in Ferguson for much of the night, stoked by Don Lemon and his gas mask. All very upsetting.

⏩ TUESDAY, NOVEMBER 25, 2014

Clayton is all boarded up and people are scared of their own shadows. It is so insular here—I am ashamed of my suburban privilege. Country-club people are locking themselves inside and everything seems to be closed, but I spent the day at Nelly's school downtown, which was full of students—it was life affirming to see those kids out and wanting to learn. I met each student and signed a book. I'm not sure it was the crowd for *The Andy Cohen Diaries*, but they all had a lot of questions about the business so hopefully they'll take something away from the book besides how gay I am.

The voices in my parents' apartment are so loud, and my mom is sick, with a hacking cough. It's exhausting and not restful. We got in a huge fight because I was trying to nap from five to six and came out and gave them a warning that their voices were too loud and I couldn't close my eyes. We were ripping each other apart in the living room—I told my mom I was going to get a hotel, then she was ripping my dad for not eating the food she had made him and for the "lumberjack shirt" he planned to wear to my event. It was a brutal three-way voice fight. Mom is very anxious for me to sit on her hot seat toilet. Just *begging*. "PLEASE GET ON THE HOT SEAT!!!!! Jeremy LOVES IT." She wants to give me one for my new bathroom. I told her I was *not* sitting on the hot seat. So that hit where it counts. When I got to the event at the Chaminade campus—a thousand sold-out seats!—the first audience question was about what a wonderful relationship I have with my family. I told them all we had been ripping each other's skin off an hour before. Took about eight hundred pictures after with a professional photographer and it went really fast. Got a lot of gifts including some great *Andy Cohen Diaries* cookies. I'll call the lady who made them tomorrow and order fifty of them for Mom's party. Raced to the Four Seasons for dinner with Anderson and his CNN crew, people who he's been around the world with several times over. Anderson clearly loves these guys so much—three producers and his whiz tech guy who gets them live shots from everywhere. We had a lot of laughs at dinner and I stayed late with Anderson and we texted a selfie to our friend Cher in Malibu.

▶ WEDNESDAY, NOVEMBER 26, 2014—ST. LOUIS

The looting and madness seems to be over and now there are tons of boarded-up buildings in Clayton. They took the art out of my parents' building—none of it by van Gogh, from what I can tell—for fear of looters entering and stealing the *lobby art*. The empty walls are a reminder of suburban panic, and I feel bad for the black lobby attendants who have to stare at the naked walls and be reminded of how scared the tenants are of their people. I don't want to be dramatic, but it feels to me like South Africa. Had a great lunch at my Aunt Judy's. She will make me any kind of food and make it better, like mac and cheese with crème instead of milk. Back in the day they had a real-life ice-cream parlor in their house and a deep fryer in their kitchen. Today it was fresh turkey sandwiches, but I saw the grilled cheese she was making for Lucy and I wanted one. Then another. And we had slice-and-bake cookies. Went by Em's after Judy's. She is obsessed with her Keurig. Came home and was actually able to nap for an hour so maybe the scorched-earth tactic yesterday worked. We went to 5 Star Burgers and I felt so gross from lunch that I ate a kale salad. Kari picked me up and we went to see Jake's Leg, and dancing to a Grateful Dead cover band was the perfect antidote to weeks of signing books. Before bed I realized my Christmas party is in a couple weeks and I haven't booked bartenders or invited anyone, so I quickly emailed invites to about eighty people on a bcc and didn't keep a list of who I invited.

THURSDAY, NOVEMBER 27, 2014, THANKSGIVING—ST. LOUIS

Loved watching the Macy's Thanksgiving Day Parade, not only because the Microsoft commercials were airing but because it was nice just being home and chilled out. Did absolutely nothing all day. Napped at two. Mom was begging me to get on the hot seat. ("It cleans your BUTT too! IF YOU NEED THAT KIND OF THING EVER.") Went up to the Goldmans' and saw the whole crew, including Nana, who is ninety-nine years old and never changes. She is the coolest grandma around. Em and Rob hosted a great Thanksgiving. I chatted with everyone; we played Balderdash and there were too many people for the game but it was still fun. Asleep by eleven.

FRIDAY, NOVEMBER 28, 2014

Woke up and went with Dad to Ballpark Village for a KMOX radio hour with an audience. They had Tony La Russa call in and he immediately brought up what I said about him in my book and I turned it around to talk about how magical Tony is and how he knew David Freese was going to hit a double, and how he loves rescue dogs. So I got out of that one. I was terrified. They let me do the weather report and I loved it way too much. It's going to get warm here this weekend, so I hyped the hell out of that. Bill DeWitt III came with his wife, Ira, and gave Dad and me a tour of the new Cardinals Hall of Fame. My bobblehead is in there, which is amazing, and half of Freese's jersey from Game 6.

Went home and got ready for the book party. Showed Blouse the guy at the *Writers' Bloc* event standing up and asking about her on YouTube. It blew her mind. Bill DeWitt emailed and said they're having dinner with Wayne Gretzky and his wife and would I come. I said to let me know where they wound up and I would meet them for a drink. The cookies arrived and they're great looking, especially the Wacha ones. I miss the dog terribly. The party was lovely. I talked to everybody—full house. Jim Edmonds and Meghan King were the hits of the party. No one can believe she's going to be a Housewife. All the kids were drooling over Edmonds, who asked me if he needs to tell my mom he's not gay. (Oy, *what* did I say about him being gay in the book again?) I told him that was a compliment, and he said he knew that but most other normal people may not realize that. Then he said not *normal*, but straight. Blouse told him she was rooting for him, so she didn't get the memo he's retired. Lawd. DeWitt emailed me saying that Gretzky decided to go to the Blues game instead. Of course he did. Why wouldn't he? *That's what he does!* Party debrief with parents, then to dinner at Mike's house which was a carb festival—tomato soup, crab dip, sandwiches, mac and cheese, more pasta, more cheese. I ate too much.

▶ SATURDAY, NOVEMBER 29, 2014

I sat on the hot seat! I didn't realize it's hot all the time; I thought it had to be warmed up or something. I have to admit it is lovely. My mom was very pleased. Laid around like a bum until Elaine Bly picked me up for my signing at the Ladue Barnes and Noble. They allowed people to bring their own books, which seemed counterproductive, but what can you do? I met a man who drove from Little Rock and had a tattoo of my face on his arm, along with the date that he called in to *WWHL*. Mom showed up and I had him stay around so I could show her the tattoo. With him, she acted like it was normal but when he walked away she gave me an exasperated look. "He can't GET THAT OFF! He's STUCK WITH IT." Em had a similar reaction. Dad was in the front of the store posing for pictures. "Your FATHER is a MEDIA WHORE!" Mom kept saying all day and night. A heavy lady in what looked like a wedding dress had driven all the way from Appleton, Wisconsin. She had a big bag of gifts including a flask that was engraved with the date of our meeting, only they had gotten the date wrong and crossed it out and engraved another date above it. Loved it. Signed four hundred books. Went to Josh's, where he had all the Allens for Emerson's birthday. Sophie was going to see some Stephen King musical at the Fox and I don't even know what that means. Went to Scape with the family and everyone was shining their iPhone flashlights in each other's eyes while they looked at the menus. Jeremy wants to know when the Ferguson police chief is going to resign. I wonder too. Met Jim Edmonds and Meghan and RJ and all the Kings at BARcelona. Unclear how this *RHOC* experiment will go. Jim wanted to take her to a firing range on the show but I said no, I had seen it too many times.

⋙ SUNDAY, NOVEMBER 30, 2014—ST. LOUIS—NYC

Surfin bartended on my show before I left and said he is getting recognized! He was on Thirty-Fourth Street the other day and someone said, "Are you Andy's doorman?" Reunion with Wacha was a big hug and licks. He smells more like a dog when I've been away from him. He looks like he's lost some weight too—so the diet is working. When I've been away from him I'm always struck by how delicious it is to have another warm living being following me, looking at me for direction. We took a glorious nap before the show. When I've been gone he gets closer to me. Absence makes the heart grow fonder?

⋙ MONDAY, DECEMBER 1, 2014

"*The View* is kind of a boring show now; you were good, though." That was Evelyn's review when I got through cohosting. And she's probably right. But it did go a lot better than my last time there. I started the day at *CBS This Morning*, which I loved. Charlie Rose asked me on air what my ambition was and I said I was going after 11:00 p.m. on PBS and that all I needed was a black background, and he said that I need much more than that. It was all cheerful, but as the day went on I started to think I offended him. I emailed him thanking him for the great interview and he didn't respond, so I guess I have my answer. At *The View*, Brian Balthazar said we're giving you an earbud and it's just to tell you guys when to bail out of conversations. Then backstage Rosie said *do not take one*, you don't need one. Don't take it. She went on a rant about these earbuds, saying that we all just need to *focus* on *each other*. She came up to me a couple minutes later and said to stick a finger in my ear and try to talk to her at the same time, that's what it's like with an earbud. I said I'm actually used to wearing one and can have two conversations at once. The first Hot Topic was Ray Rice, and I really didn't have an opinion. I'd called Liza to get one and she said he is the face of domestic violence, like it or not, and what kind of message is the NFL sending? So I said that. But I had that weird surreal feeling I've had before where my mind says, "I am on *The View* and what would it be like if I just stood up and walked out while we were on the air?" It's that career-ending death wish, but then it passes. After those two appearances the book went from number 60 on Amazon to back in the twenties, so that worked. Anderson and I were FaceTiming at 2:40 p.m. Guess where we both were? On our beds. It turns out he had his appendix out, so that was a pretty good excuse. I was comatose from the morning. While we were talking someone with a 212–343 number called me and I declined it. A couple minutes later Anderson got a call from the same number. We were racking our brains trying to think who would be calling both of us. I thought it was maybe Mark or Kelly from their house phone. Five minutes later he called me back—it was Richie from Seize sur Vingt calling to invite him to a party, and he said he was inviting me too. Mystery solved. We ain't going to that party. Finally called Wendy Williams's husband, Kevin, to clear the air and resolve his issue with me so we can do this fucking show!

I did a radio interview at Sirius XM and met with Scott Greenstein, who offered me my own channel. *Radio Andy?* I told him I was really intrigued. I could program my own radio channel and be on it and be in charge of everything. Jax and Lisa Edelstein were on *WWHL*. I went into Jax's dressing room before the show and he introduced me to his publicist and I asked him why he was wasting his money on a publicist. So that was kind of rude to say in front of the poor PR guy, but Jax is a bartender! It just seems weird not to use the Bravo person. Someone called into the after show and yelled at me for outing Kevin Spacey—which I told her I did not do, and Lisa Edelstein backed me up. After the show, which was on an hour early tonight, I stayed and had a drink in my office with the dog and an overwhelming sense of loneliness. The book stuff is winding down. And now what? Went home and just felt sad. Nobody to call. Nobody to talk to. Nothing to show for anything. What good is this new apartment going to be if it's me and the dog alone? I watched *The Lego Movie* (great!) until very late and fell asleep.

▶ TUESDAY, DECEMBER 2, 2014

Woke up with a nasty crick in my neck. And went to bed with staples in my head! (More about that later.) John came over to shower and write because the email servers are down at Embassy Row because of the Sony hack. Took Wacha to get dry cleaned and he tried to direct me the opposite way down West Eleventh Street. That dog knows where he doesn't want to go. Amy Sedaris and Deepak Chopra were on the pretaped show and *man*, was the energy weird. He is a weird dude. I can't decide if he's a total farce or just at peace or what. Maybe a peaceful farce? Why not? Amy thought she was horrible (she wasn't) and that he was way weird (he was). The live show was Kyle and Gabrielle Union. We had male models revealing what was under their skirts and they all got really drunk and stuck around after. One of them was going out of his way to be provocative and flirty, which always seems like a waste of time for a straight guy. His ball somehow came out of his underwear at one point, which Kyle—and I think her daughter (not Portia)—saw too. Kyle said it's the first ball she's seen in years that's not Mauricio's. Anyway, the guy who showed us his ball did the thing of "Let's take a selfie with your phone" and then "Oh, I love that; text it to me" so now he has my number, which I had no problem with. I started getting texts on my way home and then ultimately, as I was about to get into my bed (on top of which Wacha lay in a pretzel formation), a dick pic arrived. As I looked at it, the mirror that's leaned happily against the wall for the past ten years decided either to make a run for it or to send me a message about not chasing straight models, and tipped and fell onto my head with a SMACK! I fell on the bed and put my hand on my head— blood. Wacha was so flipped out he ran onto the couch and wouldn't look at me as I ran around the living room putting paper towels on my head and yelling at him to help me. He ran into his crate.

I got my shit together and walked over to the new ER at Thirteenth and Seventh—thank you, Lenox Health, for coming in after St. Vincent's closed. They gave me a shot, a CAT scan, and then three staples in my head! I was shaky and felt very alone. Texted with John Hill, who was going to come be with me if I needed it. I told Kyle where I was and she said, "See, you should've come to Tao with us!" Funny! She was kidding and very sympathetic and offered to come help. She then told me about a friend of hers who woke up blind the other day, so that made me feel better about my staples. Got home around 3:00 a.m. and Wacha refused to come out of his crate. He was so scared. He fucking barked at me when I tried to get him out, which pissed me off and made me so sad. I was lying in my bed screaming across the apartment, "Are you KIDDING ME RIGHT NOW? Are you REALLY not going to come sleep with me tonight? *I need you*!!!!!" And then I tried again, really chipper like nothing happened. "C'mere, buddy!

Waaaaa-cha!"—patting the bed like nothing happened. I lay awake for at least an hour. Mad at the dog. Worried about my staples. Looking at the dick pic. Wondering if Wacha would ever sleep in my bed again. Left the door of my room open in hopes he would come in in the middle of the night.

▶ WEDNESDAY, DECEMBER 3, 2014

Wacha trotted into my bedroom at eight forty-five this morning, so I was grateful for that. Called Wendy's husband, Kevin, again because he has not called me back and I need to resolve his non-issue issue of NeNe Leakes "shading" Wendy *during a game of Silk du Soleil*. It was the first day in about six weeks that I had nothing to do, so I stayed in all day being mellow and taking care of my staples—which required nothing, but I was so conscious of them all day. Got word at 5:00 p.m. that the book is holding at number 5 on the *NYT* bestsellers list. Woo-hoo!

Signing with Wacha at Barnes and Noble at the Fashion Institute of Technology. It was such a great crowd—really ethnically diverse and the youngest so far anywhere. Liza came and looked after Wacha, who got about twenty dog toys as gifts, so he was all set. All I could think of was that I have three staples in my head. "I can *feel* the staples," I thought. It started to hurt to smile. Went to the show and was a drama queen about the staples. Rachael Ray and Jenna Bush were on and they were gabby and fun. Jenna said she wants to set me up with someone and asked what my age limit is. I guess the guy is in his fifties, and I can just imagine some fancy Republican.

▶ THURSDAY, DECEMBER 4, 2014—NYC—BOSTON

Today I got two messages that Wendy Williams's husband doesn't want to talk to me and told me to stop calling him. Am I living in some kind of parallel universe where calling to make up with someone over something idiotic that I didn't do is the *wrong* thing to do? I guess that's the end of that. Lifetime wanted to buy the show, too. And I'm a Wendy fan! Maybe it's time for new management. I flew to Boston and immediately wished

I'd taken the train. I'm gonna change my flight to DC on Sunday to a train trip so I can do work and enjoy it.

If you're famous, you always want the hotel clerks and the airline people to know who you are because they control your destiny in very important ways, so I wasn't excited when the gay guy behind the desk of the Fairmont Copley Plaza Hotel asked me for my ID three times and how to spell my name. Maybe he was just being a cunt, which would explain why he put me in a back closet on the executive concierge floor while assuring me that I was eligible for free, can't-miss apps from 5:00 p.m. to 7:00 p.m. daily. I walked into the room, with its view of a wall and its smell of I don't know what, and wondered why I wasn't staying at the Four Seasons. I started unpacking, still considering whether I should try to get another room or move or what when I decided to go to the app area to get a complimentary cup of tea. A woman behind the desk there asked me how my room was and I said it was maybe the worst one in the hotel, but seemed okay. She knew my entire itinerary in Boston, had my book, and immediately put me in a massive suite!

At the Q and A and signing at the JCC, a woman asked me what my idea of true beauty was, which I thought was such an amazing question. I talked about my disdain for fillers and said that inner beauty was the most beautiful thing of all. People wrote *paragraphs* on their Post-its that they then wanted me to put in their books with my tired-ass hands (like: "To my best friend in the world and favorite Real Housewife of . . . ," "Close your legs to married men, trashbox," "Go to sleep, wig," etc.). I couldn't do it. What happened next seemed innocuous in the moment, but stayed with me: A man who'd asked a question about Howard Stern earlier got his book signed and said his lady loved my show. I looked up into his deep dark eyes and saw two permanently indented dimples on a weathered, handsome face and we had a fleeting connection. I told him his wife has great taste in men and he said that she's not his wife. He left, but there was something between us that was hanging in the air. If she wasn't his wife, did I have a chance? A minute later the man returned with a business card and said he forgot to give me his cell number and that he and his lady wanted to share a joint with me. Oh, and he said his name was Jake and when we shook hands, his was like a baseball mitt. After days of people handing me their cards, résumés, and notes, I was used to being handed stuff, but I made sure to put his card in my right pocket because there was something about him. In the car on my way to meet Erik Borg and his friends I took the card out and it was for a motorcycle repair shop in New Hampshire. *Could there be anything hotter than a motorcycle-repair dude from New Hampshire?* I don't like giving my number out but remembered I had a second phone, my Microsoft Batphone, and sent him a text asking where the party is. (I'm subtle.) He didn't believe it was me; then said he was at a Chinese restaurant with his girl, Angela, and I should meet them. I said, even better, when you drop her off meet me for a drink somewhere. He said they don't do anything apart from each other, which I found to be a very interesting choice of words. I complimented his tan (if there's one thing I love more than a motorcycle-repair guy, it's a *tan* motorcycle-repair guy) and he said they'd just been to Sandals and sent me a pic of them. The lady friend—Angela—was quite attractive, tall and blond. But wait: is Sandals a swingers-type place? I always thought it was, but I could be totally wrong. And what about the wording of his text? "We don't do anything apart from each other"—what does *anything* mean? Suddenly my mind was swimming with memories of every *Penthouse* Forum I read at summer camp. Met Erik Borg and went to a couple bars with him and his friends but in the back of my mind I was thinking of the straight couple I'd been talking about meeting for years who would take my virginity from me so I don't die without having loved a woman. When I got home, at around two, I texted Jake and told him to be honest and tell me exactly what he really wanted from me. Fell asleep with a Christmas Eve vibe.

❧ FRIDAY, DECEMBER 5, 2014—BOSTON

Woke up a forty-six-year-old virgin and checked my phone wondering if today was going to be the day I lost my gold-star status. There were several long texts from Jake with a jaw-dropping answer to my question: They have been dating for years and they have fooled around with a few women but never a man, and Angela has said for years that the only two guys she would ever want to be with outside of Jake are Paul Walker (who is dead) and me (who is gay), so neither will ever happen. He said that now that they're suddenly communicating with the one free pass on her list, they talked all night and started to take the idea seriously. As for Jake, he has never been with a man but is open to it with limits. I said I have never been with a woman but am open to it with a couple but need assurance he would participate. He said he would, but there was stuff that is off limits. He sent me an incredible picture of him and his lady that left very little to the imagination and we decided to meet up after my signing tonight and have a few drinks and see what happens. A hotel suite, a book tour, a free pass, a swinging New England couple—the *Penthouse* Forum letter is basically *written* and I began an entire-day freak-out about the possibility of finally losing my virginity. *At forty-six.* In a threesome with a tan motorcycle mechanic from New Hampshire and his "lady." What I did next should surprise no one. I told everyone I knew: Amanda ("holy shit what did Grac say"), Grac ("holy shit what did Amanda say"), Liza ("be careful and you don't have to do anything you don't want"), Bruce ("look at his cock in that picture!"), Hickey ("sweetie are you KIDDING? DO IT."), SJP (via email—she said "remember everything"), Mark ("dude!!!"), and Kelly ("Jake's very handsome and Angela is beautiful and I am very happy for you"). I texted Jake at one o'clock asking if he was excited and he said he was so excited he had to smoke pot. My kinda guy. We kept saying we were going to vibe it out, ride the wave, nothing was for sure going to happen.

I had a signing at the Palm, a lively Q and A and photos where I didn't hug anyone to death, then off to Brookline Booksmith, where I ran through a massive line that stretched around the corner giving everybody high fives on my way into the store. They sold out 450 books. My arm hurt so badly by the end but it was strong enough to text Jake and tell him and Angela to "find a cozy spot in the lobby bar" (total *Penthouse* Forum playbook move) and I would join them. When I eventually nervously went down, Angela said she had bet him a thousand bucks I would be a no-show or a catfish. The headline was that beyond being very attractive, it turned out that these two are actually really cool, normal people. Angela was having a hard time separating being my "fan" from sitting there trying to have a normal conversation that might lead to some sexy time, which added a layer of awkwardness, whereas Jake was an open book, game for anything, and even occasionally engaged in some footsy under the table. We talked about everything. It became clear, though, that Angela wasn't going to take my virginity, that for her this was about the experience and it wasn't going to go that far. This was kind of a relief because when faced with this (albeit very pretty) woman, I was terrified. She went to the bathroom a couple times and I asked Jake about his feelings about being with a guy. I reassured him that I know he is not gay. Also we talked about his hair loss, and I said his hair doesn't define him and that his face can carry off anything, which was a relief to him. He nervously asked me if I would ever write about this experience in a future book and I said *of course not*. (NOTE TO SELF: Call Jake.) We went up to the room and Jake rolled a joint and I will say this: I did things with a girl for the first time in thirty years, but I did not lose my virginity in Boston. When they left I gave Jake a big homemade cake from a fan at the bookstore. It turns out Jake loves cake!

▶ SATURDAY, DECEMBER 6, 2014—BOSTON—DC

Texted all my friends for the whole journey to DC to let them know I am still a gold star, but that my mind was officially blown by the experience. Then got in a long text thing with Jake analyzing what went on last night, and he was wondering if he is gay. I assured him he is not, he's just open and freaky. We barely did anything.

Checked into the W in DC and I guess the lady had never heard of Bravo or me—fine, but once again alarming in a hotel check-in situation—but then all the other staff members came and said hello, gave me business cards, and told me to please let them do whatever they can for me. I went upstairs and found that the lady had given me their version of the back closet I'd gotten in Boston. I didn't even walk in the room; I just went back downstairs fully realizing that I have officially become *that douchey hotel guest* and said, "I'm kind of hoping there might be a different room," and they immediately put me in a WOW Suite, where I took a bath and talked to Jake on the phone and told him again that he is not gay. Went to the Palm, where I got to hang with, and shush, Bruce's sister, Andrea, during the Q and A portion of the event. Then back to the hotel to rest for one hour before my car didn't show up for my Wolf Blitzer Q and A. Went to two Starbucks stores, both of which were closed, but got the chicks at the second one to open up for me because they recognized me. Posted an Instagram with them, which seemed to make them happy. I am exploiting all kinds of celebrity privilege. Q and A at the synagogue with Wolf was fantastic. It was more of an interview about me than about the book, per se. We thought of his tag line, which is, "I may be a wolf, but I can make a situation out of any room!" Something like that. Signed 490 books in record time.

SUNDAY, DECEMBER 7, 2014—DC—NYC

The train ride to New York was so lovely and emo. I spent it texting and putting off every bit of work I meant to do with my three hours—watching an *Atlanta* cut, reading magazines, making a photo album for family. Instead I listened to Pink Floyd and my mind wandered. Bethenny called to tell me she shot the best scene she's ever shot in her whole time on camera, with her former stepfather in Miami. As she was telling me the details I walked into my apartment and was greeted by the sweetest hug from Wacha, who just sat in front of me and burrowed his head into my chest. I had to get off with B so I could experience it fully. I can't get over the fact that this warm, soft puppy is mine and is as utterly devoted to me as I am to him. I mean, we can't actually *talk* to each other, but that's semantics. Tonight was the Super Bowl: NeNe and Kim together live. Kim walked in and said, "Fuck, I look good!" After the show she showed me her new boobs and nipples, then wanted to show me pics of her tits right after surgery and I told her not to because it would ruin any chance of me sleeping with a girl. NeNe wanted to go out gay because she had the day off tomorrow and I said I couldn't handle it, which is officially a first for me. I did wind up meeting them at Tao for some overpriced, greasy food. Do people actually like the food there?

MONDAY, DECEMBER 8, 2014

Made a plan with Teresa for lunch. I told her I would meet her anywhere—her days before she goes to jail are numbered, three weeks and counting—but she said she'll meet me in the city. So we're going to Morandi on Thursday. We both seem to want to see each other before she goes away. Taped DVF and Hugh Bonneville. Went on a date with the guy Jenny McCarthy set me up with. He has an accent and uses a lot of hashtags on Instagram. He has an amazing backstory about what it took to get a green card. Not sure there will be a second date.

TUESDAY, DECEMBER 9, 2014

It's pouring rain today. Wacha's walker, Sherman, came in the apartment and I didn't hear him but Wacha did. I opened my door and he left and I stayed in bed until ten forty-five. Lunch at Del Frisco's and then, as some sort of book promo tie-in that I still don't understand, I read "The Night Before Christmas" onstage to a group of kids during the Radio City Christmas Spectacular. I was not thrilled about being onstage with a bunch of actor-y kids, but it turned out they were very cute and turned my Scrooge-ness around. Michael C. Hall cancelled for our 2:00 p.m. pretape for tomorrow with Olivia Munn and so we are scrambling. Dan Rather can't do it, nor can Alan Alda, Christine Baranski, or Padma. I think we're gonna wind up with Willie Geist, who we should've just booked in the first place. Went to the new Italian place that opened where Cole's Greenwich Village was. They got it totally right. I sat at the pizza bar and it was perfect. All night was spent trying to book another guest. I emailed Willie Geist and texted Padma—didn't hear from either and texted Anderson, who said he has a shoot tomorrow afternoon. Went to bed without a second guest.

WEDNESDAY, DECEMBER 10, 2014

Woke up and texted with Padma, who quickly booked in, then Teresa texted and said she couldn't come into the city and could I meet her in Jersey somewhere. So I am going to Montville tomorrow to meet her on the way to my signing outside of Philly. What does she want to discuss, I wonder?

Did *The Rachael Ray Show*, where I had polenta with tomato sauce and crispy kale, plus a popover, and then they took me to the kitchen, where I picked on some crème pie and was given homemade Thin Mints to take home and some of that guy Blake's famous chocolate chip cookies.

Went downtown to defer my jury duty and the lady said, "We had Calvin Klein here yesterday deferring his!" Taped the show with Padma, Olivia Munn, and a bunch of rowers from the UK. They were very cute and shirtless and it wound up being a great show. Ryan had me take a picture where the shirtless rowers were all picking me up and it looked really depressing so I asked them not to release it anywhere.

It's the holidays and I've done nothing about it, including nothing for my Christmas party. I don't even really know who's coming. Dinner with Deirdre, John Jude, and John Hill at the Waverly Inn. The prices are just highway robbery. I don't know if I can go back—sixteen bucks for the kale salad. Got an incredible massage from Adam—one I'd waited for the whole book tour—and slunk into bed directly from the table at one-thirty.

▶ THURSDAY, DECEMBER 11, 2014—NYC—PHILADELPHIA—NYC

Woke up sore and dehydrated, and a little dizzy. Went and got my staples out. Schlepped to the Montville Inn for my top-secret lunch—and the first meal I've ever shared—with Teresa, who arrived with diamond hoop earrings and bone-straight hair that I complimented and she wistfully said, "Yeah, I thought this would be my Season 7 look"—sad, of course, because it doesn't seem like she will be in Season 7 unless we wait for her. We tried to figure out if we've ever shot in this restaurant. Teresa said she vaguely remembers it and I think it was her, Caroline, and Jacqueline talking about Danielle in Season 2. Teresa had two cosmos and I finally had a red wine. She wanted to know off the bat if I'm dating a hockey player. I told her that Sean Avery is straight. She said *Us Weekly* has her kids' Christmas lists printed, but the kids don't even have Christmas lists so she knows everything is bullshit. She hates her hair on the "Free Tre" T-shirts. We talked a lot about her case and how the lawyers fucked up. . . . I kept pushing her about what life was gonna be like in the prison in Danbury. She has a prison consultant but she hasn't talked to him yet. Who knew that a prison consultant is a thing?! I want one! She said she had a seen a psychic and the queen card came up, and the psychic said a queen might help her in her life and she thought that might be me because I'm a queen. Hmmm. She said she wakes up in the middle of the night scared. I kept asking her about prison and she goes, "You're so obsessed with this prison thing, aren't you?!" So that makes one of us, I guess. She asked what will happen with *House-wives* while she's gone and I said I really didn't know, maybe we would wait for her. She said she would be fine coming back with them all but isn't sure about Melissa. Melissa and Joe moved back to Montville and didn't tell her; she hasn't seen them since the reunion. They're "fine," but they're not talking. So is that fine?

I told her it would be in her self-interest to write a diary, and I told her in my own selfish interest that I wanted her to do an interview with me right when she got out or while she is in prison, and to start shooting *Housewives* whenever she legally could. Toward the end of the meal we started to get heavy. She said I occasionally hurt her feelings when she was on *WWHL*; she left the show crying a couple times. I apologized. She said she was hurt when I asked her the day after the sentencing how she looks in an orange jumpsuit. I said it was mean and that's why we didn't use it in the show, sometimes I don't know if something is going to be inappropriate before it comes out of my mouth and only realize after it's too late. I said she has a good sense of humor and I thought she might jump on the jumpsuit line. In front of the restaurant we had a real moment and I told her everything I wanted her to hear from me if for some reason we didn't meet again. Her eyes filled with tears and I felt like I was on *RHONJ* as I put my hands on both her shoulders and told her that she's important to me, that she has meant a great deal to me over the years, that I care for her, that I am sorry if I've ever hurt her feelings, and that I will pray for her. I meant every word of it. We hugged twice and she pulled away in her white Range Rover to sign Gabriella up for advanced soccer.

After, I went to an ebullient last signing thrown by the Katz JCC, outside of Philly. I took two hundred pics quickly with VIPs and had a lot of yentas all over me, then spoke in front of a thousand people on the bema of a temple. The lady organizers had the mic and were reading questions the audience had submitted. If I hear the title of my show misidentified one more time . . . "Watch What's Happening Live." "Watching What's Happened." It's not the best title! Then I ate half a pot lolly, which kicked in fast, while I was also sipping a massive tequila on ice and I signed more than five hundred books. A woman told me her four-year-old son, Sam, has a *Housewives* tag line: "I may be four, but I run this town." Haha! And a woman said, as she got hustled through the madness of the yentas after waiting ninety minutes, "This is my Vietnam, but it's worth it." A lady named Michelle handed me a piece of paper with Wacha's *Housewives* tag line on it: "I may not have balls, but that doesn't make me a bitch." Oh, and the couple was there that I wrote about in my book, the ones who I overheard trashing me in the lobby at my show—the lady who squeezed my ass in the photo and made me the collage. She made me another collage, this one of me and Wacha, which I love. And the husband said he was the one who was trashing me in the lobby and felt horribly about it and I said but isn't it funny that I was listening around the corner? He did think so, and we fist bumped.

I triumphantly left for my schlep home and was momentarily deflated by my driver, who was the whitest black guy I've ever met. It took him a solid three minutes (eternity) to do all his little paperwork before starting the car for the ninety-minute journey. Once under way, with the silence thumping in my ears, I asked him to turn on the radio. He asked what I wanted to hear and I said to flip around the FM dial and we'd find something. "That would be pretty hard to do while I'm driving, don't you think?" he asked. Yes, I said, that would be *near impossible* to accomplish. I got out my computer and DJed the journey home while slowly sucking the life out of a massive bag of Doritos a fan brought me.

ꙮ FRIDAY, DECEMBER 12, 2014

Sherman brought Wacha home this morning and I put him right into bed with me. I was on the phone a while later and heard what sounded like him drinking water, but I knew it couldn't be that because his bowl wasn't in my bathroom. Then I realized he was slurping toilet water, which would've been fine but it was full of my pee. Gross. Ran around getting ready for my Christmas party and talked to Jake in New Hampshire about Angela and the Patriots. Early dinner with John Hill at the new Italian place that I'm obsessed with. I went home and was really tired but Jake Shears and Kylie Minogue were doing an all–Dolly Parton set on Twenty-sixth Street at ten-thirty and I really wanted to go. John Hill had gone home by that point and I was a little stuck for who to go with. I tried Hickey; he was still at dinner. I wound up staying at home. I would've had the guts to go alone if I wasn't famous but I felt self-conscious about it. Interesting. Mark and Kelly sent me a beautiful, ornate gingerbread house and it took having a gingerbread house to realize it was something I always wanted.

Ran around getting ready for my party all day. It was SantaCon and it seemed like the wind was out of the sails for all the drunk straight people who run around town in Santa outfits, perhaps owing to the simultaneous demonstrations over police violence against black people. I stopped by two independent bookstores, Three Lives and bookbook on Bleecker, and signed their stock of my book. I went crazy on twinkly lights and looked at my apartment before everyone arrived and realized that between the gingerbread house and the gold tree from *WWHL* I've transitioned to a Christian home. I had no clue who was really coming to my party so the night was an adventure as everybody arrived. All I knew was that Jake Shears was bringing Kylie Minogue. Next year I might want to have people RSVP. I called John Hill in a panic because I forgot to redo my Christmas party playlist and he came over and did some work on it. I told him to add some Kylie, because maybe it would be disrespectful if she was there and there wasn't any on in a mass of Madonna. The first guests at the party were Grac and Neal. Then Bruce, Bryan, and Barry. Then Mark, Kelly, Jessica Seinfeld, Jake Shears, and Kylie Minogue, who was over by the cheese and crackers looking like she was in crisis. I went up to her and she asked if this was all the food I was serving. I said yes but asked if I could get her anything. She said well, what do you mean, and I said pizza? She said no. I said roast chicken? She said perfect, so I ordered out from Good and she was thrilled a half hour later eating it on the couch. She said she's never seen the *Real Housewives of Melbourne* and I said that makes two of us—I have nothing to do with the show. She lives between London and Australia. It was all the regulars: Dave, Ally, Jeanne, Fred, Jackie, Amanda, Jim, SJP, Hickey, Victor Garber, Troy Roberts, Harry Smith, and on and on. I was sitting chatting with Fred and Padma, who had her stilettoed legs sprawled across both our laps, and Jeanne stormed over to her husband, under a blanket of Lakshmi, saying, "Get your fucking legs off my husband!" And then she said, "I'm just trying to protect my family." It was a real-life scene! Exciting, though. I guess Julianne Moore was having her Christmas party down the street and we got spillover from that. Barkin was amazing; she brought Sandra Bernhard and Sara, who said they were not invited but crashing and I said, "Yeah, I realized I didn't invite you and wondered why," which kind of hung there. I made a lunch plan with Greg Berlanti. NPH was there. The bulk of the group stayed until three; we went until after four. Jon Jay and Nikki stopped by at some point in the madness.

MONDAY, DECEMBER 15, 2014

I was at *WWHL* early for Sting and Trudie Styler. They were both all in black and he was wearing black leather pants, which I absolutely loved. He was so *Sting*. I asked them a lot about tantric sex. She said he has a gay alter ego named Rene and I latched onto that like crazy.

Heard from Anderson that our live stage show is coming together, we're looking at a March show in Boston to test the water. We need a title. He suggested *AC Squared: An Evening with Andy C and Anderson C*. We decided on *AC2: Deep Talk and Shallow Tales*. We taped a show with Jason Schwartzman and Krysten Ritter. He was so lovely before the show and excited to be there but a little tongue tied on the air. The gay shark brought out a birthday cake for Ritter at the end and Wacha jumped up and ate some, which made us all laugh. I thought it saved the show, but I think my producers think he needs management or Cesar Millan. Am I becoming one of *those* dog owners? Do I not know what is obnoxious or not?

Went to Whitehall with Hickey, who said it was like airplane food and not to get used to seeing him there. I told him he is a food snob from Plano, Texas. Walked home and watched two episodes of *The Comeback*.

TUESDAY, DECEMBER 16, 2014

First visit to the dog run in months and Wacha ran around like a mother-fucker. Had lunch with Greg Berlanti; it was fun getting to know him. I left my phone aside and I guess it was blowing up while I was in there because Seth Rogen and James Franco bailed on our 4:00 p.m. taping. I booked Anderson and Kelly to replace them tomorrow.

Yolanda and Anna Kendrick were on the early show and I went into Yolanda's dressing room beforehand and she had her head down and tearily told me she was in really bad shape from the Lyme disease. She was so weak and feeling slow and vulnerable—but looking, I should add, like a million-dollar bill. I'm on the *Today* show recommending Christmas books with Brooke Shields tomorrow, and they want me there at 7:20 a.m. for a 7:45 tease and I just know that they don't need me there that early. *I know it.* But no one else does.

The live show with Vicki and Beth Stern was perfect. I grabbed Vicki before the show because we're in the middle of figuring out her future on the show. I said you're nuts to walk away, we are at a good place and you waited nine seasons to be the voice of reason on the show so why walk now? She said she agreed, but who knows. We played Name! That! Pussy! with Vicki. I gave her multiple-choice questions and she had to pick which one was the right cat name (Stormy, Millicent, or Shadow?!) and Vicki got something like six out of eight right and was all "I won; I won!" Of course she won nothing, though.

▶ WEDNESDAY, DECEMBER 17, 2014

A never-ending marathon day that started at six forty-five in order to get to the *Today* show—went to two Starbucks stores on the way and both were *out of tea* and I don't even know what to do with that. They're transitioning to different tea brands this week, so they ran out of the Awake stuff. I was so irritated, and even more so to walk into NBC and discover that my seven forty-five tease had been cancelled and no one bothered to let me know but somehow Brooke Shields got the memo and arrived fresh after eight. I was looking around for someone I could hug to death. The segment was fine and hopefully "selling," as they say. Went home and walked, then nuzzled with, the dog. Quick lunch with Hickey at Zampa and I was already stressed about having three shows today (we're in a logjam because of Christmas), but Hickey made it worse by saying I was nuts not to have started looking for a place to live while my old apartment is being combined with the new one. Called Fredrik Eklund to say I need to find an apartment to rent because I have to move out for a year starting in February and he said do you realize how late you are to the table here? I said no.

Radzi came by to get a book signed and remarked that Wacha is the perfect animal. He was just sitting there watching us sweetly with his big eyes. Cut to two hours later, and he bit *Anderson*! We were short of space at

WWHL because we were doing three shows, and it was madness so Anderson was in my office getting ready and I had just given Wacha a fresh meaty bone which I knew would take him through eight hours at least of being at the show, and Anderson leaned down to pet him and he started growling and barking. He thought Anderson was going after the bone. Anderson retreated to the couch and all was fine for thirty seconds until Wacha out of nowhere started attacking him and bit him on his side. He was cut—bleeding a little. Anderson is the ultimate trouper but I was mortified and horrified. Kelly said I need a trainer for the dog but I don't know what I'm training him to do, erase whatever bad memory he has about being territorial with bones? My mind was on the dog during the whole show, which I thought sucked but the control room thought was great. The gay shark came out at the end for a dance party—Wacha was supposed to be there too, but I nixed that—and Anderson didn't stand because his shirt was a little bloody and ripped on the side. Humiliating for me! *Maybe* worse for him, but I was a wreck.

During the break before the next show I distributed my staff Christmas present, which were Adidas track jackets with *WWHL* embroidered on the back. The whole staff put them on. John Hill and 1 were chatting about WTF could be wrong with Wacha when Daryn came into my office in tears. This girl she'd been seeing went home to Mississippi to come out, and the mother called Daryn with the girl next to her and threatened her life ("I will come to NYC and blow your brains out") if she continued to see her daughter. She made the daughter tell Daryn that the daughter was choosing the mother over her and she would never be speaking with her again. This is 2014? I have never seen Daryn so upset. It was horrible. I felt like her powerless dad. And what could I tell her that would make her feel better about being threatened by this intolerant woman *and* losing her girlfriend? (I said time would heal her, still, not great . . .)

Then we had Phaedra and Faith Evans, and Phae was freaked about the *RHOA* episode she'd just screened so there was some light damage control to do there. Dave Brecher's grandma, Libby, was the bartender and she brought homemade brisket and latkes and I was just obsessed with getting my hands on some after the show. The whole studio smelled like brisket. I became convinced that the staff was gonna eat it all before I got any, but Mike Robley saved me some and all was okay with the world. I shoved brisket in my mouth and told Mom and Dad about how the tour with Anderson could work and Mom's first reaction was, "And an agent takes 20 PERCENT?!" I yelled at her for having an immediate negative reaction to it and not focusing on the positive. So that devolved. I spent a good chunk of time prepping for Nicki Minaj, who was on live for the #AndyConda. During rehearsal I realized I should take a butt selfie with her because she has been posting a lot of ass pics and that seemed to work so well with Kim Kardashian. Also, Phaedra was going to come out to do a surprise shotski with her. I made sure to ask Nicki during the promo if she put "Fix it, Jesus" in "Yasss Bish!!" (How do I say that title out loud without sounding like an old Jewish dude? I wondered) because of Phae and she said yes. She said she watches *WWHL* every night and was excited to be there, which I loved. Right before the show her publicist and Dori came in the control room and said that Nicki wanted to know the Plead the Fifth questions—her publicist was acting like "Wink wink, I know you do this all the time," but we said actually we've never told a guest in advance. Thus began three minutes of me tap-dancing to the publicist as my entire staff watched in delight to see if I was going to be able to push this through. I said the first question was a positive spin on something negative (it was "Say three nice things about Mariah Carey"). He seemed okay with that for a second, and then I said the next one was about one of her song lyrics (something about big asses attracting big dicks, which was leading me into asking her who had the biggest dick in the music business), and the third question was something that then related to that lyric again (it actually related to dicks; this time it was, who *is* the biggest dick in Hollywood). At that point he went back to the first one and asked, "Is it about someone she's collaborating with on this current album?" I said no. Finally I just caved and told him the question and he said *absolutely not* and the truth is that after the day I'd had I was feeling violent and I was having PTSD from being a booker at CBS, *and* I was upset that my dog bit my friend who had done me the favor of going on my show *and* upset I couldn't make (always upbeat) Daryn feel better— but instead of getting mad I said, "It's gone," and mentally decided to move the question about what she knew about the elevator incident with Beyoncé to that spot. He asked what the new question was going to be and I said, "It's about someone she *has* collaborated with," and shut it down from there.

The show was a roller-coaster ride of Nicki rolling her eyes at photos we'd decided to use of her and of shady turns of phrase I was using in the script (thank you, John Hill) mixed in with her totally dodging questions and also enjoying herself. I asked about Phaedra and she started to say that she had been really mean to Apollo and I thought, Uh-oh, this may be awful when I bring her out to surprise you in three minutes—but we turned it around and it became a good moment. They took pics during the break but she wanted to approve them before Phae posted them. I was supposed to ask about the ass selfie top of act two, but I just had a premonition to wait until the end of the show. She dodged all the Plead the Fifth questions, as well as plenty more. During the second commercial break she said WTF were you thinking bringing Phae out, what if I hated her and said something bad about her? I said it was all cool, that she was already here and that I asked about the "Fix it, Jesus" thing early to get a sense of it. And she told the audience to stop taking pictures of her. She's obsessed with the pics! During the last act I asked if she would take an ass selfie with me and she said no. I am *so* glad I waited. She actually left saying she had the best time and was singing "AndyConda" during the after show. Twitter was abuzz with people sending their condolences to me after watching me trying to pull teeth. I binge-ate after—cookies and peanut brittle that Martha Stewart had sent over—and brought Jackie back to my office, where Wacha started barking at her in a rough way. I removed her and then ran him home before I returned to party with the team. I was really upset about Wacha, though. I was upset, period.

▶ THURSDAY, DECEMBER 18, 2014

Decompressed today. Slept on and off until one o'clock and hung out on conference calls about *RHONJ*, development with Embassy Row, and game show ideas. Spoke to Anderson, who is getting a tetanus shot, so now I feel even more horrible. Sherman pointed out how hungry Wacha is since we halved his food. He's scavenging aggressively on the street. What's worse, a fat dog or a violent one? I'm upping his food almost back to normal and I will find a diet food for him when I get back from Indonesia. The guy from the parking garage chased me down the street today with an envelope. I have never tipped them at Christmas before and I don't plan on doing it this year. I get my car maybe twenty-five times a year—maybe thirty, actually—and I tip them five bucks every time, plus the monthly rent there is more than 60 percent of what Americans pay a month for their homes. Maybe more.

It was Colbert's final episode, and I was invited to join the sing-along to end the show. Walked into an insane group of sixty to eighty people you can't believe are together, all famous and interesting. They divided us into groups—I was in Group 8—that would be coming out and singing together. My group was Christiane Amanpour, Patrick Stewart, Jeff Tweedy from Wilco, and David Gregory. I walked in the room and immediately told David Gregory that he got fucked out of his *Meet the Press* job. He agreed, and was happy for the icebreaker. I wandered into another room and had started talking to Charlie Rose when Katie Couric came in and said, "Let's all rehearse the song"—which we did, while she took video of us and then kind of interviewed each of us and took some selfies. That rehearsal group was Mark Cuban, Charlie, Keith Olbermann, Ken Burns, Ric Ocasek, Michael Stipe, and a blond ballet dancer whose sexuality Andrew Sullivan and I later spent a fair amount of time trying to ascertain. We went down to the studio where we were told to sit and await instruction. I sat with David Gregory and Maureen Dowd, who made my day when she said she bought my book for a lot of her family and friends for Christmas. I couldn't wait to tell Mom that a *smart person* bought my book for other (presumably) smart people. Across the aisle Barry Manilow was sitting with Lesley Stahl and that was two hair systems next to each other. I told James Franco how bummed I was that he had to cancel *WWHL* and how sorry I was for the week he'd had, being that he was at the center of the Sony hack. He had no clue who I was, but I explained. He was really nice and open. We ran through the routine twice and then they sent us back up to the rooms and I was starting to get kinda bored and anxious about making the Billy Joel concert, which was starting in less than ninety minutes. Talked to the mayor's wife (it felt endless) about her hot security detail (one of whom I was kinda cruising but who was straight) and her Christmas plans, which she said were as little as possible—she made it a point to tell me what normal people they are. She asked where I live and I said the West Village, and what I should've brought up was all the small businesses closing. (And by the way, there is another fucking chocolate shop opening next to Manley's Wine and Spirits—so there are now *three* fancy chocolate places over two blocks. *Where is the demand for high-end chocolate??*)

We all watched the show together and then finally we were backstage waiting to go on and David Gregory was dying to go over to Willie Nelson and take a selfie, but Patrick Stewart beat him to it and by the time David went over there, Willie had walked into the studio. I took a quickie with James Franco after he and Michael Stipe did one, and we did one Group 8 shot on my camera, then each of them wanted one so I did one with each of their phones. Finally we went on and I gave it, served it, and belted it. I was so paranoid about making Amanda and company late for the Billy Joel concert that I ran out just as the show was wrapping up, along with James Franco and Barry Manilow (were they going too?). Raced down Ninth Ave to where Amanda, Jim, Jeanne, and Fred were waiting with Jägermeister shots. Downed them, raced to MSG, went backstage, saw Claire Mercuri who took a pic of me and Alexa Ray Joel and then raced inside for the concert which was perfect. Tommy Lasorda was in the row in front of us and he was dozing on and off. He came back during "Scenes from an Italian Restaurant." We danced and were happy. I stood between Jeanne and Fred, who are kind of Brenda and Eddie but they never split, so maybe they're just Jeanne and Fred.

They gave me a ride home, and Jeanne and I got into it about the scene she made with Padma at my Christmas party. She said, "You called me the original Housewife, so I was proving it to you," and I respected that. They dropped me off and pulled away and then I got a text from Hickey saying, "meet us now at Indochine." I couldn't get a cab and hit my knee on a post, so I was irritated. Then Andrew Bowen drunkenly fell out of a cab in front of Lenox Health and so that was my ride to go meet SJP, Matthew, Hickey, and Scott Wittman at Indochine, whose kitchen closes at midnight, which enraged me. WTF—that is supposed to be a late night fashion place, and BTW it was five after twelve. We were all on our soapboxes about various things, actually. Hickey and SJ had seen two shitty plays in a row. Hickey yelled at me for looking at my phone. I wanted to see people's comments about Colbert. They loved it.

▶ FRIDAY, DECEMBER 19, 2014

Now Anderson says he *doesn't* need the tetanus shot. I think he is trying to shut me up because I keep texting him. Met with Eric Hughes and Gordon and chose colors and finishes and backsplashes and faucets and on and on. Made a lot of decisions. It felt great.

The *Daily News* emailed Bravo PR saying they are running an item tomorrow about how I was basically making an ass of myself backstage at Colbert, taking endless selfies with people, and even James Franco had enough and he rolled his eyes at me on camera. They say you have an hour to respond and then they don't answer their phones. Bravo emailed them a list of celebrities who were taking selfies, with corresponding Instagram accounts. They don't care. I guess they just want to write something mean about me. And Nicki Minaj fans are pissed at me for asking her to take a butt selfie and who has the biggest dick in Hollywood. They say that's racist and sexist. I was talking about a music lyric, but they don't care. It was an endless stream of insults about how misogynistic I am, and how racist, and how I would've never asked Taylor Swift that question. But Taylor doesn't sing about dicks and asses.

Spoke to Teresa. She changed lawyers; she wanted me to know. She still hasn't met with the prison consultant. She changed criminal attorneys too, she said—her third so far. Met Diane Ronnau for a quick drink, then went to Harry Smith's Christmas party, where he has that same great pianist every year and a massive tree and it feels really cozy. Came downtown, got Hickey, and went to a party at Jason and David's house. There were a few cute guys who I flirted with. The cutest was very boring. The second cutest was too young. The third wanted to come over and cuddle but it didn't happen.

❧ SATURDAY, DECEMBER 20, 2014

Dad dozed off a little during our Skype call today. I told them about Tommy Lasorda dozing at the Billy Joel concert. Every time his name comes up (which is twice yearly) Mom says, "You know his son died of AIDS, right?" and I say, "Yes, you remind me every time." Wacha freaked out at this big, nice dog at the dog park, to the point that I had to take him out and leave. Everybody was saying what a nice dog that is and that I should keep Wacha there, but he was so flipped out, his hair standing straight up on his back. It was upsetting. Incidentally, Hickey says I absolutely have to tip the parking garage people. Went to the Knicks game with John Hill and saw Scott Greenstein, who asked what I was thinking about Radio Andy. I said I had been too busy to think about it but I will now that the book is out. Bruce and Bryan hosted a beautiful candlelit dinner in the private room of

Bill's Food and Drink on Fifty-fourth Street. Talked to Ethan Hawke and had a nice flirt going with a ballet dancer, which ended when I later found out he has a serious boyfriend. Scarlett Johansson was there too.

▶ SUNDAY, DECEMBER 21, 2014

So today I walk into the dog run and Bert, who is the Gladys Kravitz of the joint, says, "You will never believe what happened yesterday"—it turns out that big dog wound up attacking another dog minutes after we left. So I guess Wacha smelled it. Hickey and I walked the dog and I told him I may do my own radio station and I want him to do a music show. I'm thinking "John Hickey's School of Rock," or something like that.

Breakfast with Bruce and Bryan at Whitehall. Remind me not to go back there for breakfast—it's all fried eggs on top of beans and toast and bacon and British breakfasts that I don't want so I felt like an ugly American. Did major gift-giving TCB today—bought sweaters at Grahame Fowler for me, Ralph, and Liam; then Save Khaki stuff for Liza, Bill, and Joanna; then to the East Village for Todd Snyder shoes for Danny and Michael; sweater and shirt at Ralph Lauren for Dad; and some more stuff I can't remember. Thought about the radio channel all through my massage. Sedaris would be great, I realized. I emailed her from the table. She's in London.

Bozzi family dinner at the Palm was lovely. Went deep with Lukas about the Housewives, which is what happens every year. Before long Hickey texted to say Lady Bunny is spinning disco at the Monster so he brought SJP and Matthew and they were waiting there for me. It was fun. Bunny played "The Boss" for me even though she said she had just played him. She also played a song that made me go nuts and I asked what it was but then totally forgot the answer. Lady Bunny would be great on the radio too—"Lady Bunny's Saturday Night Dance Party," maybe? Got home and took Wacha on a long walk all around the West Village which was blissfully semi-deserted but beautifully lit with Christmas lights all over, like an endless, rolling movie set. Talked on the phone with Dave the whole time. He had some confusing dreams about me. Maybe we were boyfriends in them? We don't know.

I emailed Bunny to find out what song that was last night. She said it was "Victim" by Candi Staton, who she said was great and then got really very Christian and that fucked everything up. Went to look at eight apartments with Fredrik and they were all wrong for one reason or another. Watching Fredrik do his facial expressions reacting to apartments—buggy eyes, furrowed brows, pursed lips—is like watching *Million Dollar Listing* in person. The best was a really small one on Christopher and Bleecker in Amy's old building—it's too small and has not-great fixtures and stuff, but a great terrace, which is all I ever really wanted. Fredrik suggested getting a contractor in there to redo the kitchen and floors and then making a new deal on the rent because the building would never want to make those improvements. So we're exploring that. It's a very *MDL* idea. Then I saw a cool place in the sky that had incredible views and made me again think I should just do something like that—a super-high floor in a building I'd never live in regularly but could work with for a year. Also ran by Adidas, Grahame Fowler, and Amanda's between apartments to do various present swapping. Went home and wrapped and packed and sorted and finally went through mail and went to the bank four times to get wads of cash to tip all my people and reluctantly went by the garage and gave the dude an envelope with a hundred bucks for the five of them to split. Luckily it was the non-greedy, non-angry guy I like who took the envelope. And I upped my tip game with the whole staff of the building. We have a long year of construction coming up! Pot delivery girl came by and Wacha seemed on the verge of flipping out. He doesn't like shady, illegal activity! It was all I could do to get the hell out of the apartment with tons of gifts to Adri's, where I met the Perskys and it was all a big Christmas explosion of love. Ordered an Uber and he was there in thirty seconds which freaked us all out. There are more Ubers than cabs in the city at this point. Palm West for Ralph's birthday dinner with Liam, the boys, Hickey and Jeff, Aefoa and Ciaran. It was lovely. We had toasts for Ralph's birthday and his Golden Globe nomination and for Danny getting into Yale. Hickey texted afterward saying that that room at the Palm was the last place he saw Natasha alive.

Very cuddly morning with Wacha that was ramping up to a sad goodbye for me, highlighted by his big sad eyes looking at me as I packed. I can't imagine having actual humans to take care of and then leave. Talked to Lauren Zalaznick from the airport and was feeling down from my goodbye with Wacha and wondering if this trek to Indonesia was the right thing to be doing—I just had a feeling of displacement. She thought we were still going to the Philippines but I said no, it's Indonesia now. She said you'll schlep there and run around on Jet Skis and you'll be back in a week. She said Barry is gonna have to start taking us to the moon to get us to be excited about something. Then we'll say, "Oh, I thought we were going to the moon"; "No, it changed to Saturn." Ha ha—she's right!

Got on the plane and was seated next to Michael Cunningham. He asked what was up with me and I told him about my book tour and felt like a fraud doing so because he is a "real" author, but I made the story about pot lollipops and then we discussed Adderall, which is too speedy for me. I landed and Ubered to meet Bruce at the Palm and the first thing the driver wanted to do was pick a fight with me about the bad weather I left in New York. I told him it was in the fifties today and he made a big joke about how refreshing that must've been. He was confusing me with someone who gives a shit about the weather in LA being perfect. Bruce was in front of the Palm smooching Sherry Lansing and John Goldwyn and I got in on the action. She says she is "a fan." Of the *Housewives*? Sherry Lansing? Of *WWHL*? I don't know what to believe in this town. While she was talking George Hamilton walked by. It's a real hard-candy Christmas in LA, I'll tell ya that. Bruce and I walked to Barneys, which was depressing—the store, not the walk, or, well, maybe both—then back to the Palm for a rosé to celebrate my arrival. Back to his house, where I napped and Ava woke me too enthusiastically to tell me it was dinnertime. We had a mellow dinner and then watched a movie called *Northern Soul* about these kids hopped up on speed dancing to soul music in England in the sixties. I understood 80 percent of it. Then we started to watch a *Laverne and Shirley* Christmas show—looking at them young and knowing how they turned out adds a layer of depression to the experience—but the TV went out and then so did we.

Woke up on Christmas Eve in Bruce and Bryan's guest house again, feeling a little displaced. If I were in New York with the dog, would I feel like I was in the right place? Hard to tell. Went shopping on Third Street where we met up with Barry, then went to Neil Lane Jewelry and Barry got jewelry for DVF, then we went to Fig & Olive for lunch, where some guy thought I was from the Food Network and wanted to talk to me about his friend Adam who "also" is on the Food Network. Then we went to some shops on Beverly; all but one were closed, which sent me into a rage because isn't Christmas Eve a huge shopping day? LA just felt dead, and that displaced feeling lingered. Those guys went home and I kept Bruce's car "Monty," and went to Maxfield to shop for Bruce, where I found a delicious cashmere kind of wrappy sweater thing with a belt that turned out to be $2,600; then I looked at vintage Rolexes which were all $6,000, and finally I spotted a stick pin that was diamond costume jewelry in the shape of a palm tree for $200. Sold. Then to Neiman Marcus, where I bought some Creed. The lady behind the counter told me to tell my friends that online shopping puts people out of jobs. It was actually bustling in there, and all of Beverly Hills was really packed so that made me happy. Back to the house, where I napped for a couple hours and Ava woke me up for dinner, which was an Italian Christmas Eve specialty: lasagna and filet mignon. And caviar. I ate a ton. Just wolfed it down. Ava went to bed and Jason, Lauren, Bruce, and I became obsessed with setting up a little Christmas village Bruce had bought on Amazon (sorry, Neiman lady) for Ava from Santa. Jason set it up all vertically on the table, which Bruce said was no good. So he set it up more spread out, then Bryan got a sheet and covered the whole thing and spread the town over the whole table. He thought it was depressing and that Ava would know there was no Santa by the looks of the table.

▶ THURSDAY, DECEMBER 25, 2014—LOS ANGELES—HAWAII

Woke up early—seven-thirty—and put on the red onesie Bruce had left for me and went to the house to find Bruce and Bry in matching union suits and Ava hard at work unwrapping gifts, ignoring the depressing town that Santa had tragically arranged. Bry said she kept asking if Santa was real and he thinks the town was a giveaway. I thought it looked perfect last night but in the light of day he might've been right. All morning and all day I got a flood of tweets from people taking pics of themselves with *The Andy Cohen Diaries* under the tree, which *made my day*. I had hundreds by the end of the day. I made breakfast for everybody—eggs, bacon, toast. Then we went to Barry's, where DVF was wearing her off-the-shoulder "Mazel" sweatshirt, and then to Runyon Canyon for a hike. I missed Wacha so much today. Saw *Into the Woods* at the ArcLight. I was fighting sleep during the movie so I could sleep on the endless flight that awaited me. I liked the movie, even though the score is a little like nails on a chalkboard. Yes, that's my review. I am officially the only gay dude who doesn't like Sondheim. Kill me. (I'm sure he would love my oeuvre as well.) Went back to the house and watched *Working Girl* with Bruce and then headed to Jason's to go to Van Nuys Airport. Downloaded all episodes of *Serial* on the way. Got on the plane and it was me, Jason, DVF, Barry, Ashley Olsen, and Bennett Miller. Intimate! We watched *Still Alice* on the flight to Hawaii and I cried.

❧ SATURDAY, DECEMBER 27, 2014—HAWAII—RAJA AMPAT, INDONESIA

We stopped to refuel in Hawaii and then Jason and I took our pills. We woke up somewhere over nowhere and I was quickly humiliated to find out I had been snoring horribly and the entire plane had heard me! Bennett asked what the plan was for the flight home. If I wasn't already flying back commercially I might've rebooked. DVF said the snoring was going to be terrible for my sex life. We spent twenty hours on the plane and I only listened to one episode of *Serial*.

❧ SUNDAY, DECEMBER 28, 2014—RAJA AMPAT, INDONESIA

Woke up and DVF said it looks like we're in Connecticut. Took a beautiful swim in the morning with Barry, DVF, and Jason. At some point I was in a corner of a cove and got a mouthful of salt water and puked up my scrambled eggs. Whoops. Later I went paddleboarding while DVF swam. She took pics of me and I hated them all. She said I will love them in ten years and she is probably right. Lunch was perfect—salade Niçoise, quinoa with avocado, meat filet, flatbread with cheese, lobster. I love lunch on the boat. Afterwards DVF and I watched *Unbroken* under thick cashmere blankets. Then we found out an AirAsia flight in the area was missing—the third missing plane in this area this year. So that freaked me out because I am flying home commercially on Friday. Lee, the bosun, brought me my itinerary and it is a mess—four planes; I'll be in the air for twenty-four hours. My heart sank when I saw it. This is not where my head should be on the first day of vacation. All day we were scoping out a megayacht around the other island and then they invited us over for drinks. We got on the other boat and it turns out they're Americans from LA who all knew Ashley—how random. The son-in-law is listening to my book on audio. Small world of rich people.

MONDAY, DECEMBER 29, 2014—RAJA AMPAT, INDONESIA

Woke up at 4:00 a.m. and tossed and turned until 8:00 a.m. when I got out of bed. My mind was racing, turning over these issues again and again: Jake and Angela, what the hell happened to that plane and its poor passengers, my own airplane situation end of week, my radio channel, Wacha, my apartment renovation and the imminent move for which I am completely unprepared, being alone . . . By the way, what happens if I meet someone and I have built my dream apartment and that person doesn't like it? Then what do I do? My life is too big and set up. I leave no room for another life coming in. Swam around a bunch of coves—incredible snorkeling in pristine waters. After the swim I listened to *Serial*, then took a nap and that went right up until lunch. I can't decide if I care about the murder case in *Serial*. Ashley and I had a scuba lesson and an intro session underwater and I only got to about twenty feet (Ashley was at fifty feet) before my ears were hurting but I saw a world of beauty—huge blue starfish and many varieties of yellow and blue and orange fish of various sizes. It was disconcerting to see trash on the surface in the middle of nowhere, though. Sat on the bowsprit and listened to the six new Madonna songs over and over and felt happy and confident, as she is prone to make me feel. I thought about what I will ask her if she ever comes on my show and over-analyzed how she'll respond. She doesn't like to dwell on the past and she isn't into feuds, so that's a bit limiting. Michael Jackson for sure I can bring up. Does she ever look at her *Sex* book? Does she regret doing it knowing that her kids can see it? Does she ever get jealous of Lola's youth and freedom and beauty? Aging—how does she view it? Will she ever stop working? Who among her former conquests does she regret: Dennis Rodman? Vanilla Ice? (That's a good Plead the Fifth question.) I'll go deep about the music. These are good questions so far! Watch, she'll never do my show.

▶ TUESDAY, DECEMBER 30, 2014—RAJA AMPAT, INDONESIA

Overnight we had crossed over the equator so after lunch there was a ceremony on the bow for the crew members who'd never crossed the equator before today. The captain dressed as Neptune/Poseidon, God of the Sea, and "punished" the crew, who had to dress as the opposite sex and dunk their heads in a big barrel of water with fish heads and gnarly stuff in it, then the captain read their list of "offenses" and they got spanked. At the end they walked a plank, which meant jumping off the bowsprit, an activity that I joined in on. Dove and made it to forty-five feet, then I took a paddleboard and swim with DVF and we saw more amazing natural beauty. I have been pining for one of the deckhands for the last couple days and when I got back from the long paddleboard tour he was taking Jason out for a swim, so I joined just so I could bail out of the swim quickly and then chat with him. He has a girlfriend. I had sensed a gayish vibe off him, but after the chat it was gone. I did take a magic-hour selfie with him behind me and post it, so all was not lost. I'm overindulging in every kind of way—which means plenty of booze, starch, and desserts. My face is really fat. But come January 4 or 5 I'm clean for a month, so I am enjoying myself now. I was alone on the aft deck drinking and listening to Madonna and had to grapple with an unusually strong attraction to the young blond deckhand who is on night watch.

▶ WEDNESDAY, DECEMBER 31, 2014—RAJA AMPAT, INDONESIA

The last day of the year: time to reflect. And I started reflecting at four o'clock this morning, meaning I tossed and turned and once again fretted about stupid stuff—my apparent feud with Wendy Williams, what the hell

I'm going to perform next month on *Lip Sync Battle*—and then not-stupid stuff: flying over the triangle of terror commercially on Saturday and moving to an apartment I don't have. Eventually I gave up trying to sleep and I went up to the aft deck and ate. We were in another corner of paradise, little mounds of islands all around us and green water, with a light rain falling. I went back down to sleep and DVF—it's her birthday today—came in my room to give *me* a present, which was that we're now leaving Sunday and I don't have to fly commercially on Saturday and go missing. So that was one great weight lifted. I napped, then went on an incredible dive with the group. There can't be a better place to dive; you see every last thing, all different colors and everything alive. I am five episodes into *Serial* and I'm getting really, really bored. Why is everyone so obsessed?

New Year's Eve dinner on the aft deck was a barbecue under lanterns. I got high on the hash vape thing and we played Balderdash, which was amusing. BD said during the game he is not competitive nor is he scary to work for, so we spent a lot of time challenging that. DVF told me she's curious about what I am like in bed, am I smiley? She thinks the idea is hilarious. I told her I am a different person in bed. They all went to bed early and I joined ten or so crew members on the aft deck as they swilled champers and I drank tequila and Sprites (side of ice). We counted down to midnight on Lee's precise clock and fireworks appeared from the next cove. There were lots of hugs and I felt a little awkward; I guess we all do at midnight but this was especially weird given that I was hugging the Thai masseuse lady and the dive instructor dude who lives in Bali. Tried to figure out who is sleeping with who below deck. The ginge-y deckhand with whom I am in unrequited love (I have a few loves onboard) asked me my New Year's resolution and I went very deep about needing to open my life up to someone and it felt awkward and double entendre-y.

▶ THURSDAY, JANUARY 1, 2015—RAJA AMPAT, INDONESIA

I am overly dependent on emojis. They're so ingrained in my head that I just think in them—mainly the face with hearts for eyes and the streamers, and party hat, but even the turtle is popping into my consciousness now. It's so lazy and childish. On the plus side, it is very Cher-like. New Year's was happening in America during our daytime and I was already over it so

I felt very Regina George whenever I got texts from the States. We had a jam-packed day: a swim and a dive in the morning, then over to the other yacht, *Suri*. Back on our boat, the group started watching a documentary about Jews on Broadway before dinner. Jews love making documentaries about themselves: Jews in science, Jews in movies, Jews on Broadway. Dinner was mellow yellow and I sat on the bowsprit listening to music for a while before popping an Ambien at eleven and getting into bed.

❧ FRIDAY, JANUARY 2, 2015—RAJA AMPAT, INDONESIA

Deirdre wants me to find a replacement host just in case I don't make it home in time on Sunday. I'm landing from the other side of the world two hours before the show—*what could possibly go wrong*?! We did a dive in the afternoon in a really strong current that was horrible—my ears were hurting and I was huffing and puffing against the current and Mike, my dive partner, suddenly raised the orange flag and pointed at me to go up. He called me out! Then Ashley and I went paddleboarding in a mangrove forest and it was an eco-paradise in there. Very quiet except the birds and fish jumping. She and I went deep about my future and hers. She said I should get into consumer products, but I couldn't figure out what. Then we talked *Full House*. She's smart. And very nice, and dry and funny. I like her.

I dropped my phone in the Jacuzzi tonight and Lee rushed it into a thing of rice to sit for twenty-four hours. Twenty-four hours without my phone, and I was actually really zen about it. So I went on the deck in my robe, free of the phone, and I had a great therapy session with DVF. We talked about how quickly time goes, how you are getting older for a period of time and then suddenly you *are* old. She said the danger about being alone with no family as an old person is that you disappear, become invisible. Just an old person. I see some of these people in my building. She asked why I'm alone and what I'm blocking. I talked about my ex, John Hill—what we were and why we split. I talked about nights of coming home from the show and feeling lonely—allowing myself to feel that recently for the first time. The dog, I fear, is a Band-Aid. In ten years he will be dead, then I'll be alone again. I talked about sex, how I love it, and how now that I'm famous it's gotten better *and* worse in a way—there is more to chase, more opportunity, but to what end? I love doing whatever I want in my life; I love my friends. She said okay, then you're happy—you don't have a big problem. She said I need to start having affairs; they don't have to be committed relationships, just a way of getting to know people. I should take a boy to the Matisse exhibit, for example. So my new rule is that I need to start doing things with new people. I think this is the most practical advice to begin getting me out of whatever circular pattern I am in now.

After dinner, I went to the aft deck, then Jason came and turned his phone on and a pic of Wacha appeared. I had dropped *his* phone in the Jacuzzi! He took it pretty well, all things considered. (And yes, I was thrilled to get mine back.) Watched twenty minutes of *Postcards from the Edge*, took half an Ambien, and fell asleep.

⟩ SUNDAY, JANUARY 4, 2015— INDONESIA—HAWAII—LOS ANGELES—NYC

Woke up and had a last swim to a little private beach near Sorong, where some locals came and took a thousand pictures with me as though I was a Martian. Showed DVF the dirty picture of Jake and she said maybe I should bring *him* to the Matisse exhibit. ☺ Got a last blast of sun, wrote my note to the crew, planned my tip with Jason, signed the guest book, and left. The flight was like floating on a cloud for twenty hours. Of course on the plane I felt like I had no tan, and everybody on board seemed to agree. WTF! To prepare for reality, I did all my work: I watched three episodes of *Vanderpump Rules*, two of *RHOBH*, and two of *RHOA*. Landed and went straight to *WWHL* and I suddenly wasn't on a boat or a plane or in the water and I didn't have my land legs. I was sober, though, and people at work said I was tan. And somehow I was on top of my game and had a great time, so whaddya know. Got home and there was a note with the doorman, in a child's handwriting, from Teresa's daughter Milania, of all people, saying she had stopped by to say hi and I wasn't home. She's what, *ten*? It was eerie and interesting.

WINTER/SPRING 2015

IN WHICH . . .

- ❱ I AM CHER ON *LIP SYNC BATTLE* . . .
  AND I VISIT CHER'S HOUSE.

- ❱ WACHA BECOMES CUJO . . .
  AND MEETS HIS NAMESAKE.

- ❱ MY DATING LIFE HEATS UP . . .
  BUT—

MONDAY, JANUARY 5, 2015—NYC

Woke up and read that Teresa turned herself in overnight. And Milania came by to see me while I was in Indonesia? I was trying to get my head around this all day. Sherman dropped off Wacha around ten-thirty and he was licking my face so much I thought he was going to take a bite out of it. Maybe my tan is making me extra salty and delicious. A crew was downstairs to shoot me walking Wacha for the World Dog Awards—which seems very Valerie Cherish, but he is up for Dog of the Year and I feel like it'll help him get a Purina deal if he wins. Ran into Hickey on the street while I was shooting and he compared me to a *Toddlers and Tiaras* mom. Went up to Bravo to pitch a scripted show. I want to pull my hair out during pitches that are being presented to me, but it's actually worse being on the other side. Went from there to a photo shoot with the NY Housewives and it was such a trip seeing Bethenny in a red jumpsuit in the middle of the clump of wives again. I love it. There was a big drama before I got there, which often—okay, always—happens at cast photo shoots. Kristen from *Vanderpump Rules* and Margaret Cho were on the show. There was a viewer question to Margaret asking what advice she would give someone about how to bottom for the first time and I immediately got a series of texts from my mom: "TOO DIRTY! STOP! YOUR AUDIENCE DOESN'T CARE ABOUT BOTTOMING."

TUESDAY, JANUARY 6, 2015

Today was the day I said no to Oprah. Slept until ten forty-five, when I felt like a truck was running over me but it was actually Wacha standing on me, telling me it was time to wake up and take him out in the first snow of the day.

When I read my email there was an offer to be on OWN's *Oprah: Where Are They Now?*—an interview by Oprah. Dream of a lifetime, right? Well, I thought about it and looked at the website—it's pop star Tiffany, the original cast of *The Real World*, Natalee Holloway's mother, and Robin Leach. Is that *my* category? I feel like people should pretty much know where I am now. *Where was I?* That's a better question. I passed. I actually considered being classified as a has-been just to be interviewed by Oprah, but my dignity won out! Fredrik is sending me listings but so far there's nothing. Starting to stress. Went to the show full of piss and vinegar; Jeff Lewis arrived and we kibitzed in my office while I paid bills. He told me they are looking for an egg donor and maybe they should use Brandi. I joked that her eggs are scrambled. On the show he was on her about her wine toss and told her what I'd said about the scrambled eggs (which I did not appreciate). When someone asked if Brandi could run her hands through his hair to see if he was wearing a toupee, he asked if he could get an STD from that. Then we played Paintionary with his new paint and he was drawing dicks and uniballs and really nasty stuff. My mom was furious! (Texts: "NOT AGAIN! STOP! THIS IS DISGUSTING!") During the last act of the show Brandi suddenly got very upset at Jeff for the STD line and threw her wine at him, turned her chair around and started crying. She said, "If you read my book, you would know this is sensitive." He was stunned, I was stunned, Wacha was stunned. After the show I got Jeff to apologize and they made up. It was really awkward and Twitter was *lit up*, but then Brandi whispered to me, "It was an act; we planned it." Jeff corroborated that they were going to go after each other, but said he hadn't expected her to go that far and that he was wondering if it was real. I didn't know what to think— we were trending on Twitter; the control room was electric, but the whole thing felt wrong. A staged fight with no "Haha, just kidding" doesn't seem like it helps anybody. I told her this was supposed to be her big redemption night; she had wisely been totally sober so she could succinctly account for having thrown the wine at Eileen on *RHOBH*. Two wine throws in one night is two too many, and I told her I thought it was a bad look for her. I got home and texted Brandi and said I wanted her to succeed at some point and was worried this had backfired. Then I couldn't sleep, and Twitter was going strong with hate for Brandi, who realized a few hours (and a few cocktails?) later that it wasn't a good look and tweeted that she'd been kidding. I woke up at 4:00 a.m. and had a text from her from 3:30 saying she'd made it better and that having a dog had made me a nicer person.

WEDNESDAY, JANUARY 7, 2015

I want to insert emojis now after every sentence—for instance, a bleary-eyed one here, as I barely slept. Frances passed on the pitch and said they'd had a "really good debate" about the show, which is a nice way of saying no. She said it's a little darker than they want to go. The good news is it looks like we sold *Match Game* to NBC stations for 2016. 2016?! Jesus. Will the world still be here? Will we have water?

Daryn's ex-girlfriend is in New York City packing her bags with the hateful mother who threatened Daryn's life if she contacted her (formerly) lesbian daughter. The girlfriend has totally shut Daryn out—blocked all her social media and her phone and wants no communication with anyone here. So the mother is brainwashing her, and apparently she brought her gun to New York City. I wanted to find that mother and confront her but the gun was a deterrent. The *Top Chef* Dave and I did aired tonight. We watched together in my office, then Dave bartended on the show, which was Nicolle Wallace and Patrick Wilson. It was a *This Is Your Life* show for Patrick—his wife, his college roommate, and two separate girls he went to high school with called in. Finally, an episode that my mom liked.

THURSDAY, JANUARY 8, 2015

I was supposed to work out with the Ninj today for the first time since the book came out—exactly two months ago—and I cancelled. It was cold and I woke up in an Ambien haze. Instead I decided to get a daytime massage, and on the table I realized that I make a shitload of money and I should just spend stupid money on a temporary apartment. I emailed Fredrik from the table and told him I want to see the super-expensive loft in Chelsea. Raced to meet Amanda at the Polo Bar, where it was Friends and Family Night, and in the Uber on the way up John Hill asked if horse was on the menu—very humorous. The restaurant is like a country club, which are basically clubs that give alcoholics another reason to drink, making my sober January all the worse. Okay, it's not a totally sober January—I was stoned off a vape pen. The place was overstaffed, and for good reason: There was a famous person at every table, so they clearly didn't want to fuck anything up. But as a result eighteen people told us to be sure to try Ralph's favorite menu item, the corned beef sandwich. We had a quick hello with Martha Stewart. Sat down and Ricky Lauren said hello and be sure to try the corned beef sandwich; it's amazing. Then Bette-Ann Gwathmey said, have you heard about the corned beef sandwich? Ali Wentworth came by to say hi; then I realized Brian Williams was at the table right behind us and said hi. It was too intense a social situation to be dealing with stoned, I'll tell you that. Mr. Lauren came by and was very sweet, says he sees me on TV, which is what he always says and totally kills me. Two managers came over and each gave me their card and told me to try the corned beef sandwich. I said that I had been inundated with talk of the corned beef sandwich, and could they please just bring me a *bite* with our order (chicken paillards and dover sole). They brought an entire sandwich, though, and we looked like pigs. I took two bites and guess what: It was good! I had them take it away because it was also draped in butter and not exactly dietetic. My chicken paillard was cold, and since it was Friends and Family Night and they were testing the restaurant out I politely told the waiter, which unleashed a flood of new managers with business cards coming over to say they were very upset to hear about my chicken. I mollified them by telling them that *I loved the corned beef sandwich!* Charlie Rose came by and we chatted. I said I was so impressed that he was still out at 9:30 p.m., Stephanopoulos had headed off to bed an hour ago. On the way out, one of the managers told me that Ralph had personally tried each item on the menu "more than twice" to determine whether it should go on the menu, and I said that I would hope that was the case because it was his restaurant. Can't wait to go back.

▶ FRIDAY, JANUARY 9, 2015

Woke up to a stack of business cards from that Polo restaurant. Which one do we actually call for a reservation, I wondered. I threw them all out. I basically crawled in the freezing cold to work out with the Ninj and it was a pathetic showing. I did thirty pull-ups and I don't know what else. I talked a lot, that's for sure. There was gym gossip to catch up on! Meanwhile, Willspace is a teeny private gym so the gossip is meager. Nonetheless, I milked it in order to defer working out, much like I deferred my Hebrew studies by leaving my tutor, Yitzi, little props (electronic football and comic books) to distract him. I hated Hebrew. I hate working out. I am old and creaky. Fredrik and I went to see the Chelsea loft that costs stupid money—it's got crazy outdoor space and is lofty and really sexy. Fredrik kept saying you work hard, you should treat yourself, you deserve this. I said I've seen your show, honey, don't do your lines on me. But I had come to the same realization mid-massage, so I'm gonna bring Hickey by tomorrow. And I told Fredrik to look for places on the Upper West Side with a terrace overlooking Central Park West. That should be simple to find. ☺ Had a late dinner with John Hill at Rossopomodoro and went home bored with myself from having no booze. Tried watching the premiere of *Downton Abbey* but it bored me even more. Mr. Molesley dyed his hair? This is part of the plot? Who wants to see Mr. Molesley dye his hair? Who?

► SATURDAY, JANUARY 10, 2015

I *hate* not drinking. I woke up in a lather about it. I decided I was going to perhaps have a tequila on ice tonight at Mark and Kelly's. Took Hickey to the apartment and he said it's like a line of cocaine and that I have to do it. BTW, I don't feel like I have to do a line of cocaine, but I understood his reference. The agent, who is very cute, let it drop that the gardener is not included in the rental cost and that's another two grand a month. So that's insane. I freaked. Hickey thought I was playing it for the agent but I was being honest. Well, I was being honest while knowing that it was an effective bargaining technique. He also said I was being rude and interrupt-y to the cute agent.

Dale's bar mitzvah was really nice. Leave it to Lauren Zalaznick to have found Dale a black Hebrew tutor. I love it. Michael Hirschorn reaffirmed that we're moments away from TV dissolving; the whole business is changing and we are all going under. So that was terrifying to hear right before the haftorah. It made me rethink the big loft. Rabbis and drag queens have one thing in common—they both never met a microphone they didn't love. This dude went on a beat too long, but Dale was phenomenal. I gave Monica Halpert's fifteen-year-old son an Uber lift uptown and drilled him with sex, drugs, and lifestyle questions about the prep-school kids of Manhattan. He was very open, and I swore I would take his answers to the grave.

Went to Mark and Kelly's, where she had made homemade pizzas, which I devoured (pizza two nights in a row). What's the point of not drinking if I am going to eat like a pig? (I didn't drink, though.) Kelly pointed out that the risk of moving to such an amazing place is that I could wind up liking the outdoor space more than my new apartment. Good point. Outdoor space is my kryptonite.

▶ SUNDAY, JANUARY 11, 2015

Lisa Rinna tweeted that it's Kyle and Yolanda's birthday today, so I sent a tweet. Then someone said, you forgot about Naomi Judd's birthday; hers is today too. Then I took Wacha out for a walk and I saw a Naomi Judd look-alike on the street. I thought it was odd, and then I saw her again twenty minutes later. So I tried to wish the real Naomi a happy birthday on Twitter, but she doesn't appear to have an account. She did give me her home number, her "private line," all those months ago when she was trying to break up my family before the holidays, but I am not going there. I put in an offer on the rental, but I can't stop thinking about what Kelly said last night. At the end of the day I found out I didn't get the place: Someone offered to pay for the gardener *and* do a two-year lease. So that's that, and I can refocus my energy on my *real* dream apartment, the one I own.

I FaceTimed the really Waspy guy I met on Tinder when I was in Boston on the book tour but didn't actually meet because I was busy trying to make my *Penthouse* Forum thing happen. It was like an hour-long blind date on FaceTime, which I quite enjoyed. You get to see the person's apartment too. He seems really nice and looks a little Don Draper-ish. He is only thirty-four but looks and seems like a man.

▶ MONDAY, JANUARY 12, 2015

Someone tweeted me a picture of an article from *The Onion* lampooning incontinent old people that used a picture of *my dad* to illustrate an older man who shits himself. I was furious. Tweeted at *The Onion* and said WTF is up with you using some random picture of my dad in this article? Then someone tweeted at me and said the picture came from a Getty Images page featuring pictures of random people on the street, including both my mom and dad with the caption "Old people on the street." I decided never to tell my parents that they are now stock photos of senior citizens.

Lunch with Scott Greenstein at Morandi to talk Andy Radio. I pitched him all my programming ideas and he said the thing to do is to close the deal, announce it, and see who comes forward and wants to work with me, to be on air. Like Cher, he kept saying. What about giving Cher a show once a month?

FaceTimed again with the Boston Wasp tonight. He loves Sherlock Holmes and wakes up at four-thirty in the morning to work out every day. I told him we have nothing in common. I am enjoying getting to know him. The early show was Kevin Hart and we had a bit of a debacle with Plead the Fifth. I asked him what he thought about all the Bill Cosby drama and he gave a perfectly politic answer. As we were going to commercial break Deirdre tells me in my ear that his publicist is freaking out and wants us to cut the question. So that drama was playing out in my ear for the entire show and, meanwhile, when it was over he said he loved the show and would be back. I apologized for the Cosby question and he said, "You can't faze me with something like that, don't worry." How are we *not* going to ask the biggest black comedian going right now about Bill Cosby?

I had emailed Lisa Kudrow weeks ago for the name of the genealogist they use on *Who Do You Think You Are?* because I wanted to hire that person to research my family as a gift to the family. TLC had long ago passed on me being on the show, but Lisa said let me go back at them and see if they'll do it. So I got an email from her before my show saying, "You're in!" I was really pumped. She said to call her and she will explain how it works. The live show was Wolf Blitzer and Scheana Marie. I think Wolf was nervous, but he did great. I didn't have to take any pictures after the show, so they held the audience for a second and I ran out and was on my couch at eleven forty-five. It was blissful!

▶ TUESDAY, JANUARY 13, 2015

Wacha is fat again. I guess I would rather have him fat than biting Anderson over a bone. Skyped with Mom about *Who Do You Think You Are?* She was initially kind of excited and then came to the conclusion, "WE ARE

BORING! They won't want us!" She was on fire. She is concerned about AC and I selling out our tour. "College kids CAN'T AFFORD a hundred dollars!" I told her I hoped three thousand people in Boston could afford this. "Be ready for EMPTY SEATS," she said. Thanks for the pep talk, Mom!

Conference call about *Lip Sync Battle* against Willie Geist, which I have been dreading and thinking about for weeks. My final song contenders are "I Found Someone," "On the Radio," "Rock Lobster," "Working for the Weekend," and "Country Grammar." They really want me to do "Country Grammar," but it may be too hard for me. I hung up and put on the Cher song and I know every single word, so that's definitely in.

The show was Bob Harper and Lisa Rinna. I had a big flirt going with Bob, and when I left the studio the entire control room was standing in a line looking like the cats that ate the canary, with eyebrows raised and an expression that said "Do you *like him*??? Are you going to go *on a date*???" We exchanged numbers and texted/flirted but he kind of shut it down around twelve-fifteen and said good night, which made me think he was with someone, which in turn made me like him. I can respect a player. I like that he is an equal—my same age, successful, got his own thing going.

▶ WEDNESDAY, JANUARY 14, 2015

Spent the day fighting with headsets. I somehow lost mine and so I went to the Apple Store, where I bought a shitload of stuff I'm not sure I need, like a new laptop and a new iPad, but rejected their headsets as a matter of principle because they're always tangled and sucky. I can't even remember what soapbox I was standing on but I went off to the Verizon store and got those ones that don't twist around and made a huge show of throwing the receipt out in front of the guy, who said are you *sure* you don't want that receipt? I said of course not. I got on the phone with Liza an hour later and the headset absolutely doesn't work. Went to Duane Reade and got a shitty pair of headsets and when I talked to Liza she said it sounded like someone was knocking on the door during the convo. Anderson was appalled that Mom said to be ready for empty seats. He said if his mom said that, he would never speak to her. I told him he doesn't know the vocabulary of a Jewish mother. Gwyneth Paltrow was on the early show and was very cool

Mom and Dad on their tour of Nazi hotspots

Wacha and Bergeron playing tug of war with Donnie Wahlberg's hat—before he nipped Tom and devoured the hat. Donnie looks on, thrilled.

Awkward. Went to temple right after this.

Pure hysterics after Wacha
jumped up on Carol Burnett
mid–Tarzan yell

Grac and I double down on Italian futurism.

Look at the amount of BUTTER
Sean Avery slathers on his breakfast!

The last four people at my book party—
Padma, Kelly, Mark, and I—all slid down
Anderson's pole at the end of the night.

I made it to Hitsville!

The ultimate book party
selfie: Monica Lewinsky
and NeNe Leakes!

Presents at my San Francisco
signing: penis cake, Snoopys,
poppers, pot, and booze!

Trying to be sexy with Sarah Silverman backstage at my LA event

My book tour, in a nutshell

Crazy selfie at Colbert finale with Jeff Tweedy, Patrick Stewart, David Gregory, and Christiane Amanpour. I was accused by the *Daily News* of taking too many, but everyone was—I swear!

Before my dreams were crushed at "Lip Synch Battle"
(*Courtesy of Spike TV by Peter Yang*)

Undersea in Indonesia

Sidewalk drag with Tiffany Fantasia in Miami
(*photo by John Hickey*)

Radio Andy dream team: Sandra Bernhard
(*Sandyland*), Bevy Smith (*Bevelations*) and
John Hill (*The Feels*)

With Amy at
SJP's birthday
at the Carlyle

I made him get out of the car to take a selfie, and he was NOT happy about it.

On a sidewalk in Manhattan at 2 a.m.
Wacha finally meets Wacha!

Wearing a romper on my terrace.
I am the gayest man alive.

Drinks with my Bravo pals in town
for the upfront

Dinner in London with Joan Collins
and Tom Hollander

Dinner with Ralph Fiennes in London

Serving face with my date leaving for
the Met Ball. Now how do we get the
headgear in the car?

This is a super insane pic of me and SJP glaring at Beebs

Birthday magic with some OG's: SJP, Jackie, Liza, Amanda, and Grac

Seeing this view caused a deep homosexual panic, in the best way.

Tongue selfie with Miley at amfAR

Weird group alert! Vicki and Jenny McCarthy, with Mom and Em behind the bar

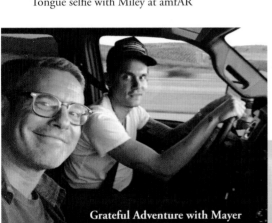

Grateful Adventure with Mayer

Rainbow at the Dead show! It's Jerry!!

What in the hell does my face convey at my *EW* cover shoot.

Saying hi to the RHOBH in the Hamptons.

With my boyfriend on Fire Island.

A haircut on the terrace by Tonee—this is the life! (*Bruce Bozzi*)

This is what you wear to a Spanish Gypsy birthday party hosted by Madonna, in case you need to know. Thanks for the smoky eyes, Kelly!

In Spain: happiest when surrounded by gingey crew guys.

With John Hickey in Amagansett

Go Cards! And how are the burgers tonight?

On the subway with Sandy. Takes six minutes to get to Radio Andy!

Outside the Beverly Hills Palm with Bruce

Selfie on the way to do
Bill Maher. Does this look
like a confident person?

He was in a kill shelter in West Virginia,
now he's getting waited on at Ralph
Lauren on Madison Avenue.

Typical moment at an airport
with AC—I'm taking selfies
and he's talking to CNN.

Mother lode of reunions
(*Trae Patton/NBC/NBCU Photo Bank via Getty Images*)

Selfie mid–*Vanderpump Rules* reunion

Nothing but fun with the RHOA

Bro'ing out at Delano
with Dave

Is it a real reunion or . . . ?

Merry woodsmen!
In Connecticut with
#BrazilianAndySamberg,
Benjamin, and Anderson

Getting ready for the ball at SJP's

and down to earth. Jessica Seinfeld came and brought friends into my office and Wacha freaked out and barked at her. He gets very territorial in that office. The live show was George Lopez, Angela Bassett, and the Whitney Houston drag queens.

▶ THURSDAY, JANUARY 15, 2015

Allison and Ricky came over and we caught up on the last few months and I totally forgot to ask her about getting her ass eaten out on *Girls*. And I found my headset in the couch while they were here and threw out the two bum ones. So that drama is solved.

During a Skype call with Mom and Dad, I broke and mentioned the article in *The Onion* and the Getty Images stock photos. Mom immediately remembered that they were bored on the street one day, killing time before meeting me at 30 Rock, and posed for pictures for a guy. I asked if they had signed a release and they both thought they did. Little did they know they would become "Portrait of a senior man on the street" and "Senior woman smiling." I told them Getty was selling these pictures and earning a profit for it. They thought it was hilarious. "THEY CHARGE 300 DOLLARS FOR THIS PICTURE, LOU!" On another note, Mom is concerned that the *Who Do You Think You Are?* people are going to find alcoholics in the family, which was rich during my month of sobriety. I told her that's not the kind of thing they look for, it's more like Civil War heroes. "Well sorry to BURST YOUR BUBBLE but we don't have ANY CIVIL WAR HEROES in the family!"

Met Bob Harper for tea this afternoon and we had a really nice talk—it got deep. We discussed my relationship blockage. I can't say there was crazy chemistry, but I loved talking to a peer. He's going through similar stuff. He likes to be alone and travel alone.

Worked on choreography for *Lip Sync Battle* with John Hill. He said to start really small with the Cher song, then build it out. I chose Loverboy's "Working for the Weekend" for my big one, which he says will be fully dependent on the choreographer. I am rehearsing tomorrow. Watched the World Dog Awards while FaceTiming with the Boston Wasp. Wacha lost to some hero dog. He didn't have a chance. I love him so much, but what has he really *done???*

Got invited to be on Bill Maher! An open invitation. Ha! Forwarded it to Mom—her absolute worst fear in writing! She said, "THIS DOESN'T WORK!!" with a bunch of freaked-out emojis. Went to rehearsal for *Lip Sync Battle*. It's gonna be great. I told the choreographer that I want my rendition of "Working for the Weekend" to be the most blatantly hetero-sexual performance ever. So girls are running over to me and I am grinding their faces and slapping their asses. The censor lady said I am not allowed to simulate slapping their faces, though. I texted Cher for advice on "I Found Someone" and what I got back was incredible:

Be Sad IN BEGINNING OF VERSE. By the time you get to "BUT YOU WALKED AWAY" START THE "AS MUCH AS I LOVED YOU . . . HOMIE DONT PLAY THIS SHIT!" By the time you get to I FOUND SOMEONE, YOUR ATTITUDE IS "YOU HAD YOUR CHANCE, YOU ARE DUMPED DUMPED DUMPED. DONT CRY! BEG! YOURE FKD! I WAITED & I'M OUTTA HERE! FYI, YOU MIGHT WANT TO PAY CLOSE ATTENTION TO MY ASS AS I WALK OUT THE DOOR, CAUSE IT'S THE LAST LOOK YOU'RE GONNA GET!" Throw your pretend hair back, lick your lips once in a while, and on "I FOUND SOMEONE" THROW YOUR HEAD BACK . . . AND STRUT BACK AND FORTH ACROSS THAT STAGE LIKE YOU OWN IT. 💪 👄 LOVE, ME

Stage directions from Cher? How can I lose?! Then we went back and forth and I said I just rehearsed and it's gonna be great, that my temptation is to do *her* but I gotta do *me* for the song. And she said:

"But ANDY . . . DOING ME . . . IS REALLY DOING THE SONG! IT'S EASY TO BE YOU, BUT NOT AS HILARIOUS. BE WHO EVER YOU WANT TO BE, BUT YOU'RE YOU 365 days a year. Step into my G-String for 3 MIN. 🎉"

When Cher is right, she's right.

SATURDAY, JANUARY 17, 2015

Breakfast with Sean Avery at La Bonbonniere. I tried to get him to go to Hamilton's because I've been dying to try it, but he said I'm always "trying to change the game." I am? *Trying to change the game?* He came straight from several hours in the gym and ordered chocolate-chip pancakes and sausage. He puts pounds of butter on each pancake and chops the sausage into little bits and bathes the whole casserole in syrup. Brought Sean to my fitting for my Loverboy routine—red leather pants—at the Leather Man on Christopher Street. Sean asked the salesman if he thought he was gay and the guy—an old bald guy in leather—said well, I don't know, I haven't slept with you yet. Sean parked his Mercedes SUV and left keys inside with the car running. He said if it gets stolen, that's what insurance is for, and he thinks leaving it running lessens the risk of it getting stolen. So I had a real wander inside the mind of Sean Avery today.

He dropped me off to see an apartment on West Third Street, where the real estate guy kept saying a big famous actor had been staying. Well, it hadn't been cleaned yet, and there was a Christmas tree and a lot of trash and he kept saying the big actor this and the big actor that . . . then I noticed a stack of headshots signed by the red-haired kid from *Harry Potter* who'd been in town doing Matthew's play. So I said I guess it was Rupert Grint, the *Harry Potter* kid, and the guy was shocked I figured it out. I said to get rid of the headshots next time. Got an at-home pedicure from Gina and read *RHONY* field reports, which were incredible. Dinner with SJP at Barbuto; we had the chicken and split some carbonara. It was wonderful. She said Hamilton's doesn't totally live up to the promise of what it's supposed to be. I went home and read the Roz Chast book about taking care of her dying parents, which was, no surprise, depressing. Then watched *Downton Abbey* and went to bed. A sober Saturday night!

SUNDAY, JANUARY 18, 2015

Hamilton's stinks. They're gonna be closed soon. Drafty, bad service, weird vibe. Went with Troy and Jonah. The waiter said sorry, we're short staffed; we didn't expect it to be busy. I asked him what the busiest days at the restaurant are and he said Thursdays and weekends. I said but you didn't expect it to be busy today, Sunday? Got fitted for the leather pants. My ass looked better in the black temp pants yesterday, sadly. Apparently the leather on the red pants is thicker.

Skyped with Mom, who wants to know what Bill Maher's gonna talk to me about: "The HOUSEWIVES? He's gonna make MINCEMEAT out of you. I don't CARE, it's not your VENUE but just WATCH IT first." She denied saying that I would be looking at empty seats on the tour with Anderson and twenty minutes later said sometimes it's good for somebody to be honest. She said to remember that Joan Rivers had agreed with her at Liza's wedding in thinking that I shouldn't do Bill Maher. My parents had just seen a lot of my high school friends at a funeral, "They were all HUGGING us. I guess they were thinking they might be at OUR FUNERAL soon. We're DEAD MEN WALKING!" On that note, *have a great show!* FaceTimed with the Wasp. He does magic too. I thought he was lying, then he sent me a picture of himself in tails doing it. Did the show without incident.

▶ MONDAY, JANUARY 19, 2015

DVF said on the boat that I'm competitive. She was right, and I also think I might be a sore loser. I never realized it. I had a great walk with Wacha, lip syncing all the way down the street. I kept saying, "I got this." Went to rehearsal and did both songs with the red leather pants. If I heard it once from the producers and crew, I heard it twenty times: "You got this, you're winning; Willie hasn't even rehearsed." The director told me to watch out for grabbing the women too hard; apparently I was making the whole routine look like forcible rape and not consensual sex. Whoops! Oh, and the whole rehearsal they're saying, "Todd will hand you the mic" and "Todd will introduce you" and I said who the fuck is Todd, and it turns out that's LL Cool J's real name! And Todd told me I was gonna win. I like that Todd! I went to wardrobe for a fitting and they said you got this, you're winning. Went home and walked the dog again. Back to *Lip Sync*, where John Hill, Liza, and thirteen-year-old James Wilkie Broderick (he was off school and wanted to come) met me and we watched Anna Kendrick versus John Krasinski. Krasinski had a tear-away outfit and sang "Proud Mary" in a dress.

But Kendrick had JLo come out (she was supposed to do a whole dance to "Booty" but just walked out and waved). James Wilkie kept saying "He was *robbed*; he *pushed his body to the limit*!" He also thought it was unfair that the winner is chosen by the audience because the person who goes second always wins.

Guess what—it was time for my show, and I went first both times. I lost my way during the Cher song and stumbled a little during my big finish. When Todd(!) was interviewing me he asked what I did to prepare and I told the story about texting Cher, and then realized what a douche I looked like for telling that story. Then Willie did "9 to 5" and the audience cheered for him more. I did the Loverboy song and it was pretty good. I might've been too concerned about not appearing to be raping the women, so it may have looked neither here nor there. Willie's next song was an LL Cool J song, and I didn't even realize it was an LL song until thirty seconds in when I saw Todd was beaming in a way that told me that I was completely fucked. I plastered the biggest, fakest smile on my face and it was a painful final twenty minutes of me smiling and watching my hopes and dreams get stolen in slow motion as Willie took the belt with *zero* rehearsal and I stood there drenched in sweat, feeling like a total loser in a scoop tank top, mullet wig, and red leather pants. The whole crew that had been up my ass all day was now barely looking at me! John Legend looked right through me backstage! *It stung*! I went back to my dressing room and raged to John, Liza, and James Wilkie, who all thought going second in the audience polling killed me. I felt like Valerie Cherish losing *Dancing with the Stars* ("Lisa Rinna told me I'd have fun—I DIDN'T!"). I was in a weird rage for a few hours after the show and I think I was additionally pissed that I had the night off, no plans, and no possibility of drinking alcohol. I FaceTimed with Bob Harper. I said I was using him for his money and gifts. John Hill wound up coming over and I had an omelet. Was asleep by midnight.

▶ TUESDAY, JANUARY 20, 2016

On Tuesdays and Thursdays I leave the door cracked, Sherman comes in, Wacha runs out, and he's gone for Brooklyn and I go back to bed. It's a beautiful thing.

I figured out today that I've been a sore loser before. Something like nine times at the Emmys. I went every year and sat like a chump with the *Top Chef* and *Project Runway* teams and lost and lost and lost to *The Amazing Race* and the one year I didn't go (because I'd just gotten back from Tahiti the day before and didn't feel like schlepping to LA to lose) *we won* and I watched in slow motion on TV from Sag Harbor and had the worst FOMO of my life.

Worked out. We boxed the whole time. I'm back in the zone. *RHOA* is on my mind. The reunion is months away and I am oddly stressed about it. Taped JLo show. She is so stunning. She was wearing one of her classic boob separator tops and it was hard not to stare at them the whole time. It felt like I was doing my show with someone with bare tits next to me. She said she could only wear that top on my show, which was flattering but the truth is she wears some variation of that top all the time. It's boring to say but she is perfect. I told her I wasn't drinking and she asked, "What do you think it means that you are angry about not drinking?" Is JLo getting to the heart of the matter? She said that buying the apartment Fredrik found her was the first time she felt like she'd made it, which makes me wonder if renting somewhere great from him will make me feel the same. The live show was Kyle and Brad Goreski. It is Hot Men of Instagram week, and what I have discovered is that the hot guys on Instagram are fugly in person. One of them had apparently not had anything to drink for seventy-two hours in preparation for me asking him to take his shirt off behind the bar, but after I looked at his face the last thing I wanted to do was see more.

▶ WEDNESDAY, JANUARY 21, 2015

Worked out with the Ninj. The afternoon was all conference calls, including a pre-call for this paid speaking thing I have tomorrow night that I barely listened to. I just zoned out on Instagram like a preteen. We taped Julianne Moore and Jonathan Groff. I walked into the lobby and there was the most beautiful man sitting there—so beautiful that I had to say hello, and when I did he informed me that he was going to be my bartender that night, to which I replied that he is the only legitimately hot guy on Instagram. He helps disabled veterans get support, so he's a good person too. He has huge blue eyes and reddish-blond hair. I was effusive in my praise of him after the show. He was very sweet back but gave me no clear signal. But Anthony gave me his number and I texted him. Went to the Rainbow Room for this NBCUniversal executive dinner and arrived as cocktails transitioned into dinner. Steve Burke showed a video that detailed how they transformed the building to make Jimmy and Seth's studios and all I could think was how much money they dumped into them and how mine is the size of a Tic Tac. The guy who won *The Voice* performed for us. He won the biggest singing competition in the country, and now he's singing to a room of jaded TV executives who are on their mobile devices. I went to the bathroom and got a text back from the bartender. We texted late into the night, and this is a boy who loves sending smiley faces but he does it the old-fashioned way—colon and parenthesis. I asked him out and he said yes with an exclamation point and a smiley.

▶ THURSDAY, JANUARY 22, 2015

JLo wants Sherman's info, so now her two boxers are gonna be part of Wacha's playgroup. Got dubious info about the bartender from my friend at the beach, but I am going to find out for myself—I booked theater tickets for Saturday night and am taking him out. He is pumped about it and sending lots of old school smileys.

Computer geek came and set up all the Apple products I don't need while I got updates from the producers of *RHOC, RHOBH,* and *RHONY.* Spoke to Liz Rosenberg, who said she will deliver Madonna if it kills her. That paid gig—a Q and A at this travel agency awards dinner (*the Travvies!*)— turned into something of a debacle. In their initial offer to come speak, they'd requested that I talk about the parallels between the changes in the TV industry and the changes in the travel industry, which I felt like I was possibly incapable of addressing. I asked for the format to be not a thirty-minute speech but a conversation with the guy who runs it, followed by audience Q and A. I was in the hall outside the ballroom waiting to go on, texting with Jack and Angela (who are going to be in LA in ten days when I am) as the guy inside was introducing me. I turned to the handler— whose name was *Courtney Love*—and asked her which seat they wanted me in. She said I wasn't sitting, I was standing. I said, wait, we're doing the conversation standing up? She said, there is no "we," and there is no conversation—it's just *you*, and you're giving a speech. So my heart sank as I flashed back to that pre-call yesterday where I was zoning out on Instagram. There was nothing I could do but completely wing it to the top travel agents from across the country. As I stood onstage I saw Courtney Love whisper to the man in charge that I was unprepared.

My speech turned out to be a little Tom Cruise in *Magnolia*-esque. I said I wanted to talk about passion—my passion and their passion. I said we had a lot in common because they are passionate about travel and I am passionate about TV. I said that they were lucky people in that room because they are so talented that they wound up at the Travvies, and that they get to work in the travel business. They don't *have* to, they *get to*. And that is a *privilege*. And I said the same about TV: You *get* to work in the TV business. I went on and on, talking about how challenging the TV business is right now and making loose and lame connections to travel. The whole time I was looking at this man in charge, wondering if I was doing what he wanted. He came up to run the audience Q and A and said it was all good. Then he announced to the audience that if they wanted to take selfies with me I would be going out in the lobby and to "just grab me," so I guess that was my punishment. After being manhandled by selfie grabbers for a half hour in the lobby, I went over to Hickey's, where I reenacted my entire speech, which he said sounded concurrently great and horrible.

▶ FRIDAY, JANUARY 23, 2015

Feeling insecure about my date tomorrow with the hot ginge. This guy is a literal fitness model. Anderson said don't be insecure; you're handsome and he should be happy you're interested. So that made me feel better for a minute but I'm still seventeen years older than him and a lot less hot. Worked out, and that made me feel even older and even less hot. Took Wacha to be dry cleaned and once again he attempted to change our course. Saw two dud apartments with Hickey and had a long FaceTime with Bob Harper. I'm trying to follow DVF's advice and have more dates, so tonight was a movie date with Andres, and the truth is that some friends with benefits shouldn't be movie dates. He showed up drunk and late and was behaving like a child during the movie. It was a real bummer. I loved Part 1 of *The Hunger Games: Mockingjay*, though. We went back to my house and Wacha snarled at him. So he verbalized what I was feeling.

SATURDAY, JANUARY 24, 2015

It snowed and rained all day so I stayed inside with the dog. I had an hour-long FaceTime with the Wasp in Boston. The big news is that we made a plan for him to come spend the night on February 14, not because it's Valentine's Day but because it's my next free weekend night. This should be interesting. I picked up the ginge for our date and the convo in the Uber required a fair amount of work, which didn't bode well for the night. But man, was he cute. We saw *The Curious Incident of the Dog in the Night-Time*, which was relentless, intense, and ultimately really good. Overhyped, though. Everybody said it was the best play *they'd ever seen*—you can't walk into something with that in the back of your mind. We had a lot of hand-holding and cuddling so that made it better. After, we went to Joe Allen, where I asked him what kinds of guys he liked and his answer was very PC and canned, about guys who know what they want and have something going on and are powerful in their own way. I was all "Yeah, but hairy or smooth? Blond or brunette?" All the while Mark was texting that he and Kelly were out with David Muir and wanted to go to the Diamond Horse-shoe, so I set up a table for them with Erich Conrad and I didn't want to go because I wasn't drinking, but I was down the block so the ginge walked me there—he had to go bartend in Queens, which had always been the plan—and we had an awkward good-night kiss and I went into the club, which was already teeming with people. Kelly was spinning like a top and Erich was in rare form; he kept saying, this is our house and it's right down the street from Poop, which is true. I realized I have been going to his parties for twenty-five years, since Grac was working the door of Poop—holy shit. I said good-bye to him and he said, never say good-bye when you're at a club; just disappear, which is so true. Kelly was on a platform dancing when I left—I did say good-bye to her—and I was out by one o'clock. It was a nice night downtown and Wacha and I strolled around meeting people on the streets. In front of the Cubby Hole a group of people got me high. People are so kind! I love NYC.

▶ SUNDAY, JANUARY 25, 2015

The Backstreet Boys are on the show this week and I actually watched their entire two-hour documentary and I can't believe it—well, I can—but I cried several times. Basically each of the BSB has a breakdown at one point or another in the doc, so I went on the journey with them.

De Blasio had a press conference and said the worst storm in NYC history is hitting tomorrow—we may have three feet of snow and he's closing the entire city down starting tomorrow evening. We immediately started scrambling to tape two shows tomorrow before the sun goes down. In the meantime, Kandi and Ne-Yo were on with some hot Philadelphia Eagle behind the bar who wanted me to Instagram a picture of us, but my caption was "I love linebackers!" and I don't think that was what he had in mind.

▶ MONDAY, JANUARY 26, 2015

Went straight into work with the dog and the snow was already starting to come down. Luckily all of our guests for the next two days were in town, so we did Eileen Davidson and Whitney Cummings at twelve-thirty and Kristin Chenoweth and Tom Sandoval at three-thirty. By the time we were done it was dumping snow on the ground. Thankfully the RHONY got out on the last flight to Turks and Caicos for their big trip. Every damn thing is shut down and who knows if we will be able to shoot on Wednesday. The Backstreet Boys already cancelled for Thursday, so I'll never get the time back that I spent on that documentary. All the talk shows are cancelled tomorrow—Kelly said they've never done that before. I felt so accomplished that my team pulled it all together and we have two shows in the can.

Ray drove Wacha and me through the snow to the D'Agostino on Bethune so I could "stock up" for the storm. The supermarket was complete bedlam—ten-minute lines at each checkout. I don't know what it means to "stock up" for a storm whatsoever, and my cart was pathetic: ice cream, eggs, frozen pizza, SpaghettiOs, turkey, cheese, chicken breasts, lots of chips, chocolate, Kraft mac and cheese, and Duraflames. Basically just carbs and sugar. Is that what you buy for a storm? At home I checked in with Liza (she'd also bought a bunch of pizza) and Bruce (under a blanket in sunny LA watching the East Coast feed of WNBC, eating his heart out that he isn't in NYC). I was all cozy, hunkered down and ready to be inside, but then Hickey and I decided to go to Rossopomodoro, which was open until 8:00 p.m., and as I sat there I realized if there was ever a moment to drink a glass of red wine this was it—superstorm hitting, two nights off from work, and tons of firewood and a warm puppy at home. I ended my sober month five days early, with two glasses of red, and it wasn't that amazing or life-changing but it sure drowned out Hickey railing on me for going to D'Agostino, which he says is a cheap supermarket. After dinner I lit a fire and FaceTimed with Bruce and then the ginge, with whom I truly have no connection beyond a physical attraction. We went back and forth on him coming over to hang out and finally decided we will see each other in the morning. Before bed I took Wacha out in the snow—there was an eleven o'clock ban on cars on the road, so the street was completely empty save the snow and we walked in the middle of Eighth Avenue, which was surreal and peaceful and gorgeous. And incredibly cold. I went home, FaceTimed with the Wasp in Boston, and compared snow stories. I ate an entire pint of Chunky Monkey ice cream, so I guess I am unable to have ice cream in my home. That being said, I didn't have any more wine. I went to bed with a niggling suspicion that the blizzard would be a bust.

▶ TUESDAY, JANUARY 27, 2015

Yup, a total bust. I woke up at six-thirty to pee and saw that it looked not that much different outside than it did at bedtime and didn't know whether to be happy or sad. Walked the dog on the fresh snow; watching him submerge his head into snowbanks was delicious. The ginge came over. He borrowed a pair of sweats because his were wet, and we made pancakes from a mix I found that turned out to be just terrible. His whole thing is putting peanut butter on pancakes, but that made them even mealier. Sad to say, we have zero connection. Took a cold walk with Hickey and spent the rest of the day rescheduling tomorrow's two (and at one point possibly three) shows, and there were many iterations of guests throughout the day. John Mayer's flight got cancelled and Martha Stewart didn't want to go on with any of our other possibilities, so that whole show went down the tubes and we wound up with Savannah Guthrie and Al Roker. We figured Al would be good because of the weather stuff. I texted the Ninj asking him what workout I should do, then got high and actually went to Equinox and did what he told me to do, which is a revelation. I saw Lance Kash, who was full of bummer financial information for me: I have more tax payments to come and he withdrew more money for me this morning. *This* is the news that's waiting for me at Equinox? Now I know why I never go there. I texted Brandi and said don't watch the show tonight; Whitney Cummings and Eileen are a little brutal on you. Sit it out and stay off social media. Adam showed up for my massage, and Bruce called and I said I officially am Sandy Gallin—getting a massage and talking on the phone. I actually cooked dinner with some of my D'Ag stuff—broiled chicken teriyaki and broccoli—and Skyped with Mom and Dad. Mom said my eyes looked red, and I said I smoked weed and Dad said is that pot? "WHAT DO YOU THINK IT IS, LOU??" was Mom's response. I explained to my parents what it feels like to get high. Then Hickey came over and we watched *RHOBH*. I love his sociological reaction to it. I went to bed and watched *Downton Abbey*. It's starting to get good.

▶ WEDNESDAY, JANUARY 28, 2015

Cold as balls. Brandi didn't take my advice about skipping last night and sent a scorched-earth tweet—"@Andy I think I've taken enough abuse on *WWHL* I dare you to pick on someone else! I'm fucking over it! It's just bullying at this point!" On the show, Al said maybe there will be a big storm on Monday, so I told Daryn to order another ticket back from Miami for Sunday. I called Al "Matt" on the air. Met my neighbor who lives above the new apartment, who told me that I owe him a lot of money because he could've started a bidding war with me for the apartment, and he didn't because he figured I would keep going up but he *could have* and *almost did* but *didn't* and it went on and on and on. So I thanked him. John Mayer feels terrible for cancelling now that he is trying to book *The Late Late Show*, which he's hosting next week and I'm appearing on. I told him Martha cancelled after he did because she only wanted to go on with him and he felt even worse. Booking sucks.

On the way to 30 Rock I got an email from Brandi wanting to know what she did to make me hate her so much and informing me that she drinks on occasion when there are cameras around so that something will happen on the show. I sent her a very reasonable and measured email back and I think she may have wanted me to go nuts on her instead. Bravo cast two docuseries around groups of women in Dallas and Potomac, Maryland, and I had a meeting with Jerry, Shari, Lara, and Frances about whether or not we should make them Real Housewives or something else. I'm on the fence about Dallas because it seems like we should've done it in 2010. Potomac seems totally unexpected but Shari and Frances worry it seems like we are trying to punk people, that the location might sound lame. I like the unexpectedness of it. We joked about calling Potomac *Real Housewives of 20854*, trying to make that ZIP code hip. Ratings are coming in and *BH* had a season high, but it looks like Brandi is done.

I went back to the Clubhouse, where we taped Tony Goldwyn and Jennifer Nettles. The virgin Bachelor was behind the bar, and I had so much fun playing with him. Went home, walked the dog, and met Keith Marshall for a drink. I love meeting up with old high school friends who I don't get to see much. Then to the Time Warner Center for a party for Jason Blum's doc *The Jinx*, where I saw Tommy and Jon Alter, who are like a father-son double punch of media. I have known Tommy since he was a kid. That would be a good radio show, the Alters fighting about politics. Even though they're all on the same team, I wonder if they fight? Sat with DVF, Barry, and their crew. Talked to Sandy Gallin at the end of the night and he said he and I are so alike, I'm the only person besides him who still meets up with high school friends.

⮞ THURSDAY, JANUARY 29, 2015— SATURDAY, JANUARY 31, 2015—NYC—MIAMI

Welcomed back drinking and welcomed back my hangover. The plane to Miami was Jews of all shapes and sizes. Hickey and I went straight to the Delano's pool, where Soledad put us in the corner by the bar, which seems like it's gonna be great but the truth is it's obscured by palm trees and there's a lot of traffic. They were shooting interviews with two telenovela stars who were concurrently repulsive and hot. #Repulhot. (I don't think it works.) Had a perfect nap, then went to Michael's Genuine, recommended by Padma. The way the go-go boys dance at Twist is just basically shifting their weight from one leg to the other and then turning around and looking at themselves in the mirror. They also each look damaged in various ways.

Reports from *RHONY* in Turks and Caicos have been coming in every morning of the week and they're spectacular. I couldn't make this shit up.

Woke up to an email Friday from Al Roker saying if it were him, he would fly back on Sunday, so it looks like the storm could be bad on Monday. I put off the decision. The pool scene greatly improved for the rest of the weekend and we watched a really chubby woman in a string bikini get progressively sloshed as the sun moved across the sky. She could barely walk by 4:00 p.m. every day and threw down her wine like it was water, which made me feel better about what I was consuming. By the way, just back to drinking and already I feel bloated and sugary and am sleeping less well. So why do I do it? I have to go to LA this week, and I texted Cher that I have a proposition for her and will be there Thursday and would she consider having an audience with me and if not would she talk on the phone. She said, "Cool!"—one of those non-answer answers.

Saturday night we went to Jon Jay's celebrity-bowling charity thing for the Boys and Girls Club of Miami. He is an angel. Matt Holliday was there with his wife and I finally got to chat with him and his enormous forearms. I met a pretty-boy pitcher for the Marlins. From there we went to the Palace. I was asleep by midnight.

‣ SUNDAY, FEBRUARY 1, 2015—MIAMI—NYC

It's never fun leaving Miami, yet I always feel like putting a match to the town as I head to the airport. I may or may not have gotten a little misty saying goodbye to the pool staff at the Delano. They are *so* nice. I got in a little tussle with an Instagram commenter who said, "Why did you even get a dog in the first place all you do is go on vacation. You say he likes his babysitter but he wants to be with YOU!" I said I actually keep him in a cage in the basement when I leave and he loves it. Everyone has a fucking opinion. Came home, walked the dog, and went to Marci Klein's for the Super Bowl.

MONDAY, FEBRUARY 2, 2015

I dreamed that Hickey was in a movie with Marie Osmond and Oprah and I made him late for his shoot, and then that I was on tour with John Mayer and I made *him* late for something too. We were in St. Louis in a van. I tweeted last night that the Super Bowl commercials were so depressing I felt suicidal, which led to a stream of tweets all day from people demanding an apology, saying I had offended the mental health community by joking about suicide. (I didn't apologize.) It was snowy and slushy and rainy today and so I went for it and had a can of SpaghettiOs in honor of Jimmy Fallon's triumph last night after the Super Bowl. It was glory in a bowl. Delightful. Delicious. I don't know when the last time I had them was, or when I will ever have them again, but the taste brought me back to the thousands of cans of SpaghettiOs I ate at the kitchen table at 7710 West Biltmore Drive. I wasn't a latchkey child—my mom didn't work, and I had an older sister, a housekeeper, and plenty of friends—but for some reason I only have memories of "fixing" myself SpaghettiOs alone at that kitchen table, using nacho-cheese Doritos as spoons to make the experience as rich as possible. We taped Tom Colicchio and Busy Philipps, then were live with Tom and Katie from *Vanderpump Rules*. It felt fun to drink on the show again. And I buried the lede—I'm going to Cher's house to pitch her the radio channel on Thursday! I set it up with Liz.

TUESDAY, FEBRUARY 3, 2015

Wacha got a few notches cuter today. It's incredible.

Cher texted twice to see what I want to eat and drink when I come to her house. I said don't worry about it, but she really wanted specifics. So I said Whispering Angel and she said, "Whispering What!?"

Had a pre-interview with John Mayer for *The Late Late Show*, then I texted him and said don't make them only talk about what I discussed in the pre; you should go off the cuff. During the show I went off on the RHOBH for saying "my gays" eighty-five times. I did a little teachable moment, saying, we are not your accessories, we are not purses, you don't own us—next time sub in the word "blacks" and see how it sounds.

My dream was that Anderson and I were going to do our show and I had a really crazy Stevie Nicks costume on with a witchy blond wig and I kept saying that people might not recognize me. He kept wondering why I didn't take it off, but that didn't seem to be an option for me. The rant about gays not being accessories is getting picked up all over and people are either saying I'm right, or I'm too sensitive, or how can I criticize my own show when I am an executive producer of it, or why am I criticizing the RHOBH and not Kathy Griffin and NeNe. So I dunno.

Flew to LA, changed at the hotel, and went to CBS Television City to do *The Late Late Show* with John Mayer. A little scandal broke about Brian Williams and a helicopter today; I called Harry Smith to find out what happened. Among other things he said that people's memories are funny things and we all remember things differently, and it reminds me of what I misremembered in my first book about being *alone* with Dan Rather in Utah when the private plane sank, and then later saw on Bill Madison's Facebook page that he was there too. I cut Rather's assistant out of the whole story! Hung out with Chrissy Teigen and John Legend, who were in the dressing room next door. I can't get over how much I see Chrissy Teigen. She's everywhere. She wanted *Housewives* dirt, and I gave her everything she needed. And she helped me pick out my shirt. John Mayer, as a host, has a really slow, nice mellow tone about him and an understated, calm delivery. It was all I could do not to rip the show out of his hands and start hosting it myself, waiting for him to get to the next topic. I'm such a backseat host.

Went to meet Bruce for a drink at the Beverly Hills Palm and Jimmy was there with Lorne Michaels and Ron Meyer. I told Jimmy about the SpaghettiOs in his honor and mentioned to Lorne where I just was. He said everybody thinks they can host a talk show. Talked about Malibu traffic patterns with Ron Meyer because I'm going to Cher's house tomorrow and I can't figure out what time to leave. He is surprised Cher is seeing me because she isn't seeing anybody. Ryan Serhant from *MDL* was there with Jenn Levy, quite randomly, and he made me really stressed about finding an apartment. I need to move in less than a month! Dinner at Bruce and Bryan's with Tate Taylor and his boyfriend. Among other things we talked about Brian Williams, ISIS, Mississippi, and molly.

The day was a slow march until I went to Cher's, and as I watched the Brian Williams thing grow and grow I spent much of the day trying to figure out what is the scandal that's going to bring *me* down. I watched *Housewives* cuts and left for Malibu at three. We got there with time to kill, and I realized I was going to Cher's empty-handed so I went to Maxfield to look for a gift. I figured a candle was the way to go, but you can't just bring Cher a rinky-dinky candle so I found one of those oversized Diptyque ones that Kelly and Mark gave me for Christmas—it was like five hundred bucks. The guy at the counter said, "Don't tell me—you're going to Yolanda's." I said, "No, *Cher's*." I felt about as cool as I could. He nodded, unimpressed. Indeed, there were palm trees everywhere and the gate is very thick wood, and my mind wandered to Cher's Sanctuary line of home goods. Her assistant took me around the house, which is gothic, with endless views of the Pacific, and has a tennis court. Paulette appeared, then the shrimp plate and Whispering Angel appeared, and then Liz Rosenberg, who said they were all just watching the "Living for Love" video that premiered today and did I want to watch it? I told her I could only focus on one diva at the moment (and left out that "Living for Love" is maybe my least favorite Madonna song ever), and then in walked the diva of the moment wearing black kind-of harem pants and a T-shirt and a cutoff hoody. I called her massive living room (with stone archways and vaulted ceilings and a view of her infinity pool and the Pacific Ocean) "understated." She said it is *not* understated, and I said I was kidding. We settled in and talked about her health, her hatred for reality TV, how hard it is to find Whispering Angel (did *Cher* actually go looking for that bottle?), and how bad the sun is for you. I explained what's going on with Brian Williams, then I explained the Harper Lee book controversy.

This was all small talk ramping up to my pitch, which she brought up by saying, "Do you want me to say no now, or should I wait to hear your pitch?" Finally, I said, I'm launching a radio channel and it's going to feature people who I care about, who I want to listen to, and who are passionate. And you have so much to say and so much you care about and I would like you to do a monthly radio show from your house where you talk about whatever you want. At this point she perked up, and Liz perked up. "I think it's a good idea," Liz said. Cher was worried about coming up with topics, and I said, well, it could be anything and we can find people for you to interview. I said I would even do a couple with her if that somehow made her feel better. "Like *Andy and Cher*?" she asked. *Exactly!* And, I told her, you can do it from your house and not have to worry about makeup or anything. She started talking about people who hate her, and how more people might hate her if she really started letting her opinions rip. I said everyone *loves* you, are you kidding, you sold out five stadiums in NYC last year and could've sold out five more.

The sun had set by this point and I didn't want to overstay my welcome, plus Sandy was throwing a dinner for me back in town, so I said to think about it and I would be in touch. Paulette said, you gotta see Cher's bedroom! But I felt like I had already overstayed and said I would see it when I come back to do the radio show. I got in the car and immediately regretted not going to see Cher's bedroom. *What the fuck was I thinking?* I called Sandy to say I was on my way and he said he had a surprise for me at the house. I walked in and there was my surprise: *Dolly Parton.* I almost fainted! She had on a wig with hair stacked on top of her head and then little ringlets with butterfly-shaped barrettes keeping them together. I said I loved her hair and she said with a laugh that it took her forever to do, that she'd been braiding it on the bus from Memphis. She said she loves the bus and doesn't get out the whole way. She writes songs and reads and eats. She said if she gets out she has to be Dolly and she just wants a break sometimes, even though she is really good at being Dolly. She introduces herself to everybody and has unending enthusiasm punctuated by lots of nervous giggles. Having been around her about fifteen times over the course of twenty-five years, I can say that her smell is unmistakable; it's a combination of dairy and perfume. The rest of the dinner was Stacy and Henry Winkler, Jane Buffett, Anjelica Huston ("Your book sold very well," she said), Sandra Bernhard, Lorraine Bracco, Frances, Eli, Jeffrey Richman, Bruce and Bryan, Donald De Line, and Aaron Fox and Perrey Reeves. Jeff writes for *Modern Family* and all the ladies were pitching themselves to him to be on his show. Frances, Eli, and Bruce discussed what would be my downfall. I said I thought it was going to be something with sex, and Eli agreed. Frances said she thought I would say something really un-PC that I couldn't recover from and she was going to have to regretfully let me go. Thanks, boss. Bruce agreed with us all. Oh, and drugs were mentioned. So we have a menu.

I got to sit next to Dolly at dinner. My brain was so fried from making witty conversation with Cher for ninety minutes that I was having to reach to make conversation with Dolly because I was essentially interviewing her. We talked a lot about her variety show. She said she didn't regret doing it, but they were trying to make her pop and she was country. She doesn't regret anything in life; she just learns from her mistakes. She kept telling me she is not exclusive to NBC, almost like in case I wanted to work with her or something. We talked about the Opry. She said she does it once a year. I asked if Loretta Lynn still performs there and she said she's not feeling well right now. Asked about Tammy Wynette and she said well, she's dead. And then someone changed the subject and I got to the point where I couldn't think of anything to ask.

❧ FRIDAY, FEBRUARY 6, 2015—LOS ANGELES

Hickey reminded me that I should've talked to Dolly about that great clip of her and Kenny Rogers singing "We've Got Tonight," and why didn't I make a pitch for her to come on *WWHL*? And why didn't I go see Cher's bedroom? So I'm pulling my hair out. Today was the *Vanderpump Rules* reunion and I was kind of on autopilot. Jake and Angela are in town and, unbelievably, staying next door to me at the Best Western. They came and said hi during the lunch break of the reunion. They can't get over how classy Lisa Vanderpump is. Jake is so attractive and she looks great but I'm scared of fooling around again. That being said, we all made plans to meet after my dinner with John Mayer. The reunion went until about six and I was fried. Got back to the hotel and there was a painting of Wacha that these fans had dropped off. I wound up cancelling on Jake and Angela. I'm just too freaked out!

❧ SATURDAY, FEBRUARY 7, 2015—LOS ANGELES—NYC

KJo emailed saying she has a friend who does dog art and she wants to give me a painting of Wacha. I said I don't want to sound ungrateful but I am overrun with paintings of the dog. I texted Sandy from the plane and he said I for sure did the right thing not asking Dolly to be on my show. Then

I texted Cher that I was unhappy I didn't take her up on the tour of her room, and that I am a fool. She said that I *am* a fool, but pointed out that *she* was not the one who invited me and that I can see it another time. Aha—my instincts were correct. Then I texted Hickey, who said being able to text on airplanes is maybe the best or the worst thing that ever happened to me.

Got home and met Amanda and Grac at the Paramount Hotel, and I walked in to discover that the big staircase is completely gone. I asked the doorwoman where it was and she said they got rid of it three and a half years ago. I said that's funny because it's kind of what the hotel was known for. Why would they get rid of the best thing about the hotel? She said she's been wondering the same thing for three and a half years. Went to prettyugly at the Diamond Horseshoe and met Bill Curtin. Billy Eichner and Jake Shears joined us, and there were too many people in the VIP area that Erich Conrad had arranged for us and the security guy was *freaking* out, kicking people out and just going nuts, so I stood outside it for a good chunk of the night. I met a bunch of people I had met before and forgotten, thus offending them and further souring my reputation.

▶ MONDAY, FEBRUARY 9, 2015

Worked out with the Ninj. Met with the architects, fought with Wacha about taking a bath, and FaceTimed with the Wasp from Boston. I just found out that Naomi Campbell's fashion show that I agreed to months ago is this Saturday, which is when he's coming in from Boston. They *just* called to tell me the date. I'd totally forgotten about it. I don't feel like I can drag him there. Melissa and Joe were on the show and we had a drink after. They really want *RHONJ* to come back, and I went through every scenario of what it would take to bring it back.

▶ TUESDAY, FEBRUARY 10, 2015

Apartment hunting with Fredrik. Still nothing. I texted Naomi and said I just heard your Ebola fashion show is Saturday and I am so sorry, I can't do it, but can't wait to see you tomorrow at *WWHL*. Then three hours later Naomi cancelled for Wednesday with Lisa Vanderpump. So I texted back and said I hope you're not cancelling because I can't do your show. No response. We asked the publicist and she said, "No no no, she has business out of the country and that's why she's cancelling; it's all good." Hmmm—I'm not sure I believe it. I hosted the Red Dress Awards and got testy with a handler, and in front of a bunch of people raged at the lady from the *Daily News* in the press line because of all the lies they keep making up about me, and had a meeting with Caroline Manzo in my dressing room about her issues with production on her show, with which I have nothing to do.

Catherine O'Hara and Eugene Levy turned my frown upside down on the show. They stayed and watched Christopher Guest's final appearance on *Letterman* and Catherine got very misty. It was cool to be in the room for that.

WEDNESDAY, FEBRUARY 11, 2015

The Ninj made me puke today toward the end of the workout, then I got to work and Hugh Grant almost made me puke again before the show when he informed me that he was surly, monosyllabic, and cranky. We got him coffee. He asked on air how the FedEx man was; I had forgotten that he knew the story of my romance with the FedEx man in the Hamptons. We did a scene from *Notting Hill*. Met the Perskys for dinner at Polo Bar. This girl came over and said, I'm Tina Louise's daughter and she loves you and is celebrating her birthday; please come say hello. There's not enough paper for me to dissect everything about that sentence, but I did go over to the table later and Tina Louise seemed to have no clue who I was or why I was there—but the daughter wanted a selfie. David Lauren and Dan Abrams were there, as was Drew Barrymore. I left early for my show, but Bill Persky told me later he was in the elevator with Derek Jeter leaving the restaurant. Bill turned to him and said, "What more can I say that hasn't been said?" Good line.

THURSDAY, FEBRUARY 12, 2015

Deirdre texted me a picture of Naomi at the amfAR event in NYC last night, so I guess they indeed were lying about her having to go out of the country. She must be *pissed* at me! I'm kind of excited for Naomi to bitch me out. I'm ready. Had lunch with Anderson to plan our tour. We wrote a funny intro video that explains both of our biographies and how different we are. Then we will interview each other and surprise each other with some funny videos from our past, and then open it up to the audience for questions. I want people to feel like they're out at a bar with us, so we're going to have a bottle of tequila onstage. Anderson doesn't really drink but has no objections. Brandi's agent called and we fought. He blames me for everything—the edit she is getting, her lawsuit against Joanna Krupa—basically he feels anything that comes out of her mouth is my fault because I provoked it. He talked a lot about her brand and how hard they worked to build it and I told him that with all due respect, part of the brand is based on her getting drunk and tweeting insane shit. She is concerned she's going to get ganged up on at the reunion and thinks I am not impartial. I told him I would do what I have done at the last fifty reunions, which is make sure everyone gets their say. I told Sandy that I don't believe Dolly's husband, Carl Dean, exists. He said he absolutely does and that he and Dolly got stuck in traffic yesterday.

Went to the Todd Snyder fashion show with Bill Owens. Poor Bill and the rest of the *60 Minutes* team are in shock about Bob Simon, who said good night to them at six-thirty last night, got in a Skyline car, and was dead twenty minutes later. Skyline was a shitty car service when I used it while I worked at CBS all those years ago, and now Bob Simon is dead. Went to Café Fiorello with Bill and we talked about CBS being the last of the producers' shops; the correspondents run the show at NBC and ABC.

❧ FRIDAY, FEBRUARY 13, 2015

It is insanely cold out. Like 5 degrees. Had a prep call for this Derek Jeter thing I am hosting tomorrow. Bruce and I had lunch at Good and discussed the Wasp's visit tomorrow. I am freaked about the amount of time we will have together. (Twenty-six hours straight will be the longest relationship I've had in a while!) Dinner with Lynn and Troy at Nobu, but Lynn mistakenly went to the midtown one and I wound up having to explain to Troy why FaceTiming with someone for over a month is more intimate than anything. I have seen this guy's home, his clothes, his office, his car, and on and on. That's more intimacy than I've had with men I've met walking out of a club. Lynn met me at my house, and this has been a week of me reuniting with my news friends and breaking down this Brian Williams thing. It's all anyone can talk about.

Sandy told me today that coincidentally he called Dolly and forgot it was ringing and ringing and finally Carl Dean picked up! He said it was the first time they'd spoken in thirty years. When I hung up I wondered if he was just making that up to put me off the scent of a conspiracy!

❧ SATURDAY, FEBRUARY 14, 2015

Even though the Wasp and I agreed that Valentine's Day was not going to be a factor in our time with each other, it was impossible to ignore. While I waited for him to come, I downloaded to Amanda about my plans. I told her there was this Derek Jeter event this afternoon that I had to go to and I didn't know whether to bring him or not. She advised that I go to the Jeter thing alone, just to give each other some space. I agreed, and as we were hanging up the twenty-six-hour date began. The Wasp is shorter than I imagined (I'm not saying I'm tall, by the way). It was a little awkward, with so much anticipation and flirting, to be finally together. It was either going to be wild attraction from the get-go or something else, and for me it was in the "something else" category from the moment I opened the door. We hung for a few hours and I headed to the Jeter event launching his new website, *The Players' Tribune*, where I moderated a conversation with a group of massive sports stars (including Russell Wilson, Jeter, Andrew McCutchen, Matt Harvey, and Blake Griffin) in front of a room of more massive sports stars and sports press. I had no teleprompter, but there was a lot of "business" stuff they wanted me to say and I felt alone in a sea of athletes. When it was done I ran out of there and found the Wasp back at my apartment reading a book with the dog snuggled up to him. It was idyllic seeming but without the actual emotion. I had tickets to *Constellations* for our non-Valentine's date, then we went to Orso, where we saw Danny Meyer and family. I'd gotten an invite from Jane Buffett to Paul McCartney's small surprise concert at Irving Plaza and we decided to go and boy am I glad we did. It was like the Oscars of *Saturday Night Live*. We stood on a balcony right on the side watching McCartney jam on all of his hits. In our area were Jimmy Buffett, Chris Rock, Billy Crystal, Jim Carrey (with bodyguard),

Steve Martin, Tom Hanks and Rita, Maya Rudolph, Rachel Dratch, Lorne Michaels, and Ron Delsener, who told me he is seventy-eight. McCartney was incredible and could've kept going and going. I always think he looks like an old lady when I see him in pictures but onstage he looks like Paul McCartney. I was standing talking to Rita Wilson and Eddie Murphy's bodyguards pushed this woman next to us out of the way in order to get Eddie through. It was McCartney's wife they were manhandling! Chris Rock told me he was introducing Murphy at the *SNL* fortieth anniversary special tomorrow night (that's why everybody is in town) and that he's gonna say he is the better version of me. Not sure that's true, given what I saw with his douchey bodyguards. Meryl Streep and I had a nice chat toward the end, and I must've been in my cups because she wanted to know how I got where I am, and I was yammering on about being really good at making decisions. Then she was saying what a great businessman I am, and I said I think I am more creative than business-y. I kept saying how *decisive* I am, and how important that is. To Meryl Streep! *Who am I?*

McCartney said, " 'Til we meet again," when he said good night, which was really sweet. We walked outside and it was snowing lightly. I think I blew the Wasp away with the perfect date night, and we had a nice time together but it was not love at first real-life sight. We came home and Wacha refused to leave his crate and was aggressively snarling and barking at me, which was infuriating and confusing. I was trying to get him to come out so I could walk him but he refused to budge. Was Wacha cock blocking me with the Wasp? But he'd spent the day with him! Every time I went in with the leash he went nuts on me, until finally I tried to just put it on him and he jumped up and his teeth grazed me on the top of my arm by my shoulder. It wasn't a bite, but I was so upset it sobered me up. Slept in the same bed as the Wasp but it was not sexy.

❧ SUNDAY, FEBRUARY 15, 2015

The date continued today with breakfast at the Village Den. It was all nice and pleasant—I think too long, but a good exercise. He left around noon. Had dinner before my NeNe show with Ricki, Liza, and Milo. Then during my show I realized that I am doing a version of *The Ricki Lake Show*. The party at the Plaza Hotel after the *SNL 40* show was not to be believed: every movie star, comedian, NYC fixture, rich person, and musical superstar under one roof. I had great chats with Sia (big Bravo fan), Molly Shannon, Amy Poehler, Lorne Michaels, Paul Rudd, Caryn Zucker, Jerry and Jessica, and on and on. Onstage, Jimmy was leading a who's who of incredible singers in the ultimate freestyle jam. McCartney was up there, Taylor Swift, Miley Cyrus . . . and then, as I'm walking to get drinks for Nancy Juvonen and me, I run into two members of my favorite party band in deep conversation. Barging in on the B-52s' Kate Pierson and Fred Schneider (for whom I once go-go danced, in a #dreamofalifetime scenario), I said, "You have got to get up there!" Kate said she wanted to sing "Love Shack" but that Fred was too scared. I said, "You come with me right now; I am *making this happen.*" Suddenly *I* was delivering the Bs to *their* #dreamofalifetime. I grabbed Nancy in a panic. *"These are the B-52s. We need to get them onstage to sing 'Love Shack' ASAP."* Nancy switched right into producer gear, said "Come with me," and brought them to the front of the stage, where she pointed at them and mouthed "Love Shack" to Jimmy, who told them where to go and in two minutes they were doing their thing. Magic! An hour later the room came to a standstill when Prince arrived, thrilling even the most jaded among us. I almost took a picture but instead decided to just dance. As I walked (stumbled) out of the party sometime before four, Cheri Oteri walked (stumbled) over to me wearing one shoe and said her date, Lance Bass, was nowhere to be found and could I give her a ride home. I said of course I will, where are you staying, and she said Ninety-something and Central Park West, which was entirely the opposite of where I was going and had she not been booked on *WWHL* literally the next night I would've called her an Uber. As we got our coats I saw Andy Samberg looking at me and I wondered if he thought I was taking her home, like, *taking her home.*

▷ TUESDAY, FEBRUARY 17, 2015

Almost barfed with Ninj; getting in shape seems more and more insurmountable. Did a ton of bookkeeping stuff, watched *Atlanta* and *NYC*, planned the show with Anderson, did a Fallon pre-interview, negotiated with Sirius, and tried to decide whether to come back to New York on Oscar Sunday. (After three days of partying out there, sometimes actual Oscar

Night feels like a postscript. I can't decide.) Saw an apartment online that had crazy outdoor space and I got in a fever pitch about it and then it was rented in a second. I am being so laissez-faire, and I have to move in, um, two weeks.

SJP came over and we met Hickey and went to the Waverly Inn, where I saw the straight waiter who flirts with me for the first time in many months. I was trying to figure out if he read what I wrote in the *Diaries*, but he didn't let on. What he is, no question, is a loiterer and a lingerer who is always placing silverware, pouring water, or replacing napkins or condiments. I am sure he heard half our convo, which was about casting SJ's new show, *Divorce*; Brian Williams (still); Housewives; *SNL*; SJP's birthday; her kids; my dating. We walked her home in a balmy 30 degrees, which given the temps the last few days is like 50. Then Hickey and I tried to think of a song to perform at her big fiftieth birthday party and thought maybe "We've Got Tonight," and I could enter from behind like Dolly, which would be a great showbiz moment except the song has nothing to do with SJ and we can't sing it. So that was a bad idea.

⟩⟩ WEDNESDAY, FEBRUARY 18, 2015

It was one thing after another all day. Worked out with Ninja and had lunch with Anderson and a reporter from the Associated Press who is doing a feature on our tour. I am always worried about going one step too far with Anderson and saying or doing something that's going to piss him off, but maybe I am just fine. The apartment I saw online yesterday, with the sick outdoor space, is *not* rented, and so I ran over to see it (three blocks from my place) and though it's in a weird building, it was pretty killer. The terrace is like Margot Kidder's in *Superman*—views north, east, south, and west, with enough room for Wacha and eighteen friends to run around. And two bedrooms inside. It is pre-war and has not the greatest bathrooms or kitchen but it's all about the outdoor space. I called Hickey and asked him to get over there and he freaked out when he saw it; I told them I want to take it and they sent an application for Daryn to fill out. Did I mention it's a third of the price of the "line of cocaine" one Fredrik showed me?! Got home and the phone never stopped ringing while I tried to shower, walk the dog, and pick out clothes for Fallon, which seemed impossible given that of the twenty-five white dress shirts I own it seems as though only one of them fits and it's the same one I want to wear on the *RHOBH* reunion tomorrow. I had a *BH* reunion call to decide seating issues (Vanderpump will be displeased if she is on the end, Yolanda may leave after a few hours, most of them hate Brandi so there aren't many options for seating her, and on and on). It is going to be intense—Kim and Kyle haven't spoken in four months. Ran up to do the *Tonight Show* and on the way, Shed Media pitched me EPing a Bethenny spinoff. I'm game. Got to Fallon—Amanda met me because we were having dinner—and was briefed. My phone was ringing off the hook, with the real estate agent calling with more and more requirements for the application: financial statements, letters from the current building, a hundred bucks cash (whaaaa?). Daryn met me in the greenroom with a pile of papers to sign and thank God for her. Jimmy was so sweet to me on air, plugged the book three times, called me one of his best friends, and just is amazing. I thought I was only fair. I kind of tried to drive the bus and should've let him do it. That being said, the *Housewives* tag lines killed. Amanda and I went out to dinner, then back to my place. I didn't watch myself on Jimmy and was asleep by eleven-thirty.

▶ THURSDAY, FEBRUARY 19, 2015—NYC—LOS ANGELES

On my flight to Oscar weekend were John Shea and Ray Booth (who I married and who are heading to New Zealand on their honeymoon), Derek Blasberg, Stavros Niarchos III with a hot girl and a cute dog (but not cuter than him), and Sunny Ruffalo, who still doesn't have a dress for Sunday night. I watched the final three episodes of *RHOBH* and tried to coordinate more of the endless documents needed to rent an apartment in NYC—tax forms, a signed affidavit from my lawyer, and endless letters of reference. You think that when someone becomes a celebrity everything is just handed to them but the truth is that ain't the case. SJP emailed and said Hugh Grant told her he's worried he was too cranky on my show. I said that's ridiculous. Landed and met John Mayer at Soho House. I was waiting for him and looking around, thinking hateful thoughts about the people loitering around me. LA brings that out in me. Discussing it further with John, he pointed out that everyone is going through the same struggle here, so if I am thinking whatever I am, then everyone else is too. He always brings me calmly back to life. We talked about Katy Perry and what is and isn't working, and about his texting with Bob Weir. Dinner with KJo at Lucques and it was great to see her. I pitched her on the radio idea and she wanted weekly, not daily. Got back to the Sunset Tower and had a drink with Mark, Kelly, and Jimmy Kimmel and his wife, who had read my book and was surprised by what I wrote about our time at SXSW. Now I have to go back and read what I wrote. Kate Hudson was there with her midriff. George and Amal were too, and in LA that's the equivalent of seeing Obama. On the way out I saw Lee Daniels, who said he had pitched me *Empire*, and my face fell, but then I realized it was actually an updated *Valley of the Dolls* he had pitched so I felt better.

▶ FRIDAY, FEBRUARY 20, 2015—LOS ANGELES

It seems like I got the apartment! BuzzFeed did a list of "Hugh Grant's Ten Crankiest Moments from *WWHL*," which he forwarded to me, and I said fuck BuzzFeed, but the list was in fact pretty funny. *Beverly Hills* reunion day today. There was a lot of buzz leading up about Kim's state of mind, but she seemed great. I assured Brandi I would be fair to her. Later I thought she was going to walk off when I compared her slap to a dog biting Lisa by mistake. (She told me to "fuck off.") Kim and Kyle got very ugly, and that was a sad way to end the day.

I went straight from the reunion to the CAA party at Kevin Huvane's, where I then downloaded to Lisa Kudrow and Michael Patrick King about the theater I'd just witnessed. Anna Kendrick told me the backstory of her time on *Lip Sync Battle*. Gwen Stefani was a bombshell. JLo was in a high ponytail and really flawless. I came face to face with Naomi Campbell for the first time since I pissed her off and she went *in* right away: "I'm so mad at you! You blew me off so bad!" I said wait wait wait, and we worked it out. It wasn't the reaming out I was kind of hoping for. Saw Aaron Rodgers who is big and kinda flirty in a straight way; Queen Latifah wanted me to say hi to Anderson, whom she loves. Chelsea Handler was on brand, falling-down drunk, and when I say that I mean she fell down into James Corden and me talking. Corden is a *WWHL* fan and really sweet, with big blue eyes. After a fun, glittery night, I was content knowing that I am leaving Sunday. Two nights of high-profile parties is enough for me. (Said me, never.)

▶ SATURDAY, FEBRUARY 21, 2015—LOS ANGELES

Moved over to Casa Bruce/Bryan, where I devoured Doritos and perused the guest list for dinner as workmen scrambled to fix the house. We went to the Diller picnic and it was Joan Collins, Shirley MacLaine, Steve Martin, and Berry Gordy plus every studio head and power player. Had an interesting talk with Les Moonves about Brian Williams and late night and news in general. Gayle and I chatted about movies and Bruce said, "Oh, yeah, last year Andy was speculating about whether Oprah was in a bad mood at this lunch," and I quickly said, "No, Bruce, that is *not* what we were talking about." Then she walked away and I yelled at him.

Took a two-hour nap, then watched some *Lego Movie* with Ava and got a massage from Nate, by which time the dinner started. Had a long visit with Nanci Ryder, who has ALS and can't speak. She was writing everything down on a card. Her mind is still there. She told me you find out who your real friends are and you can eliminate others from your life, that she's been watching a lot of news. She is inspiring. I thought she wanted me to get her ice for her coconut water but what she really wanted was some vodka, which we laughed about. Anna Wintour said the new *Vogue* offices downtown have a lot of space but there's not a lot in the neighborhood. And you're always looking down on the memorial. When she left, Nanci wrote down that she was terrified of AW. Amy Pascal was there and I said, "You got fucked," and she said thanks but then I wondered if I said the wrong thing. The Obamas of LA were there and all over each other. Gwyneth Paltrow was really nice and for the first time I realized how beautiful she is. I don't think she had any makeup on. Broke down the Housewives with Ryan Murphy, who is worried about NeNe's role on the show. Ethan Hawke told great stories. Jason and Lauren picked out jewelry for the Oscars from Billie's stash. Meryl and Don were there and also Robert Downey Jr., who is much more handsome in person.

SUNDAY, FEBRUARY 22, 2015—LOS ANGELES—NYC

Car picked me up at seven-fifteen and Bruce and Ava were already up watching *CBS Sunday Morning* and snuggling. Felt like I made the right move leaving even though I was sad to miss Jason and Ethan's party. And Guy's. Saw Bill Hader in the lounge and we gossiped about *SNL 40*. He said when you have been to *SNL* parties for so many years, you come to the point of "Oh, yeah, there's Prince performing" and kind of blow it off. I get it. Jeff Probst was on my flight. He said he emailed Gary when I was on Stern, wondering if I was kind of ruining myself by naming all those names in my book and telling stories and I tried to explain the line between selling out and not. Spent the rest of the flight paranoid. Landed in NYC and watched the Oscars at Jimmy and Nancy's—it was just the three of us—and there was a weird moment with Terrence Howard that somehow made us laugh so hard that I fell on the floor in hysterics. Literally.

MONDAY, FEBRUARY 23, 2015

Was walking out to go to the bank and saw the cutest dog coming into the building—we locked eyes and I realized it was mine! I was happy, until I had to go get certified checks in the tundra, sign the lease (the landlord prefers blue pens; people are weird), go to Grac's quickly, buy a suit at Ralph Lauren, and come home and totally freak out about moving in a week. The Wasp texted and said, "I know it wasn't a huge connection but I would like to hang out again" and I said I would too and that if I had it to do over again I would've had him stay at a hotel, which of course came out sounding horribly wrong over text. Why text this kind of conversation? Early show, then watched *Downton*, which was finally great.

TUESDAY, FEBRUARY 24, 2015

Packing and purging. Purging and packing. Throwing out posters, old beauty products, unused spices. Had lunch with Sandra Bernhard to try to get her to do a radio show for my channel and came home to find a signed

Sandra Bernhard poster as well as Wigstock posters, an *Ab Fab* poster, a Tom Hanks–signed poster from *Philadelphia*—what the fuck do I *do* with this stuff? Keep it.

We had a live keg party to celebrate Dakota Fanning's twenty-first birthday party on the show. Rinna's publicist kept emailing saying not to put her in the "second chair" and we said we have to because we don't know what Dakota's personality is going to be and she's young. After the show I did a keg stand and was horrible at it and got beer all over my tie.

▶ FRIDAY, FEBRUARY 27, 2015

More packing. I went to the new apartment and love it. It's like a tree house in the sky. I measured all over and realized I can fit almost every scrap of furniture I have right now. Dinner with Jackie at the Polo Bar. Ate like a pig, but no corned beef sandwich. Came home and Wacha was initially skittish about getting out of his crate, so I left him alone. Then he came out but was going back to it, which I didn't realize, so I clicked his leash on to take him out and he freaked out and turned into a wild beast. While I tried to get the leash off he bit me on the arm, hard. I don't know what's happening to this dog or how to fix it; it's like he's changing personalities.

▶ SUNDAY, MARCH 1, 2015

Snowing. Packing.

Show was Kenya and the Fashion Queens. Came home and spent my last night in this version of my apartment with Wacha, watching the two-hour *Downton Abbey* finale, which was warm and wonderful. I was feeling really melancholy with the dog, snuggling and trying to desperately get him to emote, talk, feel me, feel the situation, and understand that our lives are changing together. He is a dog, though. I accept his limitations.

Woke up early. Sherman came and I showed him my bite. He was shocked. It *is* pretty bad now that I look at it. Even though I paid Brownstone Brothers top dollar to not only pack my shit but also unpack it to the point that not a box is left in my new apartment when they leave, moving is still stressful and exhausting. Neicy came and helped me unpack. I don't like the bathrooms, and I haven't felt that unsettledness of being in a new building in eleven years, so the feeling took me by surprise. I was very focused on getting everything done and fixing what wasn't right. Maybe that means I'm just old. The twenty-four-hour elevator operators add a whole layer of uncomfortable conversation the minute you walk out your door. One good thing is being directly across from an Associated supermarket, where I went around seven to get supplies. Bought a lot of pre-prepared food—Hickey says it's crap, but he's a food snob and I ain't picky—while Delilah blared on the speakers. Delilah either makes me cozy or intensely sad, and tonight it was the latter. That feeling hung with me after I'd gotten home and nuked my premade dinner for one (chicken kebab, mushroom quinoa, and roasted mushrooms—yes, I doubled up on mushrooms, but it was dinner for *one* so I wasn't answering to anyone) and sat in my little eat-in kitchen in the one chair I'd brought, looking out the window at New York City from a new vantage point (directly at that lit tower in Madison Square Park) feeling alone and sad. No stereo yet, no Wi-Fi, no TV, just me and double mushrooms. The dog wasn't even here; I'd left him in Brooklyn because I didn't think I'd be moved in. I felt the opposite of how I thought I'd feel tonight. Isn't that what winds up happening in life? How am I ever going to remember all the elevator guys' names?

GG and Reza from *Shahs of Sunset* were on and they were lit up, willing to do or say anything no matter how filthy or ugly. When reality stars get to the point when they feel like they have to keep upping the game no matter how ugly they become, it's upsetting. Lisa Vanderpump surprised them, and I think Reza was pissed that the spotlight was being taken off him. Lisa had just spoken about Ebola at the UN and, I mean, I can see her speaking about rosé or dogs at the UN, but now that I think about it the Ebola connection seems a little loose! Good for her, though. I came home and suddenly it was *fun* being in the new apartment alone. I wasn't depressed.

▶ TUESDAY, MARCH 3, 2015

Hickey came by and helped me decide where to put my art, after which the guys came to hang stuff, Time Warner came to install cable and internet and phone, and then JP came to look at my computers, the stereo people installed speakers, and the shade folks put in blackout curtains. I am all set up. And exhausted.

We taped Kelly Clarkson, who is really nice, open, funny, boozy, and game. We acted out a scene from *From Justin to Kelly*. Came home to the apartment and am now completely in love. Kelly warned me that if you move to a temporary apartment with outdoor space you run the risk of not wanting to go back to your other apartment, and she's right. I spent all this time putting my eggs into the basket of combining the two apartments and now I might be in the apartment I was meant to be in. What to do?

▶ WEDNESDAY, MARCH 4, 2015

Big snow. The dog went out on that Margot-Kidder-from-*Superman* terrace and that was his exercise, running around in the fresh untouched snow. He peed and pooed on the snow too. This dog *loves* pooing on snow. I picked up the poo and snow and put it in the toilet. *Could life get better and more convenient?*

Shania Twain and Penn Badgley were on the pretape and Shania looked like she had walked right out of 1997—the hair was huge and curly and had to be highly flammable, whatever it was made of. She is perfectly nice but there is something very off about her, like she's suffered a huge trauma. Or she's Canadian. Well, actually both apply, so now I've figured it out.

Came home and my phone and internet went out, so I fought with the cable company, who said it was actually Apple's problem because of my fucking AirPort tower and Apple said I was out of warranty on the tower but that I could pay a one-time fee of twenty-nine dollars and they would help me. I told the lady that I was going to take the opportunity right then to say fuck you to Apple and hung up, at which point I realized that I was indeed the one who was fucked. You can't beat the system.

The live show was Anne Heche and Tim Daly. I'd not been looking forward to this one and didn't enjoy it one bit, but the control room really loved how nutty Anne Heche was. Trying to get her to talk about her alter ego, Celestia, I brought up her sexual abuse, which made for an awkward transition to "Game time!" but I somehow managed. Ryan kept telling me that this Real Housewife of Melbourne was coming to the show and wanted to meet me. I met her before the show and she was a 2007 version of a Real Housewife: satin dress, bad hair, heavily scented. She asked if I was staring at her boobs and I said no. I wanted to say, "I've seen huge *Housewives* tits and these aren't even in the ballpark," but I was worried she might've taken that as a suggestion to get a tit job. She kept telling me how *tired* all the other Housewives were and that Beverly Hills needed *her* to join the cast and how could she make it happen. I told her it actually was not going to happen. On the other hand, she claims to be a psychic and said that my right knee was giving me problems, and she was exactly right about that! After the show I got more from her and wanted to run away. It was our "Friday" and so we stayed at work, drinking, and I asked my team what my downfall will be. A dick pic? Something racist? They're gonna think about it. They seemed a little freaked by the conversation—I guess because if I fall, so do they?

▶ FRIDAY, MARCH 6, 2015

Met with the architect and told him he might need to see Fifteenth Street because that could be our next project. If it weren't a rental building, I would buy it. Had my first design meeting with Eric Hughes to pick out fabrics. Got overwhelmed. Pitched a show to Bravo called *Andy's Yearbook* on which I look back at a year in pop culture and see how it's affected what's happening today, like a smart *I Love the '80s*. I couldn't tell if they liked it.

Signed my Sirius deal. Now I need to find someone to run the channel— that hit me like a ton of bricks. And we have to program the channel twelve hours a day. Oy. Article on *HuffPo* that says I said Seacrest had Brian Dunkleman killed. Will *that* be my downfall? Nah. Photo shoot for Bravo Upfront. They had me dance a little and jump and stuff. I felt my knee and it reminded me that that woman was right. First little party at my new place—John Hill, Hickey, Amanda and Jim, Jeanne, Liza, Bill and Chris, Bryan. We rang the bell.

▶ SUNDAY, MARCH 8, 2015

Spent all day in the tree house. Michael Rourke came by and talked ideas for my radio channel. I am getting pumped for London next week. The night I get in, I have plans for drinks with the British actor I met on Instagram Direct. He has made it very clear to me that he has to be up early and can't stay out late, which translates to me as he is not into me and wants me to know that. He is so sexy. Ugh.

It was Jon Stewart's *Night of Too Many Stars* autism benefit and I worked the phone banks before the show, seated next to Susan Sarandon. I showed her my pot vape, which she said was "brilliant." White Castle was the sponsor and I kept asking the stage manager for a burger and Sarandon said she knows what's in them because of her time filming *White Palace* but then they brought them over an hour later and she had one. Cecily Strong said she watches everything on Bravo, as do the *Broad City* girls. Martin Short and I talked to Paul Shaffer about the end of *Letterman* in a couple months. Sounds to me like Dave thinks he made the wrong decision to leave.

▶ MONDAY, MARCH 9, 2015

I was all prepared for three days of jury duty—I had a backpack full of stuff to occupy me and Wacha was home, expecting Daryn to come walk him in four hours. I was committed! I walked in and was flagged down by a wonderful female cop who asked me if I wanted her to get me out of the whole thing. *Yes!* I told her that last time I got out but then didn't get a time-served letter and was back in the pool a year later. So I was free by nine-twenty and felt like Tim Robbins at the end of *The Shawshank Redemption*! Met Hickey at Bonsignour and sat outside in the balmy, sunny, 45-degree morning, and then we went and got Wacha and took him for a walk. These elevator operators in my building do everything—bring you mail and packages, bring people up—they have really great attitudes. I forget all their names.

Wondering if my channel should be called Andy Radio or Radio Andy—Kelly, Lauren, and Bryan all like Radio Andy.

TUESDAY, MARCH 10, 2015

Now that I don't have jury duty I was able to go to the gym, where I discovered Cristiano Ronaldo is circling: Not only is his body double (which I still don't get) working out there, so is his Russian model ex-girlfriend. He *has* to be next. Lunch with the Consueloses at Morandi. Did Bethenny one-on-one, which was good except there are a ton of crazy legal issues associated with talking about her marriage. *Rebel Heart* came out and I texted Madonna that it was amazing and I was working on Liz to get her on my show. She said, "Ha! Thanks," so that's a kind of a "no." Later in the day, after I'd listened to it five more times (and legitimately started to think it amazing), I texted her that there was no doubt that Jesus liked her pussy best, to which she replied, "hahahhahhaha."

My cable is fucked up once again. John Hill said the Jesus pussy line is like a parody of Madonna trying to be shocking. He may be right. Like what's the one thing she hasn't said, oh, that Jesus likes her pussy best. Liz Hurley and Tony Danza were on the show and it was surprisingly good. The bartender was a model dressed as a British guard—he was flirting like crazy during the show and I told him to stay for our staff cocktail party after. He turned out to be a complete drip, and straight, but the kind of straight guy who makes gay guys think we have a chance. Ain't nobody got time for that!! Anthony came in at the precise moment I turned on the fake Brit, fake gay, fake model, and told him his car was waiting to take him home. Cheerio!

WEDNESDAY, MARCH 11, 2015

It was 60 degrees, plus Madonna was on Howard today at one, so it was like a holiday all day. I worked out and then stayed home to listen to the show, which was both satisfying and not enough for me. I want this interview so bad and I can feel it slipping away. I realized today that she is saying "Yeezus," not "Jesus," in that song. So my text made me look dumb. *Yeezus loves my pussy best*. Aha. Borrowed ten bucks from the daytime elevator operator (who wears a nice white button-down every day) for the laundry-card machine. I still don't know his name. SJ and James Wilkie came over and she flipped for the apartment and outdoor space. We took a zillion pics outside and went to 5 Napkin Burger on Fourteenth Street even though James implored me to understand that the one on Bleecker and Seventh Avenue is *way* better. He was emphatic about that. Played phone tag with Jake, who I invited to Anderson's and my opening night in Boston next week. Eli came over and we discussed the radio channel, my romance with Jake and Angela, and the bottom falling out of the TV business. Packed for London trip and went to bed.

▶ THURSDAY, MARCH 12, 2015—NYC—LONDON

I got on the plane and realized I never paid the elevator operator back his ten bucks. The day flight to London is *so* the way to go. My driver at Heathrow recognized me from *Housewives*, which is wild. Stayed at the lovely Covent Garden Hotel. Met the British Actor, who actually was sweetly flirty but has a boyfriend of six years. We had a drink at the hotel. British men are so fun to flirt with. We walked to the Soho House and had a couple drinks and something to eat there. This guy is very famous over here, and so it felt like opposite day because I was the one being handed the camera to take pictures and no one knew who I was. I loved it. Then we headed to Club Room Service in Soho, where I took more pics of him and his fans, and I randomly met a Brazilian who had DMed me on Instagram a year or so ago. #BritActor said he was leaving and that we would definitely hang out when he came to America in the fall. Not sure how that will play with his boyfriend, but I felt optimistic based on our connection. I stayed and worked on the Brazilian, who seemed not so into it but then I wandered off and he found me and kissed me on his way to the coat check, very passionately and forcefully. And if I have to lip sync for my life with a kiss, I will always win, because he came back with his coat for another one, and that was all it took for him to say, "Go get your coat; I will meet you in front."

I was not so happy being woken up in an Ambien haze at nine-thirty by room service with my tea. Had a photo shoot for the British magazine *Attitude* that involved me in various stages of undressing from a tuxedo after a night out. They played Madonna, so I was happy. The reporter told me that Madonna had told him that she loves skiing because she puts on her helmet and is anonymous, and once she got pushed on the mountain and she couldn't believe it because no one pushes her. On the way back to the hotel Prince Charles and Duchess Camilla drove right past us in some weird car with a police escort! It was quite exciting. Had some pasta at a café and walked around and shopped. Am so high from my flirt with the #BritActor and just being in London. (The Brazilian also put a spring in my step.) Had dinner with Tom Hollander, his new girlfriend, and Joan Collins and Percy Gibson at The Colony Grill Room. Joan held court the entire time and we talked about everything: Ava Gardner (she lost her looks), Kim Kardashian (Joan is flummoxed by her), her chicken liver (she had to send it back because it was "almost moving on the plate"), the royals (all good), Linda Evans (not winning any awards for her acting, apparently). Joan told me I aged her up by three years when I mentioned her on my show recently; Jackie called her to let her know as soon as it happened. I felt terrible, of course. Joan is about to be Dame Joan and there are parties planned. There was an exhibit of wedding dresses at the Victoria and Albert Museum and Joan said hers was in there and I said dare I ask which one. She didn't love that comment. We explained Instagram to her. She asked how many followers I have and how many followers I have on Twitter. She wants more followers. She doesn't have a secretary, stylist, or publicist, but she is very much in the mix. She is a treasure and I loved every second of being with her.

I went back to the hotel and was supposed to meet #BritActor but he was tired, and I was tired but very bored and went to the Shadow Lounge. Lisa Vanderpump used to own it, so I kind of thought I might get in by osmosis, but I was of course unrecognized and disregarded at the front door before I got in and fought for a drink at the bar while getting no extra kindness from bartenders and being pushed aside several times by people. I've wanted anonymity when going out to a gay bar for the last few years, and I finally had it. I felt like Madonna on the slopes! I enjoyed myself but admit

I missed the perks. Met a guy from Jordan and I tried to explain what I do, but he just wasn't computing "talk show host." He said that I was lying and walked away. There was one woman who recognized me—the wig-wearing bathroom attendant. She gave me her card; she's a singer. Talked to this little twink who looked like Harry Styles's cousin and asked him if he knows who Joan Collins is and he didn't, and I showed him a picture and he said "Oh, yeah, it's the old lady from the Snickers ads."

▷ SATURDAY, MARCH 14, 2015—LONDON

Hickey arrived and we met Micheál Neeson for a really fun lunch at The Wolseley, which was a favorite spot of Natasha's. Finally it was time for the real reason for coming to London: Ralph starring in George Bernard Shaw's *Man and Superman* at the National. He was phenomenal; it was a performance worthy of the trip. And it was perfect for Ralph—a four-hour treatise on not getting married. Walked over the bridge in the foggy night with the London Eye and Parliament in the background for dinner at the Delaunay. The thing in London seems to be fifties/sixties-ish looking places. Got blown off by #BritActor again so we met Ralph's castmates at The Box. An Asian lady dressed as Prince took her pants off onstage and pissed in three champagne glasses, which she and her backup singers drank from, then threw on the audience. Theater! Hickey and I walked home. We'd taken half a molly apiece at the club and didn't think it had worked, but it turned out it did so we just wandered. It was fun.

▷ MONDAY, MARCH 16, 2015—NYC

Back home and had lunch w/ Jodi et al. They're having a seventy-fifth birthday party for Uncle Stanley in St. Louis the day I am flying home from Atlanta, so I think I will stop in and attend. Everybody is getting old. Did press on phone for the radio channel. The taped show was Nick Cannon and Bobby Cannavale and the energy felt off to me. The live show was Thomas Ravenel and MJ from *Shahs* and it was electric. He blames me for his running for office!

TUESDAY, MARCH 17, 2015

Radio Andy was announced today. Watched the intro piece for our AC2 tour and it made me really excited. It feels real, and it better because our first show is Saturday. Booked a Snapple commercial for next week. I love Snapple. Had a coffee date with a guy I met at the gym yesterday who came over with pastries and it turns out he has a husband. And I said, so WTF are you doing here anyway? With pastries, yet!

WEDNESDAY, MARCH 18, 2015

Anderson and Barkin were on the show and he and I did a bunch of work on our videos and shot stuff before the show, during which I sent Cher a pic of both of us, which she loved despite that I am using her "brother (the good Andy) to sweet talk me into doing a radio show," which she said she is still mulling. Then she asked if she could tweet the picture and said we are as cute as puppies, with a puppy emoji of course. I felt like I had the night off because Barkin and AC are so easy; it was a laugh riot. I couldn't hold my tongue on the after show when someone called in asking what Anderson thought of Kathy Griffin leaving *Fashion Police*, which has been the big story this week. He defended her but I said she is the pot calling the kettle black, that she has been body shaming for years and can't pretend she doesn't make fun of people. Afterwards we showed Barkin our intro piece, then we had drinks in my office and broke down the state of the world. I texted Cher back and said I wasn't using Coops to get her to do the show and she and I went back and forth. I went to bed thinking that she would try doing a few episodes.

THURSDAY, MARCH 19, 2015

There are so many elevator guys to keep track of! During the day there's the cute one with the nice butt who wears button-down shirts, then there is a kind of manic guy who is into pop culture and has seen me on *Colbert* and stuff, then the overnight guy is a heavy, mellow dude who doesn't say much. But the overnight guy shouldn't say much, now that I think of it. What's to say overnight?

Cracked my iPhone on way to the gym. By the time I got home Daryn had arranged for this guy to come over and fix it for two hundred bucks.

Went to Marc and Scott's to practice my song for SJP's birthday. All her friends are performing the score of *Annie*, and I will reprise my role as Bert Healy from the Clayton High School production and sing my critically heralded version of "You're Never Fully Dressed Without a Smile." Even though they're my friends, I was quite tickled being "directed" by *the* Marc Shaiman and Scott Wittman.

Had dinner with that gay weatherman I've been flirting with at the gym. He is very attractive but I'm not sure there was a connection. I will say that *he loves weather*! During my massage I told Adam that I'm amazing at getting massages and it must be so nice for him to massage me because I am so receptive to it. He said I am the only client he has ever had who turns a massage into a compliment for himself.

▶ FRIDAY, MARCH 20, 2015—NYC—BOSTON

First day of spring and I woke up to a text from Cher saying that she wants stats on who wants to hear her on the radio, what they'd want her to talk about, etc. She said she wasn't nervous, she just thought that she and radio may not be a marriage made in heaven. So we may not have a done deal after all. I said the audience is people like me and we want you to talk about whatever the hell you want.

It started snowing just in time for my train trip to Boston and I had the best ride; I watched two episodes of *RHONY* and got some Sirius work done. Set up a meeting with Sarah Silverman in a month; she would be great for Radio Andy. I should just blow my whole programming budget on her and call it a day. Got to the Four Seasons and it was a very VIP arrival with a bunch of gifts waiting in the room, like Jack Daniels, an AC2 pastry thing, and some animal crackers, which I ate—but quickly found out they were actually crackers *for* animals. There was a random envelope with pictures of an older Jewish lady with famous people like Barbara Walters that she had used as holiday cards. I used to do that! The lady from the Four Seasons who brought me to my room said maybe I should've used an alias, which seemed rash. Looked at two other rooms to switch to because I didn't like that the bathroom was so far from the bed, but wound up staying. My being a difficult hotel guest seems to be becoming a theme, which is great timing given that we're embarking on a tour. A bunch of the staff from *WWHL* came for the weekend and I took them to dinner at Liquid Art House, then to Club Café where I met the cutest boy—a Brazilian version of Andy Samberg, a twenty-eight-year-old PhD student at Harvard studying epidemiology. He is obviously very smart and he has only seen an occasional clip of my show online and has a peripheral knowledge of me, which is perfect. He is adorable—did I say that? He spent the night.

▶ SATURDAY, MARCH 21, 2015—BOSTON

As we were cuddling in bed this morning I asked #BrazilianAndySamberg what type of guy he is attracted to and he said his friends have come up with a term for it: "fattractive." "So, um, just how fat do you think I am?" I wondered as I held his smooth, taut, tight, incredibly perfect body. No, he said, he just likes a little bit extra to hold onto. Someone a little stocky. That I could handle. Liza arrived and we went to Faneuil Hall, where none of my old friends still worked! What the hell—it's only been twenty-five years since I stopped working at that pushcart! Liza couldn't find the peanut butter store either, so things weren't as either of us remembered, which is probably a good thing. We took advantage of the food court and had chowdah and pizza. I almost also got a hot dog but thankfully stopped myself even though I should've, given my new lover's interest in a little chub. We became obsessed with a twelve-year-old kid named Bradley Bartlett-Roche wailing on a saxophone—he also played piano—in the middle of the food court and watched him for twenty minutes. There was nothing he couldn't do! John Hill showed up and ripped us away from the kid and we walked to Beacon Hill. I remember getting out of the T stop at Park Street on my way to work at Faneuil Hall all those years ago thinking I was in the middle of a megalopolis, in the center of the world. Now that corner looks like a tame cozy little Olde Towne corner. We walked around Beacon Hill and it's still picturesque.

Went to sound check with Anderson and Ben and got pretty freaked out by the size of the Wang Theatre—yes, we're at the Wang; it's massive and beautiful. We have a road manager and badges and a promoter. We are on *tour*. Hilarious.

We went back to the hotel to nap but I couldn't sleep so John Hill brought his new teacup Yorkie, Linda(!), over for me to meet her. She is so cute but her breath is massively horrible, her teeth are a little fucked up, and she is wearing a diaper because she's bleeding a lot from her vagina. Among other things, it made me long for Wacha's bad, but not crippling, breath. Some lady called up to the room and said, "Did you get my CARDS?!" I said what are you talking about, and then realized it was the Jewish lady who left the envelope of photos. I said yes, and she demanded that I "come to the lobby so I can get a picture with you, and bring Anderson." I told her I was napping and we would be down in the lobby at seven-fifteen to go to the theater and she could get it then. People can be bossy! I went down to the lobby an hour later and forgot all about it until I saw Anderson with her. She'd called his room and told him to come down, that she was with me. He thought I knew her.

Got to the theater and the dressing room had Coke Zero for AC and Don Julio for me, buckets of ice, and grilled chicken. That was my rider. Anderson thinks the grilled chicken and *crudités* are excessive. We forgot to deal with makeup and so asked our stage manager(!) to get some. He and I were both nervous, pacing around our dressing room, and I made Anderson apply mine. It turned out it was either Kabuki makeup or they'd gotten it for AC's albino skin because I was *white*. The intro video played great; the crowd was riotous. I did an unintentional Valerie Cherish move when we were introduced—I thought AC hadn't gone out yet but he was waiting for me onstage so mine was kind of a delayed entrance, which can be considered a bid for applause. Our conversation was good and the audience was electric. The audience questions at the end were a little weird—how big is your dick ("I'm really happy with it"), will you do a shotski with me (we did), can we get selfies (not now), and lots of *Housewives* stuff—so we need to set ground rules next time, like no plugs or statements or pictures. We took two hundred pictures with VIPs after and I was really tired—thankfully AC was being a really gracious host to them while I kind of stood there. It was really nice being in a duo, something I'm totally unfamiliar with. He picked up the slack for me. We were both so concerned with people leaving feeling they'd gotten their money's worth that it wound up being a good balance of codependence. We changed in the car for the party at the W, which was another exercise in codependence—all my *WWHL* team plus random people I'd forgotten I'd invited. And then I regretted not inviting the Wasp and Jake and Angela to the party; I'd thought I was going to have to take care of them too much. We went to gay night at House of Blues, where Anthony had hooked us up with a special area. At some point a massive amount of confetti came down from the ceiling and I thought Liza was going to lose her mind. I have never seen her happier. #BrazilianAndySamberg came and we had another really fun night. He is *dreamy*.

▶ SUNDAY, MARCH 22, 2015—BOSTON—NYC

Woke up at eleven-fifteen and snuggled with #BAS again and it was so blissful, except that I had to poop terribly. I told him I had to run an envelope down to the lobby and instead went to the health club to take care of my business. We ordered great room service and I gave him the bottle of Jack the hotel had left me and the *Rebel Heart* CD a fan had brought, but he had nowhere to play the CD so he left it. I am so analog. Flew home to my sunny apartment, which still smells like paint. No dog. Lonely. I look at his crate and miss him. I have to work early tomorrow and am going to the *Mad Men* premiere, so it made more sense for him to stay in Brooklyn. Amanda and I enjoyed the first episode immensely and saw Jon Hamm (hair on fleek and I told him so), Christina Hendricks (she is strawberry blond), Elisabeth Moss (we talked about Hickey and Bravo stuff), John Slattery (showed me a pic of a passed kidney stone). At the party, Chris Noth asked me if I am straight. I said yes. Then I said that no, I am actually the gayest man in America. He said, "You're not *the* gayest man in America," and I said you're right and I am going home to fuck Amanda tonight. Then we talked about how NYC is dead because all the great stores and restaurants are closing, a perennial topic.

▶ MONDAY, MARCH 23, 2015

I woke up at six-thirty and finally texted Cher one last long plea for the radio show and never heard back. Shot the Snapple commercial in Brooklyn. It was me at a table in a French restaurant and the waiter and I bond over Snapple. It's national Puppy Day and all Wacha did was chase shadows. I looked it up and I think he needs more exercise and he has to be interrupted when chasing. I've been taking him to the vet just to get treats in order to desensitize him to the experience of going there. Today was the sixth time, and he was good. His tail was up and he not only took treats from the people there but he walked around the whole office. This may be working. Benjamin brought over this ventriloquist's dummy that an artist made of me; it's my evil Mini Me. Wacha initially thought it was a toy for him but now he is scared shitless of it. He goes in the other direction when I bring him out and flap his mouth. At the show tonight, Wacha was also not having Brandi. He just didn't care for her and rejected her advances. Mike, the porter from my old apartment building, was in the audience with his girlfriend and it was so good to see him.

▶ TUESDAY, MARCH 24, 2015

James Corden premiered last night—he's got two guests out there at the same time and a bar, which he called "the only bar in late night," and then they played a game in front of a green screen and as much as I want to get all puffed up and offended, the truth is there is no original idea anymore. We're all just ripping each other off. Carson was original. And Letterman.

We pretaped Sunday's show with RuPaul and Regina King and I did my first one-on-one for Radio Andy with Ru after the show. It was forty minutes of good conversation. We went right up to ten-forty, at which point I had to run in and do a live promo and go through elements for the live show, which was Kyle and Jerry O'Connell. Jerry hung out with me after the show; he's interested in a radio show, and then I made him come with me to my new building because I knew he, who grew up two blocks away in Chelsea, would flip when I showed him the apartment. He really did flip. The night elevator guy, Victor, plays jazz on his iPod. They're all so nice.

▶ WEDNESDAY, MARCH 25, 2015

Joe Giudice called because he has an idea for a cable channel with a friend of his. I said I would meet with him. I kept saying, "Are you sure it's a whole *channel*, and not a *show*?" It's a channel, he says. He said Teresa is doing really well, that the food is good and the place isn't so bad. She has a group of girlfriends, is working out three times a day, and has never looked better.

I always know a *Housewives* reunion is coming up because one of them threatens not to show up. I tried calling NeNe all day but she wouldn't return my call. The reunion is Friday and I hear that I spooked her when we spoke last month about it. We wound up emailing at the end of the day, and she said she is going to start the day at 100 because she is sick of the women who will do or say any damn thing. And here I was worried about her not participating. Went to the Polo restaurant (I love a scene, and it is one) with the Perskys and John Hill. Walked in and saw Ralph. I asked him if my tie was wearing me or if I was wearing the tie and he said, "You actually have a way bigger problem than that." I stammered and pled for an explanation and he implied that something was really wrong with me, and then he walked away and I was paranoid all through dinner. Bette-Ann Gwathmey said if you ask Ralph his opinion he is going to give you an honest answer. My theory is that he saw me interviewing someone disgusting on TV, or being a little vulgar, and was repulsed. He said something to the effect of it having to do with where I come from. So maybe I am disgracing my sweet hometown roots? People were coming up to the table all night and leaving business cards. Came home and FaceTimed with sweet #BrazilianAndySamberg.

▶ THURSDAY, MARCH 26, 2015—NYC—ATLANTA

Woke up and did extra snuggles with Wacha because I knew it was my last morning with him for twelve days. Even though I am coming back to town for twenty-four hours on Sunday, the logistics don't work for him to come back to me. By the time I started packing I think he got the drift that I was leaving. And it was like he knew I was getting out my Brazil clothes, which means I'm going extra far. He was hanging his head low. It was too much. Got an email from NeNe first thing, saying, "I hope the girls give you a good reunion," so that tells me that she is deciding to sit this one out. I'm not actually sure why. She's mad, is all I know. It's all a bit frustrating. Nick Cannon reached out about producing a show for Amber Rose together. I am interested. He thinks we are a power duo and I agree! My knee is hurting me, so that Melbourne Housewife was right. Got to Atlanta and met with Steven Weinstock and the producers and tinkered with seating. Oh, and NeNe is back in, so call the Associated Press. Went to dinner with Lindsay at Superica, which is at some very hipster-y market kind of place. He kept saying it was like Brooklyn but they have valets and a parking lot, which didn't seem like Brooklyn. On the other hand, there *was* artisanal stuff everywhere, custom haircuts, and bubbly water in some of the public taps, so I get his drift. Then we went to Blake's on the Park and an older drag queen did a dance to "Upside Down" in honor of Diana Ross's birthday, which made me happy enough to tip her a twenty, which she didn't look at and then I got upset because I didn't get the credit for giving her such a good tip. Walked home happy and buzzed.

▷ FRIDAY, MARCH 27, 2015—ATLANTA

Showed up at 10:00 a.m. and the divas didn't get to set until around noon. I lost my wits. NeNe kept saying before the reunion, "I am here in peace; I know that everything is my fault"—being sarcastic. So I figured she was going to just be quiet the whole time until she popped off. It wound up being a really non-ratchet, thoughtful reunion and NeNe was engaged and present the whole time. Around 9:00 p.m. she broke down in hysterics about her mother abandoning her, which was a dramatic and interesting turn because she had earlier refused to apologize to Claudia for calling her a "half-breed." I finally did get her to apologize to the viewers, though halfheartedly. She was a little "I SAID what I SAID."

▷ SATURDAY, MARCH 28, 2015—ATLANTA—ST. LOUIS

Stopped in St. Louis for one night for Uncle Stanley's birthday. All the talk is about Jeremy's college applications and where he will go. On another note, Mom is convinced that I *must* call Ralph Lauren to find out what he meant the other night when he said I have deeper problems than my tie. Went over to Em's, where it was more college talk and I got to see Abby. Mom and Dad modeled clothes they plan to wear to the amfAR event at which I'm being honored in June; both were their outfits from Em's wedding ten years ago. I think Dad might need a new tux, but Mom's knit was just fine. I told Dad I will get him a new tux and Mom said, "Maybe THAT will be his BOX SUIT." Macabre. To retaliate, I told her—lying—that JLo is presenting me the award and that amfAR wanted *her* to come up and accept "to be funny," which sent her into a complete tailspin. "Be FUNNY?! What does that MEAN!? With JLO!? GET ME OUT OF THIS!" I quickly told her I was kidding. She was mad and relieved, not in that order. Uncle Stanley's seventy-fifth birthday party was really nice. I got up and spoke about the importance of his stewardship of Allen Foods, how the company had been a bond that kept us together. I was glad I was there. Met Kari for a drink at Remy's, which is an incredibly depressing place. Then home, where Mom and Dad were watching *House of Cards* and when they paused it their photos came up in a slide show on Apple TV. "This is good for OUR BRAINS!" Mom cheered, trying to identify the origin of photos taken at outdoor markets from their various travels around the world. "That's VIETNAM. No, THAT'S Vietnam! Those are those HORRIBLE people from that boat in the Galapagos! That's that WOMAN with the BOOBS from China!" After twenty minutes I went to bed, at eleven-fifteen.

▶ SUNDAY, MARCH 29, 2015—ST. LOUIS—NYC

Back in town for one night for SJP's birthday party. Rehearsed "You're Never Fully Dressed Without a Smile" several times and just knew I was going to mess up the words even though I knew them by heart. The idea of all of us singing the score from *Annie* in front of Annie herself was making me nervous. Walked over to Sedaris's in my sharp David Hart suit, singing the song loudly and making something of a spectacle of myself. Amy and I caught up on the cab ride to the Carlyle; she said she would rather do a radio show where she wasn't the host. I just want her to do a show called *What's Your Problem?* and have people call in and talk about problems. The cocktails were in Bemelmans Bar and I knew I'd be on edge until we had to sing, which was still two and a half hours away. I sat with Amy, the

Rifkins, and Hickey, with SJP and Matthew on the farther end of the table. Congratulated George Stephanopoulos on a great job lambasting that idiot Governor Pence, from Indiana, about his discriminatory religious freedom law. Straight ally! Hickey, Rifkin, Sedaris, Lisa Leguillou, and Anthony Borelli started the entertainment as orphans singing "It's the Hard-Knock Life." I sang my song with a lot of patter in advance of it and I was nervous in front of that crowd. I fucked up the words, just as I thought I would, but it seemed like it was well received. Victor Garber sang the beautiful "Daddy" Warbucks song. Matthew did "Little Girls," which was funny given all the little girls in his house. James Wilkie broke our hearts and made us *sob* singing "Maybe" directly to his mama. The finale was Marc and Scott leading us in "N.Y.C.," which had been rewritten as "SJP" with special words. For someone so comfortable being the center of attention as an actress, SJP is bashful about being the center of praise. Of course we dragged her onstage to finish it off with "Tomorrow," which became a sing-along. Then Matthew got up and sang her a love song about New York City (called "Manhattan") that they once saw Bobby Short do in that very room, and it was so pure and lovely and romantic. I sobbed. If every woman could have her husband sing to her once in her life the way Matthew did that night, looking right at her the whole time, their hearts would burst.

I was so happy to be done with my song that I gobbled up a pot lollipop and went hard-core into the after event in Bemelmans. At some point late in the night the Carlyle guard said they'd just turned away NeNe Leakes, who I called and told to come back. I got her seated in the corner and had the waiter get her drinks. James Wilkie said, "I have never been more nervous to meet anyone in my life!"—he was hilarious. Nathan Turner and Prabal Gurung paid their respects too. People like a surprising late-night guest. We decided to go to Bruce and Bryan's after the party and I only lasted about a half hour before telling them all I had to go. I was overserved. Kissed SJP and Boz goodnight and ended a truly magical New York City night.

▶ MONDAY, MARCH 30, 2015—NYC—BRAZIL

Woke up with a crushing hangover, *not* in the mood to spend the day at the D&D Building looking at fabric swatches or the night on a flight to São Paulo, but such are the perils of being an upwardly mobile gay man. Walking into the D & D I felt like there was no way I was going to be able to isolate what I liked, but it's funny, when you do connect with something you just know it. Finding a bunch of fabrics and wallpaper that I loved made me excited for the new place. Eric and I started at the top, Floor 17 I think, and walked through each floor until joyously hitting the bottom, where I was thrilled to hop in a cab and go to the old building. Surfin misses me very much but the ritual of my opening my packages in front of him when I go home is a new bonding time for us. They haven't even begun demolition and I've been out for a month. The board has new questions about the floor above the staircase. I am just so relieved to be moved and happy on Fifteenth Street, I don't care. I left word for Ralph Lauren, hoping he'd call back to explain what he meant the other night. The assistant sounded like he would be calling back. Also Daryn said Dan Rather was trying to reach me, so I'm not sure what that's about. I wore a full track suit on the plane and tweeted a pic of Missy Elliott as my spirit animal. Drank a bunch of white wine, took an Ambien, and dissolved into the sky.

▶ TUESDAY, MARCH 31, 2015— SUNDAY, APRIL 5, 2015—TRANCOSO, BRAZIL

Got a solid seven and a half hours sleep on the plane and had a nice breakfast answering the questions from various flight attendants about what we were doing with the Jersey Housewives with the same answer: "I don't know." Got to São Paulo and was quite bored during my layover. Instagram Directed #BritActor trying to get him to flirt with me, which he kind of does but is withholding so not really. The snack on the flight to Porto Seguro was toasty biscuits flavored like ham. I almost puked. It's a long journey to make alone—a connecting flight and then a ninety-minute drive with a Brazilian driver for whom I DJed Madonna the whole time. We kept repeating "Madonna!" to each other until I got to Anderson and Ben in one piece.

The trip was great and upon returning, I realize that it taught me several important lessons.

1) The importance of mosquito nets! This lesson began on the first night while crashing at Anderson and Ben's, when I noticed some bats and I

don't know what else flying above my bed. I felt absolutely secure in my netwomb, though!

2) My thoughts on the importance of good hair were reaffirmed by a family we kept seeing with three Jewish brothers with outdated hair. I wanted very much to tell them that their hair should be revisited. They bonded with a British gay couple that also had out-of-date hair, so I guess they had something in common. The better-looking of the Brits whipped out his selfie stick on the beach and even brought it on a horseback ride, which made me want to throw my phone away, which leads me to . . .

3) Selfie sticks are appropriate nowhere, especially the beach.

4) Don't reuse pranks. Mom texted me on April Fool's Day and said the Cardinals traded Michael Wacha. I said, "You did that exact prank last April Fool's!"

5) Resort staff are not your best friends. I pondered the relationship between beach waiter and hotel guest when the guy at the beach remembered me from last year and we had a very sweet reunion. You feel such a bond with someone when you spend six days having fun at their disposal, and then you leave and you feel weepy about being separated. When you reunite it's like you're old friends, but your relationship quickly devolves back into you making them get you rosé.

6) If you hang out in the middle of Brazil for too long you stop dressing like an American. I had sushi with our friends in Trancoso and their crew. The expat was wearing Phyllis Lindstrom hair and baggy Brazilian clothes topped off by a Safari Countess LuAnn statement necklace. He was with a gorgeous nineteen-year-old Brazilian boy who seems to be his boyfriend.

7) Oh, and when you live in Brazil, having a super-young Brazilian boyfriend of ambiguous sexuality becomes totally normal.

▶ MONDAY, APRIL 6, 2015—TRANCOSO, BRAZIL—NYC

I was dreading the journey home alone but it wound up being kind of great. The same guy drove me the ninety minutes from the Uxua to Porto Seguro and once again I DJed Madonna the whole way and he kept saying "Ma-don-na," which is something I love hearing foreigners say. Basically it was a carbon copy of the trip there, but with a tan. On the way onto the plane the woman in front of me, a Brazilian, said she watches my stuff online and just read my book, so that was a shock. I made short work of a five-hour delay at the São Paulo airport in front of the gorgeous new Terminal 3 watching *Empire*. It is delicious. Terrence Howard is a drag queen, all the white people are dumb, and it's very gay—so what's not to like? Landed in NYC fresh as a daisy at six-thirty. Today construction was supposed to begin at the old apartment, and didn't. Why should it!? The show was Elisabeth Moss and John Slattery. Someone asked him when his pubes went gray and he didn't seem that psyched.

▶ TUESDAY, APRIL 7, 2015

I am definitely fat again. I can barely look at my face. And I have aged. It is what it is. I was on Skype with Mom today and ravenously opened a bag of Doritos. I put a handful on a plate and was sucking them and Mom said, "WHEN are you going to STOP!?"

Stopped by the *RHONY* premiere party. I'm trying to get LuAnn to record another song. Went up to Ramona to prep her for the evening on *WWHL* and let her know that she may not be sitting next to me. She interrupted me. "I don't *care* about seating, I don't *care*." It's the new Ramona! Pretaped Scott Eastwood, who revealed that Ashton Kutcher slept with his girlfriend and that's the girl that broke up him and Demi. That was a massive bombshell that he just handed to me on a platter. I felt like I was leering at him because he's so handsome. I got a tweet at the end of the night from a woman who said I need to whiten my teeth and she is absolutely right! I have been thinking to myself the yellow teeth are adding to my fat, old grossness. I came home and watched the last part of the Sinatra doc with teeth-whitening stuff slathered on before bed.

▶ WEDNESDAY, APRIL 8, 2015

Wacha got fat-shamed on Instagram! I posted a picture of him lying on the Edward Fields rug asking if he clashed with the pattern and a bunch of people commented on how fat he looks. And he *is* fat again. Like me. Lunch with my Holt team, who say they don't want another diary even though I'm still keeping one. They said maybe a YA book about being different. Cher texted me a pic of her at the São Paulo airport, all in black, bangs, with a shitload of luggage. I said this is the amount of luggage I expect from Cher abroad. Sandra and Lorraine Bracco were on the show and Sandy was on fire. I tried to fan the flames of what I see as the injustice of Letterman not wanting her on the show anymore, hoping it'll get her booked before he goes. It won't happen. Brandon McMillan was the bartender; he's a dog trainer specializing in rescue dogs and is gonna work with Wacha. He is very hot but very straightforward.

❧ THURSDAY, APRIL 9, 2015

Good workout with Ninja without taking any iPhone breaks, which seems basic but is somewhat revolutionary and indicative of my wanting to change my body. Let us all pray. Went to Bravo and worked on cleaning out my emails, which are being purged beyond three months. Kept a bunch of *Housewives* nonsense and every email from Mom and Dad. You don't like to think of your parents' mortality but I do all the time. I get a voicemail and wonder if it will be the last one I'll ever get, so I keep it. I have a backlog of mundane voicemails from Mom and Dad now. Did press with Anderson for our Miami date, which for some reason is selling sluggishly, and brought Daryn to a meeting at Sirius for the channel. We came up with some good stuff. Took the subway home for the first time in—I'm too afraid to admit how long it's been, but long enough that I'd forgotten that it's the most effective way to get around the city. It took ten minutes total to get home from midtown during rush hour. And there are hot straight guys everywhere underground. Had a playdate on the terrace with Ricky and Allison's dog, Moxie, which was a raging success although Moxie doesn't really know how to drink without spilling everywhere. But Moxie *is* adorable, and the dogs were all over each other. Dinner with Amanda at El Quijote was really nice, and relaxing. Then I FaceTimed with #BAS and had a fantastic massage from Adam and I made lists in my head.

The Scott Eastwood story is *everywhere*. Watch, he'll become a huge star and never do the show again. Great workout—three this week, and I added one tomorrow. Stopped by the apartment, where they started demolition yesterday, and *holy shit*: There's not a wall to be found in the twelfth-floor apartment, except crumbled on the floor. The walls were on the floors! They say that is the quickest thing and everything else takes forever.

The very hot dog trainer who bartended the other night, Brandon, came over to try to provoke Wacha into biting him to see how dangerous he is. The bad news is that he was so riled up he was barking and snarling in his crate like a wild wolf for forty-five minutes; the good news is that it was apparently fear-based. We got rid of the crate after he left. No more crate, which seemed to be a common denominator in a few of the biting incidents. Brandon said Wacha was definitely abused in his former life, and this isn't a surprise to me given how he flinches when I open cabinets quickly or when he sees an umbrella. Who would hurt my sweet dog? The thought sends chills.

I dropped my phone and it broke. I was going down the elevator, en route to the Apple Store and told the operator—the chattiest one, Richie—and he redirected me to Fourteenth and Seventh, where this Asian dude in some store I never noticed fixed it in one hour. It was monumental! Had dinner at the Polo Bar with SJP, Alison Benson, and Jill Matson and crew. Sonja Morgan appeared, to the delight of everyone, and she was hilarious. They asked her what was in her purse and she showed us at the table. No lipstick, they all marveled, and she said, "A gay packed my purse today." She doesn't disappoint. Jill was giving her advice about where to sell her jewelry collection, until she left and I told Jill I wasn't sure if she actually had one, and to watch the show a little closer. Still no callback from Ralph Lauren, by the way. That phone tag seems dead, and Mom asks about it every time we speak. She wants to get to the bottom of it! Wacha seemed fine without the crate.

SATURDAY, APRIL 11, 2015

Bruce says that if you take your iPhone to the Apple Store after a random Asian dude on Fourteenth Street has fixed it, they know it's been touched and won't go near it themselves. So I feel like my phone has a disease or something. Boxed seven rounds with the Ninj today, and I never work out on a Saturday. Brandon the hot trainer came back and we worked on "heel" and "stay." The truth is that as hot as Brandon is, he only talks about dogs—which *is* all I want to talk to him about but I do also maybe want to flirt or find out who he is fucking. Took an Uber to Bar Italia on the Upper East Side to meet Mark and Kelly and it took fifty minutes—crazy traffic, and I was a backseat driver the whole way. At least I had my vape. I got out of his car and the guy behind us was honking like nuts because we stopped and I started yelling at the guy but he rolled down his window and then threatened me and he looked like he could beat the crap out of me so I backed down and stormed into the restaurant, where they claimed not to know anything about a Consuelos party and I realized I was in the wrong place. Dinner, when I finally located it, was a lot of laughs; Rachael Harris joined too, and then I split to meet Billy Eichner at ASC, and then we went to Industry. Gay, gay, gay, gay.

SUNDAY, APRIL 12, 2015

I guess the guy who wanted to make me pasta all those months ago was at ASC and was texting me late last night after I'd passed out. He has been trying to cook me a pasta dinner for months and I have been blowing him off, so this morning he took matters into his own hands and sent me a pic of him in his underwear—and then, when I took the bait, a pic of his ass, then a pic of his dick. I felt kind of bad for him for objectifying himself when he is a nice, quality person but this is the time we live in. It made me a little sad. But it did make me want to finally see him, so I think he did the right thing. Maybe not with pasta, though. Met John Hill at Bubby's and talked ideas for his radio show. Took him to see the construction on my dream apartment, then went home and ordered outdoor furniture for my other dream apartment. Brandon came over and realized that Wacha had been severely beaten with a rope or leash in his past life. He recoils dramatically if you hold the leash up a certain way.

The show was on early and it was Porsha and Phaedra, who decided her business was personal and was reading all the callers to filth. The control room was abuzz because Deirdre adopted Linda, John Hill's teacup Yorkie with horrible teeth and breath issues who was in a diaper menstruating when I met her last month. Thankfully, Deirdre got her teeth fixed (pulled, I think) and Linda's not bleeding from the vagina anymore, so it's a real Hope Over Heartbreak story. We should consider pitching it to Lifetime. *Mad Men* was slow and kinda boring. But also good. Doesn't that describe every episode?

▶ MONDAY, APRIL 13, 2015

I downloaded the ethnically diverse emojis today. And my phone is completely freaked out. It is diseased. It's doing crazy things. Not because of the ethnically diverse emojis, but because I had it fixed by the Asian on Fourteenth Street, as Bruce predicted. Went to Padma's Blossom Ball and talked with Gail Simmons, met a cute doctor, and sat between Padma and Norman Reedus. Told Norman that Wacha's original name was Norman Reedus, and Norman wants me to change it back. Went to *WWHL*, which was the *Botched* guys, who refused to really weigh in on any celebrity plastic surgery so that was kinda boring. Heather said Vicki is "done" if this cancer thing turns out to be not true. Came home and watched SJP saying goodbye on *Letterman*. She was perfect and it is amazing to see how unsentimental he is.

▶ TUESDAY, APRIL 14, 2015

Haven't had a drink in a few days and woke up feeling even worse than if I had. Hmmm. My delivery guys charged me seven hundred dollars to transport the couch that Mark and Kelly lent me for the terrace, and maybe that's the cost of a new couch. Worked out. Weighed myself for the first time since last October—170.8. The Ninj and I were excited. Went up to Ralph Lauren for a fitting for the Met Ball and Travis had picked out a

Purple Label midnight-blue tuxedo, so that was easy. SJP is getting a red corsage of some kind made to complement her dress. The theme is Asian something—Chinese Whispers? She is wearing a huge headdress.

Came home and interviewed Sean Avery and Hilary Rhoda for *Hamptons* magazine by phone. Sean was twelve minutes late and I yelled at him. I was bitchy as fuck! Brandon came over and we worked on a complicated "stay"—throwing food all around Wacha and getting him to stay there and not go for it. He was decent at it. Showered and went to a night of parties— first stop was Hunter Hill's *BlackBook* party, where I saw Veronica Webb for the first time in years. She was telling me Grac's ACL surgery must've gone great because she didn't hear otherwise, and I got territorial. Then to the *Vanity Fair* Tribeca Film Festival party on the terrace of the courthouse downtown, which was lit up beautifully. Talked to John McEnroe (again wearing Björn Borg undies), Caryn Zucker, Gayle King (about *RHOA*), and Julie Chen, who gave me some unprintable gossip. Then to the show, which was Bethenny and Isaac Mizrahi. She did an off-the-cuff reverse one-on-one with me about the Housewives after the show that was supposed to be for the web but I think we can air it. Got home and immediately took Wacha out around the block and met a big fat cop from the Chelsea precinct coming out of—wait for it—the Donut Pub! His wife loves me and I said to come to the show and he will definitely get laid that night. I get guys laid, I told him. Then I walked away thinking, "Who the fuck do I think I am?" Wacha wouldn't poop on the walk and I got home and found out why— he'd gone in three spots on the rug in my room, so I did what Brandon said and tied his leash to a piece of stone I took from the construction site and made him sit next to the poo for half an hour. He did not like it one bit. Brandon said to keep doing that every time he shits in the house and he will stop. They don't like to be near the poo. Who does?

▶ WEDNESDAY, APRIL 15, 2015

This was a nutty day. Walked Wacha for an hour, stopped by the apartment construction, went to the bank, hit the Apple Store and got a brand-new iPhone because the other one has a life of its own and it's typing gibberish. Worked out with the Ninja. Came home and Wacha had pooped again in the bedroom! Same spot! I was so pissed and he seemed really ashamed, looking at me with his big eyes. He knew I was mad at him, but I didn't get crazy and he sat tethered by it. We got to *WWHL* for the taping with Suzanne Somers and Reba McEntire, who I interviewed for Radio Andy and asked how crazy the Judds are (she paused and said they are "colorful" and then "very smart"—which means "nuts" to me), whether she thinks Carl Dean exists (she said it's been a big topic of discussion over the years in Nashville) and about the plane crash that killed her road manager and eight band members ("Dolly was the first one on the phone, offering me her band"). I love country kinship!

Joe Giudice came in for a meeting with his lawyer. He tells me Teresa's prison is barely a prison and it's no big deal. He and the lawyer showed me a pic of Teresa and the family taken in the jail by *Us Weekly* where Teresa's hair is straightened and she looks exactly like a Housewife; they ran one with curly hair in the magazine because she looks more like a prisoner. He has an idea for a beverage channel and I don't know what to do with that. Went home and watched cuts of *RHONY* and *RHOA* on the terrace while drinking tea. It was so lovely. FaceTimed with #BrazilianAndySamberg, who is really easy to talk to. Walked the dog and saw a gorgeous male model who was sitting in Starbucks—we locked eyes and he came out to tell me he was going to be on my show that night, shirtless, for our game. He is a beauty, tall and blond and fresh off the boat—his second day in NYC. I started giving him advice about New York, realized he hadn't asked, and walked away. Dinner with John Mayer at Nobu. We very spontaneously decided to take his EarthRoamer from LA to Santa Rosa for the Dead shows at the end of June—how *fun* will that be? By the time I got to the show I felt like I'd lived three lives in one day. I picked a Jackhole that made fun of how slow the subways are after a guy was found dead on the subway and I said the L train made him twenty minutes late for heaven. Deirdre, John Jude, and Melissa all hated the joke but I thought it was funny and told it anyway. No one laughed. Actually, a few people groaned and gasped.

⯈ THURSDAY, APRIL 16, 2015—NYC—MIAMI

Woke up and had tea on the terrace. Feeling grateful for my blessed life, my health, New York City, the dog, my terrace, getting to travel on someone else's dime, and a great room in Miami waiting for me two days in advance of my show with Anderson. I do not want for anything. Watched two cuts of *RHONY* on the plane while the flight attendant said we were having "light to dangerous turbulence" and not to go into the aisles because we would get hurt. Got to Miami and had a half hour by the pool before I did two local news interviews promoting our appearance (we still have some tickets to sell), then back to the pool for twenty minutes in the sun and then up to get a massage. The massage therapist was stuck in traffic and almost an hour late, which was a first for me. You don't think about the massage therapist getting to the massage; they're just *there*. It was great until the very end, when he had me open my eyes so he could *give me a high five. On the table.* It was really weird. Oh, I spoke to Jake in Boston today. He and Angela are actually going to be in New York City Sunday night and coming to *WWHL*. I started to wonder all over again if I was going to lose my virginity.

⮞ SATURDAY, APRIL 18, 2015—MIAMI

Anderson arrived and I told him to meet me at the pool, which he eyeballed for ten seconds and decided he hated, which wasn't a surprise. We had lunch on the porch and by the time I got back to the pool—Anderson went to nap, natch—it was an endless parade of people who are coming to the show tonight sending me rosé after rosé. I didn't drink any, of course. *I don't drink.* I realized in the bathroom that my body is looking good again, and that's a good thing because I got papp'd out on the beach. I felt okay about it but then this woman ran up to me like a lunatic and hurled herself at me, saying, "Who are you?" Eventually I pushed her away and said, "No one." I realized twenty minutes later by the pool that now there are pictures of me pushing a girl on the beach.

Went to the Jackie Gleason Theater with Anderson for a sound check and they couldn't wait to show us Gleason's dressing room, which didn't seem like much of anything beyond a leather couch warehouse. Some people came backstage before the show—Cousin Dave and his friends and the nice guy from Phish, who brought me a joint from Vermont and was surprised when I said I would fly back with it. They're not looking for pot, I said. Anderson and I did a shot before the show as we waited, bored, in that leather showroom. He's not a drinker so I considered it something of a victory. The show was great, much tighter than in Boston. Our chemistry was really good and the audience seemed into it—except for the two Waspy ladies sitting directly in front of us, who did not crack a smile. I keep meaning to ask Anderson if he noticed them. There were many, many toupées at the meet and greet—bad ones, which sounds redundant—and very interesting, eclectic fashion. Went to House, which was really fun—a big, brand-new, highly air-conditioned club. I kept bringing different boys up to the VIP area and Anderson and company were rejecting them, saying my taste was really warped.

▶ MONDAY, APRIL 20, 2015—NYC

I'm still a virgin. Jake and Angela were at the show last night and we all hung out and had many drinks together, but I think we talked about it too much. The magic was gone somehow. Rainy day and not much happened. The table for the terrace arrived from Crate and Barrel at 8:00 a.m., then I went back to bed until 10:45 and lay around. Recounted the tale of last night with Jake and Angela to Kelly, who is fascinated by my thrupple. I emailed Anderson to see if he'd seen the Waspy ladies in front of us. He said he too saw no one else in the audience *but* the Waspy ladies. So we were both doing the show for two people who weren't enjoying it much. Mike Robley, the saintly production assistant on *WWHL*, got me a better cinder block to tether Wacha to in case of an indoor poop. It's his twenty-third birthday and he said he felt old.

▶ TUESDAY, APRIL 21, 2015

Sluggish workout at the gym. On the way home I ran into one of my camera men on Fifteenth Street and I said WTF are you doing on this shady block; you must be going to have an affair. He said he actually was indeed on his way to see a lady friend. We laughed and went our separate ways. He texted me later in disbelief about my ESP. I said there's no reason for *anyone* to be on that block who isn't up to no good. Went out again to a Holt meeting, where they want me to do a YA book about coming out. My concern is that I already told the story in *Most Talkative* and also that

I will put stuff in there that my family won't want to read. Came home and Wacha had pooped on the rug in the bedroom so I tied him to the cinder block as instructed for a half hour. He seemed humbled for sure. He was crying in the room. He never cries. I hope it works.

Mo'Nique was on the show and for some reason the staff was terrified of her. I went into her dressing room to butter her up but she was already so touched we had Mo'Nique cupcakes in her room (we give our guests personalized cupcakes and they flip over them). I told her we have been giving our guests cupcakes with her face on them for many years and we were so excited to finally give them to her. She looked at me in utter disbelief before I broke the news that I was kidding. She said I am so shady, but she knows I am a twelve-year-old boy inside. So at least she understands me.

▶ WEDNESDAY, APRIL 22, 2015

I am in a complete pickle with Tori Spelling. Twice on the show I've made fun of her burning herself on a hibachi at Benihana. It seemed so stupid— and funny. The first time was blatant—I said they added chicken caccia-TORI to their menu—but she apparently also caught my second reference and was pissed and sent me an email. To be honest, I started reading the email, saw I was in big trouble with her, and barely read it all the way through because I hate being in trouble and wanted to get out of it in the time it would've taken me to finish the email. The gist of the email was that she always liked me but that her heart sank when she saw me say, ". . . drink until you fall into the hibachi grill at Benihana. I haven't stopped laughing about that." She said she was in the burn unit of the hospital for two weeks and had to have two major surgeries, and the burn on her right arm was down to her bone and on and on and on about the surgeries and the pain. I flashed back to her Ebola scare the week her series premiered a few months ago and wondered where on the scale of reality this information fell, but I felt horrible for hurting her feelings. Like I said, I barely read the e-mail, though I *thought* she'd said that among her calamities, she hadn't been able to eat since this happened. I sent back an email profusely apologizing, referencing a pic she posted on her Instagram the day of the burn, saying besides the burn it looks like you had a great day and that her husband had commented somewhere that the burn was small so we assumed it wasn't serious and if I thought it was I wouldn't have joked about it. I ended by saying, "EAT SOMETHING!" But I guess that was exactly the wrong thing to say because I immediately got a horrified email back asking what I meant by that, and why I was insulting her weight, and that she used to love me and I should find out the details before making jokes and that she will never be able to use her arm again. I looked at the original email and there was no mention of eating. Whoops. So not only did I skinny-shame her out of nowhere, she will *never be able to use her arm again* and it was time for some serious backtracking. I said that I had totally misread her email and I wouldn't have joked about it if I thought it was serious. She said "OK." I have a bad feeling about this. And I feel terrible that I was making fun of her and she will never be able to use her arm again.

I took a nap at the end of the day and woke up at 8:00 p.m. to a text that Hayden Panettiere is puking and cancelled being on the show. I texted Jerry O'Connell, who came through in a big way—with Lori Loughlin—and it was a great one. We reenacted *Full House* and I played Michelle and the team thought I thought she was mentally challenged. Amy Sedaris came and hung out after and I might've convinced her to do a six-week trial run on the radio. We did my first Periscope together.

▶ FRIDAY, APRIL 24, 2015

I am starting to learn the elevator guys' names—the cute daytime one is David. The night guy is either Victor or Vincent, and one of them has a son also named either Victor or Vincent. I don't know. Got an email from Ashley Olsen saying my Michelle was perfect. Went to Brooklyn and hung with John Hill. #BrazilianAndySamberg is in town and came over with friends. Went to Eastern Bloc and met Anderson and Ben. Darren, the DJ, asked for a request and I said, Diana Ross? And he said, "Oh, these kids won't know what to do with that." So he said he would play more Madonna for me. And #BrazilianAndySamberg made fun of me for tying my jacket around my waist; I guess that's an old-folk thing to do. Got home and Wacha had pooped on the carpet so he was tied to the cinder block while we ate. We went to the Donut Pub on Fourteenth Street, which was divine!

SATURDAY, APRIL 25, 2015

SJP says that donut place is a national treasure and should be on the register of historic places. How have I lived so close to it for so long and never even noticed it? Went out with #BAS and again had a blast with him although I was feeling sick when we were almost home, so I sent him back to the donut shop and nearly puked on the street but got stopped to take selfies twice just as I was about to get sick. I can only imagine what those pictures look like. And Wacha wouldn't shit on his last walk with me so I came home to his poop inside. I tethered him to the cinder block for a half hour. Is it safe to say this is not working?

MONDAY, APRIL 27, 2015

I heard from Ralph Lauren this morning. He said he's a big fan of mine and he thinks I dress great but he thinks he upset me the other night. I said, "No, you didn't upset me. I thought you had something to say, and I want to hear it because I respect your opinion!" What he said is that he thinks I am dressing too flamboyantly—too brightly—but that it's nothing serious and that he is here to help if I want it. I hung up feeling like he was being nice and letting me off the hook and that he actually had something worse to say. Took Wacha on a walk and he never shit and later I went on the terrace and saw he'd shit out there, so that was a big victory and I took him out there and treated him. Then at the end of the day he shit inside. Again. He knew I was gonna tie him there so he went in the closet where the crate is stored. I called Brandon in LA and he said it could be ten to fifteen times before he stops. He said to take the shit on the terrace after his tethering and leave it out there and treat him next to it so he gets the message that it's okay to shit out there. This is all exhausting emotionally; Wacha looks up at me with those sad eyes and I know he is trying to exert some control.

Dad texted from Mendocino, California, where they are for two weeks:

DAD: Saw Kenya's picture on Ma's phone. Really nice set!!!
ME: Of boobs??
DAD: Yes of course. What else would it be?

Me: I didn't know if you meant the set for the reunion.

Dad: Anyway, she has a rack.

Me: She sure does! They are real.

Dad: That would have been my next question.

Walked the dog and took him to the show for Cynthia Nixon and Nicolle Wallace, which I thought might be terrible but was really good. Live was Asa from *Shahs*, Shep from *Southern Charm*, and three Melbourne House-wives who were grateful and excited to even be behind the bar so I liked them. Came home and puttered on the terrace looking out at the city, feeling like a king.

❧ WEDNESDAY, APRIL 29, 2015

Before the show I went to a birthday dinner for Jane Buffett at their apartment in the sky. Had a long chat at dinner with Steve Kroft, who thought I wrote for *Time* magazine, and I said he had me confused with another Jew. Maybe Joel Stein? Fran Lebowitz was a few people over and I just keep my head down around her. Barney Frank and Bob Harper were on the show. Barney was a combo of great and very curmudgeonly. I loved him, and of course the after show wound up being better than the show itself, unfortunately. Jimmy is out of *Match Game* and without him producing it, I don't know where that leaves us. Nowhere, I think.

❧ THURSDAY, APRIL 30, 2015

Wacha shit on the terrace. You would've thought he *built* the terrace—I brought him out to the shit and gave him a ton of treats in front of it. He didn't know what the fuck was up.

Taped a show at noon today with Helen Hunt and Candice Bergen, both of whom I always think of as ice queens. But the truth is that Helen Hunt just seems awkward to me, not icy, and Candice, whom I'd previously dealt with at the height of *Murphy Brown* when she was a thin, icy superstar, was so happy I'd read her book—which I very proudly announced to her in her dressing room, like a peacock—that she was warm and fuzzy and quite

182

possibly cuddly. You can't imagine how much I carried on about the book because hosts, me included, *never* read the book. And I'd only read half, and skimmed it really, but she didn't need to know that. I referred to various minutiae five times on the show to prove to the world that I had really studied the damn thing. I asked Helen what motivated her to write and direct her own movie and she said, "Sometimes you gotta make things happen for yourself," and I asked if she had seen the Amy Schumer sketch about how when you turn forty you're unfuckable in Hollywood and she said, "Are you saying I'm unfuckable?" That got real awkward, real fast.

I met Sarah Silverman at my apartment at three-thirty. We'd had a date on the books for about a month and my big plan was to pitch her on doing a daily show on Radio Andy. I've been kind of putting off committing to anyone else or booking anyone for the channel because of this big Hail Mary meeting, which started as I thought it would—with us getting high on the terrace, where we stayed for a couple hours going from tangent to tangent about everything, like discussing how Candy Bergen looks like Sharon Gless and then trying to figure out who is older, a fact which we ultimately googled to discover Sharon is two years older. Then we got further into it and started looking into the ages of everyone from Goldie to Helen Hunt. Finally we decided to take a stroll with the dog and wound up on Thirteenth Street in front of the gay center, where Sarah suggested we rap with the kids a little bit and find out what's on their minds. So we had a little rap session with five kids, one with a guitar. One asked if he could pet Wacha because it had been a long time since he'd had any contact with an animal, which broke my heart a little. He was loving on the dog, and Wacha let him. In the final moment of the third hour of our hangout I sat her down in that park on Bleecker and Sixth Avenue and proceeded to give the weakest, most half-assed pitch for radio. The answer was no. She has too much going on. It was the lamest pitch ever. Persky dinner on the Upper East Side with Bill's famous meatloaf. Mark and Kelly came for dessert but I had to split for a massage.

‣ FRIDAY, MAY 1, 2015–SUNDAY, MAY 3, 2015–SAG HARBOR

First time out east since October, and the house looked great and it felt like a crime to have left it empty all these months. What was I doing that was so important? Slept a lot and Jimmy gave me a ride home on a chopper. Wacha was really well behaved, probably because he was so happy about spending the weekend out at the beach sniffing stuff, doing what dogs do. He didn't poop in the house all weekend!

‣ MONDAY, MAY 4, 2015

Reese Witherspoon and Sofía Vergara were on the show and we really watered down Plead the Fifth, to the point where we shouldn't have done it. It was a bunch of softballs to RW and even those were stressing her out. I interviewed NeNe and she and I kind of got into it beforehand. She says all her friends say I am shady to her and I said she should get off Twitter and stop listening to these people who are up her ass. We laughed. Had a meeting at the construction site and there is asbestos that needs to be removed, and a bunch of the pipes are cojoined, so that means we're delayed again for another month or so. Put on my midnight-blue Ralph Lauren tuxedo and walked over to SJP's to pick her up for the Met Ball, where I found her topped by a massive Chinese headpiece with red-and-black ornamentation. It was incredible. She had to ride in the car with her head cocked to one side so it wouldn't break, or break off. On the way up, I peed at a random eye doctor's office on the Upper East Side and took pics with the receptionist. The red carpet went crazy for Sarah's headgear, and I told any reporter who would listen that I was going to take her home and make love to her all night. I'm pretty sure I say the same thing every year. The room was everyone from Kim Kardashian to Cher, who was with Marc Jacobs. I made a beeline to her with SJ and Bruce in tow. She made fun of my insane shit-eating grin and the fact that I introduced myself to her. She said she knew who I was. I didn't even mention radio. She looked good. We were at a tech table with rich people from San Francisco and with Valentino, who did not seem like he was a fan of the food. He has really good Italian chefs. We met Justin Bieber, and SJ asked what he thought of his first Met Ball and he asked if it "gets crazy" and I said, well, the bar is high for you on that. The truth is I walk around in a fog, recognizing no one in the joint because the dresses make it seem like everyone is in costume. You turn to one side and hug Lady Gaga, or who you *think* is Lady Gaga but maybe it's Gwen Stefani, you just don't know. Lee Daniels was there with Naomi, *I think*. Went and kissed Madonna's ring—literally kneeled by her at her table and said I didn't like all the ageism being leveled at her and that I was pissed at her for not doing my show and she said, "Don't take it personally." I said, "You're Madonna; I wouldn't take anything you do personally." I think I said hi to Katy Perry, who was with Allison Williams. Rihanna performed a few songs, including "Diamonds," with a full orchestra—pretty magical. Sat at the Boom Boom Room with SJ, Bruce, Bryan, and Paul Bettany and Jennifer Connelly, who seem lovely. Bummed around with John Mayer a bunch too. I was in bed by three forty-five.

⯈ WEDNESDAY, MAY 6, 2015

This day almost killed me. Got more outdoor furniture delivered for the terrace. Spoke at a JCC on Long Island—my people! Taped three shows in a row, got in bed feeling lonely and depleted, and looked at my phone to see that I hit a million followers on Instagram, which I had been thinking was going to be some milestone that would feel like a great accomplishment. It didn't. The dog was cuddled up perfectly to me before I fell asleep; then he moved to my feet and I couldn't sleep. Got a text from Mom, furious we'd played a "guess the crotch" game, saying, "Your show has JUMPED THE SHARK."

⯈ THURSDAY, MAY 7, 2015—NYC—LOS ANGELES

Richie, my elevator man, is officially better than Google. He tells me everything I need to know. The cute gay guy on the fifth floor is the brother of the cute gay guy in the penthouse, but they aren't twins. And the guy on the fifth floor was just denied a dog by the building but I can't figure out why. Richie will find out.

Emailed Carole and LuAnn and said to quit fighting so much on Twitter; it's taking away from the show and beneath them both. I never get involved in stuff like that but this was irritating me for some reason. There's a YouTube clip of Sonja asking me what famous person I've slept with and I said Lance Bass, which is officially the oldest story out there but somehow is getting picked up everywhere. And now it's a (fake) "controversy" because he is a married man and should I be saying stuff like this about a married man?

Flew to LA for the *Shahs* and Will Arnett was on the plane sitting behind me, all rumpled and nap-sleepy, and then when we walked out he had somehow transformed into a superstar: sunglasses, Dodgers hat, amazing denim jacket. I asked if he got touched up during landing or something. Checked in at the Tower and had dinner at Sandy's.

▶ FRIDAY, MAY 8, 2015—LOS ANGELES

Shot the *Shahs* reunion—very dramatic and I didn't wear a tie, which was personally very dramatic. Lance Bass said, "Sex is a broad term," and that I didn't penetrate him, so now websites are saying that he is denying he had sex with me. #BrazilianAndySamberg FaceTimed to ask if I'm making up stories about sleeping with Lance Bass. It's all very embarrassing.

▶ SATURDAY, MAY 9, 2015—LOS ANGELES—NYC

Breakfast with Lauren and Jason and I met Roxie Blum.

Don't fly into Newark from LA, I learned; the planes are old and the first class is no good. Landed and went to the Diamond Horseshoe—met Jorge, a beautiful, open-hearted Venezuelan. Then was flirting with a poor man's Jewish John Stamos when a handsome South African came up, and then they connected right before my eyes and I let them be and split. It's frustrating when your trick is overtaken by another trick, but it's a jungle out there.

SUNDAY, MAY 10, 2015

Mark and Kelly came over and we drank rosé on the terrace for three hours and I wore a Mr Turk romper, which I thought Kelly would appreciate (she did). I had no show so I felt like I hadn't a care in the world. Bought solar-powered twinkly lights for the terrace, which don't work great.

MONDAY, MAY 11, 2015

Horrible allergies. I cannot get *Match Game* going and I feel like a total loser. Fremantle wants a prime-time window and I think it'll fail on NBC.

Met Frances at the Rainbow Room for a drink. Walked to Giancarlo Giammetti's, where Valentino showed me his ruby-red sparkly watch and cuff links and three diamond rings. Then I quizzed him about whether he travels with his jewelry or if he leaves some in NYC. The answer is both. Came home to get the dog but he had pooped in the bedroom, so I tethered him to the cinder block and went to the *Entertainment Weekly* upfront party, where I ran into Bellamy Young, Guillermo Díaz, and Katie someone, who were all on their way to do my show, but I've never seen *Scandal* so I faked it. After the show Mom texted that she doesn't watch *Scandal* so my show was very boring, with three sleeping emojis.

WEDNESDAY, MAY 13, 2015

This morning was rehearsal for cohosting tomorrow's NBCUniversal Cable Upfront Presentation with Giuliana Rancic and Nick Cannon. In the script there's a gag where I come out and have a leotard on over my suit. I am worried that it's not funny, so I said maybe I won't do it and they all said that it's Bonnie Hammer's favorite part, so I better do some abs today because I see a leotard in my future.

Matt Lauer was supposed to be on the show but cancelled because of the Amtrak crash, so we scrambled for a guest to pair with Snoop Dogg. We got Willie Geist, who went on to witness one of my most embarrassing moments ever: mistakenly calling Snoop "Spook." The look on Willie's face matched my inner horror. Snoop said, "*Spook?*" and I pretended that it did not even happen. I went in the control room after the show and they said they'd all gasped when I said it.

After the show Snoop wanted to talk to me, and it was not about the racial epithet I uttered to him on the show (which was being edited out as we spoke) but about wanting to produce a show with me, and it was officially the best pitch meeting ever because in the middle he handed me a blunt, which I sucked down. His manager stopped me from taking a second hit because he said it was a creeper and I would be high enough with one hit. And I was! Got in the car and heard a very nice message from Matt Lauer telling me not to think he is avoiding me. Went home and took a nap so I could get Snoop's hooch out of my system.

The live show was Sharon Osbourne and Seann William Scott, who I can barely look in the eye because he's so hot. Mom texted that I need to go after him and I said I don't think it's an option, and she said she will talk to his mom for me and make it okay. Funny. After the show I met Jeff Lewis at Koi for drinks along with the Bravo crew (in town for upfronts): Kyle, Tamra, Shannon, Jenni Pulos, NeNe, Kim, and more. . . . Tamra said as good as my body looks she could tell I could lose five more pounds, and she's right. Shannon and Tamra have forty examples of Vicki lying about cancer and they say she has to go if she really lied, that the viewers will hate her. And I said, well, she's Vicki, so maybe it would be more interesting to find out *why* she is lying. NeNe came over and we barely said hi and Tamra said OMG, something is wrong; she just totally dissed you. I said honey, we're basically mid-convo; I have seen her twenty times in the last three weeks; it's all good. Went to the bathroom and saw Jax and a girl and I got in his ear and said what are you doing; one isn't enough, go out and find another one! Then I heard my name and it was Harry Hamlin saying hi and he and Rinna were checking in. I like upfront season.

Came home and there was a bottle of rosé champagne from Bonnie with a note saying she couldn't wait to see me in a leotard, so that's that and I didn't do abs today.

It was a race to get to through the upfront's mile-long red carpet, complete with a stop at E! to be interviewed by Ross Matthews and Maria Menounos. The show itself was a trip. The Housewives and all Bravo talent were sitting in front of me, which was fun but distracting. It's thousands of people at the Javits Center; you don't know *who* is there but you might know every single one of them.

During the show I went to pee and said to some guy in Nick Cannon's posse who was also peeing, "This is *boring*!" and he said—somewhat menacingly—"Are you really trying to talk to me while I'm peeing??" I really did not care for his tone. I didn't ask to see his dick! I then had a fantasy that this guy punched me in the face and then we fell in love: We met cute! Anyway, none of that happened. I had a quick change to put that leotard on over my suit and did the gag. The good news is that the room is so cavernous I couldn't tell if people were laughing or rolling their eyes.

Wound up spontaneously meeting Bethenny, her friend Jimmy, Kyle Richards, and Eric Stonestreet for dinner at Dirty French, which was crazy good. Kyle kept saying that Lindsay Lohan was two booths over and I said that couldn't possibly be her; it looks nothing like her. They waved and Kyle said "Come over," and I said you just invited a stranger over. Sure enough, Lindsay Lohan comes over and sits down and she now has some kind of a clipped European accent and says she lives between "London, Dubai, and Morocco" or maybe Monaco, I can't remember. And she is in town doing community service for two weeks, to which Jill Zarin accompanied her today and Bethenny said that itself sounds like community service. She said she loves Jill like family. But the community service is only eight hours a day, and she wants to work all day and all night so she can get it over with but they won't let her and maybe that's a cause she wants to talk to me or Oprah about. Then she tried to get me involved in an app for leasing private planes. You join for eight thousand bucks and then it's a dollar a flight or something. She left and we marveled. Later she sent me a sambuca and espresso, and I don't know what message she was trying to send me. She was smoking outside when I left but I ducked into the Uber.

▶ FRIDAY, MAY 15, 2015—NYC—CHICAGO

As is now customary with my tour with Anderson, I arrive a day early and get the lay of the land in the city. There are men around Chicago wearing preppy shorts, which I just don't see much of anymore. Went to my first Cubs game at Wrigley with Kenny Werner and it was probably the first activity he and I have done since high school. We sat with one of the lesbian owners of the team. Wrigley is a trip, super old-fashioned—she took us to the owner's box and it's a dump. A lovable dump, but a dump nonetheless! Had dinner with the Arkins at Giuliana's restaurant, RPM, which is like a nightclub. They put a security guard in front of our booth, which felt very baller.

▶ SATURDAY, MAY 16, 2015

Spent the day with Em walking all over town. There was some debate about whether Dad was going to come too but it wound up being just her, so we had good sibling fun. She is obsessed with the amount of goodies the Four Seasons left for me in my room: Swedish Fish, booze, pastries emblazoned with images of me and Anderson. AC got in this afternoon and on the way to the show I demanded we stop across the street from the Chicago Theatre to take a selfie with the marquee, which was officially the worst idea ever. People were already there for the show, and it turned into Beatlemania and then we had to be hard-asses and get back into the car and I got rightfully blamed for the fiasco. It turned out to be our best show yet, with an intensely enthusiastic sell-out crowd that included some Cubs and Dave Ansel. It felt like every story and punch line got a huge laugh, and we're getting better at telling the ones we repeat and at finding new ones for the top of the show. Went to Sidetracks after and they'd reserved a private area for us—on some sort of stage, weirdly, so Anderson lasted about three seconds and said he was going next door to Minibar. I followed and we wound up having a blast.

SUNDAY, MAY 17, 2015—CHICAGO—NYC

Anderson said we should savor the energy of last night. He's right. We won't always get a response like that. Landed in NYC and met up with Mom, who is in town with her bridge club. She was never a dog person and doesn't know how to interact with Wacha. She holds her hand up but he thinks she has a treat, and she's trying to get him to stay down but he's jumping on her for a treat. She asked me not to give her and Dad dirty stuff to do on *WWHL* and I said I couldn't guarantee it. The *Mad Men* finale was perfection.

MONDAY, MAY 18, 2015

Had lunch with Mom's bridge group at Bubby's. I had matzo ball soup. Mom came back to my house and started to get into a groove with Wacha, rubbing his stomach. She didn't get the *Mad Men* finale, that Don came up with the idea for the Coke campaign. The bridge group bartended and were hilarious. Our photographer, Chuck, brought Mom over to me for a photo during a commercial break and she said, "Are you gonna hang this in the Clubhouse WHEN I DIE?!" That kind of stopped everybody in their tracks.

TUESDAY, MAY 19, 2015

Shot the *Southern Charm* reunion and thoroughly enjoyed it. We had a whole group of Cardinals wives in the audience for *WWHL*—and after the game a bunch of the players and a coach showed up and I met the woman who retweeted that comment from Seth Maness's account during the last post season that then became a big scandal. Sounds like the management of the team was *pissed* at her and her man really stood by her. I was, of course, thrilled to have been in the middle of it. Then we met the boys after their big win over the Mets at Anfora. It was like being at a character break-fast at Disneyland: They're all giants. So it was Lackey, Maness, Wong, Jay, Big City, Siegrist, the new pitcher, Tuivailala, Grichuk, and . . . Wacha, who was really shy and I waited until we had a couple drinks in us to go deep about the dog and make sure he understood it was a sweet tribute and not creepy. He said he took it as such. The guy is only twenty-three. So is Grichuk, who is hot and sweet. I told him I want to set him up with a bunch of starlets. One of the guys taught me about "slump humps," where you have sex with a heavy girl to get rid of a slump. He's in one, he said. But he got two hits against Matt Harvey yesterday, so maybe he found a heavy girl in New York. They all wear bad jeans. I was in heaven looking around at all these tall Cardinals. They're a lot of fun.

At around two I grabbed Wacha and said, "Wanna meet your guy?" We went outside and I gave Grichuk my phone to video the meeting. I opened the car and the dog was sleeping and I got him out. Wacha was kneeling down with a bunch of treats I'd given him and the dog was sleepily eating them out of his hands and we were kind of drunkenly loving on him. It was really adorable. We got a picture of them shaking hands. Then it was last call at Anfora and I took them all to the Cubby Hole, which was certainly titillating but didn't really result in any lady sandwiches or anything. I left them around three; they were going on to 1 Oak, and I tried to get Wacha to say goodbye to Wacha but he barked and snarled. I yelled at him on the way home in the car. "You SNARL at your NAMESAKE?? THAT'S how you treat him?!?!" I have become my mother.

▶ WEDNESDAY, MAY 20, 2015

Hoda called to beg me to be with her tomorrow night at the Red Nose Day event, and I told her I would do whatever she wanted but I now really regret it. I love her, but I don't want to be on a double-decker bus all night in Times Square. Taped a show with Kellan Lutz and Vanessa Hudgens, who I kept thinking was the other one—Ashley Tisdale. Literally, she was about to walk in the Clubhouse and I turned to John Hill and said is it Ashley Tisdale or Vanessa Hudgens? I don't know that generation so well. I am so old! Kellan Lutz is a little caveman-esque but he is very hot and gave me a hoodie from his clothing line, which is nine sizes too big but I wore it this afternoon on the terrace while talking to Hickey and pretended Kellan was my boyfriend who left his oversized hoodie when he slept over last night as a ploy to get back into my apartment. Hickey is stuck in Santa Fe again shooting season two of *Manhattan* and it sucks not having him here.

Went to the Riverkeeper benefit with Dave and Allie. Cheryl Hines introduced me as the host of "Watch What Happens Next"—which made me feel like crap. Speaking of shit, I came home and Wacha had pooped in the bedroom, which was a real bummer. I'm calling Brandon. The show was Vivica Fox and Fredrik—I was tired and cranky. Went straight to my office and watched Letterman's finale alone. It was perfect, elegant; not a tear was shed. I thought of him after the show going up to his office and being alone. You always wind up alone at the end of the night, no matter how many people are cheering for you.

▷ THURSDAY, MAY 21, 2015

Went to the Mets-Cardinals game with Jerry and Matthew and discovered the magic of Waze. Jerry should be their pitchman. We lost, but the food was spectacular! Shot the Red Nose Day live special on NBC with Hoda and we made the best of it. She always makes things better. Got a massage late and pondered the world's problems.

▷ FRIDAY, MAY 22, 2015—MONDAY, MAY 25, 2015— NYC—SAG HARBOR

Drove to the beach with the help of Waze, which took me over the Williamsburg Bridge and avoided a ton of traffic. I got there in two hours, in time for my annual summer kickoff lunch at the Consueloses' consisting of lots of fried chicken and rosé. Took a lovely nap and had pizza at the counter of Sam's alone, which was blissful. On Saturday night Calvin had a beautiful dinner for Sandy's birthday. Had a long talk with Ingrid Sischy about doing a radio show for me, interviews with interesting people. She seemed really interested. Drove to Shelter Island for fried chicken at the Perskys' on Sunday and heard myself on Howard Stern. The dogs were running around and Bill told me he's feeling older and wishes he appreciated walking more when he could do it better. Big nap, Marci's for dinner, and then Bethenny was telling me to come over because she had a house full of gay guys. I chose sleep instead. Maybe I should get out more.

Tweeted about Memorial Day, but first I tweeted something about the men in uniform and then people said what about the women, so I deleted that and redid it but the bigger problem was that I tweeted "thank you" to the troops, not "Remember the troops." So everyone was up my ass and I had to redo the fucking Memorial Day tweet several times. Worked out at Tracy Anderson's studio but left the class after the cardio portion. Did my rounds: lunch at Bethenny's; Eric Stonestreet was there, and a family. The kids took the big burgers and we ate sliders and I was resentful. Then to Sandy's, where we hung out and wrote interview questions for our talk next week, then to the Fallons', where Gary and Wacha ran around. Jimmy and Nancy were in matching windbreakers and I took a Jacuzzi. Watched *Twenty Feet from Stardom* and went to bed really early.

▶ TUESDAY, MAY 26, 2015—SAG HARBOR—NYC

I am having low-level depression about my birthday, and about the Hamptons. I feel like I did it already, like it's a repeat of last summer. Drove back to the city in a fog of Howard Stern. I dropped the car off and went to my construction site and there was a note from the Waspy lesbian seersucker lady on the seventeenth floor saying thanks for the "heads up" on the work on the apartment and good luck. But I didn't give her a heads-up, and why did she put it in quotation marks? I spent a long time with Surfin and Mike debating whether she was just being passive aggressive or what. Then Carlos got there and I asked him and he couldn't decide what it meant. I miss my old building.

Had dinner with Amanda and dared Grac to come but they're going to see Joan Jett. I went to bed at ten-thirty but I made lists in my head about everything I'm stressed about and that kept me up: my birthday next week (I wanted to have a party on the terrace but it's supposed to be chilly and rainy Tuesday night), the amfAR event for which my parents and Em and Rob are coming in but they have no one to introduce me and I don't know how many seats I have and haven't invited anybody, my radio channel (unprogrammed and launching soon), my new publicist to whom I have paid five thousand dollars and whom I called on Friday and she never called me back—oh, and the area in my groin that itches where I pulled a tick off me on Sunday, and the hair loss I saw in the rearview mirror while driving home from the beach. I could almost see through the front of my hair. Tossed and turned and made lists. This could be the moment where everything falls to shit in my life.

WEDNESDAY, MAY 27, 2015

I had so many fucking lists when I woke up there was no way I was going to fail. Started the day with a pretape with Kevin Dillon and Kevin Connolly, both of whom I liked very much. Went up to Bravo, where I TCBed it on the radio station. Working on shows from Ali Wentworth and Sandra Bernhard, but I need a lot more. Had a meeting with Henry Goldblatt, the editor in chief of *EW*, about my editing an issue in August; he said we have to schedule the cover shoot and I realized I'm going to be on the *cover* of *EW*. *Wow*. I couldn't believe it. I told him it's going to be their least selling issue of the year. Went to Sandra Bernhard's dermatologist and had a Triad facial for eight hundred bucks, which he said was actually a deal. He also asked me two minutes into the appointment when I was going to send a tweet about him. Anyway, he also prescribed doxycycline for the tick and some new hair shit. Went to Danny Neeson's graduation party at the Palm. Dermot Mulroney was on the show and his only prerequisite was that we not ask about Dylan McDermott, so I guess too many people have done "Is it Dermot Mulroney, Dylan McDermott, or Dean McDermott?" (We have played it with Dylan!)

THURSDAY, MAY 28, 2015

Slept fitfully, and Wacha left for Brooklyn first thing in the morning. I cancelled the Ninj, who sent me a teary emoji. Poor Ninj! Planned my Grateful Dead trip with John Mayer. Had a long talk with my new publicist and we figured a lot out. No resolution on my birthday party, but I started inviting people to amfAR and now I feel like if the birthday party doesn't happen it'll be fine because that will be enough. Creative call with Sandra Bernhard, who seems to be on the same page as I am. I'm not sure if she and I are on the same page about the facial I got from her dermatologist, though, because I can't tell the difference one way or the other. Went to the Friends In Deed photography event and who did I run into on her way to get a charger at the Apple Store but Sandra herself, who eyeballed my face and said it was better.

I was feeling bored and SJP came over out of nowhere and ordered food, which we ate on the terrace, turning it into a magical Manhattan night—the kind where everybody is out on the street and you never want to go inside.

▶ FRIDAY, MAY 29, 2015—NYC—SAG HARBOR

Trained with a new guy at Will's gym, Robbie. He grunts when he boxes and that was exciting me. Drove to the beach—Waze took me through the Midtown Tunnel and on the Long Island Expressway, so that was no big diversion.

Went to Almond with Troy—my first time there in five years, and I expected it to be all old gay guys with cashmere sweaters over their shoulders but it was actually younger gay guys with cashmere sweaters over their shoulders, so that was a big change. Earlier in the night it was people my age and I was looking around thinking, "Look at all the old people," and then I realized I was one of them. Troy and I got in a fight about the safety of Ubers; I told him he's been working for *48 Hours Mystery* for too long because he thinks everything is a setup for murder. By the way, Uber in the Hamptons is amazing. I drank and didn't have to worry about driving.

▶ SATURDAY, MAY 30, 2015—SAG HARBOR

Was feeling a little blue but it turned into a lovely day. Went to Marci's, where we hung on the beach with Christina McGuinness. The dog was being very codependent. Then I dropped him off at Sandy's and went to the gay beach with Justin and his friend Peter. All day Sandy was saying who else fun can we have at my dinner? Well, we only wound up with me, Sandy, Brian, Ingrid Sischy, and Donna Karan.

SUMMER/FALL 2015

IN WHICH I . . .

> CELEBRATE GAY PRIDE IN A VERY STRAIGHT WAY,

> OFFEND THE BLACK COMMUNITY,

> LAUNCH A RADIO CHANNEL,

> AND HOST NEW YEAR'S EVE ON NBC.

TUESDAY, JUNE 2, 2015—NYC

It was a fine forty-eighth birthday. Last night Solly and I rang in our birthday eve with Jeanne, Fred, and crew at Benihana. (No third-degree burns.) Met #BrazilianAndySamberg and his best pals in Brooklyn, where we watched *The Bachelorette* and I apparently said something his friends thought was transphobic. So we beat that to death. Then we went to a fun gay bar where everybody was really hairy. The drag queen overtook the mic, and we had to run. Had a good morning with #BAS, and I can always count on my sweet dad to be my first call of the day. Birthday texts from a few Cardinals, some Housewives, and every one-nighter I've ever had. Had a most awesome dinner at Indochine with OGs Jackie, Amanda, Liza, Grac, and SJP and it ended with us coming up with their *Housewives* taglines, which oddly is something none of us had ever thought about before.

Jackie: I know my way around a gallery because I'm a work of art.
Amanda: During the day the doctor is in, at night I'm accepting new patients. (Alternate: . . . at night the lady is out.)
Liza: I'm a daytime gal but I come alive at night.
Grac: I rub elbows on Park Avenue but my heart is in the Mudd Club. (Alternate: . . . heart is in Danceteria.)
SJP: You may think you know me but don't get Carried away. (We forced her to add Carrie to it.)

WEDNESDAY, JUNE 3, 2015

I was so pissed at Wacha today; he was eating everything off the street. This woman saw me yelling at him and for sure thought I was abusing him. And I took him to the vet to get shit sprayed up his nose for kennel cough or something and he wasn't having it at all, so I wound up bringing it home to do myself and I sprayed it across the terrace. I guess we're all getting kennel cough because I ain't trying again. After my endless prodding, the Countess recorded a new song riffing on her "Don't be uncool" line. I told her it was a moment and she had to seize it. Fun party for Anderson's birthday tonight. When mine is over, his begins, so I ride his wave too.

I woke up to the news that Diana Ross had joined Twitter and I freaked out. I kept retweeting her weird tweets and it was pandemonium in my bed. Wacha gave me side-eye while he tried to figure out why I was so hyped. Did a radio press tour with Anderson—basically a conference call where they connect us to stations across the country to promote the AC2 tour. I got yelled at by him three times for doing other things: opening presents, eating toast, clearing dishes, reading Diana tweets to him. He told me to "*Sit* and *pay attention*." Later in the afternoon I got a text from Cher asking if I'm cheating on her with Miss Ross. (I love that she called her *Miss Ross* in the text.) I told her I don't know her but am a fan and am fascinated by her inability to manage her legacy in a way similar to Cher. The Countess asked me to come hear her song in the recording studio and I loved it.

I hosted some kind of gay pride roundtable at the W Hotel and was at loggerheads with a transgender woman because I didn't understand why she wasn't thrilled about Caitlynmania—wasn't it ultimately a great educational opportunity for America to learn about the trans struggle? She said it was because Caitlyn is so rich, it's only one view of the issue and not great for the entire community. I didn't totally get it. Then #BAS explained it. He speaks "college campus" to me. I'm going through a massive homosexual crisis because they punched open the ceiling in my apartment to make room for a staircase and you can see both floors of windows when you walk into the apartment and it feels so dramatic and open that I'm wondering if I should make the family room have a double-height ceiling and dump that upstairs guest room.

Wacha pooped in the extra room. I sat on the terrace in front of the window with him bound to the cinder block, curled up like a pretzel watching what he was missing out on, which was me watching Julia Louis-Dreyfus on *Comedians in Cars Getting Coffee.* She hates the Housewives and I'm pretty sure that's why she won't do my show.

FRIDAY, JUNE 5, 2015

The Donut Pub around the corner is killing me! I lived in the close vicinity of it for twenty years, but now that #BAS is spending some time in NYC he's really opening my eyes to donuts as a plausible late-night snack. Luckily he also likes #fattractive people. I lay in bed late last night wondering what would happen if I died in my sleep and I realized Daryn was coming here today to get some photos hung and that she would find me then. So I told her today to be glad I wasn't dead. Went to the CAA Tony party, then met Bill at an all-black club and it was the most fun ever. I was one of five white people. The energy was electric and chilled out at the same time. Everyone is beautiful, even guys with bodies that aren't ripped up. And everyone is nice, happy to see you, and not rushing over with a camera. Plus they all love the Atlanta Housewives. We met so many great guys. Why hasn't it gone totally mainstream that black people are so much cooler than white people? White people are afraid of everyone realizing the truth, right?

SUNDAY, JUNE 7, 2015

Long Skype call with Mom and Dad in advance of their NYC visit for my amfAR honor. "Where is Sirius?" they want to know. I explained the only way I know how with them: in relation to Uniqlo.

I was talking to the landlord as I was waiting to show Bryan the demolition and debate the double-height room conundrum and I found out that the studio apartment next door to the new upstairs apartment might be available. I low-key freaked out and badgered him to give the owner my number. SJP came over for a casual hangout on the terrace, and I think she finally "got" Wacha. They cuddled. John Mayer and Ricky came over with Jimmy's new Ben and Jerry's ice cream flavor, which is tremendous.

MONDAY, JUNE 8, 2015—NYC—SAG HARBOR

I'm on hiatus chilling at the beach, where Jimmy told me he made up that flavor himself and I think it's genius. It's called The Tonight Dough and it's caramel and chocolate ice creams with chocolate cookie swirls, gobs of chocolate-chip cookie dough, and peanut-butter cookie dough—so basically everything. Gordon drew up plans to combine the studio with the other apartments and make a big atrium. The super gave the guy my number but he hasn't called me, so I am putting the cart before the horse.

I am getting channel 102 on Sirius, right next to Howard! This is *big*.

▶ WEDNESDAY, JUNE 10, 2015—SAG HARBOR

Sometimes I think Wacha hates me because I'm gay. Or judges me. He played with Gary all day. My NYC neighbor called while I was at Nancy Fallon's. He's been renting out his studio apartment for years but the tenant moves out July 1 and he is open to selling. He said that *of course* the apartment would be more valuable to *me* than it would be on the open market and I said yes, I am aware of that fact. Then he said that he had had a preliminary conversation with his neighbor on the other side, who may be interested as well. A bidding war between neighbors? Can't lose there. He asked if I had met the neighbor. I said no, and he said well, *Sally Field seems very nice*. A bidding war between *celebrity* neighbors. Wonderful. This guy thinks he is in the catbird seat. Newsflash: *He is*. Dinner alone with MaryAnn Bozzi at the Palm, which was a first for us and really fun. On the drive home I called Bruce to tell him everything his mother had told me and we really are Myrtle and Gladys, just two clucking old ladies.

▶ THURSDAY, JUNE 11, 2015—SAG HARBOR—NYC

I got in an accident outside the Midtown Tunnel! A big truck cut me off. I was on the side of the road with the guy, waiting for the cops to file a police report, for hours. I had to get to a pitch at CAA, so Daryn had to come relieve me and wait for the tow-truck guys. Wonder if this is what will make her quit? In the heat, by the side of the road I saw Rachel Zoe and Rodger coming in from the Hamptons. Missed the Bethenny pitch but made it to CAA for the *Blast Your Past* pitch. Went to Anthony's birthday party, where Sonja did a memorable caburlesque performance.

FRIDAY, JUNE 12, 2015

Spent half the day terrified that Daryn was dead. She was being unresponsive to every form of communication—which is completely out of character—and by two in the afternoon I was calling everyone at Embassy Row and Bravo to figure out what was up. How ironic that I thought *she* was gonna find *me* dead last week. Turns out she was in some seminar where there were no phones allowed. Relieved!

We let Brandi go today. She was kind of expecting it; there was nowhere for her to go because none of the women like her and she hates them. I have a cold (I think I got it from Richie, the elevator guy), and Mom sent me this stuff that you rub on your chest and under your nose to help you breathe. I called her "Mom" in a text thanking her today because it was a really mom thing to do. She sent back a bunch of emoticons. We are debating who should bartend on Monday, and she keeps saying Dad is a camera whore. I mean . . . Went to Robbie Baitz and Leon's wedding at Almond in Tribeca, which was really sweet. Ken Olin gave a roast-y toast, Ron Rifkin sang, a lady scatted, and Gina Gershon has a good show idea we're gonna pitch.

SATURDAY, JUNE 13, 2015—NYC—FIRE ISLAND

Breakfast with Hickey at La Bonbonniere. He saw Sally Field on the street in workout clothes yesterday. I wish he'd asked her if we're in a bidding war or not! Missed the ferry to Fire Island by two minutes and had to wait for the next one. The twink Realtor and his boyfriend picked me up in a boat instead. Saw a great house to rent this summer that's expensive, but I'm gonna do it. The twink said he will be my bodyguard.

I still don't feel great.

Met Bill and Chris on the beach and gave Bill a custom AC420 vape and he said the one he has is better. Nice. We got invited to a birthday barbecue by these hot bearded guys. Some guy was getting out of the freezing water and I said he was brave and he said let's run in together, *Baywatch* style. I did it and felt like I had needles sticking into every pore of my body but I felt alive. *We met cute!* Until I found out he has a boyfriend. Walking away, he put on a sarong, so that was two rapid strikes against him. By the time I left the beach I felt free and full of promise, which is what Fire Island is all about. Told Amanda I was going to a barbecue. She replied, "That whole island is a bbq—are they putting a hot man on a SPIT?" It was more like bags of chips on a counter and not enough buns, all homemade in the best way. The bearded birthday boy makes wallets in Brooklyn. He had a dream of a screenplay and told me the whole thing. It wasn't horrible but I didn't understand anyone's motivation.

▶ SUNDAY, JUNE 14, 2015—FIRE ISLAND—NYC

I reset all my emojis to black people because I like them better and then took the ferry home with three brothers. One of them wound up putting his number in my phone and I texted him back applause, but they were black hands and I felt weird—like, did he think I reset my emojis to black people for him? Life is a minefield. Back in the city, had dinner with Mom and Dad at Café Cluny. Wasn't looking forward to the show—it was Quad and Heavenly from *Married to Medicine*—but I really enjoyed it. Having a vacation makes all the difference.

▶ MONDAY, JUNE 15, 2015

Tonee gave Anderson and me a joint haircut on the terrace today. That's living! But then it started raining so we went inside. What's the point of an outside haircut if it's gonna rain? I was sweeping up the hair, marveling that AC's is almost translucent. It's impossible to *see*, like shards of glass. Wacha will eat what I didn't get. Em and Rob came by and saw both apartments; we endlessly discussed the potential combination with the studio and how much I should pay. Dinner at Polo Bar, where Mom announced that she didn't find the 9/11 memorial that moving. She expected more—it's like a sad movie that didn't make her cry, I guess. Down to the show, where it was Jenny McCarthy and Vicki, with Em and Mom behind the bar. It was cute. Got an email from the seller of the studio next door asking way more than I expected, with a whole lot of exposition. I don't get the sense from the email that Sally is bidding. Went to Anfora with Rob and Em and engaged in more endless discussion about apartments. Came home and watched part 2 of the *Shahs* reunion and either I was drunk or it was my best work ever.

❧ TUESDAY, JUNE 16, 2015

Woke up with the weight of the world on my shoulders—stressed about not having written my speech for my amfAR honor and still grappling with many questions about this apartment situation. So I had a meeting at the apartment, worked out, taped a show, wrote my speech, and went to Spring Studios for amfAR in the sweltering heat.

The red carpet was all Miley questions because she was being honored too. Apparently Bethenny said somewhere that I talked her into getting married, so of course people take that seriously and I had to answer a bunch of those. Mom and Dad looked gorgeous, as did Em. Sat with Jeanne, Fred, and my date, Grac, for the pre-dinner crazy fashion show. I had two tables of friends and Anderson was hosting the evening. Sandra Bernhard presented my award with beat poetry:

> Andy is my good friend. We've had conversations in the Clubhouse that rival John and Yoko. I'd like to think of Andy as the Dick Cavett of the new millennium. He's brought culture to places we'd never thought possible. And turned feminism on its ear . . . Like a shaman, a new age healer, a magical guru, he's brought enlightenment. . . . Whether navigating the fragile atmosphere during Dorinda's fiftieth, grappling with Eileen's feeling that Brandi has gone from fan to foe, or deconstructing Vicki's fiesta party where "the piñata wasn't the only thing getting bashed," he is a natural at helping people, and I'm delighted to say that he lends his support to so many, not just Ramona, Bethenny, Luann, Yolanda, Kristen, Tamra, Vicki, Kandi, Cynthia . . .

I consider Sandra a cultural priestess, so those ironic/not ironic words from her were gold to me. NeNe left the Bravo table (in a huff?) soon after. Was it because she wasn't mentioned? I never got to see her.

During the live auction Grac had me tell Mom I was gonna bid on the Miley/Caitlin Jenner art, which at that point was at fifty thousand dollars—it went for more. "NO you're NOT!" she loudly intoned from the next table. Memories of the Shawnee prank (see: *Most Talkative*)! The after party at the Boom Boom Room was, like the room, glamorous and very fun. I loved being able to party with my parents, who at seventy-eight and eighty-three were game to keep going.

▶ WEDNESDAY, JUNE 17, 2015

Texted NeNe and said I was sorry I didn't see her. She texted that she saw me get my award but had to be up early and that she had worn new hair for me. Hmm—something's off. Did a radio special with my parents to bank for the launch of the channel. Mom said Fredrik agreed with her that I shouldn't pay just anything for that apartment and I said, he just doesn't want to fight with *you*. Emailed the neighbor with a cash offer that's 30 percent over the last comp in the building, very generous if you ask me. Eric Dane and Lauren Graham were on the show. He didn't want to spill one thing on air and then during commercial breaks was spilling the tea. Good guy, though.

▶ THURSDAY, JUNE 18, 2015

The Brandi news leaked and my timeline, which for months was full of "Get rid of Brandi!" is now full of "I will never watch *BH* again if Brandi is gone you idiot!" What can you do? Brought Wacha to the party for the Whistle app and he was humping all the other dogs. It was like a press event, so he gave the press something to talk about. Had dinner at Morandi with Ricki and Liza, during which I got an email from the neighbor that it is a very emotional decision and he needs some time to talk it over with his wife, so I don't know what that means. Mom texted during the show—"No more penis games!" (We did a "Guess their size" thing with Adam Scott and Natasha Leggero.) Took the girls to see the construction but it was dark and Ricki banged her leg. Had rosé on the terrace until all hours and I got in a rage at some guy who has been ripping off Liza's mom in LA and I found him on Facebook and sent him a scathing email. I have never met the man in my life.

FRIDAY, JUNE 19, 2015

Woke up to a very repentant email back from the LA guy and couldn't believe what I'd fired off. That is a first. And of course now I don't want to be involved whatsoever. Not responding. He will think I am nuts. Itay Malkin delivered my black-diamond chain and it looks good. What does it mean that I am transitioning into wearing diamond necklaces? Indian dinner for Lauren Blum, then a date with a Jewish South African guy with a crazy-great body who was starving himself because gay pride is coming up—something I hadn't heard in many years, given my age, but it depressed me now just like it did in the nineties. I took his phone ostensibly to look at his Instagram account but went into his direct messages and saw that he'd been sending erotic pics to countless people and barely getting any returns, which was surprising to me given how good his body was. I then felt superior. Wacha growled at him when I brought him home. He gave me a guilt trip for not asking him to stay, but I felt none.

SATURDAY, JUNE 20, 2015—NYC—ATLANTA

The driver to the airport groused when I asked him to take another route besides the Midtown Tunnel, which is under crazy construction, and begrudgingly headed towards the Williamsburg Bridge but we got pulled over for almost hitting a pedestrian, which I could tell he was silently blaming on me. I kept apologizing for the ticket but he wouldn't really accept my apology. And I asked if his company will pay for the ticket and he said no, only parking tickets they get while waiting for clients. So he was screwed and took it out on me!

In Atlanta, Anderson and I got burgers at the Four Seasons, then went to our show, where beforehand there were a bunch of CNN people backstage—Robin Meade from HLN was fuming that we'd found a way to monetize what we already do, which is talk to each other—and then Kari and family, who were driving to Florida and happened to be in Atlanta that night, which was divine intervention. The meet and greet after the show included Phaedra, a man with the most insane red hairpiece/system, and a dude who claimed he used to work for Naomi Judd and had juicy stories about her. I said I don't want to get involved. AC and I were *spent* when we got in the car and could barely see straight. Went to a place called Ten where we tried to blend in but drunk girls kept coming up, one furious at me for not taking a pic with her—we decided not to take pics all night because we wouldn't ever stop if we did. Another girl came up and asked why we bothered to come if we were just going to talk to each other all night. Then we went to Jungle which seemed like a druggy crowd but wound up being fun. Saw Lindsay and Jason Moattar.

▶ SUNDAY, JUNE 21, 2015—ATLANTA—NYC

Woke up with a cheerleader from Georgia Tech and an email from Danbury Correctional with a form that'll enable Teresa to email me; the cheerleader wasn't a surprise but the request from Teresa was. She's been behind bars for six months and I haven't heard a word. Flew back to NYC. Dinner at a horrible new Japanese place on Greenwich Avenue with the Blums and Bozzi-Lourds (and Barry for a cameo) and we all wanted to go out for pizza afterward. Was so tired and then got a second wind right before the show, at 10:55. At midnight went to Broadway Bares at the Hammerstein Ballroom. Entered through backstage and it was a sea of glittery chorus boys in G-strings, meaning it felt like home. I presented an award at the end of the night.

Got an email from the neighbor wanting seventy-five thousand more than I offered. I think I'll close in the middle, even though I got a frantic call from a drunk Bruce on his soapbox three minutes before air saying not to go a penny above what I offered.

▶ TUESDAY, JUNE 23, 2015—NYC—STATE COLLEGE, PA—NYC

Penn State invited me to do this paid speech and the only real way to get there within the time constraints, outside of a private plane (which they weren't offering), was to drive—seven hours there and back. Stopped at

McDonald's on the way, which I gleefully tweeted, and people replied that I was gonna get sick. I said I was fine. Got a response to my counter this morning from the guy, who wants twelve thousand *more*, which offended me and I emailed him something bitchy and he called just before the speech. I told him he was being greedy and to be an adult and accept my very generous offer, which is more than anyone else will ever give him.

I hate when Twitter trolls are right; I got a horrible stomachache during the speech. Got right back in the car. Was crazily excited for the show, which was LuAnn performing "Girl Code." The *WWHL* team was abuzz, and we realized that we hadn't known just how badly we needed a new *Housewives* song for our morale.

▶ WEDNESDAY, JUNE 24, 2015

Mom needs braces. My *mother, who is seventy-eight.* She emailed, said there's no other way to fix some issue with her gums. I said this was completely ridiculous and we would discuss it. Also got an email from Teresa, which was really sweet and light. Among other things she said she looks hot in jail, but that she always looks hot, and that "the girls in here watch your show every night, but I'm already in bed when it's on. They always tell me when my name gets mentioned." Am I the only one that thinks that's surreal?

Had two shows and saw the Georgia Tech cheerleader, who happens to be in town—cheering people up, of course.

▶ THURSDAY, JUNE 25, 2015

Woke up with cheerleader again and cancelled the Ninja. Got another email from Danbury Correctional Facility:

> HI HONEY, WHEN I COME BACK, I WANT THINGS TO BE DIFFERENT . . . LESS FIGHTING, MORE FAMILY AND GOOD TIMES WITH FRIENDS. PLEASE HELP ME WITH THAT. THE GIRLS IN HERE LOVE ATLANTA AND SINCE I HAVE BEEN HERE I MAKE SURE WE WATCH THEM ALL BEVERLY HILLS,

ORANGE COUNTY, NEW YORK, SECRET & WIVES & MILLION
DOLLAR LISTING. I LOVE YOUR SNAPPLE COMMERCIAL YOU
LOOK SO HANDSOME IN IT. I'M WORKING OUT 3 X PER DAY
AND I'M READING A LOT. I'M READY TO COME HOME AND
SHOW THE WORLD WHAT THEY'VE BEEN MISSING . . . ME :)
KISSES
PS I LIKE TYPING WITH CAPS I AM NOT YELLING . . .

I got the apartment!! And I still can't believe they have premium cable
in Danbury.

Lunch with Bruce. And later we saw Bette Midler at Madison Square
Garden—lots of gray-haired people there (like me), a real old crowd. Sat
next to Holland Taylor, the actress, and Sarah Paulson, who was on my show
yesterday. I think they're together; they seemed lovey-dovey. Backstage waiting for Bette were Rebel Wilson, Tommy Tune, and Billy Eichner, but we
left before Bette came out. Took Bruce and Bryan to a black bar where even
the duds are hot, then to Cafeteria for drunken burgers. Almost got killed
crossing the street on the way home. I jumped in front of traffic like Frog-
ger. Can't wait for my John Mayer Grateful Adventure tomorrow.

▶ FRIDAY, JUNE 26, 2015—
NYC—LOS ANGELES—SAN FRANCISCO

As I waited for my plane, which was delayed for three hours, I got a bunch
of rainbow emojis from mom, her signal to me that the Supreme Court had
struck down bans on gay marriage. Cabbed from LAX to John, who was
waiting for me in the Valley in his EarthRoamer. Sitting behind that massive front window with the promise of San Francisco (where it was Gay Pride
weekend) and two Dead shows at the end of our drive induced a natural
high. As the day went on, I was surprised at how overcome I became with
elation about gay marriage. I told John I'd give anything to be able to tell
my scared teenaged self that this day would come, but even if I could I
wouldn't have believed it. Saw a tweet with a picture of the White House
lit with the rainbow flag! *The White House!!!!* I told John I *had* to go out
tonight in San Francisco to celebrate and he said he was definitely game.
Yahoo! On the drive, we Periscoped, looked for an In-N-Out, tried to figure

out who was the Gayle and who was the Oprah (we think I'm Oprah and he's Gayle), discussed gay-bar options in San Francisco, and debated him emailing Oprah and saying we were gonna be in Montecito in ten minutes and to please let us come for tequila but I wasn't successful in convincing him. Listened to a lot of Dead all the way.

In Santa Clara, we parked directly backstage at Levi's Stadium with all the band equipment, did a shot, and found our driver, who was waiting to take us to the Four Seasons in San Francisco. We decided to go directly out, as it was after eleven. First stop was Powerhouse—gay bars always have strong names—where it was a lot of body heat and a guy in a jockstrap named Walter who was getting us drinks and, he said, "protecting us" while holding a clipboard where he was trying to convince people to sign up for the wet T-shirt contest without much luck. John wondered why they needed a wet T-shirt contest in a bar full of shirtless guys and I had no good answer. The dance floor was smoky, thumping with disco bass. I explained the significance of Diana Ross to John Mayer, which would've made a great article in *Rolling Stone*. Then we headed down the block to the EndUp, which was phenomenal. These two promoters were *begging* us to go to the VIP area and we just refused repeatedly. John and I danced like crazy, giddy boyfriends. He was the ultimate wingman. Checked in to the Four Seasons after three.

► SATURDAY, JUNE 27, 2015—SAN FRANCISCO

Breakfast with my high school pals Kenny and Keith, then John's engineer Chad arrived and we grabbed John and the three of us went to Santa Clara, where amidst office parks stands the gleaming Levi's Stadium, built with the promise of hosting Super Bowl 50. John's EarthRoamer was in the middle of a bunch of cops and quickly became a cop magnet—they just wanted to walk around it and look at the huge tires and discuss. We soon were visited by Phil and Jill Lesh. Wives gravitate to me, so I immediately bonded with Jill. I made us turkey sandwiches in the EarthRoamer and the Dead's manager, Bernie, came in and said tonight is definitely the night to do psychedelics, which answered my question about what drugs to take. He asked if I wanted to see the set list and I said I didn't—I wanted to experience the show like you're supposed to. They opened with "Truckin'" and I instantly time traveled back to a Dead show twenty-five years ago. I'd been worried that it was going to be all old, rich white people (like me?) but it was fairly multigenerational and smelled like Dead concerts did in the day, a mix of body heat and pot—not unlike Powerhouse, come to think of it. Someone handed me a joint and I was dancing again to "Uncle John's Band." Around the time Act One was winding up a rainbow appeared out of nowhere and everyone *freaked out. It was Jerry!* And *gay pride*!

We had these wooden all-access passes that literally got us anywhere— on the stage, front of house, in everyone's dressing room. And if I'd been told twenty-five years ago that I'd be backstage at a Dead show at intermission in Mickey Hart's dressing room meeting him and Bob and the gang— and Nancy Pelosi in a white tunic!—I wouldn't have believed it. Act Two began with a member of the Dead's posse giving me some moonrock—it's the purest form of MDMA; you bite a little off a rock. It was not speedy at all, just pure, which helped me enjoy a bunch of rare songs that I—who thought I knew every Dead song—didn't know, plus "Dark Star" and "Drums/Space"—which were trippy and long. Natascha Weir appeared— another wife!—and wanted me to be sure to hang out with her and Bob before I left town. I was in the middle of *The Real Housewives of the Grateful Dead*! Watched "St. Stephen" from the side of the stage with Jill Lesh and her kids but then I wandered back to front of house to see the rest of the show because the view was better and the whole point is to just trip out and dance with strangers. After the show we hung out in the RV for an hour drinking more tequila and Diet 7UP and then headed back to San Francisco, where I crashed quickly at the hotel.

❧ SUNDAY, JUNE 28, 2015—SAN FRANCISCO

Woke up a little speedy and ran into Tyler Cassidy, of all people. He was in the lobby bar drinking Bloody Marys and watching the Pride parade. I joined him and we caught up on fifteen or so years of not being in touch. I went down to the parade and found a spot on top of the Muni station rail where I stood for two hours watching the beautiful humanity. We headed to Santa Clara and John was feeling kind of funny (had he done something the night before I'm sure he would've felt fine, like me). I wandered around the stadium before the show, meeting crew people's families backstage, talking to a group of Santa Clara cops about the people having bad trips last night who'd been pulled into their custody (they said they were ignoring people with pot, they had bigger fish to fry), gossiping with the tech guys from the production truck who offered me set lists and again I refused. All of a sudden the show was going to start and I grabbed John, who felt well enough to go front of house.

The songs were totally on point—classic after classic, with Trey Anastasio killing it and amazing keyboards too. Highlights were "Alabama Getaway," "Hell in a Bucket," "Sugar Magnolia"(!), and "Brokedown Palace." I spent most of the concert on my own, dancing furiously like I used to. I was transported back to 1987 as I made concert buddies who got me high. It's like I forgot how to dance that freely and the music taught me again. During the show we met Trixie Garcia, (daughter of . . . !!) who introduced us to her half-sister Sunshine. Sunshine is the daughter of Mountain Girl and Ken Kesey. She invited me to the Oregon Country Fair, which is apparently the hippie version of Burning Man, if that's not redundant. It sounded so perfect to me in the moment and of course I told her I would definitely be there. During intermission Bob Weir texted John and said come hang out, so we went to his private sanctuary off his family room, where I left my cocktail at the door (he is sober) and went in. He was like a rock elder statesman shuffling over to give me a little hug. Back in the show, an intrepid concession girl somehow made her way to us during "Space" and we bought Dibs and enjoyed Dibs and "Space." Somehow it felt like marriage equality, the trend towards legalization of pot, and the Grateful Dead getting back together for a final tour were all mixed into one happy combo platter that filled the stadium with joy.

After the show John decided to stay in his truck, so we hung there and drank on the Astroturf in front and made our way back and forth to the concession stands for some hats and stuff. I heard someone being held in the police area screaming in agony from a bad trip—it was painful.

On the way home Chad's wife, Maggie, texted that if I celebrated gay pride in any more of a straight way, I'd have to go down on a girl out in front of a stadium full of people.

Landed, Wacha picked me up at the airport (with Daryn), and I took the car straight to the beach. Work intruded when we got an email saying NeNe was announcing she's leaving *RHOA*. We knew she wasn't coming back, but when you see it on People.com then it becomes really real. I realized I didn't get asked back for that MLB All-Star Legends and Celebrity Softball thing. What the hell? I emailed with Teresa in prison and she said it was hot in there and I should enjoy the fireworks, and "remember who has stayed loyal all these years, I expect the same in return." So that felt a little . . . scary?

I said horrible, dirty things in front of the Consuelos kids at the Persky Fourth of July party. First Kelly asked what Wacha's green bandanna signified and I said it means he likes getting fisted. Later Mark asked if Wacha only had one ball and I said no, but I slept with someone with a uniball once, and proceeded to tell 80 percent of the story until I realized the boys were listening. Oops. And Wacha ate five deviled eggs off the plate.

Marci Klein had a great barbeque. Really enjoyed talking to Jeff Zucker about the state of the news business and L.A. Reid about the state of Mariah, who he said used to say "turn the giggles up." I don't know what that means, but I love it. Babyface was there too, and Chris Rock and Alec Baldwin. Mom Skyped me and begged me to see *Kinky Boots*. I refuse because it seems like people wailing about acceptance. I'm glad it's there, but I don't need to see it. I told her I saw Chris Rock at Marci's and she said, "Did you tell him he almost ruined your life when you were in high school?" I said that was *Eddie Murphy*, Mom—the *other* black comedian. Then we went into the braces issue, which I've been avoiding.

"I'm old enough already; if I wait any longer I'll be dead!!!! If I don't do it, I'm setting myself up for all kinds of root canals." Then I said, since you are the most morose person ever, can I just ask you a horrible question? If you die with braces do you want to be buried with them, or what? She said she hopes she doesn't because that'd be in the next year. We agreed she would have a long life, then she made her decision: "NO—let 'em take 'em off when they're fixing me up. Tell them to rip them out! I WON'T FEEL IT!"

▶ MONDAY, JULY 6, 2015—NYC

I woke up and got reamed out by the woman from the management company of the building about something that went on with the pipes that she says we didn't have permission for, but my people say we did. They're putting a work stoppage on the construction while they figure it out, and I didn't tell them this but there kind of already *is* a work stoppage in the apartment because I need to close on the other one so we can finalize the new plans and combine them.

▶ TUESDAY, JULY 7, 2015

It was the *RHONY* reunion today and I took one look at the mass of hair and makeup staff, assistants, and hangers-on in the viewing room and told the director to kill the audio in there. That was a first, and guess what—for the first time there were no press leaks during the filming of the reunion. So it only took nine years to figure out to kill the audio to the blabbys. Ramona texted during the break to call her—I did, and she said her guests in the viewing room noticed that Bethenny was on the screen more than anyone else. (Just because they couldn't *hear* didn't mean they weren't going to cause trouble.) Ramona drank wine at lunch and fell asleep while Dorinda was talking, *on the show*. Another reunion first.

Wrapped at nine and went straight to *WWHL*, where I was on cruise control with Jeff and Jenni from *Flipping Out*. I couldn't sleep. I kept hearing the women yakking in my ear and I was stressing about construction. It was horrible.

▶ FRIDAY, JULY 10, 2015—SAG HARBOR

Had a beautiful lunch and then pool time at Marci's beach club and a Chinese masseur showed up and was incredible—ninety minutes by the ocean. Went home, dumped the dog and met Jimmy and Nancy. Their driver showed up and took us to Wölffer Estate, where we had rosé and I heard all about Jimmy's accident with his finger. He has a new perspective on everything after being in Bellevue for ten days, which by all accounts sounds miserable. Went to a party for John Eastman's seventy-sixth birthday. Sir Paul McCartney was there, and so was his vintage Rolls-Royce which has a British-side driver's seat. And Ron Delsener had a pink T-bird parked in front. Billy Joel and his new wife and Alec and Hilaria Baldwin were there. You could make your own pizza, but all the ingredients were figs and edible flowers and stuff you may not want on a pizza. I asked for mushrooms and the server said they're out of season. Mushrooms are out of season? I ordered a caramelized onion pizza and when it came out of the oven some man came up, put it on a plate, and took it. So that didn't work out. Went to Sen and Fallon is so nice to everybody who comes up. We tried to figure out what kind of man I need to be with. I wrote a list of Grateful Dead songs for Jimmy to get into because he doesn't know their stuff that well.

❧ SATURDAY, JULY 11, 2015—SAG HARBOR

Woke up and someone had thrown a fried egg on my car! A *cooked fried egg*. Not even eggs à la française! *Beasts* here in the Hamptons. BEASTS! Nonetheless it was a great beach day with my gay beach friends, George and Justin. Went into the new store that replaced Espresso and they spent a shit-ton of money on it but there's barely any merchandise. I almost bought dark chocolate ice cream until the lady told me it was vegan. I said, you know who wants vegan dark chocolate ice cream? She said, a vegan? I said no, NO ONE. And that's true, by the way.

Janey Buffett had a dinner and I sat with her daughter and her daughter's boyfriend. I had them both whisper in my ear what they thought was the percentage chance they would get married. I said I would not reveal the answer if they were wildly different. They both said 70 percent.

❧ SUNDAY, JULY 12, 2015—SAG HARBOR

Liza called and said I am the least defensive person she knows, which I liked hearing. Had a spur-of-the-moment beach walk with Bethenny and we wound up walking for miles and had to get a ride back at Marci Klein's.

Drove back to the city; Laverne Cox and André Leon Talley were on the show and I was out of it. In the back of the car to the show, I did my usual skimming through pitches for Mazels and Jackholes from the team and nonchalantly picked a Jackhole, a seemingly benign online feud about Kylie Jenner's cornrows between her and a young actress I've never heard of named Amandla Stenberg. I figured it was a way to get Laverne and André to weigh in on what they think of white girls wearing cornrows. They both said they didn't see anything wrong with it.

MONDAY, JULY 13, 2015—NYC

All day I have been getting tweets about last night's Jackhole from black people outraged that I would pick on a sixteen-year-old for starting a dialogue about cultural appropriation and more generally calling out the way I/Bravo represent black women on our air. My natural instinct when I get heat is to immediately try to make it better, but this time I realized I'd blindly stepped in something so much bigger. There's no quick fix. I'm embarrassed to admit it, but I'd never even *heard* of cultural appropriation until today, and when I randomly picked the Jackhole last night I had no clue what the big debate was even about.

Had lunch with Bonnie Hammer and asked her what was gonna be my downfall. She didn't know. I brought it up to Frances again after lunch and it was all a joke. I wasn't consciously connecting it to what was happening on Twitter, but within a few hours, last night's Jackhole situation was making me nervous. On another note, a while ago an older gay couple sent me a letter asking me to officiate their wedding. They've been together forty years, one of them is wheelchair bound, and they happen to live down the street from me. I said yes, and today was the day. It was in their apartment, with just us and a witness, who told me that Maker's Mark was like gasoline.

Conference call with *EW* people afterwards about the cover; it's gone from a picture of me in the back of a limo multitasking (we rejected that one) to me on a bed with a computer (no, again) to me with models on a bed to—today—me in front of Manhattan at night, which I like.

By the time the show started at eleven, Black Twitter (that's a real thing; look it up somewhere) was really pissed at me and I was getting a significant number of tweets calling for my head. I emailed my Bravo bosses around 1:00 a.m. saying that by the time they woke up I assumed this would have become a news item somewhere and that I need direction to make it right. I was pained to think I had attacked a sixteen-year-old girl who was intelligently trying to express herself about an issue about which I was unfortunately clueless, when I was really just trying to make a joke about a white girl wearing cornrows. Was feeling reminiscent of what happened to Zendaya, when Giuliana Rancic's critiques of her dreadlocks on *Fashion Police* started a race war. Went to bed thinking this was way bigger than me, and was going to be my downfall.

▶ TUESDAY, JULY 14, 2015

Really a horrible day. Woke up to Frances saying yes, this is an issue, which wasn't exactly what I wanted to hear. Taped our sixth anniversary show at 2:00 p.m. as Black Twitter was leading a groundswell against me. At one point #BoycottBravo was trending. Everyone said I called the young actress a jackhole. I didn't; I called the *feud* the jackhole. I sent a tweet this morning clarifying that, and then an apology tweet, which was vetted by no less than fifteen people and was ridiculed in a second ("That took too long," "That was too fast," "You're Giuliana," "You don't mean it," "You're losing money on us so now you care"). When I wanted to defend myself, I tried to remember what Liza had said recently, that I'm not defensive.

So we taped our sixth anniversary show with John Cena and Method Man and I announced to our staff before the show that with what was going on, it might also be our last show. I was half kidding and half scared out of my wits. I got off the air and BET and Roland Martin and *Ebony* were tweeting at me. Endless variations on "Have a seat," "You stole our culture," "You got rich off us," "Check your white privilege," etc., etc. I called Bevy Smith to get her advice on what to do. She said I had to educate myself on what everyone was so upset about. I told her that until yesterday I had never even *heard* of cultural appropriation, or thought about the term "white privilege," for that matter. She said the fact I had never heard of either of those terms is white privilege in itself. She said no apology on Twitter was going to satisfy Black Twitter and that I need to start getting involved in the community and educating myself. We made a date for lunch. She's a good friend, and smart. I didn't get into this with Bevy, but took it as an example of the way perceptions have changed regarding race over time, that my two very best black friends had never heard of it either, but they're older. #BrazilianAndySamberg was all about it, and gave me a further education.

Wacha came home from Brooklyn and wanted *nothing* to do with my bad day. He was looking at me like, "You don't know what *I've* been through today, brother!" because he was caught in the rain or something with Sherman. My day was worse, I tried to tell him.

I got a notification saying you have an email on this prison system—I looked and the subject was "it's Teresa," as though it could be *anyone* else. Inside it said, "Thanks for the book; I just got it." (I'd sent her *Most Talkative*.) One minute later came an email saying, "I hate the picture of me from the reunion that you put in the book." I said, "I hope you like book better than the picture."

On the way to the *Trainwreck* premiere with Dave I noticed that the non-black press was picking up the story now—Jezebel's headline, for instance, was "Fucking Andy Cohen Is Working Our Last Nerve." I fantasized about one day writing a piece called "Fucking Jezebel Is Working My Last Nerve." I did photographs but no press because I wanted to show off my denim suit I got at Ralph Lauren the other day and not talk about what an asshole I am. Couldn't concentrate on the movie—left with ten minutes to go and got in two wrong cars before finding Ray. Twitter was alight with *RHONY* and "Don't be uncool," which made me happy to no end until, to put a capper on the day, I got a text from Daryn saying she went to pick up the dog and out of nowhere he *attacked* her and ripped her shirt. I freaked out, and so did she, albeit quietly. It was bad. I could barely keep my mind on the show. Carole and Heather were on with two male models, one of whom seemed to be celebrating a birthday by making zero sense to anyone. Went on Twitter after the show and people were furious that I didn't apologize on the air, even though I did online.

A doctor came to the studio to treat Daryn and she was okay, but she was really shaken up. This was worse than getting publicly flogged. My heart was broken. Was I going to have to get rid of Wacha? How I could ever make things right with him? This was so out of the blue! He loves Daryn. And so do I! Am I going to have to choose between the dog and Daryn? I called Brandon McMillan, the dog trainer, who reminded me Wacha has bad PTSD from being abused and is protecting his property. He said he will work with him when he gets back to New York but that it's hard to erase his bad memories and triggers of abuse. I got home and Wacha was in a corner looking very traumatized and upset. I ignored him and he came to me outside. Went to bed and my air conditioner was broken. A shitty day, beginning to end.

▶ WEDNESDAY, JULY 15, 2015

Woke up at 6:30 a.m., sweaty and gross. Still getting flamed on Twitter. Taped a show with Hoda and Kathie Lee that put me in a good mood and I felt like maybe it was all over. I went shopping for bathroom tiles with Eric Hughes for much of the afternoon, having forgotten that I had told our PR to stop sending me clips and thus oblivious that there was a big wave of press all day online, including a piece on Time.com entitled "Andy Cohen's Apology to Amandla Stenberg Is Part of a Pattern: The Late Night Host's Provocative Behavior Can Go Too Far" that listed insane examples of reasons I could get fired, like calling One Direction "twinks" on the *Today* show and criticizing the kids from P.S. 22's Oscar performance. It was a friend at Bravo who described the article in detail to me on the phone at the end of the day, and I vowed then not to say anything else publicly on the topic. I called Deirdre on my way to tape the show to say don't mention any of the articles, because *EW* writer Tim Stack was in the middle of a profile on me and coming to the Amy Schumer taping and I didn't want him to realize how damaged I had been by this whole thing and make it a part of the story. He didn't bring it up and it was a great show, but I was still walking around on eggshells.

▶ FRIDAY, JULY 17, 2015

You would think I would've been starving myself and working out all week for the *EW* shoot today, but I didn't work out once and ate like shit all week, so that's bad.

Had a longtime plan with Carole Radziwill that she was going to hang with Wacha today, and she came to get the dog without incident. I worked out at Equinox with Pablo's trainer, Stanislav, who's from Ukraine. I just wanted to do something different, but I felt like I was cheating on the Ninj.

Not only does the black community hate me, today's headline in the *New York Post* was about the suit I proudly wore to the *Trainwreck* premiere: "Lena Dunham and Andy Cohen Are Disasters in Denim." It was one of the Top fucking Stories. Also, *USA Today* did a piece that said I'd destroyed a young black girl. They quoted two people who were completely intolerant of the idea that I didn't know what cultural appropriation was. Now that I know what it is, I accept it and I understand why people are pissed at the idea of white people stealing from an oppressed culture. I don't live on a college campus! And now I understand that it's the definition of white privilege that no one around me is talking about cultural appropriation. Had a long talk with mom and Blouse about it. Blouse was so comforting and was very upset people were calling me racist. But I don't think I can tell the black community my *housekeeper* thinks I am not racist. Can you imagine how *that* would go over? Her heart was as hurt as mine, though, and that went a long way for me.

The *EW* photo shoot was in an insane suite at the Palace Hotel with a Jacuzzi on the terrace. I popped and sprayed eight bottles of champagne. Wacha was with me, and I didn't realize he was standing at my foot "guarding" me, and neither did the stylist who came to take my men's sock garters off. The story writes itself, sadly; Wacha growled, then went after the stylist, who got nipped on the arm. I was humiliated even though the guy was fine. I now have to view my dog completely differently and watch for signs like a hawk. I ate lots of mesquite BBQ chips (which is the converse of what you're supposed to do at your cover shoot), turned toward the camera and pretended to pee over Manhattan, and got in the Jacuzzi in boxers and tux shirt with Manhattan behind me and sprayed more champs. I think they got some great photographs. Got a save-the-date for Madonna's birthday party in the Hamptons August 16, which is ironic given that I have been emailing and speaking with Brian, her new publicist, all week trying to let me interview her for this *EW* issue. The birthday party is when I am supposed to be on Fire Island, so this is a doozy.

❧ SATURDAY, JULY 18, 2015

Mom has announced to her dentist that she is *not* wearing braces. She told him to find another way to fix her teeth.

▶ TUESDAY, JULY 21, 2015

We were supposed to tape 50 Cent and Cara Delevingne at 3:00 p.m. but 50 cancelled an hour before. Then we moved Cara to tomorrow and booked Zac Posen. Then she cancelled. Then we booked the Countess to go on with Zac and Zac cancelled. Then I booked Melissa Gorga to go on with the Countess at the last minute. So, I mean, *Jesus*. But 50 rescheduled to go on with Dionne Warwick soon and that's a lot better. Had a great conference call with Sirius and I realized I have to nail down Ingrid Sischy for a radio show.

▶ WEDNESDAY, JULY 22, 2015

I had tickets to U2 and invited Liza, Amanda, Bruce, Jackie, Jeanne, Dave, Billy Eichner, Amy, SJP, and Jerry O'Connell and literally no one could go. Had lunch with Bevy and talked about cultural appropriation and white privilege for an hour. The controversy has died down but these are clearly issues that are important, and I need to fully understand. She's going to do a radio show for Radio Andy. Bruce and Liza came over for rosé on the roof. Bruce told me to invite Jimmy Fallon to U2; I said he'll probably be backstage or with the band. Got a text from Ingrid replying to mine about her doing a radio show, which said, "Hi Andy I would have just loved it. And loved to have done this with you. Unfortunately at this time it is not something I can commit to. I send my love, Ingrid." She had seemed interested in June, so what happened? The U2 concert was divine—I wound up taking Bill Curtin. Jimmy came out and that was a big surprise and so, yeah, Jimmy was *on*stage, not backstage. He wouldn't have loved my seats anyway. Bono is five foot four and kinda fat and sixty and still the greatest rock-and-roll superstar on stage. Bill says I *have* to leave Fire Island and go to the Madonna party.

FRIDAY, JULY 24, 2015—SAG HARBOR

I was at Marci's and I read on Twitter that Ingrid Sischy died. Breast cancer. I had no idea. I was doubly saddened by her sweet text two days ago. She was such an interesting person, always a friendly face across a crowded room, always had time for everyone and always had something interesting to say. What a loss. It was a beautiful, clear sunny day with four clouds in the sky and I sat on the beach with Christina McGuinness shooting the shit, drinking a Coors Light, Wacha by my side digging in the sand, feeling very grateful for my life.

Went to Almond with Joe and his friends. It was gay night, and these are the fashions I saw: white pants, sweaters over the shoulders, Madras tops and bottoms, and pastels. It looks like the Madonna interview is going to happen next Wednesday on the phone and I can record it for Radio Andy.

SATURDAY, JULY 25, 2015—SAG HARBOR

Went to the beach and hung with my gay beach friends, Justin and George. Justin was in rare form; we were walking to get in and he insisted we all walk together because "we look bitchier walking in a group." And then I headed to Jimmy and Nancy's for Winnie's birthday. I talked to Jimmy's mom, Gloria, most of the time. She's on the lookout for people ripping off both my and Jimmy's shows and I love it. She said someone did a shotski the other day on another show and she "had a conniption."

SUNDAY, JULY 26, 2015—SAG HARBOR—NYC

Slept *eleven hours* last night. Holy shit. I've been doing a lot of FaceTiming with my two flirts: #BrazilianAndySamberg and #BritActor, who has come back into the picture, having broken up with his boyfriend.

Dizzy all day from too much iced coffee. Watched *I Am Cait* looking for something funny to show on *WWHL*. Considered showing the moment where she's playing tennis with her sister and says, "What do we do with the balls?" and realized that was disrespectful and would've gotten me fired.

About eight forty-five I get a text saying Bobbi Kristina has died and Dionne Warwick is on her way to the show. So we all freaked out—we'd had all these funny games planned for her, like In the Benz with My Psychic Friendz, that we decided we would scrap. Dionne arrived alone, in a powder-blue velour sweat suit and fanny pack; I hugged her in the hallway and she was misty eyed. I thanked her for being there, and she said she had just gotten the news in the car and needed to make some calls. I said, you figure out what you want to do; we are here for you. She decided she would come on the show, that I could talk to her about it but the less the better. I went in and told her how much I love her, how sad I was about the circumstance, and asked if I could get her *anything*—some Cristal? Anything. She said, could I smoke? I said, you can do anything you want; *you're Dionne Warwick*. 50 Cent was the other guest and he'd just been handed a verdict in his case. So the first few minutes were serious, and I told Dionne I always knew she was a legend but tonight I had found out what a pro she was in honoring her commitment to us. Anthony Recker was behind the bar and I swear, what I would do to that guy . . . Michael Rourke's dog, Samson, died today so I spent a lot of time hugging Wacha.

▶ MONDAY, JULY 27, 2015

Met a porn star on the street from Miami while walking Wacha so that was a good way to start the day. His name is Ramón but I forgot his stage name. He is just starting to become big, he said. Finished my piece about the Grateful Dead for *EW*, then worked out with the Ninj. I'm fat right now, is the thing. Lunch with John Hill celebrating his one-year anniversary of sobriety. It was festive, in a sober kinda way. Walked home and saw that Anderson's barber has gone completely mental, with five of the same photos of AC in his chair in the window. He goes here; we get it! I texted Anderson a picture of the montage. Went to *WWHL*, where I had a two-hour interview about my career with the TV Academy that was kind of exhausting. The show was something else, Meghan King and JoAnna Swisher. Lance Bass was there too. Meghan dyed her hair pink and I told her it looked terrible and then immediately felt bad about it. I keep calling Shereé to try to get her back to the show but my efforts don't seem to be going anywhere.

TUESDAY, JULY 28, 2015

Took the subway (my new favorite transportation) to Bravo, where I met with Shari. The Housewives are all in disarray; we have casting issues in Beverly Hills and Atlanta. Spoke to Dina, who hasn't signed her release from the Manzo wedding yet. Met Tim Stack at Sirius—he is following me today. Planned our programming schedule and had an excellent creative meeting with Sandra Bernhard. Her show is going to be phenomenal. She is going to "elevate the fucking conversation." Tyler Perry called in the middle of it all to make sure Bravo would never air *Being Bobby Brown* again and I said it's gone forever. He is running interference on the funeral and negotiating between the Browns and the Houstons. Went to meet Anderson at Café Cluny and we regaled Tim with stories. In the middle of it all I get a text from Bethenny saying she doesn't think she can commit to doing a radio show right now, so that sank my day. She is too busy, but I am fucked. Six weeks before launch. Breathe. Two shows: Billy Eichner and Julie Klausner, and Ramona and Michael Rapaport. He is a *Housewives* savant, which made all the difference. Then I spent an hour interviewing Ramona for the *RHONY* special. Came home and Adam was set up on the terrace—it was hot and breezy, but I got a massage from twelve-thirty to two and it was pretty delicious.

WEDNESDAY, JULY 29, 2015

Hot as balls. Interviewed Connie Britton for *EW*, then took the subway to Sirius to talk about Radio Andy options. In play: Julie Klausner, Keith Olbermann, and Mechelle Collins. Interviewed Madonna at one! It actually happened! She said she was wearing a tattered pair of Dolce silk pajama bottoms. She called me sexist because I said she could just stay in one place and not tour. She said I wouldn't say that to a man. I'm not so sure about that. Then I interviewed Nile Rodgers about Diana Ross, the B-52's, and Sister Sledge, so I was in heaven. Walked to CAA to meet with Telepictures about hosting a reboot of *Love Connection.* Hosted a fund raiser for PFLAG, then stopped by Ramona's book party at Beautique, where TMZ asked me what sport Anderson and I would play if we were athletes. I said I don't freaking know! Did two shows and on the first one Ed Helms told me during the commercial break that I am doing *The Graham Norton Show*. The *Million Dollar Listing San Francisco* guys were on the live one and two of them got in a big fight afterwards. The gay one told Anthony he was "being Jewy" when Anthony said the car was leaving in ten minutes.

⯈ THURSDAY, JULY 30, 2015—NYC—SAG HARBOR

Keith Olbermann ain't happening for the radio. No surprise there. Walked dog in the steaming heat. Forgot bags to pick up his poop so I'm walking with a pile of shit on a paper bag in one hand, steaming tea in the other, and my earbuds in, on the phone to Sandy from Sirius trying to figure out WTF we're doing with this fucking channel and Wacha jerks and I spill the tea all over me. (I didn't spill the poop, though.) Long meeting with Gordon and Eric going over plans, electric-socket installation, tile selection, more fabrics, some wallpapers, and lighting. Made great decisions and am excited. Went to the doctor for a checkup. Asked to go on PrEP and got my blood tested. He's never heard of PrEP, so he's going to research it and get back to me. It seems like the HIV-prevention miracle drug we've all been waiting for, so I don't understand why more people aren't on it. Drove to the beach in the rain and talked on the phone the whole time. Dinner with Sandy and the Bon Jovis at Sam's. Talked to JBJ about the U2 concert and Steve Perry having the balls to leave Journey while they were still hot.

⯈ SATURDAY, AUGUST 1, 2015—SAG HARBOR

Beach all day with Justin and George. Came home and interviewed Taraji Henson by phone, my last job for *EW*. She and I were doing lines from Dominique Deveraux and *Mahogany*. Went to Nick and Toni's, where I was parking in a controversial way (backing up where I shouldn't, onto Route 27) when this guy in a convertible who I thought was Barry started yelling at me, "No, no, no!" I went into a rage and flew into Nick and Toni's, where I told the Brodericks that I was going to find the guy and say what the *fuck* was your problem with how I was parking and who are *you* to be the judge of my parking? I came in *hot*. Ten minutes later Scott Greenstein, my new boss at Sirius, comes over and it had been him yelling at me. Oh shit. As fat as I am, I had to have cookie-dough gelato at the end of the meal. I forced myself to go to the gay party to meet Justin and George, and it was a bunch of handsome men but all the good ones were taken and the rest were land mines. Came home and was in bed, spooned with Wacha, by eleven forty-five. His head was against mine. It's the little things.

▶ TUESDAY, AUGUST 4, 2015—NYC

A note for me was delivered to Surfin, unsigned, saying "Your friends Justin and George are the most obnoxious and pretentious people in the world. PS lick my ass with your long tongue." Except it said "like" instead of "lick." Bruce came over in the afternoon and said I have to bring it to the beach to show to them. Did a phone interview with a *New Yorker* reporter who is doing a profile on Bethenny and said to me, "No one who reads the *New Yorker* even knows what the *Real Housewives* is about. What is it?" *Very* snobby, and I did not take kindly to that and set her STRAIGHT.

▶ THURSDAY, AUGUST 6, 2015

The *EW* feature turned out really well, a relief. The cover looks awesome. Went to CVS and bought a bunch of stuff. The cashier handed me my receipt and said if you bring it back next time you get five dollars off. I got home and realized I had bought Gillette Sensor blades, not Mach 3s. And I put them and the receipt at my front door because obviously I should return them, but knowing me I probably won't. They cost thirty bucks! Had great drinks with Frances, then *EW* threw me a dinner, which was lovely. It's an honor to see myself on the cover of that magazine. I feel like I've made it. Had a massage on the terrace.

⯈ SATURDAY, AUGUST 8, 2015—SAG HARBOR

We had a good shoot with Shereé and the Atlanta girls last night, which made me very happy because I have been trying to get her back on the show for the last month. Today I delivered the mean letter to the boys at the beach and it completely traumatized George and made him sick to his stomach but Justin thought it was kind of funny and said he always strives to be the best, so the idea that he was the *most* obnoxious and pretentious person in the world was something. Went to Surf Lodge for Sean Avery's clothing event and he yelled at a photographer because he was sick of having his picture taken and I said sweetie, this is why you're here! Dinner at Sandy's was gorgeous and delicious. Got a long email from Brandi at the end of night whose subject line was "why do you hate me?"

⯈ SUNDAY, AUGUST 9, 2015—SAG HARBOR—NYC

Sent Brandi a thoughtful email back, which I hope she appreciates. I refuted her point by point. I don't hate her. Had lunch at the Seinfelds', where Wacha ran around the massive yard chasing birds, which was adorable and glorious. He really wore himself out. He runs like a bunny with his gimpy hip. Bethenny called because she is hosting the RHOBH at her house and Lu keeps trying to get herself invited but production doesn't want a double crossover, and Lu keeps texting to Bethenny, "Don't be uncool." I think it's hilarious, of course. Hung with Hickey at SJP's for a dip in the ocean. SJP had the most insane hairdo—a top knot/high pony combination of the Miss Hannigan variety. I loved it. She said she went to the supermarket in it. Then I surprised Vanderpump, Kyle, Rinna, and Eileen at a winery in Water Mill where they were at a tasting. Fun to see them in my backyard.

⯈ MONDAY, AUGUST 10, 2015

Worked out. It is so great having Bruce back for the summer. He came for lunch and we camped out on the terrace with Liza all afternoon while a parade of people came in and out of the door: Mike Robley to deal with the outdoor lights for my staff party; my computer geek, JP; then Tonee to cut my hair. It was a fun afternoon. I actually returned the razor blades at CVS I bought last Thursday and then got five dollars off with my coupon, so I got free milk. I felt like I accomplished something. We taped Ricki and Caroline Manzo, then the live show was Vicki and Jeff Lewis. We all went out to the Hotel Gansevoort roof after, joined by Tamra and later NeNe. Jeff and Tamra analyzed my inability to be in a relationship. Tamra thought I didn't have any sex at all or else she would be reading about it, and I said that's not the case, no one cares who I'm having sex with. NeNe arrived in a Veronica Lake long blond wig and gave me the play-by-play of why she can't do the show with Kim, which seems to involve something that happened at the same women's expo where she and Wendy Williams's husband got into it. I left at one-thirty and they were shocked that I was leaving. Oh, and Vicki showed me her boobs several times and they are very nice, with small nipples. They look great. So now I have seen hers and Tamra's. And I think Kim's.

▶ TUESDAY, AUGUST 11, 2015

Got an email from Vicki saying she can't believe she showed me her boobs, that it was totally unprofessional. I said you are the OG Housewife and it's kind of in your job description. Almost cancelled the Ninj, but it'll be my last workout before my three-week vacation so I felt I had to go. Then went to lunch with Jenny McCarthy at Morandi. I sat outside for twenty minutes waiting for her, then realized I bet she was inside and went in and there she was. We gossiped a bunch. She said Joy Behar kept a daily journal of her entire time on *The View*—so that's gotta be incredible, but I bet we won't see it for a while. Most importantly, she taught me about uncut dicks—that they get harder more easily because they are hooded and so extra sensitive. Like, a wind on the tip can make them crazy hard. Jenny taught *me* about penis stuff? Walked home and called Anderson to gossip. It was rainy so I did work and tried to nap, then BJ Novak came over to talk about his list app and stuff. He is sweet and a little intense. Interviewed Connie Britton for radio, then she was on the show with Austin Mahone, during which I said I was a fluffer for guys, which made me look pervy—I meant girls. Then I interviewed Christina Hendricks for radio, then did the live show with her and Bethenny and then a ninety-minute interview with Bethenny. That's a lot of interviewing, and I have an early morning tomorrow.

▶ WEDNESDAY, AUGUST 12, 2015

Woke up and started interviewing again. First up was Senator Claire McCaskill, for radio. Taped a show with Kim Zolciak and Angela Kinsey, then recorded the voice-over for the *RHONY* lost-footage show, during which I had to say "Jewish sushi chef" and it took about ten minutes between fits and giggles and exhaustion to get it out. Took Wacha to Canine Styles to get dry cleaned and he was *furious*. Guess what? They're going out of business! Greedy landlord. Where am I gonna take this boy? Threw a party for the entire staff of *WWHL* on my terrace and it was a beautiful night. I had seventy Steakburgers and fries from Steak 'n Shake and all of them got eaten. Two people on the staff got really drunk, so I think it was a success.

▶ THURSDAY, AUGUST 13, 2015—SUNDAY, AUGUST 23, 2015— FIRE ISLAND

I rented an incredibly chic house on Fire Island designed by Horace Gifford and it's perfect. Supposedly there is a dungeon downstairs, but I haven't seen it. Met a Jewish lawyer at tea and went to his house for dinner, which was one of those typical Fire Island dinners—random group, pre-meal Adderall passed around, and a kid who said it was his first time on Fire Island and he was having a miserable time. I said you *should* hate it, it's awful, I understand, but in fifteen years you'll like it. Then the lawyer and I took a Jacuzzi and the hosts offered me molly for the Meat Rack party but I went home and took an Ambien.

Saturday Bruce came out and we had twenty-four hours of bliss together. We decided maybe he will transition in twenty years to a Judge Judy type named Bruna Bozzi who will run for mayor of NYC, and she will keep saying, "ENOUGH ALREADY." I met a Dominican at Sip n Twirl who asked me if I like rough sex. I was like, *no*! Sunday John Hill arrived and Bruce went to the Hamptons, where I joined him hours and a ferry ride later for Madonna's "Spanish Gypsy"–themed fifty-seventh birthday party. In the galaxy of themed parties, Spanish Gypsy is not my favorite. I hated my costume, which was a puffy shirt and seventies striped pants. Mark and Kelly, both looking very sexy (despite the boot on Kelly's foot), gave me a ride, and I said I came from Fire Island because I have FOMO and Kelly said she has FOGO—fear of *going* out. Ha. Kelly gave me a smoky eye, at which point I felt better about my outfit.

The party was in three locations on her massive horse farm in Bridge-hampton. There were votives everywhere that took you through the barn (full of Madonna's horses—*Madonna needs a bunch of horses!*) to a little para-dise with Oriental rugs and hay and strings of lights everywhere. It looked like a movie set of a gypsy village. Madonna was Stevie Nicks gypsy, with a grill and a hint of Baby Jane. Another long path of votives led us up into the middle of a field, where two long picnic tables were set up under twinkly lights for a seated dinner. Sat across from Guy Oseary and next to Paul McCartney and his wife, Nancy. She was very cool—in the family trucking business. Sir Paul and I talked about how great Howard Stern is, even though he was scared at first of going on. They left kinda early. Got compliments from Guy about my Madonna interview in *EW*; he said I got her talking about stuff she doesn't talk about. I wanted a selfie with Madonna badly but never asked for one. You become *that guy*. She said she is rehearsing for her new tour at the Nassau Coliseum from 10:00 a.m. to 2:00 a.m. every day. After dinner, lights in the distance went on slowly and a tent appeared, and there was another path lit by candles and we all went there. I mean, it was *far*. And now we were in the middle of a massive field under a circus tent, and I chatted with Madonna about how sweet her kids are (Rocco hugged me when he introduced himself), how well everyone adhered to the dress code ("It's nice when people make an effort"), and how far behind she is in pre-paring for the tour. I told her thanks for the interview and she said it was nice, she liked it. She was sitting on a throne, and she said I don't know if this is for me but I tend to gravitate toward thrones. There were about forty-five minutes of performances by dancers—a Spanish flamenco dancer, etc.—then we all got sparklers and her cake came out. I bet she spent $1.5 million on this thing. Major dancing. Bruce was shirtless and dancing with Naomi Watts like they were on *Dancing with the Stars*. We left around 2:00 a.m.

Came back to Fire Island the next morning at 9:00 a.m. and Dave arrived. We had the best boy day, just drank and swam and talked and talked and talked. I loved showing him the gay beach camp; it was every Fire Island stereotype right in his face: We saw an underwear shoot on the beach, Robert and Robert across the way had a daytime sausagefest pool party going. A group of boys plopped down on the beach in front of us and I bet Dave they were chorus boys on their day off from their show. We went in the water and sure enough, they were all telling me what shows they're in. Made flank steak and took Dave to tea, where people thought we were boyfriends. Everyone was going to see Shequida but we went home and ate frozen pizzas and took a Jacuzzi. He left the next morning and word in town was that Shequida had a meltdown on stage last night and left mid-performance. There were technical difficulties—not her fault, but apparently she did an epic monologue about how the drag queen always gets blamed but it's not the queen's fault. Then she dropped the mic a few bars into "Private Dancer," which is her tip song, and just disappeared. I was going to go see Lady Bunny, but she cancelled because she lost her voice on the Wigstock cruise. So it wasn't a good week for drag queens on Fire Island. By the way, I posted a pic of the RHONY at the reunion today and every time I post a photo of the Housewives on Facebook, Facebook automatically tags Lady Bunny, so I guess they are drag queens according to Facebook. And I saw the Brazilian at tea who has the Grace Jones tattoo that looks like the state of California. He's telling everyone I wrote a book about him because I mention his bad tattoo in the *Diaries*.

Grac and Amanda came out on Thursday morning. I made them lunch, which they couldn't get over—grilled chicken, corn, and brussels sprouts (#BrazilianAndySamberg taught me how to grill them the other night on FaceTime). We talked about everything, and I was in the pool lamenting to Grac that I can't believe we are forty-eight and she told me we're forty-seven and I freaked out. I've spent the last two months thinking I'm forty-eight and now I feel like I was just given back another year to live! I'm young! Hickey arrived that afternoon and we went to tea, then to hear Lina spin, then home for dinner and we ate some of Amanda's pot brownie and I was out of it and couldn't wait to go to bed. Spent the next day sick in bed all day—horrible. The girls went back to the Hamptons and Hickey left early Saturday to go to NYC. So all the fun was aborted and I stayed in sick, waiting to go to Barry's boat off the coast of Spain on Sunday. I finished *The Girl on the Train* in a day. I didn't figure it out. Not the ending to the Fire Island experience I'd wanted. I am too tan, so there's that.

I was sick-ish with a stomach bug most of the time we were on the boat. There were many swims in the very blue water off the coast of Ibiza, dodging jellyfish, but they were short for me. The group was Bruce, Bryan, Barry, DVF, Anderson, Ben, Jason, Lauren, Jeff Bezos and his wife, MacKenzie, and SJP—who I'd been wanting to be on the boat with for so long. It was such a letdown to be sick when it finally happened. Bezos has a booming laugh and what seemed like a Midwestern sensibility, even though he grew up in Miami. Bruce figured out *The Girl on the Train* less than halfway through, which was impressive. I'm reading *A Little Life*, which is heartbreaking and fantastic. Fell in love with Mike, the impossibly handsome, and impossibly straight, new ginger crew member. One night I dreamt SJP and I were backstage at Diana Ross's Central Park concert—the sunny make-up date, not the rainy one— and it was so colorful and vivid that I woke up feeling it was real. I started thinking about Christmas and what I might do, and realized another year was upon us and here I was single and alone, and I started to become disconnected from the group. I feel like I actually *lost* some of my tan on this trip. Also I feel like I'm ready to go back to work, but I have another week off. The news from home is that Martino from Canine Styles has relocated to Beasty Feast on Hudson Street. Wacha can go to his same groomer he hates instead of having to find a new one to fall in hate with.

Landed in NYC and went straight to the walk-in clinic. The nurse had a mushroom-cap hairdo, which you don't see too much anymore, and said her name was Aspen. I said that was such a pretty name, and that I love Aspen. She said she was born in one and that's how she got her name. So at least she wasn't born in a Civic or something. But Altima would be kind of a fabulous name. Aspen gave me a kit to poop into to make a stool sample because they figured I had a parasite, but all the labs are closed until Monday. I decided I might actually choose the parasite over having to poop in a kit and bring it to a lab. Walked Wacha and met a guy on Twelfth Street who approached me with tears in his eyes and said I was his only hope—he'd cheated on his girlfriend by texting another girl (nothing else happened), but he still loves her so much. He knows he fucked up the trust. I'm her favorite. I did a two-minute testimonial video for him. Went to Indochine with Bruce, Bryan, and Benjamin. Came home and was asleep by ten-thirty.

SUNDAY, AUGUST 30, 2015—
MONDAY, SEPTEMBER 7, 2015—SAG HARBOR

Final week of vacation out in Sag Harbor. Feel like I have something *still*. Lyme disease? I got tested for it on Monday. It takes four days to find out. I never pooped in the kit; I can't do it. Finishing *A Little Life* and it is *gutting* me. I had a flirty two-hour FaceTime with #BritActor, which made me so happy. It literally made me feel better. He's so charming and adorable. Then again, so is #BrazilianAndySamberg, so my cup is overflowing with out-of-town possibilities. Is there a theme here? Wacha ate a piece of chocolate out of Kelly's purse with the wrapper still on, so I am waiting for him to shit that out. Yikes.

On Friday I met Sandy, Barry, and Joel at LT Burger, then went to Sandy's to show him plans for my apartment, which he *loved*. Big relief. He thinks Gordon is a genius. Went to Allen Grubman's, where it was a real power group: David Zaslav (who said Zucker was bragging he discovered me), Irving Azoff (talked about Dead and Company), Les Moonves (talked about Colbert) and Julie Chen (talked about *Big Brother*). Dinner with Jimmy and Nancy at Sen, and while I was waiting for them I ran into Alfredo Paredes across the street at the antique store. He said I have to have a child, that it is going to change my life and enrich it, and even while he was starting to talk I knew he was right. I keep waiting to be "ready" to have a kid, and hearing him, I knew that I was getting closer to that moment. I don't know when it will be, but I do think it will happen. I see it in my life. I know there is something deeper for me in my future. I need there to be. Speaking of deep, at dinner, Jimmy said, "There's an Olsen twin here, do you know one of them?" I said yeah, I know Ashley, and he said oh, I know MK. He went to the bathroom and came back and said it's Ashley; her hair is really blond and she's really tan. I went to the bathroom and the girl turned to me and I realized: A) it wasn't Ashley, B) it wasn't MK, and C) it was someone I knew because she said, "You're gonna walk by me and act like you *don't know me*?" So now I was fucked. Ten seconds in I realized it was Tracy Anderson, who looks *nothing* like an Olsen. I went back to the table and said Jimmy, you're an asshole. He made a Lumpy Rutherford joke and then a Keshia Knight Pulliam one, so all was quickly forgiven.

Saturday breakfast at Sandy's, then to Marci's for lunch, then to SJP's barbecue, which I kept calling "cute" and that was bugging Hickey. There was a movie playing down the beach for free and Scott Wittman first said it was "Pool Boys Should Do It" then "Pizza Boy: He Delivers" but everyone else said it was *Paul Blart: Mall Cop*. A policeman, Officer Buzzkill, came and "busted" our almost spent bonfire for 1) not being a hundred feet from the dune 2) not having a bucket of water nearby (our rosé steeped in ice didn't count, allegedly) and 3) having amplified music (SJP's teeny boom box playing Al Jarreau). John Slattery was the only one with an ID, so he got the ticket. Meanwhile, the irony of *Paul Blart: Mall Cop* playing in the distance seemed lost on this policeman. I ate almost an entire pint of chocolate chocolate chip ice cream when I got home. My blood tests all came back negative, so I threw out the stool kit.

Sunday I took a boat to the Perskys', on Shelter Island, with the Consueloses while Jake Shears danced for us in a Speedo. Ate plenty of peppermint ice cream; Liza and I threw a football. Then to Marci's for the last dinner of the summer with Jimmy and Nancy. Jimmy said "NO WAY, ROSÉ!" which I think should be a *thing*. Maybe next summer. Got a ride back to the city in a helicopter with David Geffen—the heli really takes it out of Wacha; he gets tired after. Skyped with Mom and Dad—we talked about her friend's funeral, and I said I think a big synagogue service and then a private graveside is the way to go and she said, "ARE WE PLANNING MY FUNERAL RIGHT NOW?" So maybe we were. She said she knows more dead people than living people, which I pointed out is a lie. But it's true she knows a lot of dead ones.

Dinner at Good with Hickey. I ran into Joe and then—finally—Sally Field. It was good timing, because I am closing on the apartment next door tomorrow and needed to tell her I was going to begin blasting it out on Wednesday. I predicated the discussion with the news that all I had been hearing was buzz for her new movie with Max Greenfield, so that might have made the construction news a little easier to take. She said how great that I am able to make this great new apartment. Had a massage from Adam outside at nine and got a lot of thinking done. Topics included my radio launch next week, construction, and what it will mean to share a wall with Sally Field.

▶ WEDNESDAY, SEPTEMBER 9, 2015—NYC

Martha Stewart shamed my Ferragamo shoes right before air: "Those shoes are the ugliest color. They're, like, cowboy-boot brown."

▶ FRIDAY, SEPTEMBER II, 2015

Married to Medicine reunion all day. Got a text that Serena lost, so tomorrow's U.S. Open is gonna be boring. Pup play date with Ricky Van Veen and Moxie, then Raoul's with SJP, Matthew, Hickey, and Sedaris—our 9/11 memorial club. We walked by the firehouse on Sixth Avenue near Houston to pay our respects and walked back to Fifteenth Street and wondered on the way where, among other things, all the ice cream stores have gone. We went back to my house and all hung out on the terrace.

▶ SATURDAY, SEPTEMBER 12, 2015

It was fun waking up on a Saturday in the city for the first time in four months. Stopped by the construction site—Surfin is seriously in the running to be the new super of the building! I told him I would do whatever I could to help. Stopped in a newsstand and flipped through the new *Vanity Fair* and saw the pic of all the late-night hosts except for me and my eyes crossed. They had the Comedy Central guys who haven't even premiered yet, and I've been on six years and couldn't get in. I swear I wasn't insecure before I got this job. Deep breath.

Went to the U.S. Open with Jackie and saw the two Italian women play against each other in the finals. We were in the Air Emirates box, and when we walked in they had me take pictures with some flight attendants in native garb. There was a bartender who said he didn't have any rosé, but could he interest me in some Pouilly-Fuissé? I was more interested in the way he was stuffed into his little Air Emirates outfit. Went into the match and some guy next to me looked like a superstar and said his name was Paul and he was supposed to be on my show at SXSW so I emailed my team, who said they think it's Paul Wesley from *The Vampire Diaries* and I googled him and it was confirmed. He was with his girlfriend, who is also on the show.

They said they live in LA and I asked if they had a Jacuzzi, which set off a whole thing because he has been begging her to get one since they bought the house and she says it's cheesy and I said oh, no, you *have* to get one. Jackie and I wound up inside the box to eat some cake in a jar, have a refill of the Pouilly-Fuissé, and determine if the bartender was straight or not. He was cruising me even more than I him, and just as I was wondering how I was going to give him my number he came by with a refill and put his card in my hand.

While all this was going on inside, one of the Italians won the match. We were stunned that we had so totally lost track of the score. So that was lame. We were inside for the win! But we got out in a jiff. Went home and sexted the bartender and napped with Wacha while it rained. Had made plans to meet Mark, Kelly, and Anderson at prettyugly, but I got *so* tired and I need to be ready for the crazy coming week so I watched a documentary about the Rolling Stones and went to bed.

❧ SUNDAY, SEPTEMBER 13, 2015

Village Den for breakfast. Sat near this kid I dated who was with that hot blond guy from the gym and it turns out they've been dating for months, so that got me feeling left out. Went to the DVF fashion show, where I gave Fran Lebowitz the stink eye, which I am sure she couldn't see because she was too busy giving *me* the stink eye. Skyped with Mom and Dad and tried to explain the schedule of Radio Andy and Mom said, "I don't want to have to listen THE WHOLE DAMN DAY! I'm not going to just SIT HERE and listen all day!" Yeah, I gotcha. Went to Amanda's for Rosh Hashanah dinner—I said, let's each say what we would change from our past. Mine was that when I came to New York I would've tried to settle down into a relationship instead of having casual sex, to not follow my id all over the place. Maybe I would be married with kids. Is that what I would want right now? I can't decide. Went to *WWHL* with Mindy Kaling and Bryshere "Yazz" Grey, who is Hakeem from *Empire*, and when the show started I fucked up his name, which was horrible. Couldn't sleep because I'm so excited about the Radio Andy launch tomorrow.

First day of school! Woke up for good at seven but had been up several times and kept waking Wacha up and kissing him. He wasn't launching Radio Wacha and thus wasn't having It. I took the subway to Sirius—best ride in NYC. Got there and it was quite unglamorous—there was nowhere for me to work so I sat in the hallway with Tim going over my rundown. John Hill arrived and soon enough I was live for two hours. It felt good, but also like a free fall. Carol Burnett came and SJP called in and asked about *Moon Over Broadway.* After the show I saw Gary Dell'Abate in the hallway, which made me feel like I really worked there. Then, while I was doing interviews with *ET* and *Extra*, I saw Howard walking by and flipped out—I ran to the window and he gave me a thumbs-up. That's like seeing Obama at the White House. Did a conference call with the *Best Night Ever* producers, who want me to do this skit involving the Housewives. They punked this woman who is a *Real Housewives* fan with Housewives all over her and they want me to host a "reunion show" onstage. All I know is that I had tickets for *Hamilton* that night, so I have to cancel them and they are impossible to get.

All day long I kept turning on the radio and listening to my channel. We're live! Meanwhile people kept tweeting me asking where I was in the *Vanity Fair* picture. By the end of the day I was in a total rage about it. I can't believe I let myself get in that place again. At least it was the *Real Housewives Awards* on *WWHL* and it felt like I had the night off because it was Ramona and Tamra.

▶ TUESDAY, SEPTEMBER 15, 2015

Emailed Teresa in prison to let her know she won a Real Housewives Award for best reunion shocker moment. She said:

> DO I ACTUAL GET A TROPHY LIKE AT THE OSCARS? I WILL
> BE HOME REAL SOON CAN'T WAIT. KISSES

Taped Joy Behar and Ciara. Before the live show I was interviewing Jessica Biel for radio and came out of my office and Dori said that Wacha bit

Rick Springfield. I ran to his room and said, *"My dog bit you?!?"* He raised his hand up and it had a Band-Aid on it with blood showing through! He said it was his fault, actually, that his wife always warns him that he rough-houses too much with strange dogs and that one day one will bite him. So tonight he pulled Wacha's ear hard and Wacha bit him. I felt a little better because there was cause and effect. Got home late and saw on Instagram that Bruce had liked something, so he was up—late for him in LA—and I called him. While we were yammering, a little mouse ran behind my bed in my room. He said, you're going to be okay going to bed knowing there is a mouse running around your room? I said yes; if it was a beetle or roach I'd be calling John Hickey or checking into a hotel but I feel like Wacha will kill the mouse before it gets to me. I mean, he just bit Rick Springfield—he's fierce.

▶ WEDNESDAY, SEPTEMBER 16, 2015

Sandra Bernhard is killing it on Radio Andy. I could listen to her talk all day. Interviewed Brooks. I predicted he and Vicki would get back together after the reunion but he said no, he was moving to Florida. When I said goodbye I said, "I'll see you again," and he said, "No, I don't think you ever will."

It was Madonna's opening night at MSG and I went with Hickey. I had been emailing Guy Oseary asking him to please check and make sure I had *great* tickets. It turns out he quite literally got me the very best seats in the house—right at the tip of the ramp she comes down in the middle of the show. We were next to Jessica Seinfeld, Amy Schumer, and Guy, and on the other side Ariana Grande with her brother, Frankie, and their mom. They seem really close to their mom. During the middle of it I said to Ariana, that's you in forty-five years. She was touched. I am not sure I totally believed it, but I wanted to make her feel good. It worked. Oh, and JLo was there, maybe in flannel? (Maybe my eyes were bad.) The concert was perfect—I loved her set list and she was joyous and grateful and had a great attitude. She sang "Material Girl," "Deeper and Deeper," "True Blue" (as a country song), and "Music," and when she was at the end of the ramp doing a little sing-along with "Who's That Girl" she said, "I see you, Andy Cohen!" and I looked at Hickey and we were all OMG, OMG. Hickey basically walked away from me because he couldn't handle everyone looking over at us. Of course she did "La Isla Bonita," which at this point is like her national anthem. She always does it! She closed with "Holiday" and, I mean, OMG again.

We went to Barracuda but I had forgotten my ID, so they wouldn't let me in. Then we went to G Lounge and they wouldn't let me in there, either. So we went home, got my ID, gave the confused dog a treat, and went back to Barracuda. I flirted with Angela Lansbury's assistant (I am being serious) for a bit and talked to a whole bunch of really drunk people before I went home.

▶ THURSDAY, SEPTEMBER 17, 2015

#BritActor is moving here in October. I went and looked at two apartments for him and found him one. It is highly unusual for me to look at two apartments for someone. He just got out of a relationship, though, so I don't think it's going to go anywhere despite our FaceTime flirts. He's quite charming and cute. Wacha has been extra sensitive, cowering every time I make a fast movement to grab his leash or close a cabinet. Sherman called to say he has been acting very tentative and scared with him lately too. It's clear he was abused, and that kills us both.

Had a meeting at the construction site—the first in three months! The entire studio apartment is demoed and the walls are about to go up. I asked Slavo his prediction for move-in and he said April. Taped a show w/ Kaley Cuoco and Serayah McNeill. The bartender was this trainer, and when he came in I said, "Nice to meet you," and he said, "Good to see you again." After the show he said, do you remember me? I said no. He said that we sat next to each other on a flight when I was going to visit Liam and Natasha in France eleven years ago. Turns out he's the one and only guy I've fooled around with on a plane! Yes, I said, I remember that flight! It was a good flight, right? In my defense, at the time his hair was long and he was a yoga teacher. I ran and told the entire staff, whose mouths were agape.

Went to Madonna again with Bill Curtin, Grac, and Neal. We were right at the tip of the dick again and there were stars all around us: Alicia Keys in a jaunty red hat, Sean Penn(!), Chris Rock, Amy Schumer and Jessica Seinfeld again, and Mark and Kelly. Watching Sean Penn watch Madonna singing "True Blue" was very touching. He sighed afterwards and paused, and then was clapping very slowly and sweetly. Guy said, "She wants you to go right up there when she gets to the tip." You didn't have to ask me twice—Kelly and I were right up there and she gave Kelly a shout-out. And Kelly and I were on the big screen, which was exciting. I'm basically a fourteen-year-old girl squealing at getting on the big screen at a Madonna concert, except a fourteen-year-old girl wouldn't be squealing at a Madonna concert. Maybe I'm a fifty-four-year-old girl. Grac says "Holiday" could be the theme for the UN.

Madonna had an after party at Soho House. I walked in and the whole place smelled like Madonna. Are there Madonna-approved scents, and then does she have someone in there spraying her scent before she gets there? I was talking to Derek Blasberg at the front door around twelve forty-five when the queen walked in—with grill—and I was so glad to be there at the door so I could give her two huge hugs and tell her how amazing the show was and how perfect she is. She said she was exhausted and she hadn't gotten any sleep the night before. She sat with Sean Penn, and I left gratified that they were together.

‣ FRIDAY, SEPTEMBER 18, 2015– SUNDAY, SEPTEMBER 20, 2015—NYC—WYOMING—NYC

I love destination weddings—they have the potential to be like a weekend-long drawing-room comedy. I especially love a destination wedding that's shrouded in secrecy, filled with huge stars, and has a decoy location to fool paparazzi—so Ricky and Allison's in Wyoming was a trip. I got to hang a lot with Bruce, Bryan, Jason, Lauren, DVF and Barry, Hammy, John Mayer, and Michael and Wes. Went shooting, which was fun but I had FOMO about not going horseback riding. I just wanted to do whatever activity Bruce was doing. Flirted a lot with a local waiter whose crazy blue eyes overshadowed an aggressive forehead, and even better he was a wrestler/swing dancer, which is about the winningest combination I could concoct. Actually he might've been a clogger now that I think of it. He has a girlfriend, but by the end of the wedding night I actually thought I had a chance. Young people are fluid!

The plane home was DVF, Barry, Hamilton, the Springsteens, and the

Hankses, and my favorite part was listening to Patti and Bruce plan a dinner with Jackson Browne. *I mean!* The thought of them having dinner made me happy. Patti said their son works at Sirius, and I said I just launched my own channel and Bruce said, "I have one too," and for some reason that struck me as amazing. Got home and watched the Emmys, where half the wedding ran off to—three hours of awards to *Veep*, *Olive Kitteridge*, and *Game of Thrones*. In other words, very boring.

▶ MONDAY, SEPTEMBER 21, 2015

Sleepless before radio show. I wonder if this is how it will be every Monday for three years, but I imagine I'll get used to it. First I was on Sway's morning show on Shade 45, then I did my live two-hour show—Anderson was on and was charming. We're trying to sell tickets to *AC2*, as we have dates in Minneapolis, D.C., and Columbus coming up. Then I taped two countdown shows, did a photo shoot and interview for the *Wall Street Journal*, went home to poop and get Wacha, and then went to *WWHL* to tape a show with Pam Anderson—who looks great and answered every disgusting question I asked—and Meredith Vieira, who gasped a few times. I don't blame her. Then I interviewed Meredith for Radio Andy, called Vicki Gunvalson (who is very upset about Brooks's breakup and cancer accusations playing out on camera), and went home with the dog for Chinese leftovers and to watch an *RHOC* cut, then taped an interview with David and Shannon Beador for air later, and then did the live show with Gretchen and Shannon. What did *you* do today, Seacrest???

▶ WEDNESDAY, SEPTEMBER 23, 2015

Neicy came and she said, oh, by the way, you realize you have mice here, don't you? I knew, but I wasn't allowing myself to really accept it. I said I'd noticed Wacha sniffing around, but shouldn't he have killed them by now? She said dogs don't kill mice, which was headline news to me. Now I'm wondering what the fuck this dog *does* do. Well, he kills flies, but that seems unnecessary. Flies aren't the problem. I'm on Fallon next week and

Jimmy had loved the Tori Spelling story about the email and said, oh, you gotta tell that, so I've been kind of nervous about that because she may not like it.

Fasted today for Yom Kippur and broke it at Amanda's. The live show was Rabbi Shmuley at the bar with Sandra Bernhard and Chrissie Hynde as guests. Sandra said before the show not to be offended by Chrissie; she's rock and roll and doesn't suffer fools—not exactly what this fool wanted to hear right before air. And Chrissie didn't seem into it at all, but then during the last commercial break she said, "This is so great; I love it!" Not sure that was translating to the folks at home.

▶ THURSDAY, SEPTEMBER 24, 2015

Woke up super early for the *Today* show because streets were closed for Pope traffic and wound up flying up Sixth Avenue. Had to bring the dog because we were going to Jersey after for a shoot, so the whole thing was complicated. Matt was generous with me, and so sweet off-air, in his teeny little tight suit. And I told Carson Daly I have a picture of me screaming behind him from when Madonna did a private concert at MTV promoting *American Life* and realized hours later that I tell him that every time I see him. I saw Suze Orman backstage and said, "I know you're too scared to come on my show, but you should do it," and she said Jillian Michaels told her not to and I said, that woman is absolutely nuts. Went to Jersey to shoot the Subaru "The More You Know" commercial with Wacha, who nipped the guy putting the harness on him. And then I got in a fight with the dog trainer on set, who was giving him bacon. I said, please don't—I don't feed him human food. She said, well, that's why it's a *treat*, because it's bacon! And I said yeah, but there are *treats for dogs*, which are what I prefer to give him. She never got rid of her cup of bacon, which enraged me. And the director was so specific about what he wanted Wacha to do ("We want him in the seat with the ball in his mouth, facing the front") and I was like, this dog is a rescue who just bit the prop guy putting the fucking seatbelt harness on him; he's not going to do that.

Next I had to go to Brooklyn from New Jersey—which I was very stressed about due to Pope traffic—to interview Connie Chung for *Then and Now with Andy Cohen* (Bravo ordered three episodes!), which sounds like *Face to Face with Connie Chung* or even *Eye to Eye with Connie Chung*. It turned out we flew to Brooklyn. And it turns out that black isn't the only thing that don't crack! She looks like vintage Connie. She really spilled about Dan, who wasn't nice to her, and Nancy Kerrigan and Tonya Harding, who she said were "wretched little wenches." Sherman came to pick Wacha up from there because he was stressed about getting him in the morning due to Pope traffic. (See how the Pope is just fucking us all up?) Got home at nine forty-five completely spent and the show was on tape and I had no plans, no dog, and a night free. Was going to get a massage but told him not to come because I thought I could drum up some plans but I then couldn't make anything happen so I got two slices of pizza and sat in my kitchen eating them, sipping on some of Ramona's Pinot Grigio looking at the mousetraps the super set up during the day, feeling lonely and sorry for myself. Then a mouse ran right by the traps into the radiator and I went to bed.

▶ FRIDAY, SEPTEMBER 25, 2015– SUNDAY, SEPTEMBER 27, 2015–NYC–ST. LOUIS

Ray picked me up extra early to go to the airport because of Pope traffic, and guess what—we flew there again. I was an hour early, and the flight was delayed so I was actually three hours early. Abby was completely whipped into a frenzy about seeing Taylor Swift next week, and we got to talking about her first concert—Fifth Harmony—which got her so wound up and happy she said, "Now that I'm reliving this moment, I have to do a victory dance!!" and proceeded to give me her most euphoric dance. To be nine again! Did a paid gig at the Young Presidents Organization of St. Louis and a lady was auditioning so hard to be a Housewife. "I live on fifteen acres!" she said. "I entertain for two hundred and fifty people under a tent in my yard! I host Splashercize classes in my pool every morning for all sorts of women! My husband ran for governor!" The interviewer, in front of the two hundred white people (I counted four Jews, which is four more than I expected) asked me what I thought of what happened in Ferguson. I started to go into a soliloquy about white privilege (now I'm preaching about white privilege, when three months ago I had no clue) and all the buildings being boarded up in Clayton and segregation in the suburbs and stuff. Then I read the room, took a breath and punted. After dinner met all the Cohen brothers at Kreis' Steakhouse, then went to Kari's to watch the end of the Cardinals game.

I slept *ten hours* and woke up feeling like a Mack truck hit me. Woke up at 4:00 a.m. not knowing where I was, which never happens to me. I felt for the dog and forgot he was in another city. . . . In the morning we made a bitmoji avatar for Mom, who was very vocal with her feedback: "You made my boobs huge!!!! I'm not fat! I need WRINKLES!" Went to Café Manhattan with Judy and Stanley. Ate a tremendous amount of pizza, and Lucy fixed the settings on my MLB app. On the way to the Saturday-night baseball game I Periscoped in the car, which didn't go over well with my mom. "What the hell is PERISCOPE? ANOTHER way for you to EXPRESS YOURSELF? Your EGO!!!" We were in the green seats to the left of the dugout and our waiter, Randy, was omnipresent. My parents asked Randy about the food this evening as though there was a chef who was making it differently every night. How are the burgers *tonight?* It was decided that the hot dogs were incredible that night but the burgers were horrible. My mother's monologue ran nonstop throughout the game. She comes up with the absolute worst scenario for a batter and then projects it into the world. So Kolten Wong comes up to bat and she screams, "Don't HIT INTO A DOUBLE PLAY!" and instead the kid *gets* a double. And on and on.

We won, and I was meeting Jon Jay after the game to go out with a group for dinner. The players' parking lot was all trucks and muscle cars with tinted windows. Went to the Gamlin Whiskey House and it was a shit-ton of Cardinals girls and their men. Everyone is so young: Jay, Lance Lynn, Wacha with his young girlfriend (who is twenty-two!), Wong (I didn't tell him my mom was responsible for heckling him). Wacha asked how Wacha was and I said he bit Rick Springfield. Then I said, "Do you even know who that is?" He said, "A singer." I said, "Wow." He said, "He sings 'Born to Run.'" I said no, that's *Bruce Springsteen*, and then I said do you know who *that* is and he said kind of. And none of the other guys did either. So there you go.

MONDAY, SEPTEMBER 28, 2015—NYC

I was in a bad mood for my radio show—I had woken up way too early, I was upset about the dog (who acted up again last night in front of some Boston Red Sox who were at the show), I'd had two early phone interviews and neither person showed up for them, and I had tea breath. But five minutes into the show Jimmy called in because he was listening in the car on his way into the city, and there's no way to not be happy when Jimmy calls in, so he totally turned my mood around! Taped a show with Stamos and Kathleen Turner, then worked out with Stan, my Ukrainian mistress, at Equinox. Ran into Anderson on the street and—seemingly out of nowhere—he begged me to go to his dentist. I asked what was wrong with my teeth, and he said there are a few things wrong with them and he's been wanting to tell me for a while. Oh. My. God. Interviewed Sandra Bernhard in Brooklyn for *Then and Now*, went to the Polo Bar with Jodi and crew for her birthday (saw Nacho Figueras, Charles Fagan, and Charlie Rose), and then did the live show with Annabelle from *Ladies of London* and Heather Dubrow. Neither lady was feeling the other.

TUESDAY, SEPTEMBER 29, 2015

It was like Christmas this morning because I got to do Howard Stern. I was *early* and sat in the car for ten minutes with Ray, listening to the show, and I could see Ronnie The Limo Driver waiting for me in the lobby. Hung out with Gary in the greenroom and then it was a freewheeling hour-long shoot-the-shit fest. I'd ranked the men of the Stern show in order of hotness—they asked me to—so that was a major topic. From there I went to Brooklyn to interview Kelly for *Then and Now*. She was a sound-bite machine! Then went to *WWHL*, where I taped Julianne Moore and Kristen Wiig, which was phenomenal. Kristen Wiig is beyond the beyond. So brilliant. Then we taped the *MDLLA* guys. Then I went home, by which time it was pouring. I napped. Dinner at the Waverly Inn with Sandy and Joel. Graydon Carter was there, and Martin Short and Beverly Johnson.

WEDNESDAY, SEPTEMBER 30, 2015—NYC—LOS ANGELES

I keep wanting Kim Fields to put something about Tootie in her tag line and she won't do it.

I don't even know what happened this morning, but a lightbulb went on in my head and I thought, "Why the hell am I not on PrEP?" I'd talked to my doctor about it when I went in a couple months ago and he'd said he would investigate. So I called him and he said, you're right, I checked it out and you should do it. So I'm in. I got the prescription and took my first pill. I guess it's a generational thing—all the kids are taking it, and we who have been so scared and waiting for this pill are just too shell-shocked to take it now that it's here. Worked out with Ninj.

Told the Tori story (sTori?) on Fallon and it went great. On the way to the airport I emailed her and said, "Hey, I told a story involving you on Fallon tonight in which I am very clearly the butt of the joke. I hope you laugh with me." Landed in LA and spent a half hour on the tarmac waiting for a gate to become available and I became *that guy*: wildly craning my neck and muttering, "This is bullshit," *not* under my breath. I thought I was going to rip the skin off my face. I almost threw my phone, then tried to squeeze it and see if I could break it, which I'm thankful I didn't because then I would've been a baby without his Binky. When I finally got to the Sunset Tower Dimitri was in the front and couldn't wait to tell me who had been there. "You missed an amazing night. An amazing night!" "Great," I said briskly. "I'm sure tomorrow will be great too." And he just couldn't handle it. "Yes, yes. But *tonight*. Tonight was *so special*." I told him I was happy for him. I am a nasty man.

THURSDAY, OCTOBER 1, 2015—LOS ANGELES

Woke up and the sTori had gotten picked up every damn place. Still no return email from her, so I hope she doesn't hate me. The *OC* reunion was today and the day began with Heather DuBrow railing at me about *WWHL* the other night; she had a whole list of reasons she didn't love it, ranging from being in "second position" next to Annabelle from *Ladies of London* to my offending her because I said she loves Botox. So that was the *beginning* of the day. Oh, and the rumor was that Vicki was on Xanax, not sure

I'd blame her if she was. But it was a good reunion—not too messy and a lot of dramatic shit. Tamra revealed her oldest daughter doesn't speak to her and won't live with her, I pulled out a smoking-gun-ish email from Alexis about Tamra's newfound relationship with Jesus, and there was an endless amount of "Does Brooks have cancer" talk with lots of evidence and Vicki—who indeed seemed medicated—taking endless punches from the group. During lunch I begged Vicki not to take any more. She said she wouldn't, but she took all the punches sitting quietly so who knows. Went to Bruce's and hung with him and Bryan a bit.

▶ FRIDAY, OCTOBER 2, 2015—LOS ANGELES

Conference calls in the hotel room all morning, then went to Bravo to check in with people. Saw Jenn Levy, Comey, and Serwatka. Lunch at the Palm with Dan and Jane, hung with Bruce, had a meeting at World of Wonder, and then headed back to the Tower. Finally spoke to Kim Fields and gave her a pep talk about saying what she thinks and finding her funny, finding the absurdity in what's around her. I even suggested putting her on the phone with Bethenny so she could give her pointers about being comfortable in front of the camera and she said she would love that, and then I texted Bethenny, who didn't want to do it. Hahaha. Watty kept calling, saying NBC had big news for me and wanted to tell me personally. Finally, Paul Telegdy called to say they wanted me to host a live *Hollywood Game Night* on New Year's Eve from NYC, which wasn't the news I thought it was going to be. It seems weird for me to take over a show that I consider a rip-off of my own show, and when I noted the similarity to my show Paul said, yeah, there are no original ideas; every show is borrowed from another show. So he shut that down. I said maybe it can be called *Manhattan Game Night* or something. Then I went to Bruce and Bryan's and we watched *The Martian*, which was an unequivocal piece of garbage—five movies in one. Watch it become a big hit. Went home and met John Mayer at the Tower Bar for a kiki.

SATURDAY, OCTOBER 3, 2015—LOS ANGELES—NYC

Slept on the flight home. Went straight from JFK to Marley's bat mitzvah, which Grac had been referring to as "the wedding" for months. Got teary-eyed seeing Grac being mom up there in front of everyone, with her Italian hairdo and dress. Marley was superb, and Grac pulled out all the stops. It was incredible. Went home and met #BrazilianAndySamberg, who is in for the weekend and was my date for Kelly's birthday party at Anderson's. We had a blast together. The *Broad City* girls were there, as well as Scarlett Johansson, NPH, Jussie Smollet, Jake Shears, Joe, Barry, Sandy, and Liza, who was sublime all night. She and #BAS fell in love. "Lovable" is a great word for him: he has great energy, and he's so easy to be with, adorable, and really smart.

SUNDAY, OCTOBER 4, 2015

Mom was at the manicurist and asked some woman who made her sweat suit and and she said, "It's Lululemon." Mom horrified her by saying it would be good for her box suit. So I should hold off on the shroud, she thinks, but she's in no hurry. #BrazilianAndySamberg left for Boston, and I have a date with #BritActor tomorrow night and am feeling very torn between two lovers.

MONDAY, OCTOBER 5, 2015

I dreamed that Teresa was vice president of the United States and every-body loved her. I emailed her and said no joke, you were running for VP and had an answer for everything and everyone was taken with you—isn't that wild?

Went to Anderson's dentist, who turns out to be a massive *Housewives* fan—as is his wife, who came in and gave me chocolates (at the dentist!) and got a selfie. Had an amazing date with #BritActor. We went to the Waverly Inn—he was early, which I loved because I was also early. I had bought a new shirt for the occasion at Odin and he complimented it. It was very flirty and chatty and cozy and awkward silences and leg touching and everything you would want it to be. He had a cod fillet, which he called a "fill-ET," which I liked. We walked to my construction site, then went upstairs and I showed him around the dark apartment and we had a big make-out session in the guest bedroom. Then we went to the Cubbyhole, where there was public kissing, then he walked me home and we laughed a lot. We were drunk and sweet. Went to bed thinking about him *and* #BAS, who is geographically unavailable but more stable.

⪼ TUESDAY, OCTOBER 6, 2015

Got an email back from Teresa: "You never know, your dream might come true. . . ." But then I realized that I don't think people who have been to jail can run for elected office, so I felt bad for opening that can of worms. Stupidly asked #BritActor to dinner for Friday even though we are seeing *Hamilton* on Sunday and he said well, we're seeing each other Sunday, so I kind of blew that one. I'm acting so available, but the truth is I have a busy schedule and am *not* available at all. Went to tape *Best Night Ever* and brought Liza. It wasn't the best night ever, but it was a feel-good kind of thing where they were surprising a *Housewives* superfan. Mom texted me a bitmoji of herself after the show that said "BORING!" That made me laugh out loud so hard! I texted her, "I love you." She was so right. Victor, the elevator guy who listens to jazz, has been here since 1976!!! His dad worked here too! I said OMG, you have seen IT ALL.

⪼ WEDNESDAY, OCTOBER 7, 2015

I'm pretty sure the mouse ODed on pot candy—Neicy found a half-eaten piece in my bathroom, so he's probably tripping in some pipes somewhere. Or dead. Jill Zarin is on *WWHL* tomorrow night. I wanted a rating. She tweeted about it and asked people what she should wear, and people tweeted "Some humility," "A muzzle," "A microphone," "A garbage bag." People are so nasty on social media. My plan is for it to be nice. I don't want bad blood.

Took Wacha to the vet for his yearly checkup and shots, which was a disaster, as I predicted. They had me give him doggy Xanax an hour before bringing him (which didn't work) and put a muzzle on him (which he escaped the second we got to the door of the vet's office). I was flipping out because he was growling and they said, don't worry; we will deal with this, and took him in the back and gave *me* water because I was shaking. Then they came in and said, it's going bad, do we have permission to give him a shot that will knock him out? I said do it. They explained that they then give him another shot that will make him come to again. So a half hour later they came to get me. The shot that was supposed to knock him out didn't fully work, but they still gave him the other one to bring him back too. The poor guy was legless and freaked out. Thankfully he got all his shots, so I am so happy. The second we left he just wanted to go to sleep on the sidewalk. But he stumbled home. People were laughing at him on the street!

▶ THURSDAY OCTOBER 8, 2015

I confessed to the Ninj that I've been having a full-blown affair with Stanislav at Equinox. He was fine with our open relationship. I told him it's a matter of my schedule, but that the windows and gay guys at Equinox are also tantalizing, which he understood. One thing I will not cheat on is my toaster oven. My love rages on for that machine, in which I was broiling my salmon today when I decided to finally unwrap the gift that I'd been keeping on top of it for three months. It was a book of Grateful Dead art that had *melted* because I had been keeping it on top of the *toaster oven* like a fucking *idiot*. Who would keep a wrapped present *on top of a toaster* that's used about ten times a week? To make matters worse, I have no idea who gave me that gift.

Taped Julie Andrews and Cate Blanchett, and we had four hot male models in lederhosen who were going to march in as the "lost von Trapp boys" but Julie's publicist saw them in the hall about one minute before taping and said, *"You cannot disrespect the legacy of* The Sound of Music! *We do not like that at all! You have to get rid of these boys."* So I said they were here celebrating Oktoberfest, they have nothing to do with the von Trapps. And that was that, and in the end Julie said, "Oh how lovely these boys are," or something. She loved it. You never know if she really would've had a problem with the von Trapp thing or if it's just the publicist mouthing off.

Jill Zarin was on the live show, and it seemed like it should've been a lot of drama, or a lot of something, but it was pleasant. She never arrives empty handed, and she had a gift for me, which was jelly beans from Dylan's Candy Bar. We had a birthday party for John Jude after and there was McDonald's, against which I was powerless—I ate a cheeseburger and fries. Jill kept telling me how she is legitimately friends with all the women, that the thing with Ramona is just an act on Ramona's end and they actually get along, that she is playing the best tennis of her life so she is ready to play tennis on the show.

▶ FRIDAY, OCTOBER 9, 2015

Cohosted the 10:00 a.m. hour of *Today* with Hoda and I was kind of on fire. They told me after the first break that I couldn't say "cocked up" or "screwed" because there were kids watching. Hickey was a guest, so that was fun and easy. Met Lauren Zalaznick for tea at that hotel on Eighth Street and when I left at 5:20, Dark Sky told me it was going to downpour at 5:26. Six minutes later I'd made it to Fourteenth Street and Sixth Avenue, where I got caught in the massive downpour. Is Dark Sky going to put Janice Huff out of business? I have mixed feelings, as one can imagine. Got home and discovered I had left the terrace door open and Wacha was standing there looking at me, then back at the door with the rain and wind pouring in, with a look on his face that said, "You have no idea the HELL that has been breaking loose in this apartment." Stayed home watching the Cardinals-Cubs play-off game (we won) and Dave called, very upset that a client had ruined his weekend. I tried talking him off the ledge but he was very angry, so I summoned him to my apartment for a scotch, which did the trick. It was all very freshman year at Boston University.

▶ SATURDAY, OCTOBER 10, 2015—NYC—MINNEAPOLIS

Walked Wacha by the construction. The temporary staircase is set up, but he was too scared to go down the stairs, which was humorous to me. He just stood there watching me on the downstairs level. Does he know something that I don't?

You can't order a tea in the Delta terminal by asking a person for the tea, you have to do it on an iPad, which they keep telling you is so easy, but it's not, and a lady had to show me how to do it. So it would've been easier just to tell the lady I wanted a tea. Then we took a selfie. The whole thing was a process. We have been working our white *asses* off selling tickets for tonight's show and we're still only at 85 percent. Some cities go immediately, like D.C. and Chicago, and others involve work. I guess 85 percent is nothing to sneeze at. Landed in Minneapolis and Anderson and I went to Ike's for burgers. I ordered two kinds of onion rings for fun. Anderson was mortified I was eating onions, and I said that Minneapolis is known for their onion rings, so how could I not indulge, which he believed, and then I said I was kidding. We went deep about the upcoming presidential primary debate, his relationship, my date with #BritActor, #BrazilianAndy-Samberg, our careers, and my New Year's Eve offer. We walked around aimlessly for a while and then went back to the hotel, where I watched the Cubs kill the Cardinals and took a quick nap during which I dreamed that I went down on Katy Perry.

Our show was phenomenal. I had to pee throughout the second hour and started wondering what it would be like if I just left AC onstage for a minute while I peed, but I didn't. The meet and greet was nuts. I was asking people if they are an Anderson or an Andy—many said Andy, but man, the ones who like Anderson want *nothing* to do with me. After a really intense scene at the stage door, we went to Jetset, where we lasted twenty minutes or so and then split.

▶ SUNDAY, OCTOBER 11, 2015—MINNEAPOLIS—NYC

Tried and failed to write my speech for Tuesday in Texas on the plane home. Hung out with #BritActor, who told me he slept with this guy I know last night after Horse Meat Disco, which led me into a maze of emotion. On one hand, there is a cornucopia of boys in New York, and he's newly single and enjoying it. But on the other hand, you want someone you have a crush on to only have eyes for you. We were supposed to see *Hamilton*, but I had to work. The whole thing was kind of a bummer. The show was Joe and Joe—Giudice and Gorga. I asked Joe Gorga if he blames Joe Giudice for his sister being in jail and he said, "Yeah, who else am I going to blame?" and Joe Giudice said he blames Joe. During the last commercial I told him,

"People at home are pissed you're not taking responsibility," to which he replied, "Who the fuck cares?" But he accepted it when we came back and I asked him about it again. A day late . . .

TUESDAY, OCTOBER 13, 2015—NYC—AUSTIN—NYC

Woke up at 5:00 and was at Newark by about 5:35. I was nervous about the speech I was supposed to give to media executives at the Spredfast Summit, because the organizers had given me crazy guidelines like "RUDIMENTARY ADVICE about social media will NOT ENTERTAIN this crowd." So I had to step it up for Spredfast, I guess. They gave me a pair of cowboy boots, which I wore onstage. I thought I was bombing during the speech because no one was paying attention, but it turned out they were all looking down at their phones tweeting everything I was saying, so I guess that's a success. Jill's team put together a PowerPoint presentation for why she should come back to *RHONY*, including text messages among her and LuAnn, Sonja, and Ramona. She made a compelling case! Landed back in NYC and the Cardinals' do-or-die game against the Cubs was on. Watched with Wacha. They died.

WEDNESDAY, OCTOBER 14, 2015

Two shows. We had a meeting to decide whether to make Dallas a *Real Housewives* city and I can't decide if we're making the right decision. I'm more excited about the promise of Potomac but feel like I am in the minority. There is something missing from Dallas. But we're doing it. Bruce thinks Anderson and I should move hotels this weekend to the DuPont in D.C.

THURSDAY, OCTOBER 15, 2015—NYC—LOS ANGELES

Time to make my number unlisted. I had another 4:45 a.m. airport pickup and my home phone rang at 4:00 with some stranger wanting to know if I'm the Andy Cohen from Bravo. Anderson doesn't want to move hotels;

he thinks we will like the Four Seasons in Georgetown better. I invited #BrazilianAndySamberg to come and I'm really excited. Decided on the plane that I was going to wing my keynote address at the LinkedIn Talent Connect conference. They wanted me to talk about my career, and if there's one thing I excel at, it's talking about my career. I got there and it was massive—3,500 people at the Anaheim Convention Center with my face blasted onto huge screens behind me, a Britney Spears kind of microphone headpiece, and no podium or anything to put notes on. So I paced around the stage and winged it. Kathy Griffin texted that she's "in D.C. at the 4S" and I didn't know what she was talking about. She said, "You've been in St. Louis too long." I figured out it's the Four Seasons. So I guess we'll see her there. Celebrated John Mayer's birthday with him.

❧ FRIDAY, OCTOBER 16, 2015—LOS ANGELES—D.C.

6:00 a.m. pickup, so that was late for me. Slept a chunk on the plane to D.C. and I think I snored, so I apologize to all affected. On the way to the hotel Liza said, where is your *WWHL* team staying, the Econo Lodge? I said I didn't know and got to the 4S (I've got it now!) and saw Anthony, Chelsea, and Danny at the front desk checking in. So I loved that. Of course I saw lots of red coming towards me when I checked in and it was Kathy, who is right down the hall from me. How small is the world? She told me Billy Corgan is here at the hotel, and I think he might be a nemesis of AC's. They had some fight about cats. When I got to my room there were four Coke Zeros, which I thought was funny because that's Anderson's thing. He loves Coke Zero. Then there was a knock on the door and someone brought in chocolates with Anderson's face on them. I said oh, I think you put me in his room. They said no problem, stay in this one, we will switch you out and put his stuff in his room. So then they wheel in a huge tray of stuff for me: Jolly Ranchers, Swedish Fish, Goldfish, Doritos, Cheez-Its, tequila, Fresca, ginger ale, and Maker's Mark. It made Anderson's four Coke Zeros and chocolates look pathetic. I was amused. Took a big nap, literally Dorinda style—naked under the covers. Then I took the *WWHL* team out for dinner and to a gay club. AC met us and we all had fun. They gave Anderson an interior room, and I'd gotten his!

▶ SATURDAY, OCTOBER 17, 2015—WASHINGTON, DC

The hotel is crawling with comedians in town for the Eddie Murphy tribute at the Kennedy Center. Dave Chappelle left a message for Anderson to call him; he said he wants to come see our show. AC told him it's a lot of drunk women and he said that sounds perfect. #BrazilianAndySamberg arrived, cute as ever, and we were out the door for the show when I saw Jon Stewart, who said what are you doing here, I just saw Anderson, and I said we're on tour. He said, what do you do? I said I don't know, it's hard to explain. He said, "I'm busy too! I have stuff going on!" Kidding. Made AC stop at the Lincoln Memorial to take a pic of our heads for Instagram. (It's our *thing*, the tops of our heads with a landmark behind them.) He wasn't thrilled. Lots of people backstage before the show including *Real Housewives of D.C.*'s Lynda Erkiletian and Ana Navarro, who worked for Jeb Bush. The theater was pretty charged up—the show was sold out—but I felt like I was going to puke for the first hour. We always make a big deal out of the straight guys who come to see the show because we say they're dragged by their wives, so during the meet and greet AC says to this couple, "Oh, you're the straight guy," and he says, "The last time you saw me I was a WOMAN. We met after Hurricane Katrina," and I flipped out. We went to Town after and walked right into the middle of the drag show and I immediately got pulled onstage. Anderson was outside, and I gave my phone to #BAS and said, "Text Anderson not to come in—he's gonna get pulled onstage." He didn't get the text and came in. She tried to get him to come up, but he wouldn't. Feeling all lovey-dovey for #BAS.

▶ MONDAY, OCTOBER 19, 2015—NYC

Radio show with Monica Lewinsky, Sienna Miller, and Dr. Drew. There's a big Radio Andy launch party Thursday night, to which I've given zero thought. Went to Anderson's dentist for some intense whitening. Took a few selfies there and realized that at some point I'm going to have to break up with my dentist of twenty-five years. How does one do that? Whoopi was sick, so we booked Anderson for the show with Molly Ringwald, who asked how I get my teeth so white. I was thrilled and Anderson was proud.

TUESDAY, OCTOBER 20, 2015

My agent emailed that NBC agreed to let me do *New Year's Eve Game Night* live from the Rainbow Room, and then going to Times Square with Carson, which is exciting. I think it'll be fun. Had dinner at the Perskys' and I brought Wacha. Bill said I am bigger than everything I am doing (meaning the *Housewives*) and I said no, actually no one is bigger than anything; this is the world we live in. Came home and saw the Potomac show and loved it! It's a *Housewives*! It's all about rules and etiquette and it's funny and feels like early *Housewives*.

THURSDAY, OCTOBER 22, 2015

Tonight was the Radio Andy party at the top of the Dream Hotel. I broadcast live for three hours from the middle of the room, interviewing the whole lineup of Radio Andy talent (Sandra, Bevy, the Alters, Jason Biggs and Jenny Mollen, John Hill, etc.) plus friends who came to support me (Hoda, Gayle King, John Mayer, BJ Novak, Mark and Kelly, Susan Lucci!). It was kind of frustrating because there was a table of my friends who I *wasn't* interviewing (Jeanne and Fred, Amanda, Dave) sitting at the table next to me and I couldn't talk to them all night. Sometimes those parties aren't actually fun to go to, but you do it to be a good friend. And I was grateful to those who did.

SUNDAY, OCTOBER 25, 2015

I feel awful about the fact that every time Em is in town, we have someone booked who she doesn't care about seeing. Tonight was Amber Rose, and it didn't go great for anybody. She didn't want to answer any of my nosy questions about Kanye or the Kardashians. Oh, and she wore her sunglasses on the air. A viewer said, "Will you take them off so we can see your eyes for a second?" and she said no. We were going to break and I said well, we're going to figure out what we *can* do with you when we come back. She said, "Am I the worst guest ever?" I said you're in the running. I wound up liking her, though. She had a good sense of humor about being a bad guest.

MONDAY, OCTOBER 26, 2015

We're in big discussions with several of the New York Housewives about their future on the show. Mike Tyson came in to Radio Andy and was hilarious. Saw #BritActor at the gym. We are going out tomorrow night but I am being cool. He should be able to sample the buffet while he's here and I'm busy anyway. Talked to Bill Maher's producer to see if I could be comfortable with going on the show despite Mom's dire warnings. The concept became about me as a reality producer looking at the election as a reality show—I can handle that. I called Mom and told her; she was very skeptical. 6:00 p.m. rolled around and we emailed two New York women saying the offer has been pulled and they are no longer Housewives, but I have a feeling this isn't the end of the discussion. Dinner with John Mayer and Ricky.

WEDNESDAY, OCTOBER 28, 2015

Last night, after a mediocre date with #BritActor, the lights were out and it sounded like Wacha was barfing or coughing. I said, "Are you okay, buddy?" and he looked at me like he was okay. Woke up and there was barf everywhere on the bedspread. So I guess I slept in that. We sorted out the New York Housewives—they're all back, and Ramona called to say that LuAnn is actually not very bright when it comes to business deals. I told her to save it for the show. Randy and Fenton came over to work on *Then and Now*. It poured all day. NBC needs me to go to LA to rehearse on the *Hollywood Game Night* set and Maher will fly me out, so it seems like the smart thing to do. The temp elevator guy wanted to kick some guy's ass for saying hi to me on the street. He literally said, "Do you want me to go kick that guy's ass?" He wants to be my bodyguard.

THURSDAY, OCTOBER 29, 2015

So it turns out *Hamilton* actually lives up to all the hype. I finally went with Benjamin. What an achievement. Went to a party after for the cast and talked to Lin-Manuel Miranda, who seems very lovely and humble.

▸ FRIDAY, OCTOBER 30, 2015

New Year's Eve Game Night meeting at 30 Rock. Went to John Varvatos for a fitting and I'm fairly certain I have moobs, although the PR guy said I don't. What's he going to do, agree with me?

Drag show with #BrazilianAndySamberg and his friends. We were in a little box on the side of the theater next to NPH, David Burtka, and Daniel Vosovic. They set us up for bottle service but I freaked when they said it was six hundred dollars for a bottle, even though ours was free. I don't do great on vodka. It was all the stars of *RuPaul's Drag Race* and the kids were going *mental* for them—just screaming like crazy, and #BAS's friend kept saying it was so cool of me to have an open mind to drag since I really didn't know who any of the queens were and I said honey, I moved here in NINETEEN-NINETY and used to go watch Wigstock for NINE HOURS in Tompkins Square Park, so don't lecture me about being open-minded about drag. I went there! Shangela introduced me and I got a smattering of applause, and she said, "Did any of you see *WWHL* last night?" and no one clapped. These kids don't have cable! Oh, wait a minute—how do they see the queens on *Drag Race*?

When we left, the huge bouncer kept telling us to get off the sidewalk, that he had to clear the sidewalk. He was saying this to us *four* people in front of the basically empty club with no line out front. I lost it—do NOT tell me I can't be on the SIDEWALK, I am a CITIZEN of NEW YORK CITY. I turned into Reese Witherspoon in the back of the police car, just as awful and righteous as I could be. I said I don't do well on vodka! This isn't me! I was like Dorinda! Went to the Phoenix and had a blast. #BAS and I were boyfriends all night and it was great.

▸ SATURDAY, OCTOBER 31, 2015

Happy Halloween. I showed #BAS the apartment construction and kept saying, "This is your bathroom; this is your oven." I am sure I will see that bouncer at the next event I want to go into and he won't let me in. Vodka! Went to the Dead show, which was very high school—Dave, Tom Reko, and Jeanne. Later we were joined by Fred—in a long blond wig—and Jim

Shuman. It was awesome. We heard "Terrapin Station"(!), "Samson and Delilah," and more. Mayer was a game changer. Gave him the biggest, proudest hug after.

▶ SUNDAY, NOVEMBER 1, 2015

Dead show again. John is breathing new life into the band! It's incredible! The third song was "Bertha" and they could've called it a night after that, that's how good it was. Went to *WWHL* and #BAS and his friend came. The audience was dead and so I kept punctuating things with "ha ha," like Nelson Muntz from *The Simpsons*. I didn't notice but #BAS did. When #BAS walked into my office after the show, Wacha went right to him and was all over him all night. He loves him!

▶ MONDAY, NOVEMBER 2, 2015

Anderson said, "Dogs know!" So that's a good sign about #BAS. If it were up to Anderson, I'd marry him tomorrow. Did two hours of radio in the morning, then went to Bravo. I was Padma's date to the Elton John AIDS Foundation benefit, which consisted of many speeches reminding us how amazing Elton is. Padma pointed out that Elton wears long coats like Hillary's, only his are bedazzled. Susan Lucci came by the table to say hi and we talked about her Fred Leighton necklace for a while. Saw her talking to Judith Light and it was a very *One Life to Live/All My Children* crossover moment. Gus Kenworthy was sitting between me and Anderson. He is very pretty. And Matt Lauer looked crazy handsome in his tux. *WWHL* was the *Vanderpump Rules* guys, so it was like a night off.

▶ TUESDAY, NOVEMBER 3, 2015

Publication day for the paperback of *The Andy Cohen Diaries,* which means I'm going on a mini–book tour over the next couple weeks and I'm tired already. Pretaped Giada De Laurentiis and Jerry Rice—we were gonna do Teach Me Your Talent with him, where he would teach me how to snap a ball. It seemed like it was going to be very gay and hilarious. Then we got to taping the show and he was like, I'm a wide receiver; I'll just throw you the ball. So that was boring.

Here's what happened at my book signing at the Tribeca Barnes and Noble: A lady made me a ceramic sculpture of Wacha's head using only dental tools, two Australians separately gave me their numbers with notes saying "Drinks later?" (the answer was no), and three trans gals pitched me a trans version of *Real Housewives*. There were two Lindas who spell their name "Lynda," a Christine who spells her name "Kristeene," and that old lady with long blond hair who comes to every signing I have and gives me some kind of a chip that looks like a poker chip but has something to do with astrology. She always says, "Here's your chip!" like I've been waiting for it or it's a rite of passage at a book signing. And the truth is I like it.

Topher Grace and Maura Tierney were live.

WEDNESDAY, NOVEMBER 4, 2015

Wacha was on some holiday pet segment on *Live! with Kelly and Michael* and I was terrified he'd do something weird but not only was he fine, they had us standing behind a table so you couldn't actually see the dogs. So that was odd. Now they wanna move the New Year's Eve show to the *SNL* studio because the Rainbow Room won't work. I let it slip on Amy Phillips's radio show that there would be a new *Housewives* "sooner than you think," and so that fucked everything up and Bravo is rushing to announce *Dallas* and *Potomac* next week.

Book signing in Jersey. Sold 350 books.

FRIDAY, NOVEMBER 6, 2015—NYC—MIAMI

I left the house very early to do *CBS This Morning* and when Sherman's assistant, Ronnie, came to pick up Wacha he was acting like a snarling, wild wolf, barking and growling from the back room. Ronnie wouldn't even go back there, and I didn't blame him. Sherman wound up having to come in and get him—thankfully he ran to Sherman. I guess the dog was furious at me for leaving him and decided he wouldn't play along? I don't know. Otherwise the advice Cesar Millan gave me a few weeks ago seems to be working—just let him come to other people, don't let them come at him when they are on his turf, and if he growls or barks, listen to his signal. Flew to Miami and got in one hour at the Delano pool, and it was blissful seeing Soledad and Diego and the whole nice crew. Some woman sent me a tequila but I couldn't drink it; I had to work. Had a fake business meeting at the Palace with Jenn Levy and the *Below Deck* producers. Here are names of people I signed books for: Genesis (not a stripper; I asked), Brittnie, Rhonda and Herb (Rhonda told me she has the sexiest wonky eye in Miami and Herb nodded in agreement), Arika, Kimmy Wimmy, Jenny Poo Poo (she came with Kimmy Wimmy), Murisa (an even *more* phonetic way to spell Marisa!), and Latarsha.

▶ SATURDAY, NOVEMBER 7, 2015—MIAMI

Below Deck reunion all day. Emile is so dreamy, I want to eat him with a spoon. Did I say that? Got in one not-totally-satisfying hour under cloudy skies at the Delano pool before it was time to go to the JCC in Fort Lauderdale. The intensity of the Jewish woman cannot ever be overstated. "I want another picture! Let's do it standing up, I'm wearing a jumpsuit!" I was *played out* after the signing, and then I got up to speak and the first question was what did I think about the Harry Hamlin Halloween costume and I explained that he went as Sid Vicious and wore a swastika T-shirt, which is what Sid used to wear, and that I wasn't offended because I didn't think Harry was condoning the Holocaust or anything. This was the wrong thing to say at the JCC—and I mean *the entire room* turned on me immediately, so I just changed my opinion right there and said I was terribly offended. They all clapped.

▶ SUNDAY, NOVEMBER 8, 2015—MIAMI—NYC

Got two hours in the sun this morning and then flew home. All the gals at the security area in the American terminal in Miami know me. We kibitz. ChaCha had cancer, but she is better now and her hair grew back. Landed at LaGuardia and the parking lot was closed so we had to walk about eleven minutes to the car, which I guess was the last straw for me because when

I finally got home I was feeling so tired and overbooked and lonely and why-am-I-doing-all-this. Just overextended. The light at the end of the tunnel is Thanksgiving, but the next two weeks are going to be bad.

We were about to go on the air with Kandi and Vivica Fox after the *RHOA* premiere for a forty-five-minute supersized episode and I was wondering what we were going to talk about when Vivica dropped a bomb— she alleged that 50 Cent was actually a "gay booty snatcher." I was floored, Twitter blew up, and Vivica and *WWHL* were quickly trending all over the country. Mama Joyce was the bartender and the gay shark came out with a Bertha-Day cake (we love Aunt Bertha). Met John Mayer and his brothers for a drink after the show and it was amazing—like Mayer Brothers Riff Fest 2015, three tall straight guys with different levels of full hair and excellent personalities. I told them about the Harry Hamlin kerfuffle, and what ensued was a most informed discussion of motive and reaction.

❧ MONDAY, NOVEMBER 9, 2015

I love the promise of a beautiful early morning in NYC; I walk Wacha and see people emerging from their buildings, ready to conquer the day. Doormen are surveying the scene outside their doors. This morning I was on Sixteenth and Seventh when this hot doorman looked at me. "My wife loves you," he snarled in a thick Russian accent. "She wants to have sex with you." I said we should have a three-way and he said okay, bemused. Then I got home feeling tired already, and the elevator guy who is always trying to be my bodyguard and take me out the back door said, are you okay? Do I need to break somebody's arms for you? And he was serious. I said, "I'm tired!"

The radio show, for which I remained exceedingly tired and cranky, wound up being fantastic. John Hill was late—the L train broke down— and huffing in an Uber, so I was solo for the first hour and fifteen minutes, talking to myself, and then Paul Bettany came in and was charming. Seal and John Hill arrived at the same time and I'd told Tim to play Seal during the whole interview and he wound up singing along with himself, which brought tears to my eyes and bumps to my goose. No joke! His team had said no Heidi Klum questions, but I asked him why he renewed his vows so many times—I said I thought only Housewives did that. He said he hated it and only put up with it and it was a circus. So that was fodder for the blogs all day. Then Sandra came and we dissected the Kris Jenner birthday video and that was a joy. A JOY! She had Lady Bunny on her radio show and I sat in for it gleefully.

My Ukrainian mistress just did a fitness competition and was all spray tanned. I tried to get him to stop with the fitness competitions. Went to Hickey's play opening with Amanda; he is the star. He's very specific about the reviews—you're not allowed to mention them, good or bad.

After the show I FaceTimed with #BAS *and* #BritActor for twenty minutes each. #BAS's friend thinks I am Caesar Flickerman. I get that a lot. It's not a compliment. Mom texted after the show—Tom Sandoval and Caroline from *Ladies of London*—saying, "not in our realm."

❧ TUESDAY, NOVEMBER 10, 2015

The day finally came when I had to decide about the heated toilet that my mom has been *at* me about for over a year. She said she would buy me one and Eric said you know what, nobody's ever been upset with a heated toilet, so do it. I texted Mom saying okay, I'm in. I said, I can't believe you're gonna buy me one of these—they're between five and six thousand bucks. She was like "WHAT?? Mine was 900 bucks." So now I have to decide whether I want a cheap heated toilet or the top of the line. This is how you go bankrupt, and this is why I am going to keep making paid speeches.

Two-hour meeting at the apartment with everybody—Eric, Gordon, Fanuka, blah blah blah. A hot worker who I have never seen was eating lunch in the corner, where the bar is going to be, and I was pretending to take pictures of the construction but really I was taking pics of him. It was pervy. When I tell you this guy had no interest in me, I mean *no* interest. Anyway, so what I haven't factored into this whole apartment-expansion equation is the installation of furniture, wallpaper, and painting that will happen *after* the construction is done. So I've been saying it's gonna be done in April, but it's actually *June*, says Eric. So the parody of construction delays continues. Does that mean July?

Taped Daniel Radcliffe and James McAvoy, who both seemed gayer than me. I am so fat in the face it's beyond comprehension. Came home and got deep with Lynn on the phone—I'm lonely, tired, at the end of my rope. Luckily the show, with Hickey and Christina Ricci, felt like another night off.

WEDNESDAY, NOVEMBER 11, 2015

It's Dad's birthday; I got him the same Ralph Lauren lined sports coat that I bought myself. I hope he doesn't hate it. Shot wraps all day for *Then and Now*. Got home to the news that the jacket didn't fit Dad and it is "too stylish" for him; he doesn't know where he would wear it. Mom and Dad are driving to Columbus this weekend and will finally see *AC2*. We're gonna meet there the night before for dinner, so I can look forward to more details on the jacket. Mom also wants to have a "FACE to FACE discussion about BILL MAHER and WHAT you plan to SAY." Drew Barrymore was on the show and unleashed an unprecedented river of words; we were 4:30 over, which never happens. We had a Drag Barrymore contest with three queens—Mimi Imfurst was Drew as Gertie from *E.T.*, Brooklyn Ford was *Scream* Drew, and Sherry Vine was *Grey Gardens* Drew. Sherry won. Face-Timed with #BAS and discovered he has never seen four gay classics: *Grey Gardens*, *Mommie Dearest*, *The Women*, and *All About Eve*. Is this proof that I'm too old for him? The live show was Ralph and Elizabeth Hurley. Wacha growled at Ralph and I got freaked out. We went to Anfora after the show and I said, "I'm sorry he growled at you," and Ralph brushed it off. "He was threatened; don't worry about it." Why am I always having to remind myself that this is a dog I'm dealing with, an animal?

THURSDAY, NOVEMBER 12, 2015—NYC—DC—NYC

Took an early train to D.C. for a book event. Emailed with SJP about being at the end of my rope. Every time I complain about how busy I am, I think of her and add three kids into the mix and scratch my head. And she retains her composure, which is incredible.

The Brooks story is hitting the fan. He admitted falsifying documents after City of Hope came out and said he was never treated there. Shannon is sending me articles, Tamra is sending stuff from E! news, Vicki is saying, "You would think I had been dating a member of the Taliban."

Signed five hundred books at the venue when I got there—in twenty-five minutes. The Q and A was fine, and I took photos for a half hour after. There were a few cute guys, actually, which is kind of a new thing at these signings. And a lot of people wanted to tell me they knew someone who once worked at Bravo, once appeared on a Bravo show, or that they knew someone who kind of knew me or knew someone who knew me. Everybody wants to make a connection, but they don't realize that by doing that they are preventing us from making our *own* connection by bringing someone I barely know into it. I get the impulse because I do it too. You want to separate yourself from a random fan, but you wind up taking away from your own moment. Catch-22! They gave me a Fresquila, which was great, but then I couldn't continue drinking because they didn't have tequila on the plane home—it was all I wanted. Speaking of that, Dave announced that he's quitting drinking, which is making me question my relationship to alcohol—how sometimes before a show I will feel sick at the thought of drinking but will have one anyway. It's so obvious, the idea of me becoming a serious alcoholic. I hope it's just obvious and not inevitable—those are two different things.

Landed at eleven and the man waiting for me with a crumpled sign with my name on it looked like he was my dad's age. Actually, he pretty much looked like my dad, although he was stooped over and wearing a driving cap, which my dad doesn't wear. But he had a wide-wale brown sports coat on and had to be seventy-five. (I don't think the Ralph Lauren sports coat would work on him, either.) So he reminded me that the parking lot is closed and we had to walk about a mile to the car. First no tequila, and now this? The struggle is very real. I felt that my life was in danger the entire drive home, like when I would sit in the back seat while my grandfather drove me down the Inner Belt to Allen Foods with his blinker on the whole way. Got home and went to bed. Wacha was in Brooklyn because I leave again in the morning, and it felt weird not having him bundled up with me. Can't believe I have to schlep to Columbus tomorrow for the *AC2* tour. I am ready for June to be here. I wanna go home.

▶ FRIDAY, NOVEMBER 13, 2015—NYC—COLUMBUS, OHIO

Peeled my ass out of bed to fill in for Kathie Lee, and luckily they let me skip the 8:00 a.m. meeting so I could arrive at 9:00. Had the greatest time with Hoda on air although I made two generalizations about lesbians, said there are no Jews at NASCAR races, and said "screwed up," which the producers there don't love as a term. #BritActor was at home watching—his first time seeing me on TV. Went to Bravo and threw shit out, then spoke at a lunch at Mediacom or Mediavest or one of those ad-buying agencies. Wolfed down two pieces of pizza and went home to pack and then to the airport for Columbus.

There's a store at LaGuardia called America! that I was mocking, but by the time I landed I was ready to shop there because Paris was attacked tonight. Horrible. The first text I got was Anderson saying, "I have to go to Paris; what do you want to do?" He suggested I go on alone tomorrow night, which I couldn't imagine doing. Waiting at the Columbus airport was a cute Will-and-Grace couple with signs welcoming me and an offer of a ride to my hotel with Fresquilas and pot. We had a bunch of hugs and took selfies instead. My parents dealt with the news that they'd driven seven hours just to have dinner with me very well. I was worried they'd make me stay the whole weekend with them, but we decided to get the hell out of Dodge tomorrow and AC and I picked a date in January to reschedule our show. Had a nice dinner at The Sycamore, then the driver dropped me off backstage at the Grateful Dead show, which was the greatest overlap in tour scheduling ever. I entered right after they'd finished the first set. Hung with John in his dressing room, got high, drank whiskey, studied the set lists and found I was okay having missed set one (except for "Cumberland Blues") and excited for what was to come ("China Cat/Rider," "The Wheel," "Good Lovin'," "Playing in the Band"), which I watched with Chad in the carpeted sound-board area right in the middle of the arena. Then I joined John on the side of the stage for "Drums/Space" in a black crepe area with Bob and the keyboardist. Fun! I stayed there for a few more songs and went back to the sound area for the rest and remarkably ran into the "Grace" woman from the airport. Hung in John's room post-show shooting the shit, then he split to get on the bus to Greensboro, North Carolina. I took an Uber to the gay bar Union and met a twenty-two-year-old on my way in, who introduced me to his friends.

▶ SATURDAY, NOVEMBER 14, 2015—COLUMBUS, OHIO—NYC

Went to breakfast with Mom and Dad and who were in my hotel restaurant but Will and Grace. How small is Columbus? Mom spoke to me about Bill Maher; she's skeptical of my confidence. "It's the SEASON FINALE? Oh no, that's BAD!" Landed back in NYC and took a three-hour nap, naked in the sheets like Dorinda every day at four. Went with #BritActor to a Scottish pub, which was sweet. At Bar Centrale the door was locked and I felt like I was in the Twilight Zone. Hickey came out and opened it, and Mary said they lock it to keep people out and just to call next time and say who's at the door.

⯈ TUESDAY, NOVEMBER 17, 2015

Three shows today. Two radio interviews, not to mention *two* pre-interviews for Bill Maher, which now have me worried I'm either overprepared or underprepared. This thing has too much buildup, and this is coming from a guy who loves an overhyped event. I was honored tonight by the Hetrick-Martin Institute and Bevy presented my award with heart and humor and big-bustedness. Dennis Quaid was on the live show and I fell in love with him.

⯈ WEDNESDAY, NOVEMBER 18, 2015

Woke up and judged a gay phone-sex contest on Howard Stern; they'd had all the guys on staff try gay phone sex and I judged who was best. Howard declared me Top Gay at the beginning of the segment. I called in from my bed! Mom texted that she knows I'm gonna be great on Maher, so maybe it will be okay. Natalie Dormer is coming on the show and her people didn't want her to play Katniss Everpeen, where she would guess her costars' identities from pictures of their crotches. Hmm.

⯈ THURSDAY, NOVEMBER 19, 2015—NYC—LOS ANGELES

Flew to LA and headed straight to rehearsal at *Hollywood Game Night* while I spoke to Mom, who reiterated she knows I will do great and she is just giving me trouble and not to worry. It was really sweet, and I said, "Thank you; I appreciate it," and she said, "NOT!" Checked into Room 1207 at the Sunset Tower but they have the penthouse available for tomorrow. I texted John Mayer to ask him for advice on whether it's worth moving because I know 1207 is his favorite, but he said to take the penthouse as long as I don't unpack. Dinner at Bruce's.

► FRIDAY, NOVEMBER 20, 2015—LOS ANGELES

Went by Jason Blum's office for a tour and a kiki, then to the Palm for lunch with Bruce, the entirety of which we recorded for Radio Andy because what could be more gripping than our lunch? I had such agita about looking like a moron on Bill Maher tonight that it made Bruce edgy. It was like we were waiting for test results to come in. Jason Bateman was there, and Brian Grazer. And you know what? The lunch *was* entertaining. It was reality radio.

Went to World of Wonder to do voice-over for *Then and Now*. Got back to the Tower and my phone rang and it was Scott Carter, the executive producer of Maher, who ran me through my segment again and was super specific about where I was sitting and about not having to jump in during the panel after my interview and the choreography of everything and I almost hung up feeling really good about it, but then he said he wanted me to come early and I started wondering why they kept running me through it and got panicked again.

Walked into the artist entrance at CBS at five-thirty and immediately smelled the familiar TV City smell, which is like an elementary school. It was where the CBS News LA bureau was, and I always loved the smell in there. They had me in one of the *Young and the Restless* actors' dressing rooms and when I went in, there was a note from Doug Davidson, who I hadn't seen since my days at CBS fifteen years ago. Scott, the producer, came in and said Senator Angus King had seen Doug coming out of the door with my name on it and said, "I'm looking forward to going on *Real Time* with you, Andy." So that was the first time someone mistook a soap star for me. Scott briefed me again, of course. Doug came by looking like vintage Paul Williams from the day, and I was so excited to get the tea on his life, *Y&R*, what he thinks of Eileen on *RHOBH*, and the horrible pay cuts they've all had to endure because the soaps aren't what they used to be. I asked what he'd done to his face and he said nothing, and I said, would you tell me if you had?

Bill Maher's show leaves you packets of information in your dressing room, so I was studying about Syrian refugees and national security in the age of ISIS before I went out there. I was the icebreaker funny segment after the panel, then I was expected to stay and join the discussion. As I was waiting to go on the discussion was so heated and so over my head that I was feeling flashes of "Mom was RIGHT!" I was thinking about how she asked Joan Rivers at Liza's wedding if *she* thought I should ever go on Bill Maher and Joan said, "Don't do it; it's a really hard show," and then the stage director was telling me to stand on my spot because Bill was about to introduce me.

I came out with a lot of energy and he immediately asked about my mom not wanting me to go on the show, which I ran with. The audience laughed. They were ready to laugh after all the seriousness, as Scott had told me they would be, and I had them. I went into my spiel about the election as reality TV, talked about Trump being like a Season One Housewife (delusional, will say anything, bad makeup yet to be fixed) and the debates as *Real Housewives* reunions (I compared Hillary's tirade about Wall Street and 9/11 to Teresa's table flip—effective, but didn't make any sense). I told Caissie's joke about Ted Cruz having the voice of a regional theater director. Then Bill brought up Lindsey Graham and I started to panic because I know nothing about Lindsey Graham, so I changed the topic to how great Gavin Newsom (one of the panelists) is. He went back to Lindsey Graham and I figured he had a joke he wanted to tell, which he did—that he thinks Lindsey Graham is gay and doing it with John McCain. I went with it.

I was sitting next to him after our segment when he went into his comedy bit, which included a thing about a prostate massager, and I started mugging for the camera, knowing they were going to cut away to the gay guy. Of course they did. The rest of the show was great. Lots of texts and emails after. Mom's was, "Good job 👌. Whew. You sure looked handsome 😊." Cher texted, "REGIONAL THEATER 😄 ANDY YOU'RE FKNG KILLING ME. YOU WERE ADORABLE. FUNNY . . . AND TELL YOUR MOM I SAID WAY SMART ENOUGH. SO PROUD OF BOTH MY BOYS THIS WK." (She was referring to AC in Paris.) If I can get approval from my mom *and* Cher, I'm good.

Went to dinner with Bruce and Bryan at the Tower. Saw Greg Berlanti and Robbie Rogers—they're so cute. And Patrick Stewart, who got a bad table. I felt like I was walking on air, I was so relieved that the Maher thing was behind me and I didn't embarrass myself or betray my lack of worldly intelligence. Twitter was really happy with the appearance too. RELIEF! Met Billy Eichner at the Maher wrap party (it was their season finale). Had a long talk with Maher, who was really complimentary and wants me back. We talked about pot, being single, aging, our schedules. He was great. There were a few gay jokes thrown around the party in a way I haven't heard for a while. It was old school. He told me my drink was faggy looking, and it was—I'd ordered a Maker's and ginger but they gave me something that looked like a Hawaiian cocktail. I asked for a new one—I wanted them to butch up my cocktail for Bill Maher! Had fun talking to Gavin Newsom (who started following me on Twitter), the hot Ben Domenech guy (who got a selfie for his aunt or someone), and Senator King, who invited me to the capital for a tour. I made friends with the panelists! Billy and I left the party and went to Revolver, which was a sad scene, but we had fun.

❧ SATURDAY, NOVEMBER 21, 2015—LOS ANGELES

This morning at the Tower, I complimented the waiter, Cody, on his hair and he proceeded to give me a monologue about how bad his haircut actually was. Cody said he feels *great* when his hair looks great, his teeth are white, and he's tan. But he never feels all three of those things at once! He is from South Florida and can't tan! His last name is White, and he thinks that's a curse! He doesn't have a pool in his complex in Hollywood, which adds to his tanning problems. So there is a lot going on in Cody's mind. Can you imagine how exhausting it is to be Cody's girlfriend? When the mood of the day is dictated by how tan he is, or how he feels about his hair? Cody is not a singular case; this is probably true of every man in LA. And woman. Nice breakfast with Jason and Lauren and Roxie, and the truth is that Cody is a cool guy and I'm glad he doesn't struggle alone.

Kind of wondered if I'd been a gay pawn on Maher—they kept cutting to me at every gay reference. He did make a big thing on the after show about me being so close to Gavin Newsom. . . . Maher is so gay positive, but it was weird. And mugging during the jokes is one thing, but why did I send my drink back?

Took three big hits of my vape on the way to the book signing at The Grove. The Barnes and Noble guy told me that Khloé Kardashian had seven hundred people there last week; that's what the YouTubers get. This is after he told me I had two hundred people, so I felt like a total loser. LA brings out the worst, most insecure version of me. And Cody. So I'm waiting for tea before the signing in the little storage room that I'm sure he didn't put Khloé Kardashian in and there's a big basket there with my name on it full of high-end artisanal pantry supplies that normal human beings who use more than the toaster in their kitchens would've loved, with a note saying that the lady who plays Mrs. Patmore was going to be in their kitchen store from one o'clock to three o'clock and would I please come over and say hello and that yes, this big basket of crackers and sea salts (that I was planning on giving to the man who'd just made me feel small by telling me about Khloé's crowd) was indeed a bribe (to which I did not plan to submit). Then he brings me out amongst the little crowd to introduce me (Camille Grammer was there in the front row with her kids, having stumbled across a sign saying I was coming) and I was getting my picture taken when one of the photographers played me a video message on his phone from Mrs. Patmore herself, saying she was next door and to please visit her. The problem was that the message was like forty-five seconds long and I was standing in front of two hundred people who were watching me watch the message from Mrs. Patmore. It was all very awkward, and I made him shut it off halfway through because it was rude to make the crowd wait. The talk and signing were lovely and sweet and, I'm sure, nothing compared to Khloé's, and it wasn't until I drove off that I wondered what the fuck Mrs. Patmore needed to tell me that was so urgent that she was moved to send a video message *and* basket to get me over there.

After the book signing I appeared on this dog-rescue award thing that's airing on Thanksgiving on Fox. I saw Kathy Griffin backstage, Betty White (of course), Kaley Cuoco, and, on my way out, Paula Abdul, looking very "Straight Up" with a high ponytail. Then went to Bruce's and we watched the Seth Rogen stoner Christmas movie, which I dozed in and out of but liked.

❧ MONDAY, NOVEMBER 23, 2015—NYC

Back in NYC. I stepped on Wacha's foot no less than five times today, once in front of the bodega on Fifteenth Street, which really hurt him. He kept lifting his little paw up and looking at me with squinty eyes. Picked bathroom light fixtures and fireplace mantels. Worked out at Equinox at rush hour and it was amazing people watching. Got Mexican food with Hickey and came home feeling kind of dizzy and FaceTimed with #BAS, who is going to stay here tomorrow when I go to St. Louis. Emily Lazar called and said Bieber cancelled and could I go on Colbert tomorrow? I said sure, if they find me a later flight. Then I basically made love to the dog. My face was so close to his our eyelashes were touching when we blinked.

▷ TUESDAY, NOVEMBER 24, 2015—NYC—ST. LOUIS

Trump was kind of humorous to me up to now, but he's saying all this racist shit and lying and people are believing him. I tweeted a *Times* article and got a raft of hate. Schmoozy lunch with Steve Burke in the executive dining room at 30 Rock. Went home, packed, and went to Colbert, which was really fun. He had me read camp letters and played a clip of *Then and Now*, and I plugged the radio and the book and it was laughs all around. Like on Bill Maher, I came on at a time in the show when people were ready to laugh—in this case right after Spike Lee, who was not exactly light entertainment. Made my flight, after much anxiety.

▷ WEDNESDAY, NOVEMBER 25, 2015—
SUNDAY, NOVEMBER 29, 2015—ST. LOUIS

It's a year since the Ferguson meshugas, so Mom and I went there to support local businesses and give back to that community. It wasn't what we were expecting: The main street is really nice and refurbished and we found two bakeries which were almost sold out of everything and had only white employees.

I got an earful on the drive:

"It's time for Tony Bennett to STOP SINGING! He's too OLD!"

"I will NEVER watch DON LEMON. If he's on, I turn the channel. Who would've thought I'd watch MSNBC for breaking news?"

"I don't care for Matt's facial hair; why does he DO THAT?!?"

"You need a wine refrigerator for your apartment!!! You NEED IT!!!

Don't buy a new mattress for the guest room, just FLIP YOUR MAT-TRESS!!!!"

"Who LIES about CANCER?!?"

"If you're going to POO will you PLEASE do it on MY TOILET so you can see how nice that HOT SEAT is?!?!!"

This was an offer I refused to accept.

Thanksgiving at Em's really turned into a Balderdash festival. I cleaned everybody's clocks. Cousin Dave and I took our annual picture for Instagram, which usually elicits many feverish comments about how hot Cousin Dave is, which we read aloud and enjoy. This year we posed with the little candles we've had on the table since we were kids, and I posted the pic and quickly realized the candles were little Native Americans—1960s white America's version of Native Americans—so I immediately deleted the image before the pic became a case of old-school racist imagery that ruined my weekend. (#BAS is getting in my head.) We posed with turkey candles instead.

We watched *Steve Jobs*—overblown and exhausting—and I read two hundred pages of *City on Fire*, which gets kind of the same review. . . . Texted with #BritActor, who met someone he really digs. Even though I was barely seeing him, the news depressed me. I don't meet people I actually *like* too often. On the plane home I emailed my entire Christmas party list to let them know I was taking the year off due to renovations at the apartment. Except that I wrote that it was "massive" renovations and then after I sent it I thought that seemed really douchey.

▶ MONDAY, NOVEMBER 30, 2015—NYC

Got home to two letters—one from Teresa, wishing me a happy Thanksgiving, and one from my dentist of twenty-five years whom I have been avoiding since switching to Anderson's without any acknowledgment of the fact. After however many years serving his patients, the letter said, he was retiring and everyone could go see his brother if they wanted to. So I crossed that awkward call off my list.

It was my first show back and I literally couldn't read and speak. I just had a really hard time putting the words together. Got a lot of tweets asking how stoned I was—more than normal.

It rained all day; it was depressing and blah. I gave a breakfast speech at the Russian Tea Room for a group of ladies and being there reminded me of my fortieth birthday party, which was my own version of Oprah's Legends Ball. Had a really tough workout with Will. I ran. I hate running. But I kind of love the idea of it. Went home and just blahed around on my bed waiting for my show and texted Anderson saying I am torrentially bored, to which he never responded. I found out an hour later there's been a horrible shooting in California. Sadly, he wasn't bored.

All day the kids at *WWHL* were abuzz about today's 5:00 p.m. taping with Carrie Fisher and Justin Long—our own special *Star Wars* episode. We had special graphics (a crawl for the cold open, like the *Star Wars* opening), we flew in some drag queens to be various Princess Leias, and Mike Robley made a Chew-Wacha costume for the dog. I was all set to give him a mild sedative for his appearance when Carrie Fisher cancelled two hours before the show. Sadness reigned at *WWHL*. Poor kids. I stayed lying on my bed all afternoon. Meanwhile, I'd had Daryn reserve stationery for everybody on the *WWHL* team for Christmas—nice note cards with everybody's name on them—and then realized these kids don't want *stationery*. I'm not their grandma! I watched four hours of coverage of the shooting and followed along on Twitter. Social media is proof of how divided this country is, right down the middle.

Gloria Steinem was on live with Mariska Hargitay (I had to spell it phonetically in the teleprompter so I wouldn't fuck it up). We didn't know how game Steinem would be, or if she'd be funny or what, and I was especially excited and honored to do a shotski with her; it seemed so cool. It turned out she was game for everything except doing the shotski, so we asked Mariska's hot, tall husband if he'd do it with us and then Mariska didn't want to do it because Gloria didn't want to do it. (I wound up doing it with the feminist bartenders.) Gloria is eighty-one and was wearing red hip huggers. I was extra sensitive on the Plead the Fifth questions because I didn't want to say anything that could be considered sexist, and it's amazing either how many things can be considered sexist, or how many sexist things I say. So I settled for "Say one nice thing about the Housewives," knowing that she considers them the bottom of the barrel and thinking that would be a way of addressing her hatred of them without having to go deep into it.

She can't name one nice thing about the Housewives because they're so awful, she said. They are the lowest of the low and bad for women. I thanked her and ill-advisedly said I was going to try to change her mind on the After Show. I brought that up three times during the show, thinking it would get people to the web to watch me and the Ms. of all Ms.es go head to head about the Housewives.

I began the After Show with my pro-Housewives arguments (they are entrepreneurs; they speak for themselves and are not dependent on their men; they are mothers; though they may not all get along and are sometimes horrible role models, the show is ultimately about friendship). She replied that it's actually a minstrel show for women who are overly plastic, mutilating their faces and bodies and performing like idiots in order to brand themselves, as if that's the only way to do it. I was very sweaty, but I knew it was amazing TV for me to get served by her. Speaking of shade, at the end I asked her about Camille Paglia, who loves the Housewives, but it turns out Camille has said nasty stuff about Gloria. Wacha didn't care for Mariska's hot husband.

▶ THURSDAY, DECEMBER 3, 2015

I spend so much time looking at my phone that I wonder what Wacha thinks I am staring at all the time. Liza asked me if I talked to Gloria Steinem about driving her in my car on Shelter Island all those summers ago, when Bill told me to pick up Phil and Marlo from a boat at the dock and they were with Gloria Steinem and her husband. All five of us were jammed into my Honda Accord. I'd forgotten all about that!

Wacha ran all over the Ralph Lauren store while I bought duplicates of some suits that were six years old. I walked him around the block afterwards so he could take his first shit on Madison Avenue and he did, and then the twinkly lights in the Christmas greenery on the window short-circuited from his healthy stream of pee. We fled the scene rapidly. Met Grac at the construction site and she flipped for the apartment. She says the guest room is for her and Lynn. She is the only person I've told that I'm having a big gold disco ball made for the top of the staircase, and she approved. We did a photo shoot on the temporary staircase. Went to Rossopomodoro, which is always either totally empty with not-great service or packed with awful service. It was the latter, which didn't matter one bit because I had Grac all to myself and what would have been an hour-long dinner with good service was almost two and I wasn't complaining. She said if she gets hit by a bus tomorrow she has done everything she wanted in her life. She's been in a rock band, she said, what more can she do? And she drums in a band now, and so she's at her peak. I said, "You know what? I agree, which is really a beautiful thing for us both to be able to say." I mean, I haven't jumped out of a plane or had a kid, but I waffle on both of these ventures anyway and I've done everything else. Wait, I haven't fucked a girl. But I almost had my chance and I didn't push it! I started thinking of her funeral, and how we would have to bust it open with a rock band or disco ball or dance party or something crazy, get Ann and Nancy Wilson to come out and sing. I told her where my mind had just gone and she said, "I really hope you and Neal do something like that." So I was glad I was on the right track. For the record, I hope neither of us gets hit by a bus.

Got home just in time for Mary J. Blige in *The Wiz*. I texted Mom asking her what she thought and she said it was boring; she's never seen it before. I said to rewind five minutes and watch Mary J., to which she responded, "You are so gay. Every single one of my gay friends are wild for this show! ☺ ☺". I said, what do you expect?

► FRIDAY, DECEMBER 4, 2015

Lots of self-hate on the massage table, thinking about the pic I posted yesterday of me getting fitted at Ralph Lauren . . . it's just so douchey. Maybe I'm actually a loser. Saw Ninj and gave him shit about three workout pet peeves: his inability to count, the fact that he hasn't rebranded/renamed the "burpee" to something more desirable so that people *want* to do it, and claiming that we're warming up when we're going at a hard pace at the beginning of the workout.

I was bringing Wacha in from a walk and was in the elevator with Richie when a gay guy got out and I asked Richie who he was—he said, "Oh, he plays around. He has a boyfriend, but when he's outta town he grinds like all the rest." He says he knows everything, which he absolutely does.

He said he could write a book but he couldn't tell all the stories. I told him you don't have to give it *all* away, that I know from experience. Later Bill and I integrated that all-black party that Sean and John throw; we were the only white guys in the place. It was a paradise of hot, cool guys; it had a great energy. I left at four when the lights went up and could've stayed longer.

▶ SATURDAY, DECEMBER 5, 2015

Left my coat at the party last night and John Cotton had it at his salon, so Wacha and I walked first to Macy's—where I bought underwear, which was a total zoo—then to Forty-Fifth between Fifth and Sixth to pick up the coat, and then home, where he had a playdate with Moxie. We were both pooped after!

Dinner with Mark and Kelly at Dirty French—I got them going about *All My Children*. Amazing stories about Palmer, Natalie, Adam, Erica . . . on and on. Just when I think we've talked about everything, we hit upon some new information. I got in a cab as these two girls were getting out and my cab driver immediately started telling me that white girls have gorgeous big asses these days, and that he doesn't know exactly why it is but it's possibly because they're eating more. He said, "White girls used to have asses like pancakes, but now they're *big*." He was excited about this new development among white women. He's lived here twenty years and is originally from Ghana. He hates the Kardashians because they have no talent ("besides getting naked on the video"), but if they are in part responsible for the new wave in big asses, then he will accept their positive contribution. He told me he has banged a lot of white girls and gotten laid in his cab "more than four times," and that he's done it in the very back seat I was sitting in. He said women are very lonely these days and they just offer it up. White girls say what they like and they need to get fucked, he said. Last week a lady going to Thirty-First and Park invited herself to sit in the front seat, where she was all over him, and then invited him up to her apartment but he declined because it was too unsafe to go into her space; he didn't know what would be waiting in there! He feels very comfortable doing it in his cab, though. His friend who is a cabbie picked up a lady at JFK two weeks ago and on the way home she stopped and got a room at a motel, where they fucked, and then he dropped her at home. And the tip was good too! He said there are a lot of lonely white ladies that need to get laid. He had a cute smile. He loves being a cabbie, and I can see why.

TUESDAY, DECEMBER 8, 2015

Wacha is running like a total gimp. I think I gotta get him the second hip replacement; I've been putting it off forever. Had a meeting at the apartment, where construction is moving like molasses. I can't even tell what headway they're making. Sometimes I suspect they load the place up with people when they know I'm coming and it's empty the rest of the time. I said, "What's happened since our last meeting?" and they said, "Don't you see the wiring in all the walls?" but I thought they did the wiring weeks ago. I asked Sandy permission to send personalized pads of paper to the Housewives as Christmas gifts (it's his thing, and I don't wanna steal someone's thing) but he said it's totally fine.

Taped a show with Trisha Yearwood and Babyface that was low energy. Went to the NBC Christmas party at 30 Rock, where Willie and I squeezed each other and I took a pic with the Telemundo people. The guy who busts the sex offenders on *Dateline* is all white hair. Got a good pic of the tree. Ran over to Bob Saget's scleroderma benefit, where I'd agreed to run the auction with him. I was seated with Bob, Ashley Olsen, and Candace Cameron. Bob said he's looking for someone to date and I said, what about a gorgeous Irish girl? He said, she sounds great; tell her I have young semen, so now I don't think he's right for the woman I'm thinking of. Joan Collins was AMAZING on *WWHL* and radio. I have been watching *Imitation of Life* for the last month, like once a week late at night until I get tired. The movie is *endless* and so dramatic. I have a crush on the guy that Miss Laura is blowing off and the daughter is so into.

WEDNESDAY, DECEMBER 9, 2015

It smells of pot on every block and every corner you turn and I absolutely love it. Richie worked 8:00 a.m. to midnight in the elevator so I had ninety conversations with him today. He smokes but he only likes joints, has never had a vape, and gets a sore throat on pipes. In other drug news, Richie thinks the lady down the street we see in the morning is on an eight ball but I think it's pills. He asked what I'm doing on New Year's Eve and I said, "Going to work," and he said, "Yeah? I'll watch you—I been to Vegas, I been to Miami, what do I need to do? Now I can watch you." I didn't mind being an option in a catalog with Vegas or Miami.

Did the *Today* show with Hoda and Kathie Lee, who asked me why I was yelling for the whole segment and I said, you should talk. I'd told the makeup lady to only put it on under my eyes, so she kind of wound up doing the top half of my face and when I saw myself in the monitor I looked like I was halfway made up, with a Richard Nixon guilty-ass upper lip. So that wasn't a good look.

Later I worked out with my Ukrainian mistress and ran into this hippie dude I met on Fire Island, who asked if I was wearing makeup and I realized I'd never taken off what little I had on. I'm on *The View* tomorrow and they wanted me to play Plead the Fifth with Raven-Symoné and I gave them three questions (including "What would you say to Bill Cosby if he walked in right now?" and "Who was the worst guest since you've been on *The View*?") and the ones they brought back were so lame that I said let's not do it.

Barry had invited me to the Grenadines for Christmas break and it looks like it's going to work out—so I invited #BAS, who is coming. I said, would you rather love only once than never love at all? He said yes, so I said okay, then I'm gonna take you on this trip but it's going to ruin travel for you forever. I haven't brought a date on one of these trips in ten years! I'm so excited! I predict everyone will fall in love with him. Dinner with Amanda at Boulud Sud. It was heavenly. We had caviar for two, which was delicious, but I had stern words for the blinis, which were too doughy. Dinner was great—branzino for two and mushroom risotto. The chef came by after and said he was glad we both got caviar because they just started doing it, and both of us almost told him the blinis are fucked up and then we bagged it. Got home and Richie said there was an ESPN party on the sixth floor but there were no famous people. I said I don't need famous people to be at the ESPN party and that I didn't know what that meant anyway. He also said the guy I asked about yesterday has a one-bedroom and that I have the nicest apartment in the building, so that made me feel good.

SATURDAY, DECEMBER 12, 2015

SantaCon today (*again*—it feels like it's twice a year) in the 60-degree weather. Gay people don't seem to take part in it, which is interesting because it's all about costumes and drinking. It's all straight, buffoonish guys who I'm pretty sure wind up doing it with dudes at the end of the night. I don't know why. Went to the Seinfelds' party and talked to Howard about Radio Andy and my expert judging of the phone sex contest, the latter of which he was trying to explain to George Stephanopoulos, who I think was horrified. He says he hasn't decided whether he's staying at Sirius, but I think he's out the door. Skyped with my parents—I told Mom her boobs look huge. "I know!! They're NOT FAKE EITHER!" Dave came by with Catie; it was very cute hanging out with father and daughter. Then Allison and Julia stopped by, and then John Mayer came over with Ricky. Horse Meat Disco with Anderson and Ben et al., where I met a cancer doctor who seemed nice.

MONDAY, DECEMBER 14, 2015

For years I've been proud of my ability to rebound after a big night and power through the day. I'm not a hangover guy, but today I think I might've reached my limit. Against all better judgment, I let my happiness about last night's premiere of *Then and Now* and our live show with Patti LaBelle and Phaedra guide me to Easternbloc, where Benjamin was celebrating the bar's tenth anniversary even though AC and Pablo had bagged it because of our late night on Saturday. I think it was the blessing that Phaedra's mother, Pastor Regina Bell, did for Miss Patti at the end of the show that had me feeling Jesus enough to go to the East Village. Anyway it was a messy shit-show, in the best way. Mistress Formika was there in drag for the first time in years, and Hattie Hathaway performed and she's about ninety so that might've been drag history. I had a blast with Benjamin, though there were some real land mines in there, either people that I knew and didn't want to see or people I didn't want to know. I happily went home around two and unhappily was awoken at 8:00 a.m. for the radio show with a text from Bill Persky saying he was sick and couldn't make it today, which meant it was gonna be a lot of me talking into a mic for two hours. We made it through, and thank god for John Hill. Went from there to a meeting at the apartment—walls are starting to go up. Jennifer Lawrence taped *WWHL* at 3:00 p.m., and I wish every guest had the same enthusiasm for coming on the show! She was more excited for this than anything, she said. As she got made up she pummeled me with questions about Brooks and the cancer, Giggy, and my interactions with the women. She was an open book on the show, she said she was high at the Oscars and a bunch of other stuff. We traded numbers after and I put her in my phone as "Katniss Everpeen," which is a game we finally got to play (costar crotch guessing, of course).

Went to *The Daily Show* and I was so tired I was falling asleep sitting up. And the producers don't tell you anything, which is both fun and a little off-putting. Trevor Noah is so adorable I can't handle it. We just talked, which might've been kind of boring but it was what it was. Went home and got the dog and he waited in the car while I went to Radzi's holiday party, where I talked to Kristen and Josh about how they made it through the Ashley Madison thing, then to the True Entertainment party at the Dream Hotel, where I met the Real Housewives of Potomac for the first time. They are in the exciting phase—about to launch, lives about to change, like they're waiting to jump off a cliff. I told Karen and Katie not to get invested in Twitter and gave my whole spiel about developing a hard shell. We all took a pic. Phaedra came and Steven and I tried to talk her into letting us follow her when she takes the kids to see Apollo in jail. Back to *WWHL* for James and Lala, who both cursed up a storm, and I yelled at them about it so many times and was so frustrated that I wound up giving them the Jackhole on air, a first. It was a really gross show. Lisa Vanderpump texted and said she was in the boonies with no TV but she was getting a lot of tweets and wondered what happened. I said they made Jax look like *Masterpiece Theatre*, that's how gross they were. I went home and was asleep by twelve-thirty.

▶ WEDNESDAY, DECEMBER 16, 2015

Did a great hour-long interview with Barry for Radio Andy in his office at IAC. Heard creative for some cold opens for New Year's Eve that all seemed to be about me being gay, so I killed them. I'm trying to push them to book some more edgy people for *Game Night* but I don't think they love my ideas. Teresa gets out in one week and I got an enthusiastic email:

THE TRACK HERE IS THE BEST I AM OUT THERE ALL THE TIME AND THIS DECEMBER HAS BEEN AMAZING SEE GOD LOVES ME HE KNOWS I HATE SNOW AND IT SNOWS ALLOT HERE. THANK YOU FOR REACHING OUT TO BOB I WANT HIS DVD'S FOR WHEN I GET HOME SO I CAN KEEP WORKING OUT . . . 11 MORE DAYS TILL I AM HOME. YEAHHHHHHH-HHH!!!!!! SO EXCITED!!! XOXOXO

She really wants these Bob Harper DVDs that he sent for her but that seem to have gotten lost in the mail. I was surprised there was a track at all! Did the radio show with Billy Eichner and Whoopi Goldberg, then taped a show with them. Passed out staff holiday gifts, which were very cool speakers. Maya Rudolph and Will Ferrell were on tonight and were as funny as you want them to be. We finally dressed Wacha up as Chew-Wacha in honor of *Star Wars*.

➤ THURSDAY, DECEMBER 17, 2015

I don't know what got into me but I FaceTimed #BritActor for the first time in at least a month and we had a sweet, flirty convo. I hung up and sent him a saucy text saying, "Before you become a lesbian and move in with your beau can we please get together," and he replied that he was afraid it was too late for that. I said, "I'm happy for you" (I may not be), and he said, "Cheers!" which made it worse somehow. Thankfully I went directly to lunch with John Mayer, which was a Christmas lunch, we decided, and that meant we were going to have a glass of wine, which meant cancelling Stan, my Ukrainian mistress, for the second time this week. John thinks it is great for me to be soundly rejected, that it will keep me in check. I don't totally agree but appreciate the thought. I also think it's good to focus on #BrazilianAndySamberg, who has not exhibited one flaw. On the way out we ran into a table full of Bravo ad-sales people and clients and John and I dueted "Have Yourself a Merry Little Christmas" for them, so if that doesn't make them buy an ad on my show I'm out of ideas. We went to some by-appointment vintage store on Wooster in the pouring rain and I lasted about two minutes and then left him there.

Did a live Radio Andy Christmas special for two hours—a "Holiday Hangout with Amy Sedaris" was how it was billed, and it was exactly that. A blind guy called in and Amy was giving him all sorts of shit. And a guy who had size 16 shoes, which Amy called "baby coffins"! Her gift idea was these fake testicles you buy at medical supply stores to see if yours have testicular cancer. They cost $150. After the show we went to the Bowery Hotel and met Justin Theroux—he just got Instagram and is obsessed—and then to meet Jim and Meghan Edmonds at The Spotted Pig.

▶ FRIDAY, DECEMBER 18, 2015

Worked out with the Ninj. Forgot to bring him a present. Lunch with Bethenny; we talked about #BrazilianAndySamberg. I'm excited about the trip with him, and to introduce him to more of my friends; he has only met Anderson and *WWHL* people. Fitting at Ralph Lauren—the sales-model served the dog a treat and water on a tray.

Went to Harry Smith's Christmas party, then Liza's. My Dominican Uber driver was so cute, and I got it in my head that he was flirting with me the way he was looking at me in the rearview mirror. He started talking about how people are up for and into anything in the DR and I said yeah, that's my impression with all my Dominican friends in the city (as if I run in exclusively Dominican circles). He said yeah, women will do anything, and I said yeah, and guys too. And that shut that down with a slam, so I don't think he was saying what I thought he was saying. All my drivers are horny these days. I think the holidays make everyone horny. He did tell me how hard life was in the DR, and he sends money home to his family all the time; that's why he came here, to help his family. But he said no matter how many troubles you have, you always have time to enjoy your life. That's the Dominican way.

SATURDAY, DECEMBER 19, 2015

Worked out with my mistress. He is *so* Ukrainian. I give him assignments every time I work out with him; today I told him to look up the words "repressed" and "asexual" in his Ukrainian-English dictionary because they both came up in our conversation. I came out of the locker room and he was doing it.

I shopped like crazy today, having bought not one gift up to this point. For myself I bought: a gold ceramic gun (I might give it to Bryan), a vintage pair of Nikes, two ties. I got a bandanna for Wacha at the Levi's Store. The lady who has helped me at Black Fleece for the last five years said they're closing—no more Thom Browne designs for Brooks Brothers. She thinks Brooks didn't want to pay him anymore, or something. I only loved his ties, but I mean, I probably have fifty of them. I bought eight more for friends; they were half off. Then the lady ear doctor came to do a mold of my ear for my New Year's Eve earpiece because it's gonna be so loud in Times Square, but I have so much wax in my ear she couldn't do it. Apparently I have to go get them cleaned out. I took the dog out and told Richie that the beautiful lady who was just at my apartment was an ear doctor and he told me all about his "lazy ear," which I never knew existed. He said, "Right, like you know how you got a lazy eye?? I have a lazy ear! It rings when a baby cries and stuff." So even my elevator operator knows that I have a lazy eye, and apparently it's fine to just sprinkle that into general conversation.

I was Barkin's date to Julianne Moore's Christmas party; then had a long hang at the Bozzis'. Daniel Craig was there, looking like a piece of cake right out of the oven.

SUNDAY, DECEMBER 20, 2015

Wacha is a hero. I'd just gotten a long massage, was late to dinner, and was fixing his when he saw the mouse that's been terrorizing us for the last few months. He jumped into action and chased it into the living room. I actually saw the mouse running from him, and like *that*, Wacha POUNCED and I don't know how he did it but he killed him fast, with no blood. Suddenly there was just a cute lil' dead mouse, belly up. Wacha turned and looked up at me and it was like the "brand new day" number from *The Wiz*. It was a euphoric moment for both of us! He knew he'd done good, and I flooded him with treats. I buzzed Richie, who said, "What happened what happened???" His excitement was diminished when I asked him to please remove a mouse from my living room. He said, "Mices are my phobia! I can't with mices!" I was too excited to deal with the double misplurification of the word "mice." He overcame his phobia and there were no more mices.

Stopped by the Bozzi family Christmas, then went to Blue Ribbon with Jimmy and Nancy. I delivered Bruce's present to Jimmy, which was the original Carson caricature right off the wall of the West Hollywood Palm on Santa Monica. Jimmy freaked.

▶ MONDAY, DECEMBER 21, 2015

Woke up to a day I'd been looking forward to for a few weeks—Bruce live on the radio with me for two hours followed by a Persky lunch. Then it all happened and it was kind of a letdown. Not because it was bad, but it was like I saw it happening in front of me but I wasn't in the moment. I want a do-over.

Got my ears cleaned out by Gwen Korovin and I felt like I was giving birth out of my ear. A lil' wax fetus came out. She has that magic machine that sucks it out with no pain.

Michael Patrick King's Christmas party was great and very adult. Talked to Adri and Susie Essman by the Christmas tree, and SJ pointed out Michael's writing room, where he wrote every episode of *Sex and the City* at this little Puritan antique desk. Guests included Hickey, Slattery and Talia, Bridget Everett, Jonathan Groff, Mario Cantone, Julie Halston, Jhoni Marchinko, Judy Gold, and on and on. Got a script in my email for the cold open I'm taping in the morning for the New Year's Eve thing and skimmed it in the bathroom and couldn't tell if it was funny or not. Walked home with Hickey and SJP. It's like 60 degrees outside again; I slept with the door to the terrace open.

TUESDAY, DECEMBER 22, 2015

Woke up and revisited the script and it's cute. Went to 30 Rock. I said hi to Carson Daly, who had vodka in his dressing room—he was in the *SNL* host dressing room and I was in the musical act dressing room—and I said, "We're gonna get along just fine," and he said, "We already *do* get along well." We shot a cold open all day that inserted us into all the big news events of the year. I asked him questions about *Total Request Live*, Christina Aguilera, his commute, the *Today* show, whether he made a lot of money at MTV, and on and on. He asked me if I cook, which I thought was funny because I only use a toaster oven. Old-school hangout later at my apartment with Dave, Jeanne and Fred, Amanda and Jim, Bill and Chris, Liza, and Bruce. I didn't cook. It was perfect.

WEDNESDAY, DECEMBER 23, 2015

Took Wacha to the Animal Medical Center to have them look at his hip and see about getting the other one done. The second Ray turned onto the block the dog seemed to know we were somewhere he didn't want to be. He was hyper going in, though he didn't put up a fight, but by the time we got in the office he was cowering in the corner. I said since he got the first hip replacement he is now Cujo at the doctor's office, and Dr. Hart said, "He seems like a five out of ten," and took him away. He returned twenty minutes later and said, "He's at eleven," and that they weren't able to do any X-rays or anything. Wacha had shit on the floor and stepped in it, so it was mainly about cleaning the crap off his paw. The vet gave him medicine and said we can do the other hip now or wait for it to get worse; we just have to decide. So I'm gonna see how he does on the medicine and go from there. The doctor is kind of hot. Would it be hot to date a vet?

It rained all day. Lunch with Hickey and Jeff at the Village Den and then pished around the construction site. Worked out with my mistress.

► THURSDAY, DECEMBER 24, 2015

It's a 70-degree Christmas Eve. I was in and out of the blues all day, just generic holiday melancholia.

Worked out with my mistress again. Dinner with Bruce and Bryan and Ava at Waverly Inn; they were really backed up so the service was blah but it was fun. So I've been loving my blabby elevator operator spilling the tea about other people in the building, but guess what? It works both ways! Will told me that his friend heard from my elevator man that I have guys in and out and that he gets me pot, neither of which is true, so now I don't know whether to believe anything he's told me, but it's not going to stop me from gossiping with him. And it's not like I don't love men and pot, so he's not so far off.

Billy Eichner and Heath came by on their way to Jewbilee—an all-Jewish gay Christmas Eve party—and we had drinks while listening to Christmas music and weighing the pros and cons of going to Jewbilee. It was my last night with Wacha for a week, so in the end I walked them to the corner and sent them off. Some guy on the street with his three-day-old dog was lamenting that the pup wouldn't shit and then said, "Are you Andrew Cohen? Mind if I tell you that your programming is the end of civilization?" I said you can say what you want, but I wouldn't love it. Then he went back to talking about how frustrated he was with his puppy and Wacha, right there in front of the guy, took a massive shit. I said, "Oh, *he* has no problem shitting." I was glad I chose Wacha over Jewbilee.

► FRIDAY, DECEMBER 25, 2015

Debated wearing a red flannel Cardinals onesie to walk over to brunch at Michael Rourke's house. Bruce was on the phone and on the fence, he said to "maybe go for it." Hickey said, you can't do that on the street. Wacha was obsessed with Beckett's rabbit in a cage. His mouth was watering—he is a confirmed killer. Went over to Amy's and we had a conversation that, upon further analysis, would only happen between single adults. We talked about trivets (specifically the felt-ball one I got for SJP), how I finally figured out I want my mom to get me a terrarium, and feeling blue on Christmas Eve.

We walked over to SJP's for dinner. The twins were like dolls, and James was hilarious. The food was really good. From there I met up with #BAS, who was coming from Christmas with his family. Amy asked him if he had "a touch of Negro" in him. In fact he has 18 percent, he said. He's smart and has answers for everything. The four of us walked over to Bruce and Bryan's, where we stayed for several hours. #BAS passed everybody's test.

SATURDAY, DECEMBER 26, 2015–TUESDAY, DECEMBER 29, 2015–MUSTIQUE, SAINT LUCIA, GUADELOUPE

Had a great time with #BAS, and the truth is I wrote nothing down so I could just focus on being with *him* for our entire vacationette. We were so chill together; it was lovely. It was just us and Barry and DVF, so it was a four-day double date. Watched *Amy* (double-loved), *The Diary of a Teenage Girl* (loved), *The Walk* (I had notes—for example, I hate straight-to-camera narration) and ten minutes of *Annie Hall* but #BAS wouldn't shut up about whether Woody Allen was a pedophile. #BAS is the voice of the PC generation. Also, it seems Brazilians are very clean, which is a virtue—lots of showers. We scuba dove, and it's even more romantic with your *own* fella undersea as opposed to a paid employee. Ain't that the way, though?! Left the boat mid-trip to get ready for New Year's Eve, and when we returned to the city went straight to Café Un Deux Trois so #BAS could meet Hickey, Jeff, Matthew, and SJP. He once again passed everyone's test. I will say he looks a lot younger than twenty-eight; I thought they were going to card him at one point. Saw Bob Saget, who's gonna be on *New Year's Eve Game Night* with me and said he's not drinking to support Stamos, which is sweet.

WEDNESDAY, DECEMBER 30, 2015–NYC

Rehearsed all day in the famed Studio 8-H at 30 Rock and if it doesn't go great tomorrow, at least I can say I hosted a live show on NBC from *SNL*'s studio. I'm hosting *New Year's Eve Game Night* at ten, then at eleven they're going to walk me, Rob Riggle, and Whitney Cummings into the middle of Times Square, where we are joining Carson and NeNe to talk about the events of the year and count down to the new year. Among other things, I am worried that this *Game Night* show is too square—the guests and categories and games—but it's a big mass show for NBC; it's not supposed to be edgy. After rehearsal I took a big group (#BAS, Amanda, Jim, Liza, SJP, Grac, Neal, Jeanne and Fred) to see Sandra Bernhard at Joe's Pub. She was incredible; she turned my day around. Also, I got to introduce #BAS in one fell swoop to everybody he hadn't met. He gets along with everybody, of any age. I did worry that Sandra's references were maybe too old for him and his friend Daley, but they got the gist.

▶ THURSDAY, DECEMBER 31, 2015

The Day from Hell started with me wide awake at five-thirty worrying about the night. I wasn't getting picked up for the *Today* show until seven-thirty, so I had two hours to envision everything going horribly wrong. Saw Bob Harper in the lobby; he said, "Oh, are you here for the *Today* show?" and I said, "No, honey, I'm here to see the tree." He was with a very cute guy who it turns out is his boyfriend, so there's another one that bit the dust. It's okay, I've got #BAS! Carson was very nice and solicitous; he gave me a bottle of Maker's Mark and some ginger ale with a nice note saying he had enjoyed getting to know me and looked forward to tonight. That's *class*. From there I shot a cold open with Stamos, Whitney Cummings, Carson, and Saget. Stamos is crazy nice—so's Saget. Cummings went through a list of black celebrities and told me they're all on the DL. I mean, she called out everybody! That was exciting.

Met Hickey and Jeff for a cheeseburger at Village Den, then went right back uptown to do blocking for *Game Night*. Then we went to Times Square for a meeting with Carson and the others, where they tested our earpieces and ran through it all. I had a bad feeling. Then we did a run-through with all the celebrity guests at 8:00 p.m. (including Bob Harper, J. B. Smoove, Sasheer Zamata, Cummings) and it was really low energy. Stamos had a really bad back pain and it just felt *off*, not to mention that I said so many gay things that Stamos turned to me and said, "You're the new Harvey Fierstein"—which was not meant as shade, but I took the note and cut a bunch of gay jokes from the script immediately. Around nine, I sat in the *SNL* host's dressing room having a major crisis of confidence about myself. Jimmy emailed me from Jamaica with a poem he wrote, and I sent one back.

His:

The moon is up, the ball is down
2016 is new in town.
May your dreams come true—wish on a star
And Bernard and Stanley are working the bar.
    (And currently we are out of gin)

I said:

Sitting in the SNL host dressing quarters,
About to host a show but I need a doctor without borders
Right about now I could use lots of lucks
Although I really really like my tux
Soon it will be over and I won't feel so dark
Cuz I'm gonna drink all of m'ginge and Maker's Mark.

After I sent it I realized I had to get out of my funk. I listened to John Hill on Radio Andy, which was a step in the right direction. Then Bob Greenblatt came into my dressing room, which was a step back because the head of NBC showing up before going live on the network could rattle a secure man! He was nothing but enthusiastic, so that made me feel great. The PA with an accent who I thought was British but is from Long Island arrived to tell me there's no drinking in Times Square, so I can't have Maker's Mark on set. I said get a Thermos and put some in there, sweetie, so I can have some juice while I'm sitting out there at midnight with the folks.

I was a little shaky at the top of the show; I started talking too soon and called Carson Daly "Carson *Davy.*" *With the chairman of NBC there.* I recovered and the rest was just general fun and games. I have no clue how it was on TV but I'm pretty sure I was screaming loudly the entire time. When it was over I walked to Times Square with my canteen, Whitney, Rob Riggle, three security guys, and Caroline, my makeup artist, who wasn't giving me a read on how the show was, which was not exactly a confidence boost. Then I got a text from Mom saying, "That was fun. You looked great. Somewhat of a shitshow. Break a leg with the next half."

While sitting in the middle of Times Square, I got a text from the British PA from Long Island saying the cars from the car company are all running forty-five minutes behind. I said, No, honey, I have been working since 7:00 a.m. and I am gonna bet that NBC is going to find me a car that will be on the corner of Forty-Sixth and Sixth at 12:31. Then I went on the air and said, "I am feeling so grateful and blessed, and we are all so lucky that we have what we do in this country." I was Mr. Pious after bitch slapping the PA via text about a stupid car. What a fraud I am! Midnight was euphoric and incredible even though I stood up and watched NeNe and Carson hug, while Whitney hugged Rob Riggle. I hugged the air, which I'm praying isn't some kind of nasty metaphor for 2016. I'm still not sure if it was worth it for the crowd standing there holding it in for nine hours but it was wonderful for me to be there and be a part of it. Text from Mom who did not enjoy Whitney Cummings.

The car was there at twelve-thirty and I left to meet Anderson and Ben at ASC. We traded New-Year's-Eve-on-TV stories, and Anderson made me feel better about my performance. He'd just come off four hours live with Kathy Griffin. It felt great to be able to see my friends at the end of the night.

WINTER/SPRING 2016

IN WHICH I . . .

> REUNITE THE FRIENDS FROM *FRIENDS*,

> GET THE GOLDEN TICKET FROM OPRAH,

> OFFEND TAYLOR SWIFT,

> AND THROW OUT ANOTHER PITCH.

Woke up way too early analyzing last night's shows. Part of my problem is that I'm not used to surrendering creative control, except in the case of a beauty pageant, which is *meant* to be ridiculous. But the whole reason I did it was to invest in a future with NBC, and maybe we can make it better next year.

As I was leaving the building for the airport, Richie, in the elevator, told me how much he loved *New Year's Eve Game Night* and repeated a joke Bob Saget said, so maybe I'm being too hard on the whole thing. My attitude adjusted when I saw a hot guy at my gate at LaGuardia—blond, kinda Southern-looking, bowl haircut, good skin, and pecs—and got in line behind him to board. I felt like the gods were with me and we were gonna be seated next to each other, but actually we were across the aisle. Then a lady came to my seat and begged me to switch with her. She was sitting next to Will! (That's what I'm calling him—he looks like the actor who played Will Cortlandt on *All My Children*, who is now a weatherman.) In my head I was like a preteen at a One Direction concert, but when I sat next to Will I acted very busy and retreated into my music while he played Tetris. I was beginning to feel like 2016 is my year.

He ordered a Cobb salad, and I switched from the cheese ravioli to "what he's having." Will and I are starting the year right! He ordered a cocktail (okay, *one* of us is starting it right) and I used that as an opportunity to start talking. He said he'd had a mellow New Year's Eve with friends and was going to Miami solo but has friends there. We broke off the convo and I noticed that he has long eyelashes, with which I became obsessed. And his skin is great. He ordered his second vodka and I got back into it with him. I asked if he has a girlfriend and he said no, but then I asked if I could set him up with one and he said he is seeing someone, which was immediately confusing. He really didn't seem gay, though. He likes sports and seems a bit square. But he's from Chicago, so maybe he's a Midwest gay? Will told me he is an optometrist, and then explained to me what that means. I said, "I'm familiar with an *eye doctor*," and asked him about my contacts and then thirty seconds into the explanation was very bored of hearing about my eyes. He ribbed me about wearing gas-permeable lenses and we guffawed over my having to still travel with contact solution and cleanser. *Optometrist humor!* His eyelashes were so pretty. I told him! He said they are real and not Latisse. He is thirty-five.

We went back to solo time and then I said, "So I can't set you up, huh?" and he said, "No, but I could set you up because you're single, right?" And I said yes, kind of—I still didn't know exactly what was happening between us. Will asked if I am a ". . . guy or mix it up?" I thought he was asking if I was bisexual, but I didn't hear him say "Soho House" before the word "guy" and that is an entirely different thing, though it got me thinking that Soho House is indeed littered with bisexual men so maybe it isn't so different. I got up to go pee and when I came back I said, "So your lady is in NYC?" He said yes she is. So that was that. Our conversation petered out. As we were landing I realized I still didn't have his name. Did I want to burst my fantasy of "Will" by finding out? I pondered. . . . "I'm Andy," I finally said. He extended his perfect, if not a hair small, hand and said, "Randy." And I thought, "OMG, he's *Randy*. Randy! Random! Fun! Flirty! Retro! Randy!" He had just gotten hotter. We landed and went our separate ways, forever. A few hours later at the Palace in Miami I got a text from Mom saying, "Get a hold of yourself. Kissing twinks at a gay bar ☹" "Excuse me?" I said. "On Facebook. At Palace bar," she texted. I felt like I was seventeen and in trouble. I looked at my Facebook and this Brazilian friend had tagged me in a short video of him and me in which I drunkenly turn to him and kiss him. It went to all my followers including Evelyn Cohen, who must've been traumatized in her robe in St. Louis! I yelled at my ex-friend, untagged myself, and texted my mom: "That's not a twink it's my friend Eric it's fine. Go watch a movie!" She said, "YOU go to bed!" When I did finally go to bed I saw that I had forgotten my contact solution. That would've been fun to tell Will/Randy, but we broke up.

➤ WEDNESDAY, JANUARY 6, 2016—NYC

Mom sent me an email saying, "You seem exhausted and uncleansed." When I dug deeper I learned she meant that I usually clean myself out in January and I wasn't doing it this year. She's right; this year I just decided to monitor my drinking better rather than give it up altogether, which may be a cop-out.

Ran into #BritActor on the street. He is in Love—capital "L"—and

I felt better having just had a great holiday with #BAS. Plus I heard from Jake in Boston today; he had lost my number. He is selling a lot of motorcycles. Bravo did focus groups on *WWHL*, which were all pretty positive, but they also asked people who had stopped watching the show why they'd quit and, among other things, several said that I seem "disengaged." That was like a slap in my face. Here I am doing my *dream job*, and for anyone to sense anything short of euphoria coming off me means I'm doing it badly. I'm worried that they are right—sometimes I *am* disengaged and need to change my outlook. It's been six and a half years. There were some other good suggestions for ways to tweak the show. We're going to change how our calls work because viewers said it was holding up the show. So now instead of me saying "What's your name and from where are you calling?" the control room will just tell me the caller's name and city and that's how I'll introduce the call. It's quicker.

▶ THURSDAY, JANUARY 7, 2016

Boxed with the Ninj. Boy, do I feel old. I couldn't wait for it to be over. Had a call with Hunter Pence from the San Francisco Giants, who seems interested in doing a radio show. Was supposed to meet with Holt today but Gillian said Steve, her boss, had eye surgery and couldn't do it. I thought that meant he was getting his eyes done, but it turns out it actually was eye surgery. Dinner with Justin and Jason at the modern-looking new sushi place that took over where Miyagi was on Thirteenth Street, which I've been checking out for a few weeks. There are only three tables inside and a sushi bar, and as soon as we sat down we knew we'd made a terrible mistake. The menu is basically either a sushi sampler from the chef for $150 per person or some random à la carte items. I had tuna with caviar for forty bucks and got two slices of pizza on my way home. Massage by Adam.

▶ FRIDAY, JANUARY 8, 2016

Went by the apartment and found out Surfin officially got the superintendent job! He showed me his new apartment—he gets to move into the building, so now he's my neighbor. Checked in on mine and there were at least ten workers there. I don't know what the hell any of them were *doing*, but there was a lot of activity and they enjoyed seeing the dog. Wacha found pieces of pizza in three separate sidewalk spots in the Village today. He is disgusting. Saw *Star Wars: The Force Awakens* again with Hickey and it seemed less great than the first time.

▶ SUNDAY, JANUARY 10, 2016

Wacha is the best. We slept in while it poured out, until 11:00 a.m. He'll stay in bed with me until I signal him that we're going to the kitchen. Tonight was one of those nights where everything went wrong on the show. I chose from lists of questions to ask Shereé and Sherri and someone mistook my marks for questions I *didn't* want to ask, so when I got on air there were two cards full of questions I didn't want to go near. Then a caller switched his question and asked something we'd just exhausted. I got a huge offer last week—well over seven figures—to do an ad about irritable bowel syndrome. I said no but told Mom that I was considering it, just to see what she'd say. She flipped. "You can't talk about your BOWELS on television, ANDY! YOU CAN'T!"

▶ MONDAY, JANUARY 11, 2016

I woke up and looked at Twitter to see that David Bowie had died. I had a pit in my stomach about it all day. David, the elevator operator, said he didn't know about Bowie and he'd have to google him. He's gonna google *David Bowie*? Wow.

▶ TUESDAY, JANUARY 12, 2016

Had a meeting at Holt; it seems like they want to publish this diary. NBC announced a new deal with Seth Meyers—they're giving him 10:00 p.m. on New Year's Eve. If I had to think about improving NBC on New Year's Eve, a 10:00 p.m. show with Seth Meyers is certainly a great solution! Hopefully we'll figure something else for me to do with NBC this year that doesn't involve leaving a boat with #BAS. Why do I need to do New Year's, anyway? I am having fun doing every one of my five current jobs, and that should be enough. And I can't wait for my West Coast weekend on tour with Anderson. Bruce is meeting us in San Francisco. Fun!

We were rehearsing the show and Zookeeper Rick was gonna be behind the bar with a baby kangaroo, a hawk, and then a tarantula. I am *deathly* afraid of tarantulas, so I put the kibosh on that and wound up with the kangaroo on my lap. When I got back into my office Wacha went crazy—I must've smelled to him like Lady Gaga in the meat dress. The Rams' greedy owner with the bad hair system, Kroenke, announced he's moving the team back to LA. I called Mom and said I want to give him the finger on air on behalf of St. Louis. She said, "I think that's PERFECTLY APPROPRIATE."

▶ WEDNESDAY, JANUARY 13, 2016

Khloé Kardashian—my favorite Kardashian, in case you were wondering—was on the show and there is simultaneously nothing and everything to discuss. At Bar Centrale I met Hickey, Matthew, Laura Linney and Marc, and our friend Tony from the UK. Tony's very young, severely handicapped niece just passed away, and we were all being very sad about it but after a while he assured us somewhat guiltily that in some ways it was a relief to his sister and family—so much so that he took a picture of his niece in her coffin because she was the first dead person he'd ever seen and she looked peaceful and beautiful and without any pain in her body. He said he was tempted to post it on Instagram as some kind of an art piece to shock people out of their fake-amazing show-off lives. I got it, as an art piece. We all agreed he couldn't do it, though. I asked, Is the picture in your phone? And indeed it was. I was freaked out just seeing the phone on the table. "I want to see it," Laura said. "Show me." Hickey and I huddled like scared school-girls while Laura inspected the sad picture. She took it like a man. She said maybe he could post just the hands. Then we moved on for a half hour, talking about everything but sad things until Tony reached for his phone to look at his calendar and when he turned it on the photo was there and I saw it by mistake and was horribly traumatized but of course we were all in a fit of giggles because it was so random.

▶ THURSDAY, JANUARY 14, 2016—NYC—SAN FRANCISCO

Landed in San Francisco and walked around town with Bruce and shopped. We had dinner at the Slanted Door with Lynn. I took Bruce to Powerhouse, where the aesthetic was hairy and a little overweight and the clothing was light. There was some kind of a wet-underwear party where people strip down to their underwear and are sprayed with a water bottle. Two of the contestants were trans. It was all very 2016, but we left before the winner was announced and fell into a Bowie party at the Cat Club, which was phenomenal.

▶ FRIDAY, JANUARY 15, 2016—SAN FRANCISCO

We added a second show in Oakland for Sunday that's not sold out, so I did morning TV in Oakland early to promote it and when I got to KTVU this lady wanted to tell me she knew exactly who I am even though a lot of people don't. Then she showed me a video she made of her going around the newsroom asking people if they know who I am. It was a lot of people saying, "I don't know who Andy Cohen is." So that made me feel really happy about schlepping to KTVU at the crack of dawn. Then when I was ready to leave the driver had taken off to pee, so I was standing in front of the station for fifteen minutes like a ninny while the few people who had figured out who I am came out to take selfies with me. Visited Uncle Dick and Aunt Kay's house, where I have never been (the Oakland Hills are like the Hollywood Hills but with bridge views instead of stars), and then to the Mission with Bruce, where we walked around, and to the Castro, where I bought a gold sequined sweat jacket. Visited with Anderson when he got into town and brought the sweat jacket up to his room to horrify him. Mission accomplished! He doesn't know where I'm going to wear it and neither do I, but when I do it will be the right place. It may take years, by the way. Dave Chappelle is in town performing and is texting AC that we should come meet him. He keeps showing up in cities we are in and doesn't get how we could possibly be playing similar venues or what the fuck we *do* onstage. (We don't either.) Had a two-hour massage with Nate that first made me exhausted, then really woke me up. San Francisco is always my crowd, and they were so raucous that one man had to be taken out by security. He was screaming Anderson's name, so I think he was an Anderson fan, but Anderson disagrees. He thinks he was yelling at Anderson because he could help get security off him. I had high school buddies backstage (Sam, Mark, and JJ), plus Lynn and Brian O'Keefe, Daniel Descalso from the Colorado Rockies, and Uncle Dick with Aunt Kay and Amy. AC had Sanjay Gupta's brother. Not a lot of wigs or hairpieces at the meet and greet, but Patrice Wessel was there and that was a sweet reunion twenty years after Harry Smith "did her job" on *CBS This Morning*. A lady in the VIP line had the best *Housewives* tag line: "I may look crazy, BUT I AM." And she *did* look crazy. Went to a hip-hop party at Oasis. Oddly, there were only about five black people, but it was fun anyway.

SATURDAY, JANUARY 16, 2016—SAN FRANCISCO—SEATTLE

Breakfast with Bruce, Bryan, and AC at the Four Seasons, then we hopped on Virgin America to Seattle—we did radio on the plane, it was really efficient. The Four Seasons in Seattle is brand new and beautiful. I love the people in Seattle; they are smart, naturally beautiful, and earthy. I think of all the cities we've been to, Seattle's Q and A at tonight's show (and maybe D.C.'s) was the best, with thoughtful questions about our families and backgrounds. AC was on fire onstage; he was shading me and reading me like an Atlanta Housewife. In the VIP line, I complimented one couple and the woman said, "We're not a couple; this is my dad." Meanwhile a lady was trying to pimp her son off on us, but I didn't think he was gay. She kept saying, "Look how big his bulge is! Meet us for drinks!" Yikes. We went out to the Cuff Complex and I guess the sight of the two of us walking into a random gay bar is enough to cause a bit of a scene. We were standing in a corner and Anderson said, "Do you realize the entire bar is looking at us?" and I said, "I'm trying not to notice." I flirted with this big ginger lumberjack-y guy, exactly the type you probably should flirt with when in Seattle.

SUNDAY, JANUARY 17, 2016—SEATTLE—OAKLAND

We were exhausted on our morning flight back to Oakland and beginning to regret booking a matinee, but our Asian-Kris-Jenner flight attendant on the plane was calming, and also made me realize that Kris Jenner looks like a flight attendant herself, and has in all her iterations. (Wait, was she *actually* a flight attendant?) Lunch with Lynn and Anderson a few blocks from the theater, so the place was full of people on their way to see us, which was sweet and awkward. The Paramount Theatre is beautiful and old, as was the crowd! At the meet and greet there was a seventy-three-year-old lady in a wheelchair who wore a side pony for me, her first in her life, she said. A blind man with a seeing-eye dog was at the end of the line wanting to interview us about the tour for the *Huffington Post*, and how do you say no to a blind man even though you literally can't speak anymore? I started tweeting during the interview because I realized *Real Housewives of Potomac* was about to start on the east coast, and I thought Anderson was going to yell at me for disrespecting a blind man but we got in the car and immediately jumped on the radio (why waste a car ride back to the hotel when we can make a show out of it?!) and AC said what I did with the blind man was fine. Went back to the Four Seasons, took a long bath, FaceTimed with #BAS, and watched *Downton Abbey* over room service while it poured down rain outside. Went to bed at eleven-thirty. It was a pretty heavenly chill-out, as they go.

▶ MONDAY, JANUARY 18, 2016—OAKLAND—NYC

Fell asleep during the flight home and had a dream that Tamron Hall got sloppy drunk at my house and she and I made out on my bed. Woke up and there was a man snoring like a walrus across from me. Couldn't wait to see the dog. Went home, changed, and went to the Clubhouse where I had two shows.

▶ WEDNESDAY, JANUARY 20, 2016

Worked out with the Ninj, and I haven't weighed myself in many months—I mean, I can't even *remember* the last time I weighed myself—but I've been on a tear at work about how fat my face looks. Out of nowhere today I decided to do it, and lo and behold, I was 172.1! I am good with that! In related news, I had ice cream for dessert after lunch to celebrate. Out of nowhere, Sean Hayes called this afternoon to see if I'd be interested in hosting reunions of casts from James Burrows shows (like *Taxi*) at the tribute he's producing for NBC in LA on Sunday. I would be *thrilled*, was the answer. I said I'd heard there was a *Friends* reunion happening too, and could I do that one? He said Jane Lynch was doing *Friends* but that I would be doing *Will and Grace*. I said, That's great; can you get me *Cheers* too? He said he would do his best. Went to see Natalie Joy Johnson perform at Joe's Pub, as directed and written by John Hill, who also plays the kitar onstage, and it was brilliant. Who knew John could play the kitar? Who knew what a kitar was? Went to *WWHL* and we scrambled to move our Sunday show to tape tomorrow because not only might I have to be in LA Sunday, there's also gonna be a massive snowstorm. It's all a juggling act. Dermot Mulroney and Jenna Fisher were the guests and he was manspreading like crazy, so every time I turned to him my eyes went to his crotch, which was embarrassing. Had a Tinder date at Anfora with a hot pianist who lives in Harlem, though it's unclear why I'm still going on Tinder dates when I am feeling so much affection for #BAS. He's not here, is probably the answer.

▶ THURSDAY, JANUARY 21, 2016

Got a haircut from Tonee and Wacha ate all the hair off the floor.

The pianist sent me a video of him playing and he's like a hot, butch Liberace without the diamonds. I didn't tell him that because I thought he might be offended. Taped Marlon Wayans and Gizelle. Haven't been feeling amazing, so I cancelled my workout and ate pizza—ever since I weighed myself I'm bingeing. Had dinner with John Hill and showed him my apartment. I don't want to gloat or boast about my dream apartment, but it's hard not to want to show it off. Sherman came to pick up Wacha and the dog was *so* excited to see him; he looked at me like "Bye; I have no feelings about walking away to be with the guy I really want to be with, and that guy is not you." I felt like I had been punched in the gut but I talked it through with Richie in the elevator (who, not for nothing, was eating a carton full of the smelliest shrimp lo mein I've ever encountered) and we decided it's better Wacha has a second daddy who he loves instead of the alternative.

► FRIDAY, JANUARY 22, 2016—NYC—LOS ANGELES

Early flight to LA for the Jim Burrows tribute—the final verdict is that I am reuniting *Will and Grace* (sans Debra Messing), *Frasier* (sans Kelsey Grammer), and *Taxi* and Jane Lynch is doing *Friends*, *Mike and Molly*, and *Cheers*. I wanted *Cheers*, but how can you complain with that lineup? *Friends* is the big-ticket reunion of the night so it's all gravy from there. Went straight to the Palm for a lobster bisque and salmon Caesar and, let's be real, to see Bruce. He had Sherry Lansing, Ron Howard, Larry King, and Bellamy Young in there. Went back to the Tower, then took an Uber to Shed Media in Burbank, where we storyboarded the first seven episodes of *RHONY*. The Uber guy of course had no clue how to get around LA and was just blindly led by the GPS which took us on Nichols Canyon to Burbank, thus completely blowing his mind. It was a challenging drive. Took a sunset pic of Sunset Boulevard, which I Instagrammed and then got a flurry of texts from all the people in LA who I *don't* want to see, asking if I'm in LA, but the happy result was hearing from John Mayer, who recognized the view and texted that he's in the room above me at the hotel. Ran over to Sandy's to see Stacey Winkler, then had dinner with Bruce and Bryan at the Tower, where we discussed the depressing election, the boycott of the Oscars by the black community, and our trip to Miami for Bruce's big birthday at the end of March.

► SATURDAY, JANUARY 23, 2016—LOS ANGELES

Woke up to the news that Michael Bloomberg may be running for president, which got me excited until I realized it might fuck up Hillary's chances instead of Trump's. It's a snowstorm shitshow in New York, and all anyone here can say is, "Aren't you glad you're here and not in the snow?" Then they get a monologue from me about not liking to miss a snowstorm and *enjoying* being hunkered down with my dog in my apartment and how quiet and romantic the city gets, how Wacha would be so happy running around in the snow on his terrace and I'd be enjoying my gold Christmas tree, which I still haven't taken down. I lose them when I mention the Christmas tree. Liza and Bruce have been terrified about my flight getting cancelled on Monday but I can't put in the energy. It'll be fine.

Rehearsed for tomorrow's Jim Burrows tribute. The producers reminded me that this was all fun and that I wasn't up there to get dish or scandal from the reunions; they're scared that I'm going to treat the *Taxi* cast like the Housewives. On the way out I saw a pink Corvette and realized it was Angelyne (the license plate and blond wig were important clues) and ran over to ask her for a photo. She said I could have one if I joined her fan club and bought a T-shirt or a bumper sticker. I said of course and she grabbed her fan and opened her trunk. She was out of bumper stickers, and then I realized she probably never had any because the T-shirts were all forty to sixty bucks. I got one for Graciela and then Angelyne told her friend exactly where to stand to take the picture, said to take only one, positioned me and told me how to hold her leg up, put the fan over her face, approved the picture, and sped off. I posted it and got a flood of people saying that it looked like her balls were hanging out. I thought she was a natural woman? Meanwhile, if those *are* balls I don't care because she was kind of mean and she approved the picture. Kelly texted immediately wanting to know what she looked like in person. Like an old, mean drag queen, I said.

Dinner at Tortilla Republic with Bruce. Someone sent over free drinks, but there's no such thing as a free drink because then it's a whole conversation with the person who sent over the drinks.

▶ SUNDAY, JANUARY 24, 2016—LOS ANGELES

I was asked to come back to the Hollywood Palladium and rehearse some more for the Burrows thing, which gave me a complex that I'd done horribly at rehearsal yesterday. But I didn't care, because being in the room with this level of talent talking about shows that I love is an opportunity for me to prove that I am more than a shit-stirring *Housewives* producer. Before I could do that, though, I had to run to Burbank to be interviewed for a *RHOC* and *Vanderpump Rules* uncensored special because I *am* a shit-stirring *Housewives* producer. Went back to rehearse and I was as good (meaning as bad?) as the day before. Napped and headed back to the Palladium where I saw Jim Parsons, Kaley Cuoco, Melissa McCarthy, the cast of *Cheers* (Shelley Long!), and Charlie Sheen. Just as I was looking around the room wondering what the hell I was doing there, Michael Patrick King walked up and asked me to remind him what show Jimmy directed me in.

The stars were all seated at tables with their castmates, and I was alone with Bill Nye the Science Guy, his date, and seven empty chairs. Jane Lynch did the first reunion, *Cheers*; I was too busy staring at Shelley Long's face to really notice but it seemed kind of actor-y and technical.

Then I was up for *Will and Grace* and it went off well. Right before we went on I had a recollection of Megan Mullally not liking to do the Karen Walker voice, so I whispered to Sean, "Is it a bad idea that I was going to have her do it?" and he said, "Yeah, she hates that." So that was that. When the cast came up, I noticed that Eric McCormack seemed to want to sit in the seat next to me and Megan Mullally was looking at it as though, as the only lady in the group, it would be her natural seat. He "won out," and I had a thousand flashbacks of Real Housewives jockeying for the "A position." The interview was fine, and most important, I didn't betray my nerves when I was introduced and walked to the mic while I heard five hundred minds questioning, *"What the fuck is he doing here?"* When it was over I walked down the stairs of the stage and said hi to Lisa Kudrow and was trying not to look to her right, where Aniston was, because I don't really know her and I don't know what my drama was but I didn't want to make her think that I thought I was cool, or that she should know who I am, or that she should have to acknowledge me. Clearly I had some sort of major Jennifer Aniston–itis where I was getting premature erectile dysfunction even though my pants weren't coming down. And as I walked away I turned towards her slightly and saw that she was standing to be gracious and say hello to me, but I was already walking away and gave her a very awkward half-wave and she gave me a classic Aniston befuddled look, which she should trademark. I ran into the arms of Bill Nye, who gave me props before he went up to reunite the *Big Bang Theory* cast.

Next for me was *Taxi*, and they said in my ear that the cast is kind of old so I might have my hands full, but they were perfect and I got to sit next to my angel, Marilu Henner. When I got back to my seat a producer came and grabbed me and asked me to come backstage, where they asked me if I would be comfortable doing the *Friends* reunion. I felt like a JV quarterback being put into the game before a huge play! In over ten years of reunions for me, *this* was the mother lode. (Yeah yeah yeah, I know Matthew Perry wasn't there and I know I never really loved *Friends* but I can smell an overhyped moment with both nostrils clogged.) *YES!* I said. Then I immediately started probing why Jane Lynch suddenly wasn't doing it.

They wouldn't tell me, but what I gathered after fishing around and even talking to Jane backstage ("Thanks for doing this, I really appreciate it; I don't think it's my thing") is that she didn't think it was her thing. Well, that worked perfectly for me, because it happens to be exactly *my* thing! *I reunite!* It's *what I do*!

Before I got too excited, I had to get through *Frasier*, which was fine except that, well, Kelsey Grammer wasn't there. When it was done I had a nice chat with Jim Parsons and his husband about renovations and went backstage to get ready for *Friends* and was told not to mention Marcel the Monkey and something else; I can't remember what now because it was so arbitrary. I had forgotten about Marcel the Monkey anyway, but now I was fascinated to know why he was off limits! Of the cast, I had just met and had a lovely conversation with Schwimmer at the premiere of the O. J. movie, I know Kudrow, I had danced around Aniston but know Justin Theroux, and I don't know Cox or LeBlanc (who has passed on coming on *WWHL* a few times because it "wasn't a fit," which is always scary). As I was running through questions in video village, Sean Hayes came back panicked because the Rembrandts were setting up to play the *Friends* theme song and he had the distinct impression that the Friends weren't thrilled about the performance, which was news to them. I went out and introduced the band, then ran back to watch what were the funniest facial reactions since the last *Atlanta* reunion. The Friends looked like they were in *agony* as the ubiquitous earworm they probably were sick to hell of came to life once again. They came onstage for the interview and I immediately wondered who was going to sit next to me. Kudrow went right for the farthest seat and Schwimmer followed; they each successively seemed to be lunging for the middle of the couch, away from me, the substitute teacher. LeBlanc and Aniston wound up fighting for the seat second from me, with Aniston even sitting on his lap for a second before succumbing to being my neighbor.

I let the moment of seeing them all sitting together really play out and kept saying what a big deal it was. And in the back of my mind I thought, "Oh, man, how great would it be to get a selfie with these guys when the interview is over?" Then I thought, "You can*not* get a selfie with them, you have to be *cool*." Two items on the question cards didn't go great: I asked Aniston about the episode where Rachel gets drunk and marries Ross, to which she replied, "What about it?" and I had to say, "Tell me about it, did you like it?" *Awkward.* And the question to Courteney Cox about the rumor (that was news to me) that they had signed a contract saying they wouldn't sleep with each other for the run of the show went over like a lead balloon, and I felt the entire audience collectively think "Once a *Housewives* guy, always a *Housewives* guy." It was over in a flash. I'm not sure why I'd had such Aniston-panic, because she was lovely and I felt like it went as well as it could have. The producers felt like I'd done them a favor by stepping in, and as an added bonus for me I got to close the show standing in the middle of the entire group of stars with Jim Burrows to my right and Shelley Long(!) to my left. I thanked Mr. Burrows during the commercial break for letting me take part in the evening and asked if it was the most surreal night of his life. He said it was beyond; he was floating. So was I.

After the show I headed to Sandy's, where he was having a dinner party that I knew Dolly Parton was at. I texted Matthew Broderick and Jason Blum to find out if it was still going on and if Dolly was still there. Double yes was the answer and I headed over. As I rode up Marmont Avenue an SUV pulled out of Sandy's driveway and, alas, in the back was a bright yellow wig. I didn't get to see the Queen of Country, but I did get to see Sandy and the group and eat his wonderful food before heading to the Tower to meet John Mayer for a drink.

I joined John at a front table of the candlelit restaurant, entirely empty save one table in the corner—occupied by who else but the cast of *Friends*, minus Matthew Perry of course. Suddenly I became a reporter from *Us Weekly* and began asking John when was the last time he saw Aniston, how awkward this was, and if there were ways I could make it more awkward. We realized they had to walk by our table to leave and that would be a "moment." We wondered if it was more fun at our table or theirs. How could it not be *amazing* at the *Friends* table? As John paid the bill I told him I was going to bust into their fivesome—on what other night could I go say hi to the cast of *Friends*?—and begged him to join me. He told me with a look that the Queen of Smartwater would not be having it. Side note: *Oh, to be an ex-girlfriend of John Mayer!* I table-hopped on my own, and Aniston said, "Oh, wow, I didn't know you were here" (which I analyzed as the words came out of her mouth wondering if they were true; Mayer is really tall—hard to miss). I told them that my favorite part of the night was watching their terrified reactions to the Rembrandts singing that song. They seemed half-mortified that I could tell. One of them (Kudrow? Schwimmer?)

said that one of the band members told them after that they'd kind of expected the Friends to come up and *dance* while they sang the song. I commented on how beautiful Kudrow's purse was and Courteney Cox said they had just been discussing it, and then I left. I told Mayer they were talking about Kudrow's purse so it was debatable whose conversation was more scintillating. As much as I would've loved to see the ultimate reunion—Aniston and Mayer—we left before they did and went to bed. Separately.

► MONDAY, JANUARY 25, 2016—LOS ANGELES—NYC

Woke up with the news that my flight to NYC had been cancelled. I've never missed an episode of *WWHL*, and many people went scrambling to make sure I didn't tonight. I don't know how it happened, but they found me a seat on an American flight where I was reunited with the flight attendant who threw me all my food a few months ago. Today he was all "Heads up—hot towel" with a tray of them in my face while I typed. He's always handing the food to you, not setting it down. And he makes military-style kind of announcements like, "It's table time!" He threw me the tablecloth, for example, as I was pulling the table out. "There's a big hubbub you're on the plane, but you're not my demographic," he announced with my entrée. I figured out midway through the flight that he has the exact same voice as Moe, the bartender on *The Simpsons*. As we were landing he came over with his business card. "If you ever get the need for an older guy," he said as he handed it to me. "I have a headshot here somewhere if you want it. Some of us older guys are still doing the work." Got to the show and the cherry on top of a great weekend was that Mom and Dad were in town and bartending.

► WEDNESDAY, JANUARY 27, 2016

Mom and Dad saw *Hamilton* (loved) and *A View from the Bridge*, which apparently put Dad to sleep and Mom kind of liked. Ricki Lake's dog, Jeffie, died and all week I've been thinking about her and that sweet goldendoodle, and I look at Wacha like he's a ticking time bomb. I love him so much. We were walking on the street yesterday and I saw his reflection in a window and thought, "What a pretty dog." That's love. Taped Matt and Savannah for *WWHL*, then spent about an hour fighting with Trump supporters on Twitter—kind of satisfying, but never fully. Recorded a radio show with Mom and Dad giving advice. Dad gives great advice, but Mom was kind of disinterested.

I booked us dinner at the Polo Bar thinking they'd never been, but it turns out I've already taken them there and they both pointed out twice that it wasn't very crowded last time. They are very big on pointing out how full a place is, as though that validates the entire experience. Thankfully it was packed to the rafters for their second trip with people like Wendi Murdoch and Lionel Richie (not together). Dad went to the bathroom and Mom said she had told Dad that if she dies tomorrow she will have lived a full life, and that growing up in a small town turned her into the person she is today. I said the only thing you haven't gotten to see yet is me getting married and I know it's going to happen. She said, "You gotta hurry it up, I will be in A CHAIR for that, at this rate."

► SATURDAY, JANUARY 30, 2016—NYC—COLUMBUS

This was the *AC2* make-good date for having to cancel because of the Paris terror attacks. Got a pre-show burger with AC at the Pearl oyster bar. The show was good. We went back to the hotel after and ordered breakfast for dinner, always surefire fun! I live to make Anderson giggle. It fills my heart.

► SUNDAY, JANUARY 31, 2016—COLUMBUS—NYC

On the plane home the woman next to me kept asking me who I was and I kept saying "Nobody." But then another woman came by and poured her heart out about her son coming out to her and telling her that he thought since I am the mom's friend—in her head—she would be okay with his coming out, which naturally touched me but confused the lady next to me. I finally told her I host a talk show. If someone doesn't know me, then isn't it weird to have to explain who I am? I mean, who are *you*? We're even.

◆ MONDAY, FEBRUARY 1, 2016

You can just walk by a doorman in the morning and say hi, but you're stuck with an elevator operator for the whole trip. My morning conversation with David in the elevator is always the same: "Hey, how's it going?" "Good, I'm just chillin'." Then we're stalled. Bruce and I had dinner and then back at Fifteenth Street. Victor (working the elevator night shift) told us that Lucie Arnaz lived in this building in the late seventies; she had the whole top floor. I asked if Lucy came to visit her and he said yes, which blew my mind. Then after the show I brought up Lucy again and he said, well, he *thinks* she came but he can't remember that much.

◆ TUESDAY, FEBRUARY 2, 2016

I was getting photographed at the Joseph Abboud fashion show and an incredibly handsome man came by and a photographer put us together for pictures, as happens, and I asked how he was doing and he said, "Well, I would rather be *playing*," which was my first clue that this blond, blue-eyed stunner was a sportsman. I asked around and it was Julian Edelman, the Jewish New England Patriot. I was excited to be pulled back for about four more rounds and permutations of photographs with him, and then to be seated between him and Russell Tovey at the show, where we further kibitzed. During the off-season he lives in West Hollywood and when he told me the intersection I said, "Wow, that's pretty much ground zero," but I'm not sure he knew I meant *gay* ground zero. The queens must *live* to see Julian Edelman on their turf. He says the best trainers are there. He pointed out his girlfriend, who was sitting behind us—she's blond and blue-eyed too, from Sweden; they met in Israel—and I said, "Oh, she's not Jewish?" But it turns out that she is. I said, "Look at you blond, blue-eyed hotties rebranding Judaism for 2016!" An image refresh for the Jewish people: Almost Aryan!

Took Wacha to the vet to get his anal glands cleaned and it was a disaster—he did his thing where he turns into a snarling Cujo and the guy told me the last time he was there two people had to get treated for bites, so it didn't look like they were going to treat him. I said, "Please tell me he is not the worst dog you've seen here," and he said he's one of them. How did that make me feel? Embarrassed, ashamed, crushed, upset, sad . . . I could go on. And when I left I realized that my vet was essentially dumping me because of Wacha's white-coat syndrome. Maybe I never should've gotten that damn hip replaced. My now ex-vet said it could be a good idea to go somewhere that he has no ill association with, so we walked straight to the West Village Veterinary Hospital and I made an appointment. I warned the new crew that he can turn into Cujo. We'll see. We came home and he was as sweet as a little angel, lying on me and looking at me with his soulful eyes while I lectured him on his behavior, and I'm sure I sounded to him like Charlie Brown's teacher.

The show was Lisa Rinna and Harry Hamlin and for some reason when it was over I slid into a sinkhole of depression. Before the show, Dave and I were texting and I said to him that sometimes I love being single, I only have to think for myself and I can do anything I want with no responsibility. He texted me back that I do need to have kids, I'll be a great dad. So hours later I was lying in bed looking back at the choices I've made and the things I've valued that have led me to being very successful, but alone, at forty-seven years old. I feel like I've had a repressed or delayed early adulthood and never moved on to the next phase. I came out at twenty-one and for the next many years experienced all the sexuality I'd been repressing for so long with little intimacy and certainly no goal line of marriage or kids, which simply didn't exist in that era. Fifteen years later, I've been having too much fun to get off the train when people around me start to settle down and have kids. I have either chosen work or every sparkly object and fun experience that's been dropped in my path. Em recently sent me the date for Abby's bat mitzvah in August three years from now, and I thought to myself, if in three years I'm doing the same routine—running around solo in Sag Harbor, Fire Island for ten days in the summer, and then a boat trip, just me and the dog in the new apartment—then there's a big problem. So I'm having doubts but am not doing anything to change the way I live or what I value.

I fell asleep really wondering about myself. Things could grow with #BrazilianAndySamberg but he has another year and a half in Boston, so can a relationship grow long distance? I have a trip to Miami coming up at the end of February, Oscars weekend actually, and I don't know who to take. I might go alone but that seems too depressing.

WEDNESDAY, FEBRUARY 3, 2016

I woke up to a text from Dave wanting to go to Miami this weekend. I said no, but what about in a month? He's in. So that's solved. I feel a little better. Had a great workout with Stan the Ukrainian Mistress. It feels good to be at Equinox—windows, gays, flirting, drama, activity, stimulation. I'm still *married* to the Ninj, who is just happy that when I'm not with him I'm still working out. What a good wife! (Is this my idea of a functioning marriage?) Lunch with Doug and Alex from Evolution Media. Two shows today: Cuba Gooding Jr. and the handsome guy from Lady Antebellum, and Cynthia Nixon and Ethan Hawke. At one point Wacha was barking in my office and I went in and gave him a treat. He got on the couch and I was going to put the leash on him but he snarled at me like a wild wolf and I left him alone.

THURSDAY, FEBRUARY 4, 2016

The shame of essentially having been kicked out of the other vet's office was starting to sink in and I told everyone at the new vet all about it and they couldn't believe that sweet Wacha would eventually turn into Cujo. The vet was really great and took him back to see if they could get a cone on him and express his anal glands. He was back there for about fifteen minutes while I got on the dog scale, which I decided was horribly inaccurate until the receptionist got on and said it was in fact very accurate. So I've been eating a lot since my successful weigh-in last month and now I see that I'm actually getting fat. Moron. They came back out with the dog, having been unsuccessful in doing anything with him because he was snarling and insane. But they were not deterred, and we made a plan for me to give him doggie Xanax one day next week and see if that works. If we don't get his anal glands cleaned out they can explode! So I have a ticking-time-bomb Cujo on my hands. This whole thing is exasperating and exhausting. I feel helpless. And then we got home and he was as sweet as he could possibly be.

Show with Leslie Mann, Dakota Johnson, and Alison Brie. Love that Alison Brie; she is a live wire. Worked out. Met Amanda quickly at Good on the way to a celebration for Surfin's promotion at the old building, but before I did, I stopped by my apartment and walked around in the dark. I do that occasionally on my way to or from dinner, trying to visualize myself living in each room or looking at the views from certain angles. I decided my closet was impossibly big and I might actually be embarrassed by it when it's done. What man could possibly need a closet this size? If this talk show goes away I will have no use for this closet whatsoever because I won't have to wear a suit every night.

The party for Surfin was at the apartment of the nutty but wonderful gal who always seems to know everything about the parking situation on the block, but she was quick to point out it was Surfin's guest list. It was a take-your-shoes-off-at-the-door apartment and of course I was wearing impossible lace-ups. The party was full of neighbors I'd either seen in the hallways and chatted to a little or had never really spoken to, but the most important thing is that it was such a warm, lovely, celebratory vibe, due to the fact that this is a group of people who not only love our building, but we love our Surfin. The host asked me to make a toast to Surf and I basically said that walking in the door and seeing him always makes us feel like we're at home and that we all have our own relationship with him as our doorman that we each think is special, and that it's so wonderful when good things happen to good people. Everyone was asking when my apartment will be done and when they can see it. It seems gluttonous to show it to anyone. Am I the same person who has talked to Margaret Russell about getting it into *Architectural Digest*?

Dinner at FishTag with Liza, Brian, and Kelly. Then home for a delicious two-hour massage. I fell asleep a couple times toward the end and then accused Adam of not doing the backs of my legs. He swore he had. I have no proof. Maybe there was lotion on them that I could've felt. I can't start distrusting Adam, then where would I go?

❧ FRIDAY, FEBRUARY 5, 2016

Went to John and Sean's monthly "First Friday" party tonight with Bill. Once again we were the only white guys. We got there around midnight and the party didn't get full until around one forty-five. The brothers take their time! And they were worth waiting for.

SATURDAY, FEBRUARY 6, 2016

Recovered all day. Stayed home and watched the Republican debate. Chris Christie ate Marco Rubio for lunch! Trump was relatively subdued. They are all a bunch of clowns, except Kasich.

SUNDAY, FEBRUARY 7, 2016

Sunday Funday with Amanda on the Upper West Side. Watched the Super Bowl home alone. Richie, in the elevator, said it was the first Super Bowl he had ever missed and offered the other elevator guys two days for one if they worked for him but no one wanted to miss the game.

MONDAY, FEBRUARY 8, 2016

I told David about Richie lamenting missing the game and he said that was bullshit, he never asked David to switch shifts, he would've done it and he's gonna text him and call bullshit on the whole thing. So I started an elevator-operator fight without even trying.

TUESDAY, FEBRUARY 9, 2016

Worked out with the Ninj. Went with John Hill, John Jude, and Deirdre to Livingston, New Jersey, for Teleprompter Dave's mom's shiva. All the goyim in the control room were googling "shiva" to find out what the hell it was and what they were meant to do. I said to bring an appetite and be ready to schmooze. Though I had already eaten lunch, I ate a bagel and lox plus a lot of cookies. Met many family members and, as Bruce says, it always means something when you show up. The rest of the day was spent preparing for the big live reunion with Teresa, which was shaping up to be Bravo's version of *Frost/Nixon*. I haven't seen her in over a year so I decided not to see her before the show, to reunite live on TV.

We taped a show with Olivia Wilde and Ryan Reynolds at eight and his publicist, Leslie Sloane, was terrified it was going to be a half hour of questions about his ex-girlfriends and I wound up watering down Plead the Fifth so much that even *he* was shocked by how easy it was. So I fucked that one up. Not so the interview with Teresa. All day I was getting tweets from people wanting to know that she held herself accountable, that she understood what she did, that she owned it, basically. When she came in the studio for our live reunion it took me a few moments—you can see the whole thing play out on the tape—to realize that not only was she wearing a jumpsuit ("I wore it for you, Andy!"), but it was *orange*. At that point, any judgment that I had about her taking responsibility for her crime, etc., went out the window. This is *Teresa*. This is why we love her. She later said of course she would never go on a reality show with skeletons in her closet and I said, "Well, that's debatable." I was drained by the end of the night but it was amazing theater.

▶ WEDNESDAY, FEBRUARY 10, 2016

Taped with Ben Stiller and Penélope Cruz—she is very private so I was extra sensitive, and he freaked me out for some reason until the end when I realized he is very nice. He loved the Geraldine/Flip Wilson doll Grac gave me. I mispronounced a bunch of words—I'm thinking four or five—on the air because I am an amateur and an impostor, or at least that's what I was telling myself in my head during the show. Drugged Wacha to take him for his anal glands and I think I timed the meds wrong, because he was actually *more* hyper ninety minutes later and at the vet I was trying to put a muzzle full of peanut butter on his snout and he snarled and went for my leg and ripped the pants of my amazing Michael-Bastian-for-Gant Christmas-y suit with the red patches on the elbows. I think I can get it fixed, though. As for the dog, I remain doubtful. We got home and he was suddenly legless from the drugs and as sweet as before, if not a little humble because he knew he fucked up.

Went to pick Padma up for the amfAR gala. There was a crowd in front for Kanye, who I guess was in the building. Padma told *Extra* I have spent a lot of time motorboating her, so that was a moment. I did the bit onstage where I have to thank the sponsors and list them, which I did with a smile. I got back to the table and someone said, "You did what you had to, which was just get through it." And even though that was exactly what I had done, it was exactly what I didn't want to hear I had done. Ran into a bunch of people including Fredrik Eklund, Rachel Zoe and Rodger, Cheyenne Jackson, Harvey Weinstein, Lizzie Tisch, and Ryan Reynolds and Blake Lively on my way out. And I met Jay Z! (The only time I fumbled during the thing onstage was when I thought of Jay Z being in the audience.)

Went home, walked the drugged dog, FaceTimed #BAS, and then met Bruce, Bryan, Machota, Matt, Joe, and Paul at I Sodi on Christopher. Then home, where I was brushing my teeth and on a whim ran outside onto the terrace butt naked while brushing my teeth in the 20-degree tundra weather and ran a lap around the whole terrace. It was exhilarating. When I was cozy in bed, Wacha came up and slept with his face right next to me. What am I going to do with this dog?

▶ THURSDAY, FEBRUARY 11, 2016

It was Kelly's fifteen-year anniversary on *Live!* so a bunch of her friends surprised her in the morning. The greenroom could've doubled as a holding room for some twisted version of *The Bachelorette*, with me, Anderson, Mark, NPH, and David Muir waiting with our roses to go on. David Gregory interviewed me for his podcast. Tonight was the Lorne Michaels tribute at Lincoln Center. Talked to Tina Fey, who makes me nervous because she is so brilliant but in truth seems just super down-to-earth. It was all the *SNL* people: Jimmy, Maya Rudolph, Steve Martin, and on and on. Went for burgers at the Corner Bistro and some drunk woman who looked like Chloë Sevigny was causing a scene, screaming at me that she doesn't know or care who I am. I said that's fine. She gave her yogurt to Bruce on her way out. Came home and watched an old episode of *The Merv Griffin Show* saluting Lucy, featuring Lucie Arnaz and Mr. Mooney and Little Desi. Lucy was smoking and was being very mean to Desi about dropping out of college. She had her purse with her and touched up her makeup at one point while she was telling a story. It was riveting. I wondered how long after that Lucie Arnaz got an apartment in my building. The show kinda made me not love Lucy.

FRIDAY, FEBRUARY 12, 2016

The drunk Chloë Sevigny lady Instagram Directed me that she wants to talk to me about last night. What is there to discuss? The yogurt? I didn't find out. Dinner with Bruce and Liza at the Rocking Horse Café felt very old school.

SATURDAY, FEBRUARY 13, 2016

Valentine's Day date with SJP at the Waverly Inn. Saw Talita von Fürstenberg, Meg Ryan, and Sandra Bernhard, who came by the table with Melanie Griffith. I said, "I just had your daughter on my show." She said, "Oh, you're *that* guy?" Melanie told SJP she and her daughter had watched *Friends* together for years. Then Sandra texted me later to say Melanie wanted me to tell SJ of course she meant *SATC*.

TUESDAY, FEBRUARY 16, 2016

I guess February 17 is my breaking point for having a Christmas tree. Woke up and decided I couldn't face it one more day. On my way to meet Frances for a drink I got a message saying there was an emergency in my apartment. They are replacing the windows this week, and I thought for sure someone fell out. Everyone was alive, but a workman had punctured a gas line—through a big yellow metal plate that said "Gas Lines." Cut drinks with Frances short and went down to Horatio Street, where my apartment was full of plumbers and workmen who had been called there by the building manager, who handed my ass to me. I was shaking when I left. My upstairs neighbors are without gas for what may be a few weeks. I am sending them hot plates and bountiful food baskets tomorrow. Oh, shit.

WEDNESDAY, FEBRUARY 17, 2016

Gillian emailed me to say Teresa's book was number 5 on the *New York Times* Best Sellers list, and I texted her to congratulate her and it was news to her.

Lunch with Grac at Cafeteria, then we went to the new downtown Barneys which is so beautiful but there's not a ton of merchandise and the men's stuff sucks unless you are a Eurogay with a sugar daddy who is buying you clothes. Maybe that is indeed the clientele. FaceTimed with #BAS and asked him to come spend the weekend. Spoke to Brandon McMillan about Wacha and the vet. He said you have to admit that you have a violent dog; many owners won't admit it and will look past it. I said yes, I admit it, but I feel like I know when he's gonna get violent. He said he can help but he has to show Wacha that he's not gonna win with him—he has won every time being violent and needs to lose. I don't know what that means, but I don't want to be anywhere near it.

Went to Teresa's book party with Liza. It was unlike any literary event—packed to the gills in the basement of a restaurant on Grove Street I've never heard of. She arrived in a white limo wearing a white fur and her tits out—very *NYT* bestseller chic. We stayed five minutes, kissed her, posed for a pic, kissed Melissa and Joe and Dorinda, and left. Went in four restaurants and got turned away from them all, and the truth is it made me so happy that I live in New York, where there are so many crowded restaurants on a Wednesday night. We finally went to Morandi, where they made room. Then I went to bed with my (violent) dog.

▶ THURSDAY, FEBRURARY 18, 2016— NYC—ST. LOUIS—LOS ANGELES

Stopped in St. Louis on my way to LA to announce to the local media my date with Anderson in October. We're playing at the Fox, which is four thousand seats, and Robin wants to pull out all the stops to guarantee a sellout. I pushed Robin to book St. Louis because it's my town, so we better sell it out! Did an hour on KMOX radio and they had two bars in the studio for me, and someone brought three mushroom and onion Provel cheese pizzas. I almost killed an entire pizza while on air, which I'm sure sounded lovely. Showed up at the Fox for the press conference and waiting for me was a bottle of tequila, plus Mom, Dad, and Em (my family didn't provide the tequila, nor did I have any). Did the press conference without drinking any tequila and then did a bunch of local radio interviews, including talking to a lady who said she was interviewing me for a local website about pet parents. I felt like Valerie Cherish. The lady from Channel 5 said she wanted to interview Mom for Mother's Day, and from across the room I heard "NOT INTERESTED!" We were walking out of the theater and when Mom saw all the empty seats she laid it on thick that we weren't gonna sell out. I said not only would we sell out, we would add a matinee. Mom and Dad have been gloating because my pics of them generate the most likes on my Instagram page, so I posted one of us driving in the car and it wasn't burning up Instagram. I told Mom if we add a matinee she is doing the Channel 5 thing. She said NO I AM NOT! I said yes you are!

Landed in LA and went straight to meet Bruce at the Palm; Judge Judy was having dinner and left without me being able to say hello. I die for Judge Judy! Met John Mayer at the Tower for a couple drinks. He'd just performed "Shakedown Street" with Dead and Company on *Fallon*, and between rehearsals and the show the band went back to John's house and all took naps. Can you imagine the Dead napping at John's house? Amazing.

▶ FRIDAY, FEBRUARY 19, 2016—LOS ANGELES

Vanderpump Rules reunion today. Lisa was a little miffed with this See You Later, Vandergator game we'd played on Tuesday with Yolanda. But she said, "I accept your apology," even though I'm not sure I apologized. It was a hilarious reunion, and Lisa and I were whispering side comments to each other all day. We wrapped at seven; I went back to the Tower for a quick nap (without the Dead) and then to Sandy's, where he was hosting a dinner for me. It was Bruce and Bryan, Jason and Lauren Blum, Jeff Lewis and Gage, Jenni Pulos and Jonathan, Jerry O'Connell, Mary McCormack and Michael, Carole Bayer Sager (who just finished her memoir today and was happy), and Bette Midler and her husband, Martin, who is lovely. Had a long talk with Bette about the election, and I somehow got into explaining Kim Fields to her and how we could make a documentary of breaking-the-fourth-wall moments: For instance, when she said, "I don't want to be on a girls' trip; this isn't what I do!" which to me really meant, "I don't want to be on a reality show; this isn't what I do!" I told Bette that she was Tootie, and I was trying to think when *The Facts of Life* was on and I said it was somewhere between *The Rose* and *Beaches*. She said, "Honey, that was a twelve-year period," and I said, Okay, well, it was somewhere in there.

Presale started in St. Louis and we sold 1,100 seats today, so that's good. Mom said she was wrong, which was even better.

⟩ SATURDAY, FEBRUARY 20, 2016—LOS ANGELES—NYC

Landed and saw *The Humans* with Hickey, then #BAS met us. We all went out and we dragged Anderson into the fray too. Had the best time with #BAS.

⟩ SUNDAY, FEBRUARY 21, 2016

Slept in. Showed #BAS and Anderson the new apartment; I remain embarrassed by the closet. Took #BAS to the premiere of the Tina Fey movie *Whiskey Tango Foxtrot* at the Museum of Modern Art. It was a lot of news ladies, like Diane Sawyer, Barbara Walters, and Ann Curry (who seems so intensely nice but possibly just a hair nuts?), and then guys like Tom Hanks, Lorne Michaels, and Steve Martin. We liked the movie and afterwards we talked to Tina, who suggested coming on *WWHL* with the real woman she plays in the film. Went back to *WWHL* for our live episode with NeNe and told our bookers what Tina said and they were psyched because Tina's rep had passed. Then we got into a whole meshugas about the massive movie star (NOTE TO READERS: Every so often I have to throw in a blind item so I don't get run out of town) who was booked to come on in a few days whose rep was being *so* intensely difficult, rejecting all the creative we pitched, telling us he won't *stand up* on the air and won't discuss several things he's discussed on every other show including his most famous role. I said let's cancel him, it's not worth it and it's not a fit. So we did. We cancelled a massive movie star because it wasn't a fit *for us*. It felt really good.

⟩ WEDNESDAY, FEBRUARY 24, 2016—NYC—ATLANTA

Brandon McMillan has been coming to work with Wacha. He reaffirmed that Wacha is acting out from PTSD. He was beaten with a leash and we don't know what else, but his behavior can be changed if we teach him how to react differently to things he is afraid of, like the leash, a cone around his head, and ultimately, the vet. We have to reteach him all this stuff.

Wound up booking Jerry O'Connell and Lala from *Vanderpump Rules* (I gave her another chance) to replace the movie star we cancelled. Today we taped the women of *Full House*, and I've never seen that show so I was pretending the whole time and the producers were telling me stuff in my ear. Exciting! Fakery! On the way to the airport for my flight to Atlanta I got texts from Phaedra, who wants to pitch me some shows at some point while I am in town and hopes we'll be done in time to go to Swinging Richards (me too!), and also from Sereé, who wasn't thrilled with Bravo's deal for her to come to the reunion. I hope I talked her into it, but I really can't tell if she's going to come or not.

As we were about to take off the flight was cancelled, which began a five-hour delay at LaGuardia, during which I was booked on four different flights. As I politely asked a gate agent to rebook me on another flight, I got into a fight with a man the size of my couch standing behind me. I had a million questions for the agent, and at first she seemed annoyed and said I was asking too many questions too loudly, but then I quietly prefaced, "This may be a dumb question, but . . ." and then proceeded with the questions—like "Why is the flight not listed on the monitor?" and "Would I be in a middle seat on that one?" And the couch said, why do you keep asking dumb questions; you're wasting everybody's time in line, and I said I am not being dumb; I'm being *polite*, which you have no idea about. I told the airline ladies that there was an *asshole* behind me in line and to be careful, and I walked away feeling very proud of my behavior.

I had about forty minutes to grab some food and get to the flight, which was oversold and I was just grateful to be on it even though I had traded in a first-class seat for coach. I went up to board and the woman said, "We don't have your seat," and it turned out that the lady to whom I thought I was so polite had completely voided out my ticket. I had to buy an entirely new ticket right then and there, and it was only when I was sitting on the tarmac in steerage as a queen from Mississippi six rows in front of me took pictures of me on his phone, which he made sure to let everyone know he was posting directly to Facebook, that I realized that I *had* pissed her off. That bitch intentionally voided my ticket! I still felt victorious by virtue of landing in Atlanta at all. When you have bad travel karma all you can do is be grateful when you arrive. See that? I'm as zen as Oprah.

THURSDAY, FEBRUARY 25, 2016—ATLANTA

Is it wrong to say that I actually might've *enjoyed* today's endless taping of the Atlanta reunion? Kenya and Cynthia remarked that I was saucy and shady and mouthy; maybe that's why I had so much fun. Kenya did tell me late in the day that I didn't have her back and played favorites, and I countered with a couple examples of times I had had her back, but I'm not sure I convinced her. NeNe had a big foil tray of fried chicken in her dressing room that she had somehow gotten one of her glam squad to drive an hour outside of Atlanta to get, and man, was I glad she did. It was a great day, even though I feel like Kandi and Phaedra's friendship is over for good with Kandi's admission that she wondered if Phae called the feds on her and Todd. That was sad. After the show I met Lindsay at Swinging Richards and we had a blast. I got a ride home from a former marine, now a stripper, in his pickup truck. (Nothing happened between us, and he complimented me on being a gentleman.) I went to bed feeling like I was actually a little mean at the reunion (not to mention the airport) and I worried about it.

FRIDAY, FEBRUARY 26, 2016—
SUNDAY, FEBRUARY 28, 2016—MIAMI

I skipped Oscar weekend in LA in favor of meeting Dave at the Delano for a boys' weekend, which amounted essentially to us sitting in the sun for two days of kibitzing like old Jewish ladies. I guess we are, at this point. You just sit and watch people and speculate on them: there was a straight Leonardo-DiCaprio-if-he-had-no-body-fat, a seemingly humorless but white-hot dad with a Harvard hat who was a dead ringer for Tom Cruise, a few beat bachelorette parties, and one dude from NYC who has a place in Miami and was reading my last *Diaries* the night before and saw that I love the Delano and got a room for the day so he could hang by the pool and, lo and behold, ran into me. I asked him what the appeal of the book was for him and he said it was like reading TMZ before bed. By the end of the day I had blurry, zoomed pictures of Hot Leo DiCaprio and Harvard Guy that I will never look at again but that seemed urgent at the moment. I took Dave for his inaugural visit to the Palace, which he called the Bird-cage. Tiffany Fantasia was on fire; she told the crowd that if Trump is elected she'll move to Curaçao, and she told Dave that she would've done more but she was on her last pair of pantyhose, to which he replied, "How many times have I said *that* to someone?!" Didn't have any FOMO about missing all the big parties in LA, and it was only when I thought about it that I realized that I hadn't even been *invited* to *Vanity Fair*'s this year, so that was one less option.

Landed back in NYC and went straight to Jimmy and Nancy's to watch #OscarsSoWhite which turned out to be #OscarsSoBlack. I smelled a horrible poo smell before the show started, and Cameron Diaz was sitting next to me and I wondered if she had farted. "Good for her," I thought, "hot girls fart too!" It was kind of empowering until the smell got even worse and I seriously thought Cameron Diaz had pooped her pants. I felt horrible for her! How was I going to acknowledge *that*, I wondered. Then the smell became markedly worse and the whole room started freaking out, including Cameron. It turned out Gary Fallon had pooped in the corner and I had stepped in it and tracked it around the room. So it wasn't Cameron. It was Gary! And *me*!

▶ MONDAY, FEBRUARY 29, 2016

Radio in the morning, then a creative call about *Blast Your Past*, which is a game-show pilot presentation I'm working on for NBC. Shit is getting real with the RHONY. They're all in Florida, and Bethenny has some incriminating photos of LuAnn's fiancé. You cannot make this stuff up. JLo was on live and as sweet as ever, looking like a million bucks even though she said she didn't like how she looked. Her bodyguard can *get it*. Troy and Jonah were there, as well as Jackie and Pony Boy from Willspace, who I brought up to get a pic with JLo during the commercial break. I was kind of hoping she would fall for him, but she was with Casper and Pony Boy with his fiancée.

▶ TUESDAY, MARCH 1, 2016

Spent the day surrounded by spray-tanned, glittered, wigged ladies fighting about food blogs and sisterly issues. I am in such reunion mode that I can't really tell a fake one from a real one. This one was fake—the *Inside*

Amy Schumer reunion. During breaks I talked to Amy about her boyfriend, who she is very hot and heavy with. She had a massive blond wig and crazy spray tan on, so that added a layer of hilarity. Her nails were so long she was pounding her phone with her knuckles. Her sister, Kim Caramele (I mispronounced her name several times on the show before she corrected me), was on my other side and she is crazy funny and was doing a riff that I was being unfair to her and favoring Amy, which was the exact thing that Kenya was doing five days earlier regarding Phaedra. Bridget Everett was great. She's about to blow up into a superstar.

Quick dinner with Hickey, then to *WWHL*. Had a bum show and came home to Victor in the elevator, who sweetly asks every night, "How was the show?" Tonight I said *I* was good but the show was fair, which he seemed to think was hilarious. Watched the new Loretta Lynn doc, then joined Snapchat in the middle of the night for some godforsaken reason. I could barely sleep because not only is tomorrow my one thousandth episode but I'm also taping Loretta and Tina Fey.

▶ WEDNESDAY, MARCH 2, 2016

This morning I was like Rhoda Morgenstern on the subway on her way to her wedding: Neither of our cars showed up on our big days. I was trying to hail a cab with bags of crap and a suit and no coat plus five ties hanging around my neck and Wacha dragged like an afterthought. Got to the Clubhouse for my one thousandth episode and I needed a little attention on account of being the host and my car not showing up, but no one seemed to want to give it to me. Anthony and Daryn both feigned concern about the car. There was a buzz at the office; Mike Robley was making toaster hors d'oeuvres to put on the bar and walking with a spring in his step because he was going to appear as the gay shark. Mark and Kelly sent balloons and Dave sent a thousand cookies, which was insane but amazing, and my jeweler who came to show me necklaces to buy Bruce for his birthday brought four massive trays of cupcakes from Baked by Melissa. And Chrissy Teigen brought us an ice cream cake. So it was a day of celebratory baked goods! Tramona, the turtle we used to have on set, was there and I was excited until Deirdre said it was a fake Tramona. They couldn't locate the real one, apparently. They said it's on a nature reserve, which translates to me as turtle soup. I said I was going to say on air that it's a fake Tramona but they said not to. We agreed I would say I was *concerned* it was fake, but I forgot to anyway.

The show was wonderful—very fun. Liza was there, and Wattenberg, who I have very directly told not to come to any of my special occasions because I would rather have my agent in his office making me money instead of making me feel good by being present. But then I saw him at Kelly's fifteenth-anniversary show and told Daryn to call his office and invite him. You don't want the attention, but then maybe it turns out you do want the attention. Push/pull! Chenoweth was great. Chrissy Teigen pulled out the best gift ever from a plastic shopping bag: one of John Legend's Grammys (his first, actually). She said he has ten and wouldn't miss it.

Finished that show on *such* a high, then walked into my office and right into Dave and Hickey, who were there to see the Loretta Lynn/Isaac Mizrahi show. I had concocted a plan to sing "Louisiana Woman, Mississippi Man" with the Coal Miner's Daughter and in rehearsal I did it millions of times with Tori Vullo sitting in for Loretta. They'd never seen me rehearse anything so much and Deirdre thought I was doing a bit, but I actually wanted to do it perfectly. She said my best part was at the end when I go "Heyyyyyyyyyy." Went into Loretta's dressing room and gave her *so* much love, told her how much I loved the *American Masters* episode and said, "Are you gonna sing with me?" And with that she started to sing the song, right at the spot I picked out. We sang it together twice, and she suggested I go *up* at the end like a yodel when I go "Heyyyyyyyyyyyy," but when I hit it right I sound so good as a bass. I told her I'd yodel it but I secretly had no plans to.

Loretta is little, with a big head, and was looking great, wearing jeans, a denim cowboy shirt, and cowboy boots. There was a massive aqua ball gown hanging up and she said (referring to her dresser), "Teeeeyum wants me to wear that gown, what *you* want me to wear?" I said, "Teeeeyum has been dressing you for thirty years, Ms. Lynn, and I am not about to start throwing my opinion around now." Teeeeyum really liked that. Teeeeyum, incidentally, was going to be the bartender and so this had to be a TV first: Loretta surrounded by three gays. Then we found out Tanya Tucker was on her way, but she's the Bad Girl of Country so of course she was running late and wouldn't make it in time for the show. When Loretta sat down in that big ol' ball gown (she actually looked better in jeans), she said she'd gained five pounds this week in NYC and could barely get it zipped. She said she eats everything in sight in this town; she loves it here. Singing "Louisiana Woman, Mississippi Man" was cute, if not exactly musical. But she indulged me, and I was smiling hard. I didn't do the yodel thing. During the after show the doorbell rang and it was Miss "Delta Dawn," Tanya Tucker herself; Isaac almost fell off his chair. She is a hot mess in the best way. She's a *WWHL* fan, crazily.

Took a lot of pics after the show and I was so tired I could barely move. I just shut down, but I had to power back up for the Tina Fey show two hours later. She is so unassuming, always smart and funny. After that was over Michael Davies came and we all toasted his fiftieth birthday, then retired to my office to watch the one thousandth show, which wasn't as great as it seemed nine hours earlier when we did it.

► THURSDAY, MARCH 3, 2016—NYC—PALM BEACH—NYC

Off to The Breakers for an "Old Bags Luncheon" with six hundred fancy plastic-surgeried Palm Beach ladies in attendance. I guess I told Victor last night that I was getting picked up at 6:45 this morning because he rang my bell to wake me up at 6:15, which was really sweet, although little did he know I'd given myself seven minutes to get ready and set the alarm for 6:38. I was, amazingly, not too tired and worked the whole flight. At The Breakers, I said, "You are all so attractive, one of you could be Trump's fourth wife." *Crickets.* Then I said, "But that would be a nice thing." I dunno. I moved on to my camp letters. Had a meet and greet after and it was about fifty women saying, "I'm the co-chair," "I'm the co-chair," and you have to make a big deal of each one because *they're the co-chair.* It happens every time.

Made the driver stop at a McDonald's and savored two delicious cheeseburgers, a large fries, and a Diet Coke while gabbing to Bruce on my headset. Stomachache kicked in about when I landed. Went home, grabbed the dog, and went to the Clubhouse for the Kim Richards interview, which was not great. She looked good, but her addiction is of course a sad topic and she's a little scattered. John Legend wants to do a bit on Sunday where he rings the doorbell and walks in and steals his Grammy back from the set. Mom is furious at me for making Trump jokes in Palm Beach.

FRIDAY, MARCH 4, 2016—
SUNDAY, MARCH 6, 2016—NYC—SAG HARBOR—NYC

Drove out to the beach and built a lovely fire, then ate at the counter at Sam's. Watched the Sally Field movie *Hello, My Name Is Doris*, which was weird. Heidi Schaeffer called to say no Burt Reynolds questions for Sally Field, which wasn't top of my mind. I asked if I could say we are neighbors and she said sure. In the meantime, Wacha was restless all day, so I went to Jimmy's to run him with Gary Fallon. Jimmy and I had a quick Jacuzzi and once back home I tried to nap, made tea, got high, put on Ibiza Sonica, and got in a great couple hours of productivity before meeting Bethenny at East Hampton Grill for an end-of-shooting dinner. We tried coming up with her tag line and she wrote them all on the paper tablecloth. We liked something about "all show and no go" or "all go and no show." Went home and dreamed Bruce had to step in to interview Hillary Clinton on *WWHL*, and I showed up halfway through act one and I asked him if I should step in and take over the show and he said no. Then in the morning I told Bruce the story and realized maybe it's because I'm giving him a radio show and maybe I'm worried Radio Andy will become Radio Bruce. Met Marci at Poxobogue for lunch and inhaled, I mean ate, at the counter. Pancakes, eggs sunny side up, and bacon. Nancy Reagan died.

MONDAY, MARCH 7, 2016

I had two massive fits on the subway today in front of crowded trains. I was on the way home from Radio Andy and had to get home to dose the dog at a very specific time for his vet appointment, but there was an injury on the train in front of us so we had to get out and I mistakenly got on a subway that was running express. So that was fit number one. I publicly stomped my foot! I was so lame. Then the second train was taking forever and I did it again, on the platform.

We had success at the vet! Well, Brandon took him, and somehow they were able to do what they needed. Sally Field was on the show and greeted me with: "What *more* can you do in that apartment?!?" Dinner in Brooklyn with Jeanne, Fred, and the boys.

TUESDAY, MARCH 8, 2016

Took Wacha back to the vet to show him it's not a scary place. It worked. Saw my Ninja. Got a tweet from a lady saying she was bored with my guests last night and I need to step it up. I said, "Well, I've had Tina Fey, Loretta Lynn, and Sally Field in the last week." She responded that none of them interest her. I wrote and deleted three nasty responses to this lady with impossibly high standards. Then I looked at her profile and she's a massive Trump fan and that's all I needed to know. I responded that I would try to round up a gaggle of Donald's ex-wives, maybe that'd entertain her. All I do is fight with Trump supporters on Twitter. I cannot stop myself. The man is disgusting me in ways I didn't know I could be disgusted and the media is playing into his hands. He's a thin-skinned, flip-flopping orange sham who has manipulated them perfectly. I remember after the Miss Universe pageant one year he offered me a ride home on his plane and I didn't go because I didn't want to be beholden to him. I flew *commercial* instead. *I knew then!* The vulgarity at the debate the other night went too far—and this is the *Housewives* guy saying it. I thought politicians were supposed to have class and dignity! Interviewed Padma about her new book at Barnes and Noble, then had the *Broad City* girls on *WWHL* and they were magnificent.

WEDNESDAY, MARCH 9, 2016—NYC—LOS ANGELES

It was a long flight to LA, and I went directly to the Beverly Hills Palm to tape the pilot for *Lunch with Bruce* for Radio Andy. Ran around going to furniture stores that Eric Hughes had recommended, which was overwhelming, but I found a few things. Drinks with Serwatka at the Tower, where I ran into Jason Kander. He is running for Senate in Missouri and I'm going to help him raise money. Dinner at Bruce and Bryan's.

THURSDAY, MARCH 10, 2016—LOS ANGELES—LAGUNA BEACH

Taped the *Beverly Hills* reunion today, which was emotional. Vanderpump felt ganged up on and so did Yolanda. We wrapped at 9:00 p.m. and I went directly to the Montage in Laguna Beach and had dinner alone outside by the beach. It was romantic. On that note, I invited #BAS to Bruce's birthday week on the boat at the end of the month. Anderson gets in tomorrow for our Orange County show.

▶ FRIDAY, MARCH 11, 2016—LAGUNA BEACH

I knew that coming to Orange County was going to throw me in the middle of a hive of OC Housewives, but I didn't know how it'd play out. When Anderson and I announced the date, Tamra texted saying she'd love to come and I said of course, it's my pleasure. I had not invited the others because I didn't want them to feel obligated to attend, but now I knew that they'd see Tamra's Instagram and possibly get pissed at me for not inviting them.

It all started the second I Instagrammed a picture of the beach in Laguna this morning. Alexis Bellino texted to tell me that my "favorite former OC wife is coming to see you tonight," and I replied that she should come backstage and say hi at 7:00 p.m., knowing that I'd told Tamra to come at 7:15 and hoping they wouldn't run into each other because they are enemies. And then I realized that the montage of reunion-show moments we run during the show features Tamra calling Alexis "Jesus Jugs." So then I texted her and warned her that there was a clip of that moment, which took some explaining. It was supposed to pour all day but we got bright sun until about 1:00 p.m., so I was by the pool when Slade Smiley texted (yes, we occasionally text) saying that he and Gretchen wanted to come "support" me (people on the *Real Housewives* "support" each other by going to their hair-care line launches, etc.) by coming to my event. I said I would've loved for them to be my guests but that we were completely sold out, which was the truth.

Anderson arrived at 2:00 p.m. from Miami, where he had hosted yet another debate. I was so happy to see him; it felt like it had been forever. We had a deep, nonstop gossipy lunch, then I Jacuzzied in the rain with a twink named Bailey who turned out to be straight. At the show, a ton of people were backstage for both of us—Diane Ronnau, Nanci Ryder, Amy Introcaso-Davis. Tamra arrived with her friends and kind of camped out by our bottle of tequila in the dressing room (Tamra wasn't drinking because she's prepping for a body-building competition—you heard me) and Alexis showed up in the hallway and didn't see her inside. Crisis averted, until I got a text from Tamra minutes before the show saying, "Thanks for putting Alexis in front of me." I said, "Sweetie, I didn't do the seating!" Apparently they kind of made up, for the moment. So I felt good about peace in Orange County.

SATURDAY, MARCH 12, 2016—
LAGUNA BEACH—SANTA BARBARA

On the drive to Montecito I told Anderson who was coming backstage tonight: Brandy and Julie from *The People's Couch*, Doug Davidson from *The Young and the Restless*, and Oprah's flight attendant (set up through Gayle). We deduced that since Oprah's flight attendant is in town it must mean that she is too because he would be where the plane is, and I lamented that we most likely wouldn't be getting an invitation to the site of the Legends Ball (I'm obsessed with the Legends Ball) for a sunset shot of tequila. We checked into the Four Seasons and walked right into a mother of a bride who wanted Anderson to take pictures with the bridal party. She didn't seem to know who I was, so I bolted to the pool. Returning from my vitamin D fix, I ran into all the tuxedoed groomsmen (there were twelve!) and we took photos together. Titillating!

When I got back to the room I saw that Oprah had Instagrammed a picture of herself on a porch with some of the girls from her school. I could smell from the picture that she was there, practically in the same ZIP code as me! Moments later I randomly received an email from Gayle, who must've been catching up on *RHOBH* because she had a lot of thoughts for me, which meant it was a perfect opportunity to remind her that AC and I were in Santa Barbara and essentially available for sunset tequila at the site of the Legends Ball. She thanked me again for agreeing to say hi to the flight attendant but otherwise didn't take the bait.

The show was interesting; neither of us had a sense of whether it was any good or not although everyone at the meet and greet after was very drunk and happy. Second night in a row that we didn't go out or party after the show—we're getting old.

⟫ SUNDAY, MARCH 13, 2016—SANTA BARBARA—NYC

Awoke with a start at seven-thirty to this text message from Gayle: "Do you and AC want to have brunch at Oprah's at ten-thirty? Let me know!" Are. You. Fucking. Kidding. Me? I replied that not only do I typically have FOMO but this morning, as I rushed to LAX to get a flight home for a live show (Kandi and RuPaul), I had FOMOBO, which is Fear of Missing Out on Brunch at Oprah's. She said that was a shame because it was going to be small, just Stedman and some girls from Oprah's school, and that the food is always delicious. I was almost in the belly of the Legends Ball! For breakfast! Pancakes with Oprah! I emailed SJP on the plane and she said I'll get an invitation another time and I said won't. Would I have been a "young'un" or a "legend"? *I will never find out!* William H. Macy and Melanie Griffith were on the plane. They ain't Oprah.

⟫ MONDAY, MARCH 14, 2016

I went from one fun thing to the next today, feeling grateful for my life. Radio Andy this morning was Sally Field and Henry Winkler. I got Stacey to come on with him and it was fun hearing about their marriage. On my way out I told Sally I was taking the subway and she said her son won't let her. I said you *must*, it's the fastest. Went home, changed for my show, kikied with Bruce and walked over to the apartment for my weekly meeting and Sally was just walking into the building from Sirius. See that?! The subway saves time! The floors are going into the new apartment and they're beautiful. Tiles are starting to materialize for the bathrooms, tubs are going in. It's coming together—slowly. Reunited with Wacha in the sweetest way at *WWHL*, where I taped Catherine O'Hara and Eugene Levy (pinch me), then headed up to the Jewish Museum for the opening of Isaac Mizrahi's stunning retrospective. Then it was back to *WWHL* for Lisa Vanderpump, who was a lot of fun. Is that a good day or what? It sort of makes up for missing brunch at Oprah's. *Sort of.*

TUESDAY, MARCH 15, 2016

Had such a heart boner at the gym today. I was boxing with the Ninj and we were talking about life, and I was saying that there are no guarantees that anyone will be interested in me in a couple years so I am taking every job and opportunity right now. He said *his* long-term goal is to buy his son a house and that's what he's saving for, and that with his daughter going to school and his nephew out of the house he was thinking of taking in some foster kids. With everything this guy has going on—showing up to work at 5:00 a.m., putting a daughter through school, a son and wife—he is thinking of taking in some foster kids. I almost cried while I was boxing at the generosity of spirit of this wonderful man. It reaffirmed everything good that is possible in people and life and love. I had so much love for the Ninj it was almost hard to hit him. Not that my cross hooks make any difference to him.

WEDNESDAY, MARCH 16, 2016

Dreamed I was dead, wandering around the afterlife with Lisa Rinna, who was wearing white jeans and a white top. The dream stayed with me all day through rehearsals of *Blast Your Past*, which is a mix of *WWHL* and *This Is Your Life*. I don't know how the show is going to be—I was walking out and asked Dave Brecher (he's doing prompter on the pilot too) what he thinks of it and he said, "Well, you have to do something to pass the time." Not what you want to hear.

THURSDAY, MARCH 17, 2016

Taped the *Blast Your Past* pilot, which went well. All the NBC guys loved it, but then you hear in a week that it ultimately isn't right. TV development is like a fishing expedition; you just can never tell. Met Eric Hughes at the apartment and chose colors and stuff. Loved it. The guest bedroom is kind of a Mexican beach house with sunset wallpaper. Hunter green in the guest bath, red in the powder room to complement the cherry-gold Warhol wallpaper. Dinner with Amanda.

FRIDAY, MARCH 18, 2016

We shot the *Potomac* reunion in NYC, so I only had to go uptown. It started at eleven and wrapped by six. Civilized! It was funny, too. They were all in sequins. They don't know the show is picked up, but it is.

Started thinking that maybe #BAS doesn't want to go on the trip for Bruce's birthday. He is in hell with his thesis and hasn't fully committed to coming, and it's next week. I texted and said, "In case you don't know it, I really want you to come and I think it'll be fun." Dinner with Hickey, Jeffrey, Matthew, and SJP at Via Carota, which was wonderful, then hung out at Scottie's house. On the way home SJP suggested getting a slice at that great place on Sixteenth and Seventh—you don't have to twist my arm. I came home and ate a pint of peppermint-bark gelato. I cannot believe I'm now keeping ice cream in the house. *Who am I?* Have been on a documentary tear: Nora Ephron, Michael Jackson, Robert Mapplethorpe—all great.

SATURDAY, MARCH 19, 2016

Took Wacha to Joe's and pondered titles for this book. I've been thinking about *I'm Not Really This Vain*, but he said I can do better and he would text me ideas by the end of the day. Considering he came up with the subtitle for my last book (*A Deep Look at a Shallow Year*) I shouldn't have been as shocked as I was two hours later as I smoked a joint with Amy Sedaris and received two genius ideas: *Artificial Intelligence* and *Superficial*. Somebody give Joe Mantello another Tony.

#BAS texted that he figured out his thesis stuff and he's coming. So I guess I got through to him. Richie wants to bartend on *WWHL*. Integrated an all-black party with Bill again.

MONDAY, MARCH 21, 2016—THURSDAY, MARCH 24, 2016

Lots of errands this week getting ready for Bruce's weeklong fiftieth birthday trip. There were little fits of *Housewives* drama popping up all week: Kyle texted me during the show the other night that Bravotv.com had posted something crazy about Mauricio; LuAnn's a little upset about what is going to be said about her relationship on the new season of *RHONY*. We are working on casting *RHOA* and *RHOP*, and just when we were having the discussion about *Atlanta,* Kim Fields called into a radio show and said she was done with the show. So that answered that question!

Iggy Azalea was on the show Wednesday and at first I found her a little standoffish, but she was very open and we discussed all of her (many) feuds. SJP's birthday dinner for Matthew was fun and Matthewesque. It was at Giorgione, right around the corner from the Clubhouse, with Scott, Marc, Hickey, Nathan Lane, Martin Short, and Kenny Lonergan, and I spent most of the night talking to Eric and Nathan Turner about design stuff and Nathan made me terrified that the Mexican sunset–themed guest room is insane but then I turned and asked Eric, who said it's gonna be great.

Aunt Judy and Uncle Stanley were here all week, and little Lucy was at the Erica Girardi/Rachel Dratch show and I'm worried it was too dirty for her. Is thirteen too young for a lot of "pat the puss" talk? Took them to see the apartment and realized I got my appreciation for themed rooms from hanging out at Judy and Stanley's when I was growing up—they had an ice-cream parlor, a room with an Astroturfed floor, a swing on a tree, a fountain, and clouds on the ceiling. Now that I put it in perspective, I'm feeling like having a Mexican sunset room is totally normal.

▶ FRIDAY, MARCH 25, 2016—SUNDAY, MARCH 27, 2016—MIAMI

Of course Sarah Jessica was right that I should get Bruce pearls from Mikimoto for his fiftieth. He loved them and wore them all weekend! Only Bruce can butch up a string of pearls. The party weekend for his fiftieth entailed two full days of rosé and people-watching at the Delano pool and a dinner at the Soho House on Saturday night, during which Bruce went around the table and said what each person meant to him with Ava by his side crying and patting her face with a handkerchief. She was like an old lady trapped in a little girl's body, taking in the deep emotional connections that inevitably she was right in the middle of.

Liza and I met a very hot straight kid from Rhode Island by the pool, Kyle, with whom we became obsessed. A major flirt, great teeth and hair, a veterinary assistant; also maybe a thuggish womanizing drunk. Basically the total package. We told him he looked like JFK Jr. and he said he was going to take that as a compliment and we said, how else could you possibly take that? We kept saying, *"That's so Kyle!"* to each other all weekend. #BAS arrived on Sunday just in time for the Palace, which after much buildup put on a shitacious drag show. One of the worst. Ava was in the middle of it all coloring—you can take her anywhere and she will adapt. I remember Bruce and I being in the last row of a plane home from St. Barts with Ava, who was not even two years old, just calmly asleep all over us, not realizing Daddy had forgotten to bring any snacks. (Veronica Webb was on the flight and rescued us with crackers.) Went to Prime 112, which was as shitty and overpriced as you can imagine. I feel sick thinking of it.

MONDAY, MARCH 28, 2016—SUNDAY, APRIL 3, 2016—FRENCH CARIBBEAN: ST. BARTS, GUADELOUPE, DOMINICA, SAINT LUCIA, MUSTIQUE

How novel to actually be part of a couple on a couples' trip! It was Jason and Lauren Blum, Sandy Gallin and Joel, Bruce and Bryan, and of course Barry and DVF. The headline of the first day in St. Barts was that a big group came to the boat for lunch including Letterman. A paparazzi picture of his beard broke the Internet last week and the first thing out of his mouth was, "Despite what I look like, I'm doing quite well." And except for that big white Moses bush on his face, he *did* look very well, actually, Waspy and in shape. I didn't have any sort of meaningful conversation with him for the two hours that he was there; I was just so tickled, and a little freaked out, to hear his iconic voice from down the table (he was sitting with Steve Martin and Marty Short, who were over from *Rising Sun*).

Towards the end of the week we almost got a Mick Jagger sighting in Mustique but were happy with Mark and Kelly and the kids, all celebrating the last few hours of their vacation. Otherwise, we took lots of long swims, slept, slogged through *London Spy*, ate copiously, hiked, and in talking endlessly about the election, each pledged to find some young candidates to get behind. Bruce and I had several conversations about whether or not I should have a kid. #BAS assimilated with the group brilliantly. I cannot find a single thing wrong with him.

Horrible re-entry. Stumbled my way through two hours live on the radio and went to a meeting at Bravo. Vicki and Tamra were in a dune buggy accident and got hurt. I spoke to both of them and was relieved they were okay. What these women have been through on that show!

Meeting at the apartment about my closet. They have tiles on the walls in the guest bathrooms, but other than that it looks like nothing happened while I was gone. I started to go crazy and ask the non-English-speaking workers if my place would be ready by La Navidad and they seemed to think it would be. Then I said what about *el verano* and they said yes to that too. But summer could mean August to them. Eric sent a lot of great ideas for my Mexican-beach guest bedroom, like covering the bedframe in Mexican-blanket material. Concurrently I started to get crazy about waiting for the elevator at my temporary building, but then every time it opened it was Victor and there's no way to be mad at him. By the way, Richie asked to bartend on *WWHL* a few weeks ago and I guess I said yes, when *RHONY* premieres. And that's happening Wednesday night and who knows how that will go.

Went by Anderson's premiere to "support him" and finally met his mom, who seemed lovely and delicate, like a beautiful antique vase. I then spoke to Lee Radziwill, who asked where I'd been on the boat and I felt quite comfortable telling her about all the islands—this is a lady who has been island hopping all her life! It was all the great ladies. Marti Stevens (gal pal of Dietrich), who I'd met through Natasha, was there. She said, "Oh, how I miss her," and I said, "Every single day, right?" Then we talked about missing Joan Rivers too. Also saw Bill Owens and Mary Noonan. Didn't stay for the doc, which I'd seen (and loved) on the boat. Raced home to get the dog and heard people yelling my name on my corner and I gave a big fake hello and kept walking and a familiar voice screamed, "We're not your *fans*!" and it was Cameron Diaz with Brad Cafarelli. I said, "But you *are* fans! You are and you always have been!" I told her I hadn't seen her since I thought she'd pooped her pants on Oscar night and we laughed. Coincidentally, I'm interviewing Cameron on Radio Andy tomorrow morning. Full circle.

Quiet audience at the show tonight. Wacha licked his ass for about twenty minutes, then threw up.

WEDNESDAY, APRIL 6, 2016

Did a personal appearance for Excedrin. Interviewed Sandy Gallin for the radio. Attended a *RHONY* premiere party for five minutes, enough time for Teresa to tell me she didn't like the picture I posted of me with a mustache. I didn't get past the red carpet. Ramona is "snapshatting." Literally, that's what she said to me. *Snapshatting*. Bethenny was on *WWHL*. Richie bartended and was as tight lipped on the air as he is loose lipped in the elevator. I couldn't get him going about the weed dealers in the building and what percentage of residents are on Grindr, so he's smart—he wants to keep his job. He had a blast. Cameron Diaz was on *Fallon* and told the story of Gary pooping on the rug, but the punch line for her was that I told her on the street that I thought it'd been her and that was the first she'd heard of it. I guess I'd only *thought* she pooped her pants and never verbalized that thought. So she and Jimmy had a big laugh about why the hell I would assume that it was *her*. And why *did I*? I'm booked on *Fallon* next week and was going to tell that story and now I've got nothing to say!

THURSDAY, APRIL 7, 2016

The headline today was actually the headline on the *Daily Mail*. Someone did some pretty exhaustive Instagram snooping to uncover that #BAS is my fella, and reported extensively about our two times on Barry's boat and then uncovered his entire biography including reprinting about eight pictures from his Instagram, which he quickly made private. He was slightly traumatized. The issue is that now when you google him, this is the *only thing that comes up*—he'd had a clean slate on the Internet and now he is famous for dating me and going on Barry's boat. I asked him what his friends were saying and he said he was getting a lot of texts from people saying they're sorry, which made me feel awful because I thought the implication was that they feel sorry for him for being associated with me. He said it's not that, it's that they're sorry he's being put on blast. The comments are of course brutal: making fun of how he wears his hat, my age, both our looks. Gay people are so supportive on social media!

I have never received more calls, emails, telegrams, etc. imploring me to attend a party as I did today for the one at the Diamond Horseshoe celebrating Naomi Campbell's book publication. So I went, and of course no one cared that I was there. I got mightily stoned beforehand, though, so it was an adventure. Talked to Naomi (who is sober and has a fucked-up foot, but was in good spirits), Bethann Hardison, Derek Blasberg, Cindi Berger, June Ambrose (some queen came up to her thinking she was Naomi and was going on and on), and Gayle King, who I walked out with.

Headed to the Polo Bar for a dinner that Jay Sures from UTA put together with Hickey, Jeffrey, Noah from the *Today* show, this guy from *Shark Tank*, and Larry Wilmore. It was a sausage factory in there—Donny Deutsch at the table next to us and on the other side Dan Abrams, who, continuing his streak of always going around with hot straight guys, was with Jesse Palmer, who is the hot football guy from *GMA*, and Rob Marciano, the hot weatherman. Marciano is in fact blindingly hot. Dinner was fun and also maybe weird but maybe that's because I was high. Got a two-hour massage from Adam after dinner and had the most hilarious phone call with Bruce for the first half hour. We were in hysterics!

▶ SATURDAY, APRIL 9, 2016—NYC—PHILLY

Radar Online called #BAS's dad at home to ask him if he knew his son was at a homosexual yacht party with a man twenty years his senior, which is bad enough but he and his dad have barely discussed his sexuality. I almost cried when he told me. I feel so awful about this—I never ever considered that this would be the consequence of dating me. It just doesn't seem like a story. It got picked up on gay blogs and because I joked on Stern that I'm a power top, it's "Total Top Andy Cohen Is Off the Market" with a picture of #BAS. I want to kick the ass of the guy from the *Daily Mail* who started this.

Train to Philly. The hotel was very depressing, and it was really hard to get a tea and other assorted meshugas. It was the Ritz, so I was surprised. Anderson was all wound up because his driver forced him to wear a seatbelt in the back seat and it got testy. All day I was getting tweets from women in the area saying they were pregaming, so I knew the audience was going to be very drunky. The show was a smash, sold out and in the most gorgeous theater we've played yet, the Academy of Music, which was built in 1857. Anderson thought someone was going to get shot because it was super

John Wilkes Booth–y in there. We added new material and it was all wonderful until the questions, which were either comments, which are banned, or really bad questions like "What makes your heart beat?" The meet and greet after was a lot of people. I love working as a team with Anderson; it's less pressure.

ᐅ SUNDAY, APRIL 10, 2016—NYC

#BAS spent the night with me and it was all good even though he's famous now. We decided officially once again that we are seeing each other and figured out some rules and guidelines.

ᐅ WEDNESDAY, APRIL 13, 2016

I was bumped from *The Tonight Show* for Ted Cruz. Why is Mrs. Doubtfire always stealing m' thunder?! Had a conference call with Dan Rather to see if we can get him to do a show on Radio Andy. He is so glowing to me ("You just go from one triumph to the next . . . my admiration and respect for you knows no bounds") that I wonder if he has absolutely no idea that we only worked on one story together at *48 Hours*. He said he wants to do it, but then he said, "I say yes to everything—my wife says that if I were a woman I'd be pregnant all the time." Oh, Dan. Looks like I'm heading to Dollywood in May to interview Dolly for a Radio Andy special, and I had a call about that with her publicist, whose name is Kurt but he spells it Kirt, which is so country I can't handle it. He also works with Crystal Gayle, so we had to talk about Loretta Lynn for a bit.

Every day I step on Wacha's paw or almost slam the door on him because he follows me around everywhere. Today I was taking food out of the broiler of my beloved toaster oven and dropped a scalding-hot sweet potato on Wacha. He freaked. It was so funny, though. Spent the entire day on the terrace. Went by the new place—the staircase is going in and so is the kitchen, but now with spring coming I don't want to give up this terrace! Rich-people problems.

Skyped with Mom and Dad. Mom said if I were twenty-eight and dating someone twenty years older she would *freak out*! #BAS and I had a good laugh over that. The show was Dorinda and Marie Osmond. Mariah Carey booked in, which shocked me—I never thought I would see her again. Went out with the boys after *WWHL*. What's going to happen now is that I'm gonna be canoodling with a guy somewhere and it'll get reported that I'm cheating on #BAS.

➤ THURSDAY, APRIL 14, 2016— SUNDAY, APRIL 17, 2016—LOS ANGELES

Just when spring finally comes to New York, I skip town. Went directly from LAX to John Mayer's incredible, super-sexy rental in the Hollywood Hills for a birthday dinner for Allison Williams, where Bruce and I were wearing the same shirt (the gray pullovers we bought in St. Barts). Other people would be horrified, but we loved it. The winds were insane and somehow one of the flames from the fire pits merged with one of the pool lounge chairs, which was quickly engulfed. Ricky saved the day by throwing it in the pool. So that was a mess *and* delightful party fodder, but truthfully it could've torched the entirety of Nichols Canyon. Friday I had breakfast with the hilarious writer Emily Spivey, who went deep with me about the Housewives, and had lunch at the Palm with RuPaul and Randy Barbato. Barry was at the next table and Brian Grazer next to that. Ava and Bruce were there too. Shopped with Eric for the apartment all afternoon, and it turns out everything is six thousand dollars—every chair, every table, anything you want is six grand. I bought four chairs and some glass elephant baubles that were way too expensive.

Friday night I went to a screening of *The First Monday in May*, a wonderful new doc all about the Met Ball and the curator of the Costume Institute. I'm in a quick shot going through the exhibit with SJP, and it's a good thing I got to relive the night because SJ isn't going this year, which means I ain't either. Saw James Corden for a second at the screening and it was either awkward or it wasn't; I can't decide. Also Les Moonves and Julie. I liked Julie's hair but she thought she looked like Mavis Staples. Dinner with Ricky and Allison and John Mayer at Ysabel on Fairfax which is a combo indoor/outdoor lounge and restaurant full of straight guys who look you right in the eye like they aren't straight at all. I was getting energy from people who should've been paying attention to their ladies, and I loved it. Rhyheim texted that there was a great party happening across from the

Abbey and I got John to go with me and it turned out it was a rollicking black gay club. We had a freaking blast. Being the only white people at parties is the best, but I don't want to tell any of my white friends because they'll show up and ruin it for me.

Saturday was a shoot for some interstitials that'll air on Bravo promoting the new movie *Alice Through the Looking Glass*, featuring me as the Mad Hatter hosting a tea party with Real Housewives Sonja, LuAnn, Erika, Phaedra, and Melissa. It's always intriguing to see women from different cities interacting, and we had a few hours of downtime together so I was like a scientist watching my sociology experiment unfold. Erika, the newbie, was getting hazed a little by the veterans. Lu asked what Erika does on her show. "Live my life," she said. Lu said what do you *do*, I mean. And she said she is a recording artist, and Lu said she is too. I interrupted and said Erika has a ton of dance hits and she should check her out and Lu wanted to know if Erika knew *her* music. Erika said she knew "Money Can't Buy You Class." There was a lot of low-key shade going on but the headline was that all of them fell in love with Sonja and were watching her with mouths agape. Lu and Sonja were a show unto themselves.

That night Sandy Gallin had a beautiful dinner party with Allison, Henry and Stacey Winkler, Mick Jones and Ann Dexter-Jones, Bryan Singer, Lorraine Bracco, Brenda Vaccaro, Alana Stewart, and on and on. It was a hotbox in the house with a big fire blazing, and Sandy said he did it on purpose so people wouldn't complain about having dinner outside. It worked; everyone was thrilled to go outside. Henry Winkler graciously endured a good twenty minutes answering my questions about *Happy Days* and his relationships with stars of the seventies. He is a mensch. Allison and I met John Mayer, Ricky, and BJ Novak at the Tower for a fun chat and debrief about the black gay club. John got a vitamin IV today to get over his hangover. He's such a rock star. Literally.

▶ THURSDAY, APRIL 21, 2016—NYC—MIAMI

Kelly drama at *Live!*. ABC mishandled her in a pretty epic way and she's uptown trying to figure out what to do. I feel for her because she's getting a bad rap for missing the show, but they seriously fucked with her. And I don't understand for the life of me why Strahan would want to be one of five people on *GMA* fighting for airtime when he was the costar of *Live!*, a job you can keep for life and make crazy money. He had it made! All the press is mentioning me as a possible replacement. I am sincerely flattered but it's not actually the case. I got TMZed stumbling out of *WWHL* last night at one-fifteen and I hope I was okay. I said I have ten jobs so how could I possibly do *Live!*—which is my way of deflecting what I know isn't even reality. I hope they let me sub, though. It's fun. I wanted to scream to TMZ about how Kelly got screwed but I held my tongue. I think I'm going to mouth off on the radio on Monday.

Landed in Miami for this tenth anniversary gala for the Adrienne Arsht Center for the Performing Arts that I'm hosting and learned that Prince died. How is that possible? Radio Andy became Radio Prince—Hickey went live for an hour and Sandra and I called in, then Nigel Barker, Jason Biggs and Jenny Mollen, and finally Bevy. It felt like a real team effort. Having Seder at Jeanne and Fred's tomorrow night.

▶ SATURDAY, APRIL 23, 2016

Today was one of those New York City days you spend all winter waiting for—perfect weather and aimless fun. Jason came by with Roxie to see the new apartment and his reaction buoyed me immensely. He thinks it's perfect.

The *New York Times Book Review* By the Book piece I did came out and there's a pencil drawing of me in which I look fifteen pounds overweight. Mom was very excited and relieved about the whole thing because she heard me talking about it on the radio a couple weeks ago and thought I was setting myself up for a Bill Maher–type moment of looking like an idiot in the *Times*. She said, "IT SURE WAS A HORRIBLE DRAWING! That same guy must do it every week because last week's was horrible too!" So there. Now she can go back to worrying that I'm spending too much money on my apartment and it won't be worth the amount I put into it. She's comparing it to things she sees on *Million Dollar Listing: New York*.

Hickey came by and we walked over to SJP's, where she was having a lemonade stand with the twins in front of her house. It was normal, with the exception of the three paparazzi across the street and the customers all wanting a picture with purchase. The girls looked adorable. Hickey didn't get change and was giving her a hard time. Some lady said, "What are you raising money for?" and SJ jokingly said, "Ourselves!" So next week she thinks she'll do one for the elephants in Africa or something. In fairness to her, she spent sixty bucks on ingredients and I'm not sure they made it back.

From there we wandered to the piers, then home, where Adam had let himself in and was waiting to give me a massage. Dinner at the Waverly Inn for Liza and Jamie's birthday—they got spray-tanned and I told them they look like soap stars, to which they replied in unison, "Thank you!"— then a party at Scott Wittman's for Bridget Everett's birthday. They had pizza and donuts. I walked SJ back to my house, where I got Wacha and we walked her home. She got inspired at the very last minute and now does want to go to the Met Ball. I have to switch a bunch of stuff around, but I hope I can go.

▶ MONDAY, APRIL 25, 2016

I had to poo all day today and was nowhere near home. On the radio for two hours—mouthed off about Kelly and Michael and by the time I got to the Matrix Awards, which I was hosting, I was like a ticking time bomb. I was seated right in the middle of the dais—Katie Couric on one side and Lena Dunham on the other, with every female in media sitting in the Waldorf ballroom audience—so it was a very low-key place to sit for two hours of uncomfortable shifting and ass clenching. I began the event by playing Plead the Fifth with each of the eight honorees, walking from one to the next. I guess the cards got stuck, so I wound up skipping Mellody Hobson, who happens to not only be George Lucas's wife but also the only African American woman on the stage. I went back to her and made it okay, I guess.

The emails started coming in with clippings of press about my radio show: "Andy Cohen Slams Michael Strahan's Decision to Leave Kelly," "Andy Cohen: You'll Be Sorry for Leaving Kelly," and on and on. And sitting at the table in front was Strahan's publicist. I had to run out to tape Anderson and his mom for *WWHL*, and on the way out Gloria Steinem said to one of the honorees who wanted a picture with me for her daughter, "He's running a *minstrel show for women! Are you aware of what he's doing? He's running a minstrel show for women!*" I said I know, I know, Gloria! She said she was going to convert me to the good side.

I made the driver stop at my place to grab the dog and, more importantly, drop the kids off at the pool. Gloria Vanderbilt was amazing and Anderson was terrified. He'd never told his mom about our tour and she kept saying, "I only just found out about your tour and I'm desperate to come see you boys." I loved her, and she was just as Anderson has always described her, a wonderful creature from another time. Before the show I was kinda brushing/picking my teeth with one of those mini toothbrushes, and she'd never seen one and she inquired about it. *"Anderson, isn't that just divine?!"* she exclaimed. *"Where ever did you get it?!"* I told her it's from the drugstore. *"But who makes it?!"* Crest, I said. *"Well, it's marvelous."* Later they both confessed to having just discovered peanut butter and jelly—she turned to her son, who very sweetly was holding her hand on and off throughout the show—and said, *"Isn't it divine?!"* He had prepared her by saying that I was going to ask questions about everything, and before the show she whispered to him, *"Is he going to ask me who had the biggest penis of everyone I've been with?!"* AC told me and I wanted to ask it but I couldn't get the words out. But she did reveal that Howard Hughes gave her the best orgasm of her life. (Anderson says he just went to his special place.) We all fell deeply in love with her. I want to buy my mom one of her paintings for Mother's Day.

From the show I went to Grac's for dinner with the family. Sam knows everything about music, weather, and movies. Went back to *WWHL* for another show and my brain was jelly by midnight. Mom sent me a funny emoji that said "Sleep tight" and I sent her an "I love you" one back.

▷ WEDNESDAY, APRIL 27, 2016

All the "news" has me or Anderson cohosting with Kelly even though I've not had one discussion with anyone about it and I *can't*. I'm exclusive to NBCUniversal. But it's got to be good to be mentioned, I guess. Had a fitting at Ralph Lauren for the Met Ball—we're going!—and went in wanting this brand-new navy peak-lapel tux they'd just posted on their Instagram but they said it's been taken by someone else going to the ball. (Even menswear designers don't like more than one person wearing the same thing.) I made them tell me who and it's Bobby Cannavale. So I'm ranked lower than him, is what that means, and I can't say I thought I was higher ranked than him but it's always interesting when you see where you stand in life. We all decided on a midnight-blue shawl-collared brocade jacket and black pants, but then the RL woman came in with bad news: someone has it on hold and will decide tomorrow whether he's wearing it or not. I told her she had to tell me who it was and she said she couldn't. I pushed. It's Johnny Depp, and I have no problem with that whatsoever. It made me dig my heels in about Cannavale a little, to be honest, and try to fight for *his* tux. As it turns out, there's a kind of Art Deco–patterned black jacket that Bieber just wore on the cover of *GQ* and it fits better than the blue that Depp has on hold so I put that and the Depp jacket on hold and I'll find out tomorrow which one I'm wearing. I may go with the black anyway.

Stopped by Gloria Vanderbilt's art opening and saw Mark, Kelly, Anderson, and Ben. Mark and Ben noticed this black dot that's on my lower lip, so that freaked me out. What *is* it? From there I headed to Holt's 150th birthday party at the Morgan Library, where Stephen Rubin gave Bill O'Reilly and me a shout-out from the stage for our contributions to the company. O'Reilly and I are such a publishing duo! I tried to meet him but just missed him. Then to the *Below Deck* premiere party in the IAC lobby, which was huge and included stars from a bunch of Bravo shows that it's impossible not to love seeing together: Captain Lee, Shep, Jax, Ramona, Tabatha, Luis, and on and on, who were each apparently asked on the red carpet if I should take Strahan's job. Took a lot of selfies—sometimes I feel like a cardboard cutout. Fun party, though. Gavin Newsom was on the show last night and our final pledge in March on *Eos* was to get behind the next generation of politicians and I think he's it. I'm having lunch with Jason Kander from Missouri tomorrow to talk about doing some fundraising for him, so that's another one.

▶ SUNDAY, MAY 1, 2016—SAG HARBOR—NYC

Spent the weekend editing these diaries—#Meta. Also kind of tiring. I've been keeping a diary for about three years and it's starting to get under my skin. Would I feel more free if I was just *living*? Dinner with Justin and George at Sam's Friday night and ate like a pig. Am packing it on for the Met Ball, I decided. Worked on the book all day Saturday except for a half-hour playdate for Wacha and Gary Fallon and a half hour in Sag, where I ran into every gay guy I know buying home décor. Dinner at Sen with

Jimmy and Nancy. I arrived wearing a striped polo pullover and down vest and JF took one look at me and said, "Hey, wanna get the Jeep and stop by Mork's house?" I looked so *Mork and Mindy*! Sunday I drove straight to Ralph Lauren for my fitting and the woman said, "I have great news for you! You can wear the black!" Her choice had been the *blue* two days before, so I guess that means Johnny Depp is wearing the blue. No, she said, he doesn't know yet but she thought on it and is sold on the black now.

❧ MONDAY, MAY 2, 2016

As is our Met Ball tradition of sorts, I picked SJP up at her house in order to watch the final moments of her preparation, and she was in a Monse tribute to Alexander Hamilton with perfect hair. In the line to walk the red carpet I saw Michael Strahan from afar and knew I was going to wind up talking to him about my comments on the radio. I do love an awkward moment, just maybe not involving myself at the Met Ball. Shook Taylor Swift's hand in the receiving line (she was one of the "hosts") and remarked on her strong handshake and she said it's like a dude's. I said it's perfect, and it is. Saw Barry and he said, "Wait for my wife to come out of the loo with me," and lo and behold out she comes with butterflies in her hair and Kris Jenner by her side. You don't know *who* will come out of the loo at the Met Ball, that's what makes it fun.

Going into dinner I walked right into Michael Strahan, who said he can't believe I did him that way, that he was so surprised I joined the pileup. I said, "No, no, no, dude, did you actually read what I said? What I said wasn't bad; you're just reading the headlines." He said it hurt his feelings, and I said, "Dude, I really like you and I wasn't going in on you." He said, "I like you and I like *her*, I really do." I said I know that. I said, "I'm gonna send you the transcript and I stand behind it; you tell me if you think it's bad." We hugged it out at the end. I will send it to him tomorrow—all I said was that I couldn't believe he was leaving a show he starred in with his name in the title to be one of five people, and what would happen to him if the ratings didn't go up? (*Um*, maybe he *is* gonna be pissed?) I told Gaga she is Beyond Thunderdome and I miss her. She said she didn't like what the women did to Yolanda this season, but maybe it will teach someone something about Lyme disease.

I was sitting between Lizzie Tisch and Anna Kendrick, over whom Paul Rudd and I kept leaning to discuss baseball. Also at my table were SJ, Stephen Colbert, Grandmaster Flash, Derek Lam, Jonathan Tisch, and Sergey Brin and his wife, who is a Chatty Cathy in a good way. Told Kanye I almost wore what he did. Stupid. The highlight of the after party was Megyn Kelly, who SJ and I commandeered and she seems so smart and her own person. She's doing my show in two weeks. She went way off the record. I told her I loved what she did with the governor of North Carolina last week. She said she has to pick her battles. I walked SJ out and wound up in a Katy Perry–Bradley Cooper logjam in the lobby, then walked right back in and up in the elevator with Madonna. I asked her if London went well, if she got the kid back, and she said she got to see him and I said baby steps. What do I know? She smelled like she always does—fragrant, perfume-y, but somehow milky. Talked to Miles Teller, Kate Mara, and Jamie Dornan, then Paul Rudd some more. Bruce and I decided Alexander Skarsgård should play Willem if they ever make *A Little Life* into a movie.

Bryan and I were at the bar and Taylor Swift was in a logjam next to us wondering aloud where there was a spot for her to hang out to watch Gaga perform. Why I felt I needed to get involved I will never know (maybe I was auditioning for her squad?) but I innocently said exactly the wrong thing to her, which was: "Your friend Katy is sitting in the corner and there's plenty of room around her." She asked "Katy who?" and I said, "Perry," at which point she clearly let me know that she's the exact *opposite* of her friend. I kind of gasped, realizing she was in the most famous feud of all the feuds, one that I'd talked about myself endlessly on *WWHL*. I said that at least now she knows where *not* to go, which I thought was a nice button on the conversation and made it all a laugh. She didn't agree. I turned away completely mortified that I'd said something so moronic *to TSwift*, who I don't know from Adam but who has been the topic of many of my Plead the Fifths. And the capper is that she now thinks I'm a dick and *I wasn't even trying to be shady*, I was just sticking my nose where it didn't belong. And I saw Katy Perry alone in a really good area! And on top of that *I failed my squad-ition!* As she was walking away, she turned back to me, commanding me not to say a word about this on my show, and said that she's watching. *She's watching?* Is that a threat? And *is* she watching? That made me feel momentarily *good* until I realized there might've been a "fucking" thrown in there before "your show," or was that my scared imagination? (If she's watching my "fucking" show, that makes it a little less exciting.) I sputtered that I had no plans to say a word about it on my show—as a matter of fact, I silently vowed to stop playing into the hype that *she created* around her song "Bad Blood." Hadn't I beaten it to death anyway? She didn't threaten me about putting it in my book, so here we are.

Gaga performed the Talking Heads' "Burning Down the House" and TSwift seemed to be front and center for it. I didn't see where her enemy was watching from, nor did I care. Hopefully she'll start a new feud soon that I can invest in. Didn't go to any other parties and was home by three.

❧ FRIDAY, MAY 6, 2016—DOLLYWOOD, USA

I am home: swimming in the amniotic fluids of the Queen of Country, surrounded by old wigs and costumes, awards, gift shops, extended members of the Parton family, roller coasters, and cotton candy. I came to interview Dolly for a Radio Andy Town Hall in front of a theater full of contest winners, and to establish some kind of on-air rapport with DP so she'll one day venture downtown to the unchartered waters of the Clubhouse, an offer she keeps refusing.

I made the tactical error of flying to Nashville and driving today because someone (a New York City cabbie? A child?) said it was a two-hour drive to Dollywood—try three and a half, so I was in the car at seven and by ten was looking at a massive rotisserie of cheesedogs and sausages encircled by pancakes; in other words, I was close. My first stop was the gift shop, where I had orders to fill for everyone from Sandra Bernhard to my *WWHL* team. I got lots of mugs with people's names on them, Dolly tees, butterfly keychains, and a country cookbook for Grac. At the appointed time, I was taken to a photo op with the lady herself, and she looked like a cross between Dolly and Ronald McDonald on account of her yellow vest and red puffy shirt with matching sequined miniskirt. She smelled of that recognizable smell again and as I type I can smell it on my hands, and as I smell it on my hands I realize it is in the same ballpark as that Madonna smell! Could it be from the same place? Is it the smell of *breasts*?

The interview itself was fun—ninety minutes—and at its best when we were talking about her music. The truth is I have heard most all of her stories because she is guarded about what she reveals. We talked about Sandy a bit backstage beforehand. She kept saying she knew me, which is what she has said before, but I get the sense that she really did remember seeing me a year or so ago at Sandy's. I wanted to get her to admit to being a pot smoker so badly, but I couldn't do it. Flew back from Knoxville through Charlotte, and the Charlotte airport is full of hot guys. Endless. Like a sausage factory, but not like that sausage wrapped in pancakes fifty miles from Dollywood; this was really great, premium sausage. Going to Anderson and Ben's in Connecticut tomorrow with #BAS.

▶ SUNDAY, MAY 8, 2016—CONNECTICUT

Spent the weekend with #BAS at Anderson's impressive house (castle?), which reminds me of Palmer Cortlandt's on *All My Children*. If it were up to Anderson I would marry #BAS tomorrow. We went to DVF's for dinner on Saturday and watched *Captain America* (in 3-D) in her incredible screening room. I didn't understand it, which is funny because aren't those movies kind of made for idiots? I was stoned and fell asleep twice, but Benjamin didn't get it either and he was awake, sober, and knowledgeable about that stuff. It was my boyfriend's first time in a car with me and he is a nervous passenger. Still don't think that counts as a fault, though.

▶ WEDNESDAY, MAY 11, 2016—NYC

I was walking to the gym on Perry Street this beautiful morning and saw an old man on his stoop in his PJs and robe who I thought was enjoying the day. "I'm locked out," he bemusedly bellowed down to me. He said his girlfriend is in Tucson so he was going to have to eventually walk to the locksmith's in his robe. I said it'll be fun. He didn't seem to believe me. Made a ton of furniture decisions today and was back and forth to the apartment a lot. There's a new refrigerator and Wacha is terrified of it. I was on *Fallon* tonight and went into it dubiously because the woman in the pre-interview didn't laugh at anything I said. It went well, though.

SUNDAY, MAY 15, 2016—SAG HARBOR—NYC

Had dinner last night at Jane Buffett's and it was, as Marci said, "a Buffet at the Buffetts'." I drove back from the beach in time for a rehearsal with Mariah Carey at Radio City for the big NBCUniversal Upfront, where we were meant to do stage patter and introduce her new E! show. I arrived on time and then realized I was a sucker because I would spend the next untold amount of hours waiting for someone for whom time is just a concept. She was only thirty minutes late, though, and quite nice. The first thing she said when we kissed was that my guests have been rather boring lately and I think she was talking about JLo, who was just on, and we went through the whole "I don't know her" thing again. JLo says she *does* know Mariah and Mariah says she does *not* know JLo. Mariah said she knows Beyoncé but she does not know *her*. So I think MC will be making that clear when she's on the show Tuesday night.

We rehearsed the bit, which involves me coming out to Madonna's song "Jump" and introducing Mariah, who is sprawled on a big divan with shirtless dancers who walk her over to me. I walked and got her the first time we ran through it, then said, "Would you rather have the boys bring you over?" and she said, "Yes, that's more of a moment, don't you think?" I said, "Yes, of course, and you are all about the moment." She looked good. Thin.

Jeff Lewis and Gage came by to see my apartment and had a couple good suggestions about couch placement, table length, and depths of cabinets in the hallway outside the kitchen. We chatted on the street for a half hour after.

MONDAY, MAY 16, 2016

This morning's upfront started with an early red carpet and I ran into everybody from Henry and Stacey Winkler to Khloé and Kourtney Kardashian, who I imitated staring into their phones in their cars, to JLo, who I kissed and asked if I gave her the coat she was wearing. Every reporter asked me about replacing Strahan, and then I went to the greenroom, where I saw Jimmy in full *Hamilton* gear for his opening number. Talked to Matt Lauer about the Hamptons and Kelly's situation. Waved to a Spanish telenovela star with huge hair who seemed to know me. Took forever to go on and right before I did the stage manager said that Mariah was running late and that she "wanted to do it" but they were not sure she'd be there. I said, What exactly are you talking about, I am about to go on and I have ten seconds of patter before she comes out, so what am I supposed to do? It was all very convoluted but then he said, Oh, no, it's fine, they're placing her now. My intro music had been changed from Madonna to Mariah, and she was wearing basically a sequined bathing suit and stockings. Our bit was fun (for me) and probably insane to people watching, because I am not sure everyone gets her, but I was up her ass onstage, being the perfect lamb of a sidekick.

When I got off I was told to go back to my seat for this next bit, and where was I was sitting? Directly in front of JLo. I suddenly felt guilty for being such a lamb onstage now that I was with JLo. It was as if I was a double agent in the middle of the two of them, like they were from the RHODivas or something. Seth Meyers made a joke about wanting to see a Mariah reality show starring her dancers and JLo said, "Now *that's* a show!" and I turned around and was all "Mmm-*hmm*!! You go, girl!" *I wanna be friends with everybody!* The *moment* it ended, or maybe a second before, JLo turned to Ray Liotta and said, "It's one and I gotta *go*!" and I turned to Jeff Lewis and said, "It's one and I gotta *go*, too!" and ran out just as JLo and Khloé and Kourtney Kardashian were leaving. So that was the move, leaving at one and beating the rush by thirty seconds.

Upfront parties all night. First was *People* magazine's, where I introduced myself to the Spanish telenovela star from this morning, who said, "I'm Vanessa Hudgens. I was on your show." And I said "OMG, I didn't recognize *your hair*!" Then to the NBC party, where I was up JLo's ass again. I asked what she thought of the Mariah reel and her team all seemed to kind of like it. Then the CAA party, where I hung with Consuelos and Bethenny, who was hammered. So was I.

▶ TUESDAY, MAY 17, 2016

Mariah arrived two minutes into her live *WWHL* show, which was exciting, giving long-winded answers for the first six minutes including an extended argument that she *does not know* JLo, which was kind of brilliant. She is clearly very bugged by this whole thing! I asked her during the commercial break to keep her answers short, and got the sense that not only was she not enjoying our MC drag queen pageant, she didn't want to walk over and announce a winner. Indeed, she remarked that the light over by the bar seemed very precarious, so she stayed seated for the end of the show and pronounced a winner from her well-lit spot. Unlike the last time she was on the show, she had no ground rules for questions and seemed much more free and happy and open to everything. Once again I switched seats to accommodate her better side. I was asked to go have a drink with her after the show in her greenroom (Michael's office), which I realized was probably because they needed content for her reality show. It was fun in there, though, and I left the night really liking her. She was trending on Twitter all night too.

FRIDAY, MAY 20, 2016—SUNDAY, MAY 22, 2016—ST. LOUIS

Came home for Blouse's wedding but wound up multitasking in a few other great events, including what three years ago would've been cause for much consternation and discussion but now was just something pleasant: throwing out the first pitch for the Cardinals Friday night. Much has been written (by me) about my past two attempts, and this time I took a completely opposite pre-throw tack: I didn't think about it one bit. It was booked as a way to promote my St. Louis *AC2* appearance in October and so it just felt like more promotion. Mom and Dad, Em, Rob, and Abby were in tow and I got up and threw the damn thing as quick as I could after taking one moment to stand on the mound and look around, which is just about the most amazing feeling you can imagine. The ball was, for the third time running, *very* high and *very* outside. I am being kind. You know who is there to actually see a first pitch? No one. Although it obviously lives on forever if it's especially horrible, so I shouldn't be flip.

Before the game people kept saying to me, "You're so lucky you still have your parents," which was pissing my mom off to no end. "They expect us to be DEAD! It's like they're SHOCKED WHEN WE WALK AROUND THE CORNER!" She is so right. After the first inning I bit a chunk off a pot lollipop just to be festive, and a few innings later was feeling no pain until the marketing woman from the Cardinals came to get me for my interview in the broadcasting booth with Jim Edmonds and the other play-by-play announcer. I make my living in front of the camera and at this point it is my happy place, where I am a version of my best self. Not so in that broadcast booth, where from the minute I sat down I thought: *"Oh shit I am in the wrong place and I am stoned as hell right now."* The inning started and immediately the guy who isn't Jim Edmonds started asking me about the Housewives, which came as a shock to me even though I was sitting with a Housewives husband on my right. He asked how it started, and I said the women's hair was blonder and their boobs were bigger than anything we'd seen at Bravo. Jim commented that I am not really involved with the Housewives anymore, and I had to correct him on the air and suddenly defend and explain my role as executive producer, which would've been fine if I wasn't paranoid.

The top of the inning ended fast, and a producer said in my ear: "Hey Andy, we love having you here, but remember the audience. This is a Major League Baseball game; lots of families are watching." Oh, great, I offended the MLB people. Awesome. I felt horrible. But they said to stay for the bottom of the inning. Back on the air, Jim accused me of not liking having Meghan on my show and I said, I love her and she's been on, and he said, But you haven't invited her back. I said, *"Are we really doing this during the baseball game?"* I ruined the whole thing with a pot lollipop. Damn me. I got back to my suite and Mom said they couldn't get the volume up to hear my interview and I said *good*! I went out for drinks with Jim after the game and he said it wasn't bad at all, and Twitter seemed to agree.

Blouse's wedding Saturday night was phenomenal. Here's a seventy-four-year-old widow, previously married for fifty-three years, who found love with someone from her past! As I sat at a table with all my cousins wondering how this wedding was going to play out, I reflected on what an important a role she played in each of our lives. The truth is, it wasn't a wedding like any of us had been to; we were out of our suburban comfort zones, and more importantly we found out that Kattie (Blouse's real name) of course had an entire life that we knew nothing about. We all danced and it was really loving. Sunday I went to a party at Companion for Sophie's high school graduation and hosted a benefit for Jason Kander, the Democrat running for Senate in Missouri, and Senator McCaskill showed up as well to push it over the top. Got back home and went to a barbeque at Benjamin's.

► MONDAY, MAY 23, 2016

What happened tonight was a fitting topper to a nonstop sprint of a day. Woke up at 6:00 a.m. to be live on the radio from 7:00 to 9:00 and John Hill was sick, so it was just me and the microphone for two hours. From there to *Live with Kelly*, where I pretaped a segment for Friday's show. Then to my show, where I taped tonight's episode. I hosted the Parsons School of Design benefit and, as I was getting dressed, chuckled at the sight of that denim suit I mistakenly wore to Marc and Scott's black-tie thing at Carnegie Hall. For tonight's Parsons event, I chose a mint green suit to celebrate spring and relived the nightmare when I pulled up to an ocean of black tuxedoes at Chelsea Piers. *Oops, I did it again!* I was actually furious and immediately wanted to blame someone—anyone. When I agree to host something, I ain't looking at the invitation, but *someone* should! I wanted to blame Daryn but I'm not mean enough. SJP and Hickey had a good laugh at my expense but were supportive, and I used it as fodder in my spiel onstage. What else can you do?

► TUESDAY, MAY 24, 2016

Woke up to a takedown on GQ.com about my mint suit! "From late March until early August, clothing racks and online stores are rife with blazers and pants in pastel hues—like mint, seen here on talk show host Andy Cohen. But just because they are sold in stores does not mean you should buy one. Cohen's pastel linen number, worn to the 2016 Parsons Benefit last night in New York City, was aggressively pastel—like a Smarty or a Jordan almond. And his tie, like a barber shop pole, didn't help steer the look away from those old time-y candy shop vibes. . . . Cohen's jacket and pants are making him look shorter and wider than he actually is." To make matters worse, Mom sent me an email with a photo of me in the mint green suit: "Seriously Andy, maybe you should see someone about that right eye. I don't mean the wonkiness part but you half close it all of the time and it seems to be getting more pronounced." When it rains, it pours!

THURSDAY, MAY 26, 2016

Hosting with Kelly today—we taped two episodes—was so fun and not stressful, knowing that I wasn't auditioning for the job. But it made me wish for a minute that I wasn't locked up by NBCUniversal and could try. They trotted out Lucci, and I got to act out a soap-opera scene with her and Kelly. Wacha stepped on a piece of gum today and I got a little too much enjoyment out of watching him contemplate what was on his foot and try getting it off. He was limping, trailed by the gum. I was in hysterics. Poor Wacha!

Went by the new apartment and saw some pulls in the kitchen that I picked out over a year ago but which I now can't decide about. Timely! And it's clear now that I'm not moving in until late August. Also the closet is installed and it's insane; I feel very East Coast Lisa Vanderpump. As I walked around the apartment, seeing the wallpaper go up and the bar taking shape, I had a sensation that I had made it. The apartment was so nice— it felt like it should belong to someone else. It's mine, though, and I felt proud. And as good as that made me feel, I had another realization as I got back to Fifteenth Street: Though I've been endlessly planning every detail and fantasizing about this amazing palace, it is not going to change my life. When you put a year and a half into something, how can it live up to your expectations or solve your problems? I think I'm preparing myself for my new normal: I may be a little fancier, but I'll still be me.

FRIDAY, MAY 27—MONDAY, MAY 30, 2016—SAG HARBOR

Finally I'm not alone out here. #BrazilianAndySamberg spent Memorial Day weekend with me and having him here made things I'd been doing alone seem fresh and fun again. Thursday night was dinner at Sam's with Sandy. Friday we went to a dinner at the Grubmans' for Sandy's birthday. Debbie Grubman said the luxury real-estate market is in a slump. We sat with Hilary Gumbel, who was fantastic. David Geffen was across from us. Then we headed to Almond, and as we were parking #BAS said he really wanted to see a Housewife. Twenty minutes later we were face to face with Sonja Morgan. He was happy.

The next few days were feedings (as Amanda calls them) all over the Hamptons that I've done before but were more fun with #BAS. His friend asked him about the rich people out here and he said they like saying how much richer other people are. Went to Tony Melillo's store opening and met his little baby and as I was cooing over him I thought, "I have to do this." I don't look at babies the same way I used to. I think it's called baby fever. My birthday is in a couple days, and I remember thinking I turned forty-eight last year, so I'm turning forty-eight again. I have no problem reliving a year, but in truth I'm feeling really pensive about the last couple years, and as I sat here today writing about the beginning of summer, I went back and saw what I did the last couple Memorial Day weekends. It looks like a lot of the same stuff, which on the one hand makes me feel happy and on another makes me feel somewhat inert.

What's been great about keeping this diary is that I *can* look back—there is a record of where I've been, who I've seen, and how I've felt along the way. That record is a gift. In this year, as I've been going back through what I've written to make it ready for publication, I've been forced to think a lot about where I am in my life. That ability to reflect does not come naturally to me. I'm usually too busy having fun! But what hasn't been great about writing the diary is the feeling sometimes at the end of a busy day that there's still one more thing to do. And also it's strange to live your life with a consciousness in the back of your head saying, "This would be great for the diary." That gets tiring.

I said at the beginning of this process, in September of 2013, that writing and publishing this is as close to being on a reality TV show as I will get. Now I'm afraid it's time to cancel the show. I need to break the fourth wall and thank you all for living my life with me for three years. We had fun, right? But I think you'll appreciate the fact that I've got this really cute guy staring at me, waiting for me to finish writing so we can hang out. I feel like on the other side of this keyboard my life is waiting for me, and I want to go out and just *live it.*

ABOUT THE AUTHOR

ANDY COHEN is the host and executive producer of *Watch What Happens: Live* on Bravo. He is the executive producer of the *Real Housewives* franchise and hosts the network's highly rated reunion specials. He tours nationally with Anderson Cooper in *AC2*, hosts and produces *Then & Now with Andy Cohen* on Bravo, curates and appears on Radio Andy on Sirius XM, and has won an Emmy and two Peabody Awards for his work. The author of two *New York Times* best-selling books, *Most Talkative* and *The Andy Cohen Diaries*, he lives in New York City with his dog, Wacha.